WONDERFUL WEST VIRGINIA

WONDERgrams

A collection of reader-submitted images

#wondergrams

Instagram

CONTENTS

Photography is the cornerstone of *Wonderful West Virginia* magazine.

For more than 85 years, it has inspired those of us who love the Mountain State with captivating stories and breathtaking photography, showcasing our flora, fauna, and natural beauty. In 2015, we introduced WONDERgrams—a page in each monthly issue dedicated to showcasing our readers' photos from all over the state. We've learned that the best photographs don't just tell us about the picture, they also tell us about the person behind the camera. Great photography connects us to our community and inspires strong emotions. In celebration of our beautiful state and the people in it, the following pictures celebrate the majesty of our mountains, the serenity of nature, and the historical importance of our Appalachian heritage. Be wild and wonderful and travel with us through the eyes of our people.

Nikki

NIKKI BOWMAN MILLS
Wonderful West Virginia Editor in Chief

Carla

CARLA WITT FORD
Wonderful West Virginia Photography Editor

fauna

A good snapshot keeps a moment that
has gone from running away.

- EUDORA WELTY

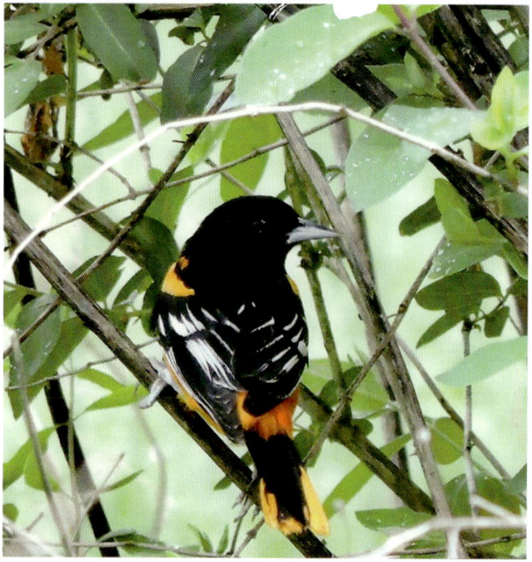

CHRISTIAN BELMONT

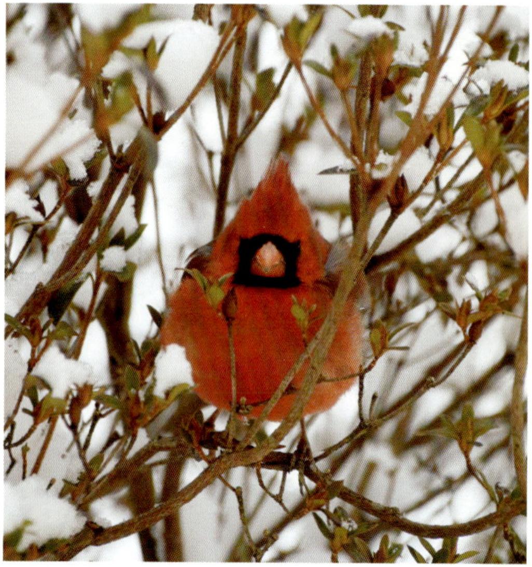

PHILLIP D. MILES

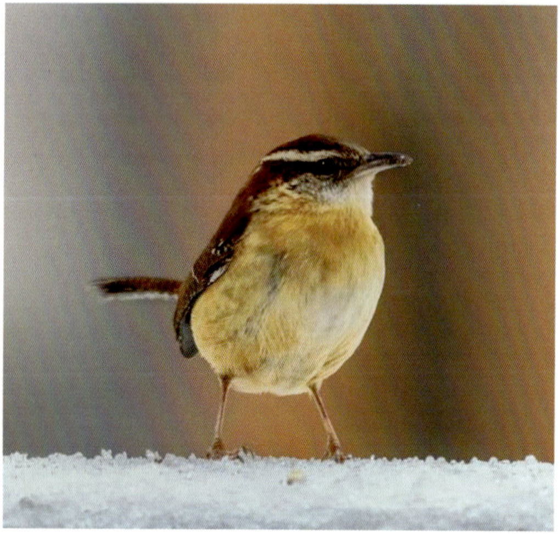

BETH SPENCER

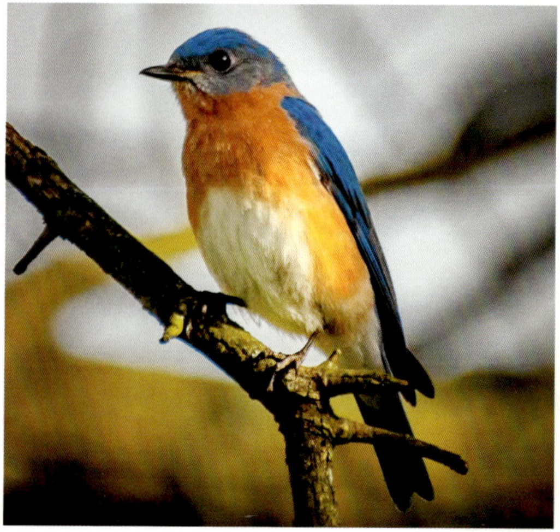

WENDY PARKS

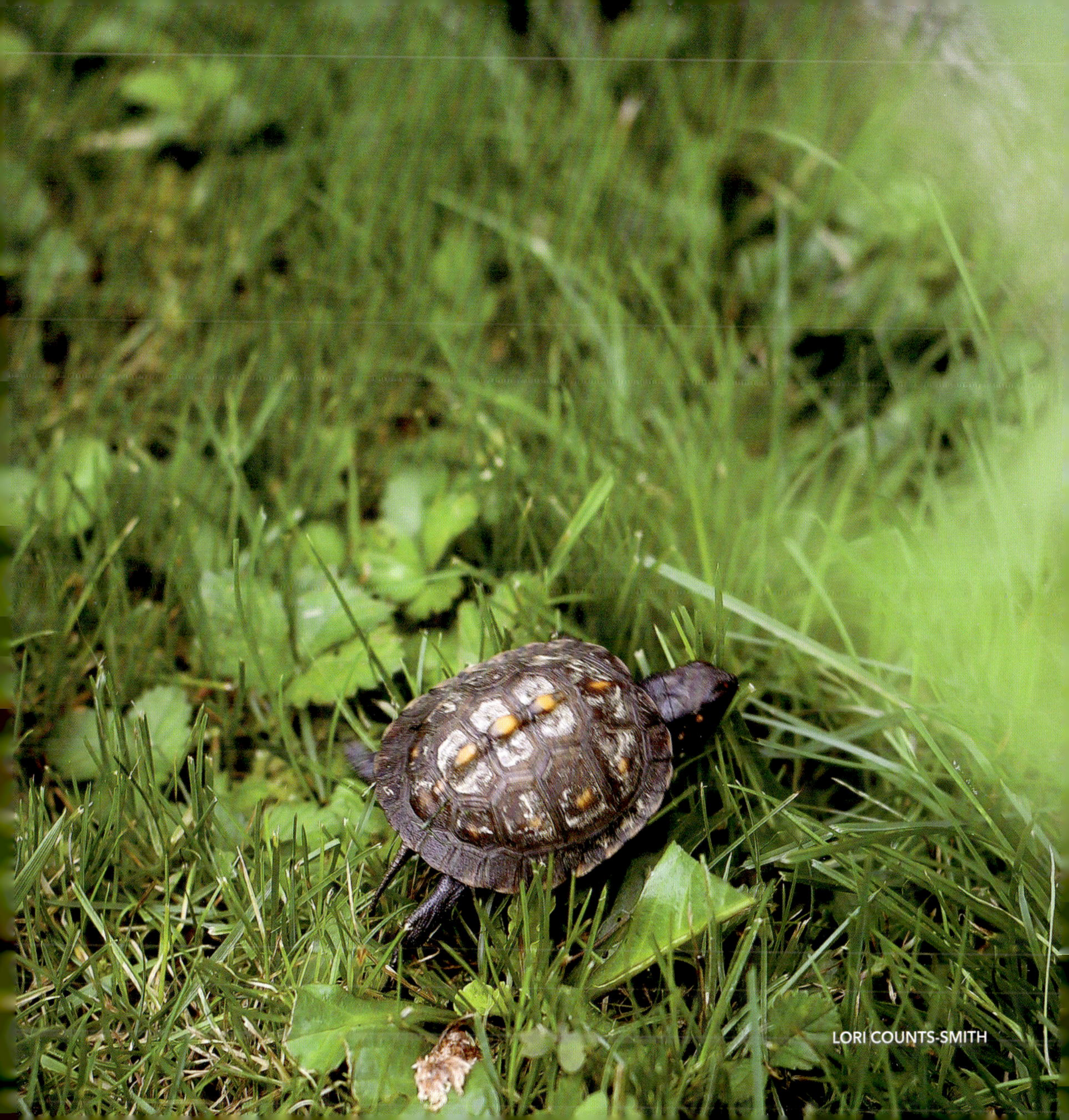

LORI COUNTS-SMITH

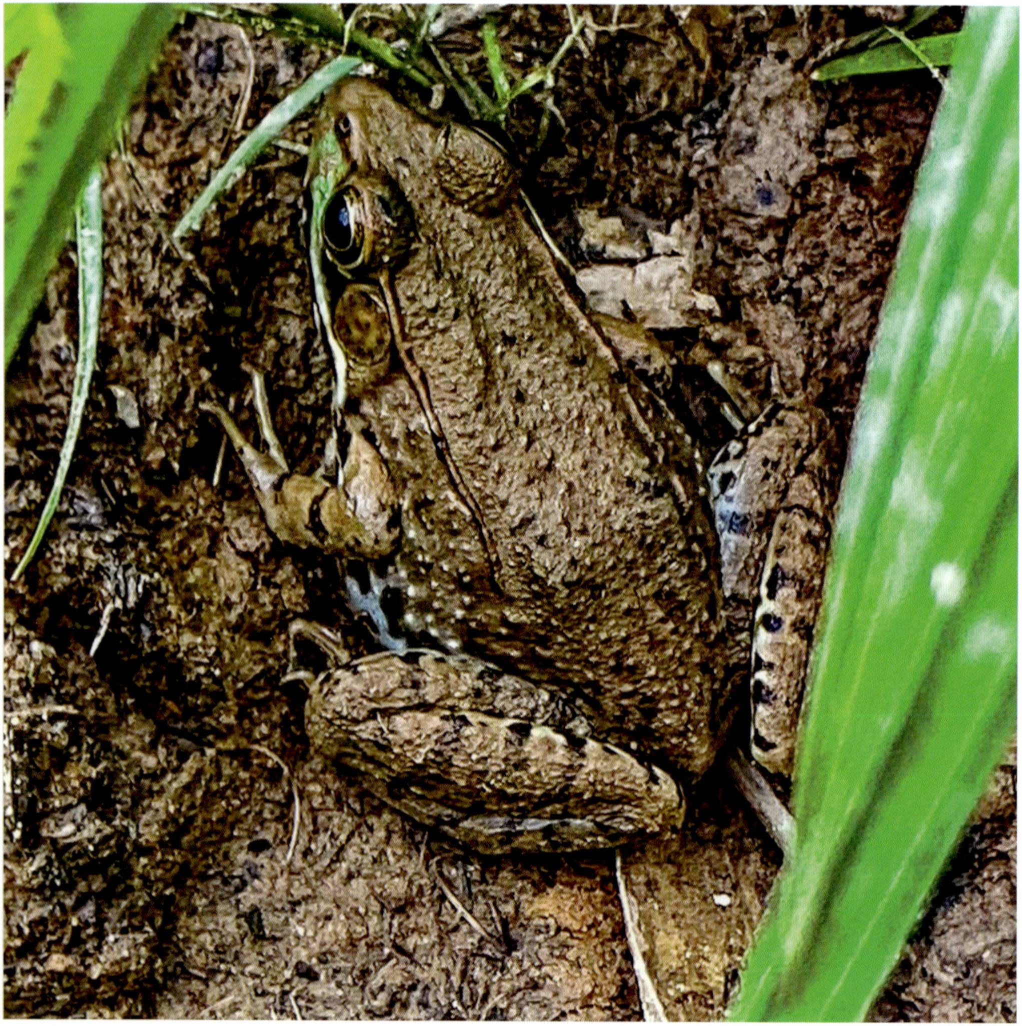

LEAH BOWES

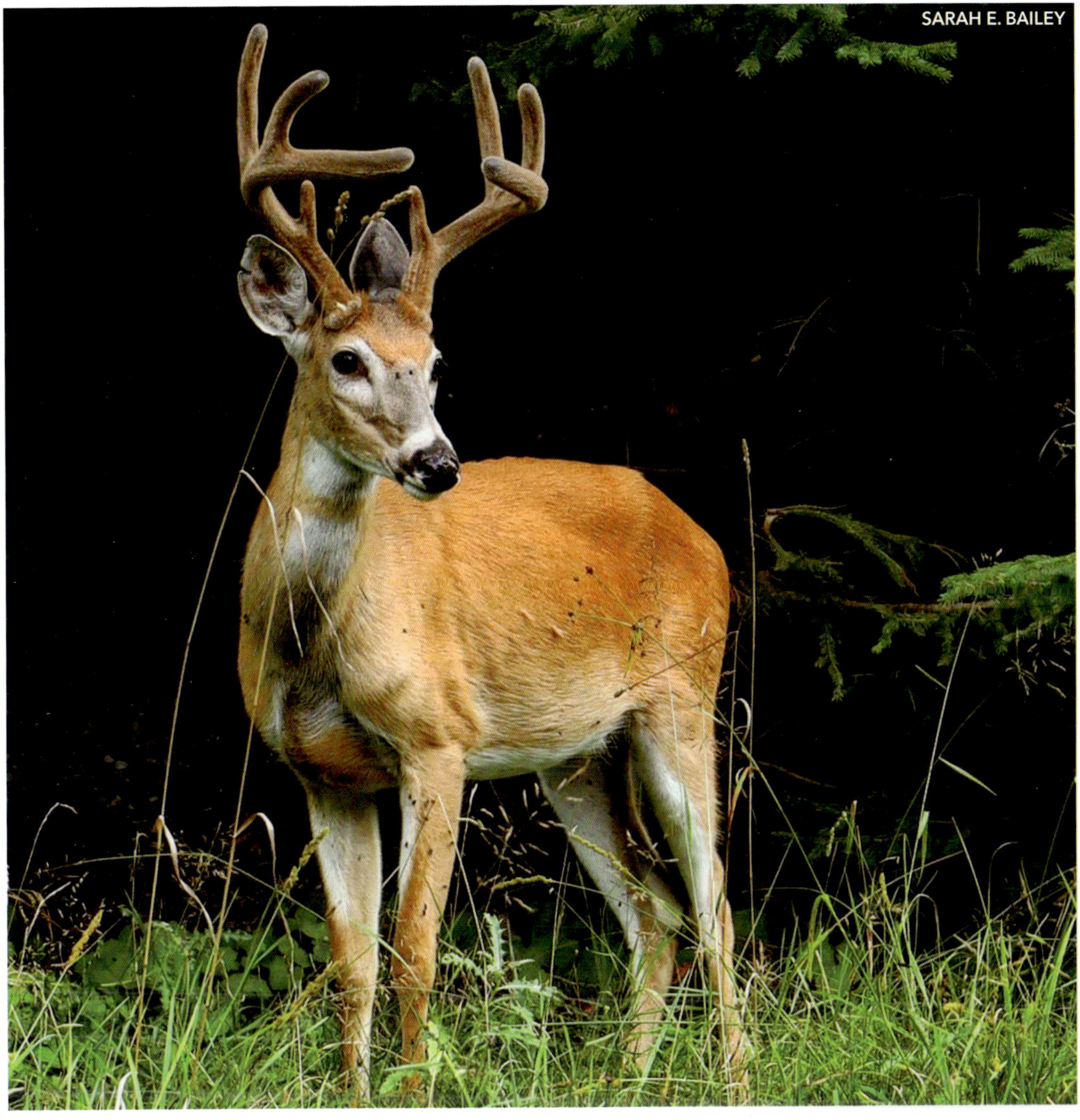
SARAH E. BAILEY

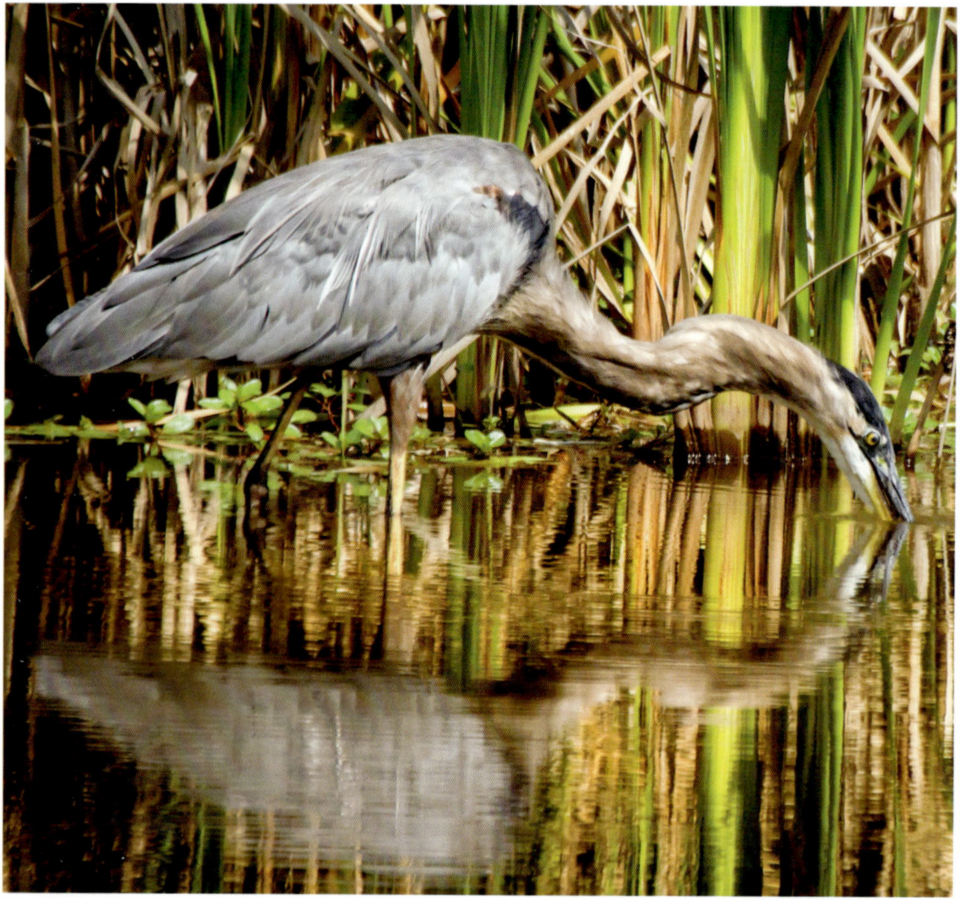

DANNY CARPENTER

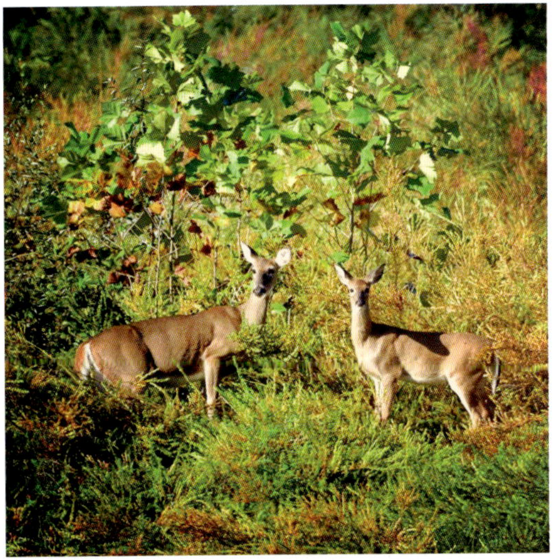
LEAH BOWES

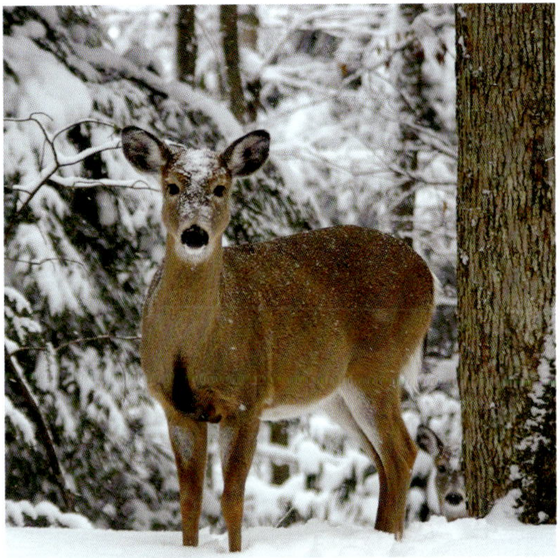
LAURA MOUL

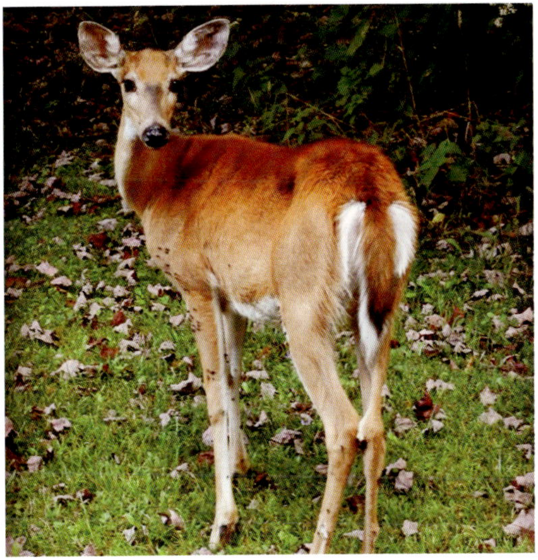
AMBER MESSICK

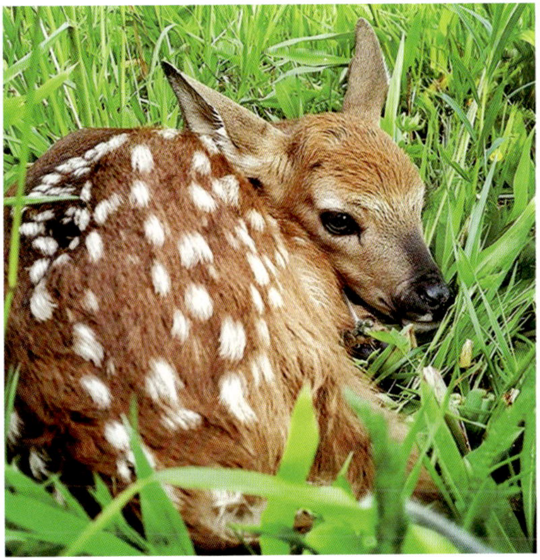
LIZ STOUT

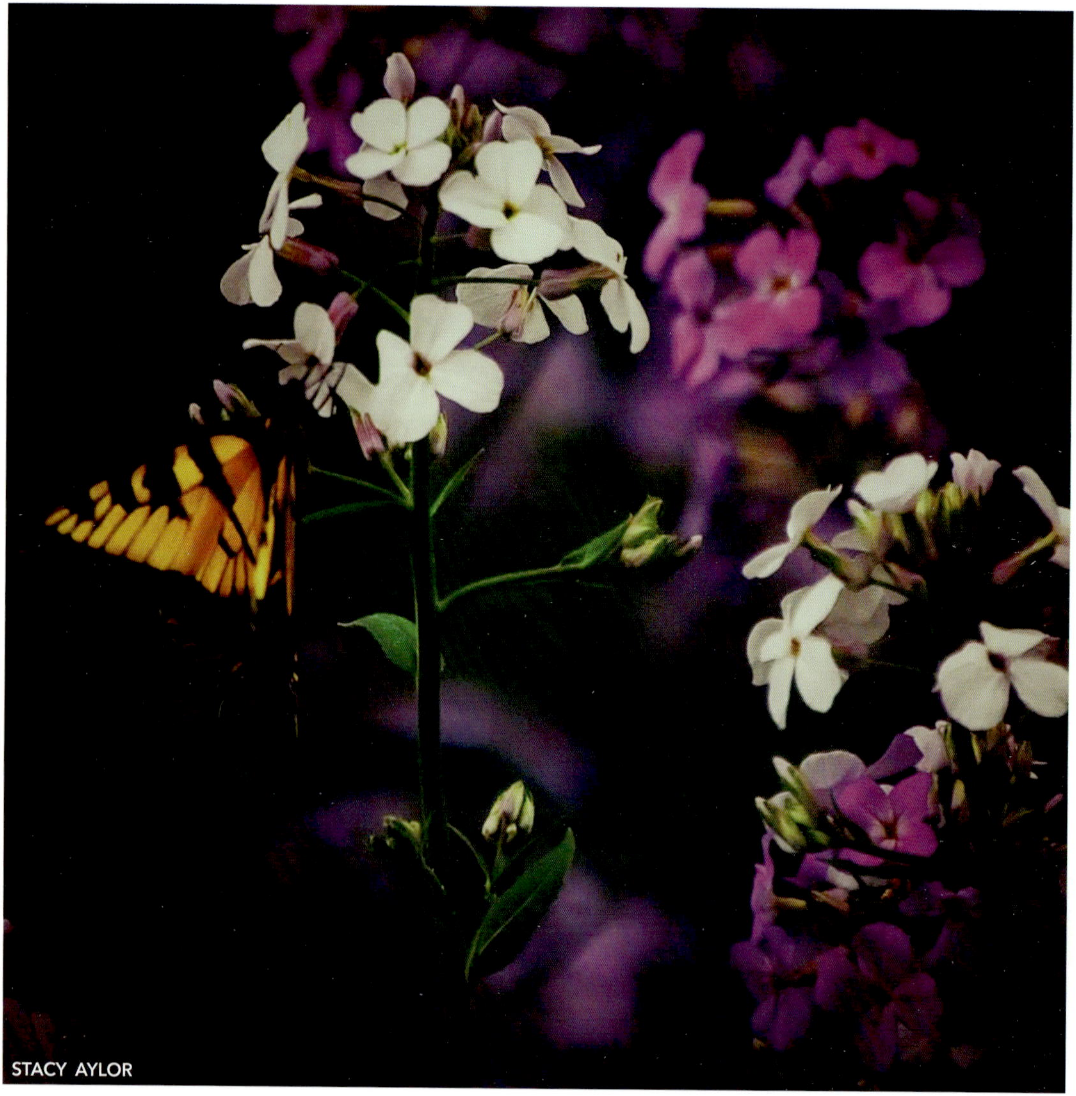

STACY AYLOR

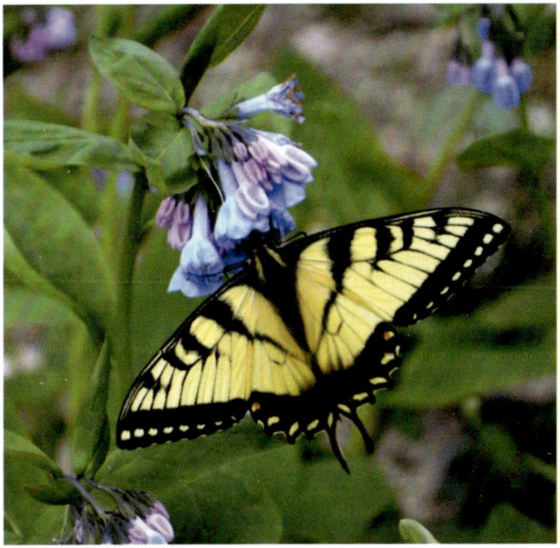

MELISSA EISENHAUER

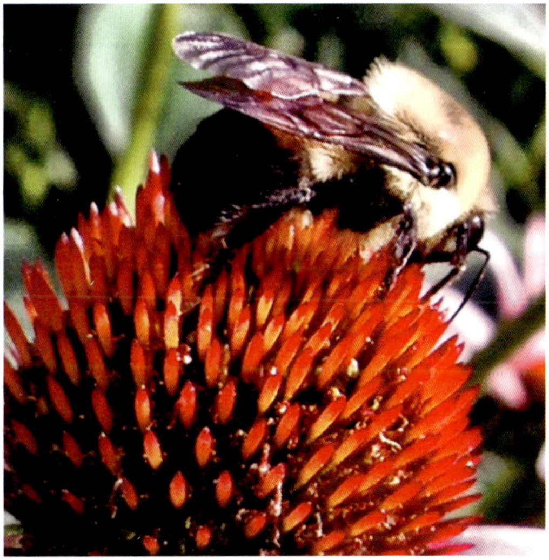

MARY SUE HEISHMAN

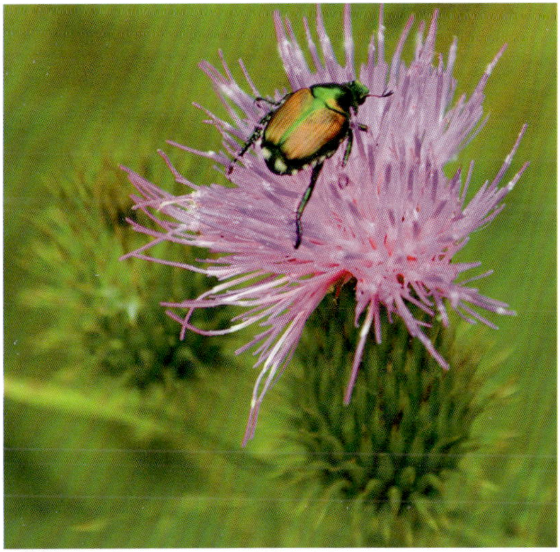

ELAINE CLARK

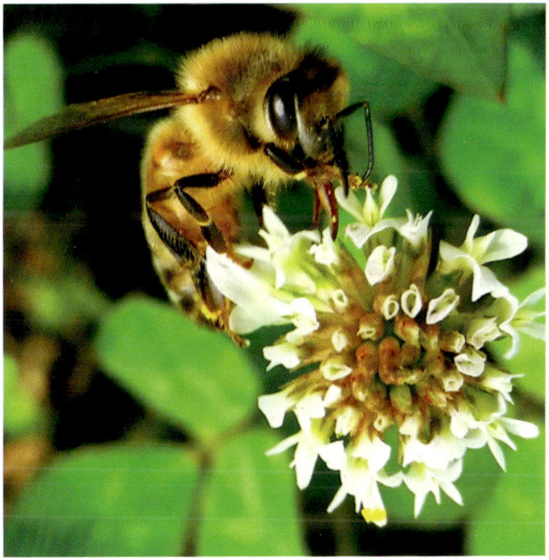

JANICE SCOTT

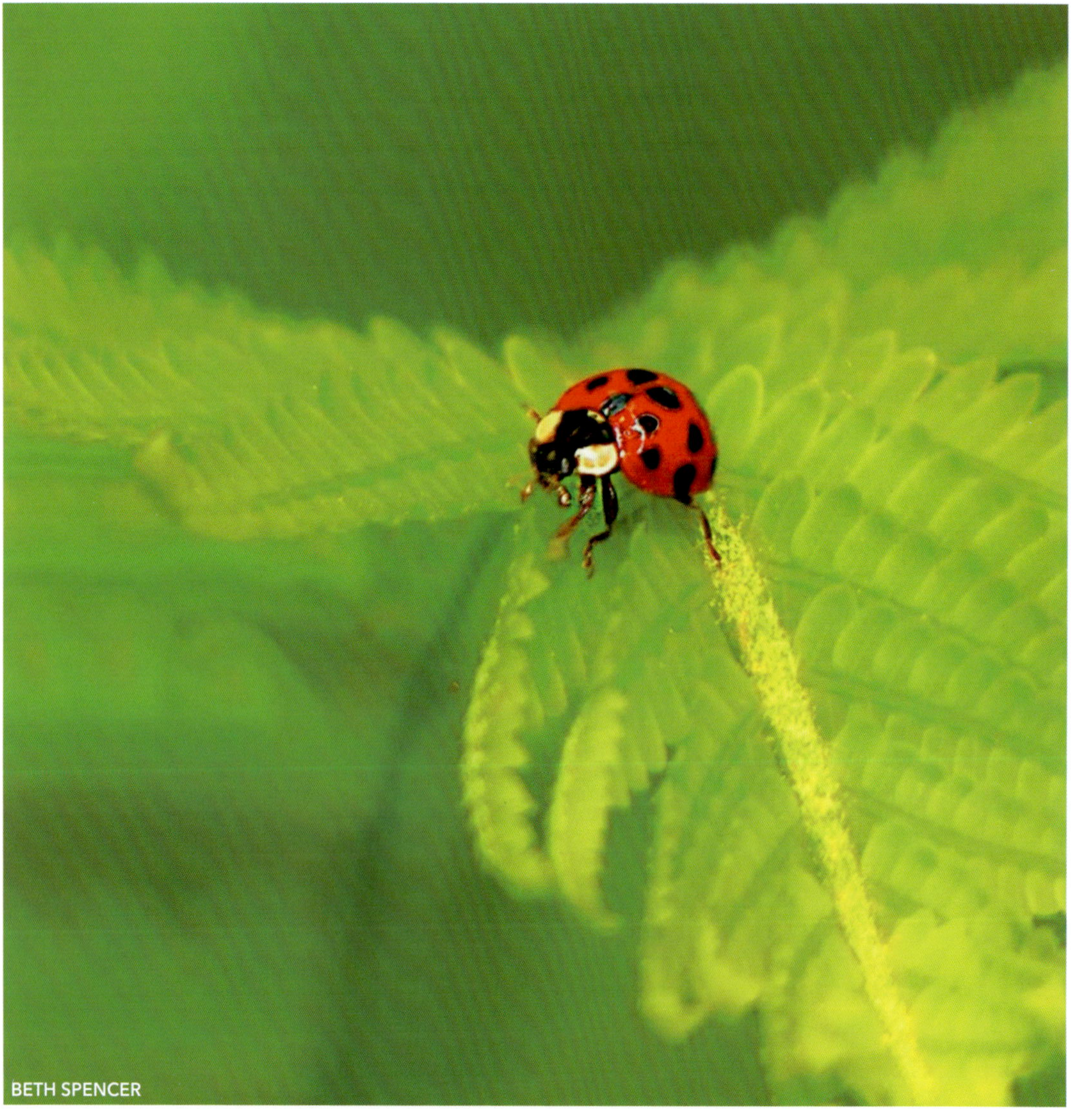
BETH SPENCER

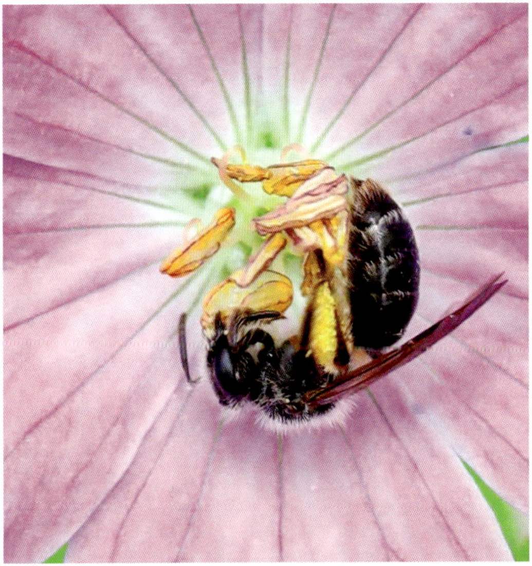

SARAH E. BAILEY

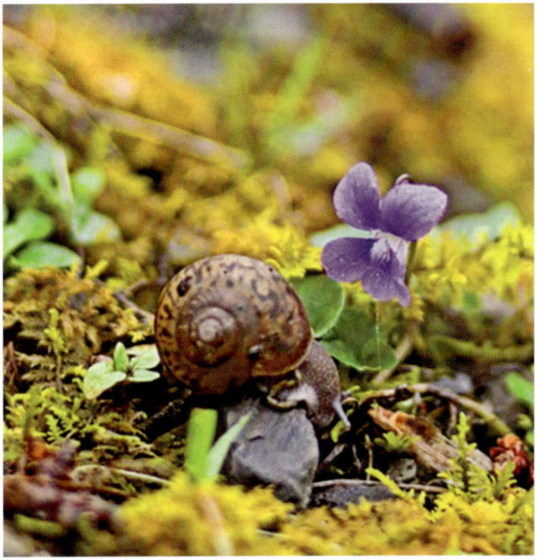

ERICA FISHER

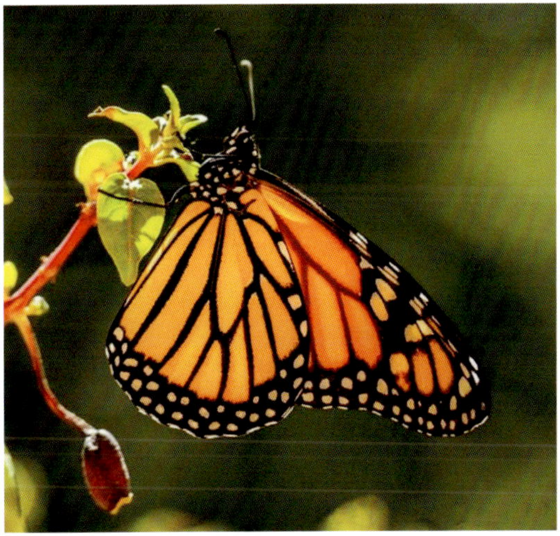

BETH SPENCER

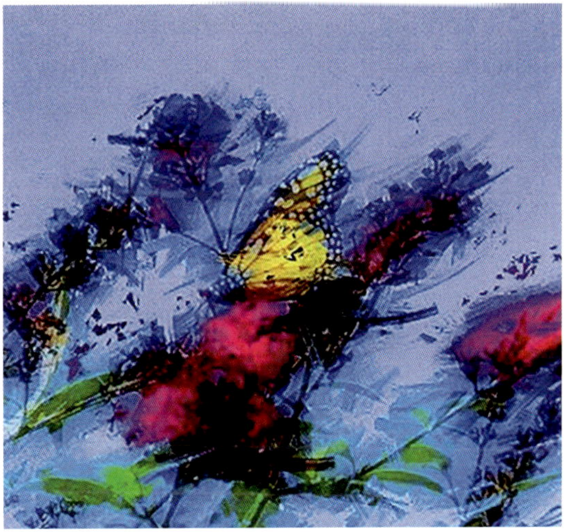

WESLEY PHILP

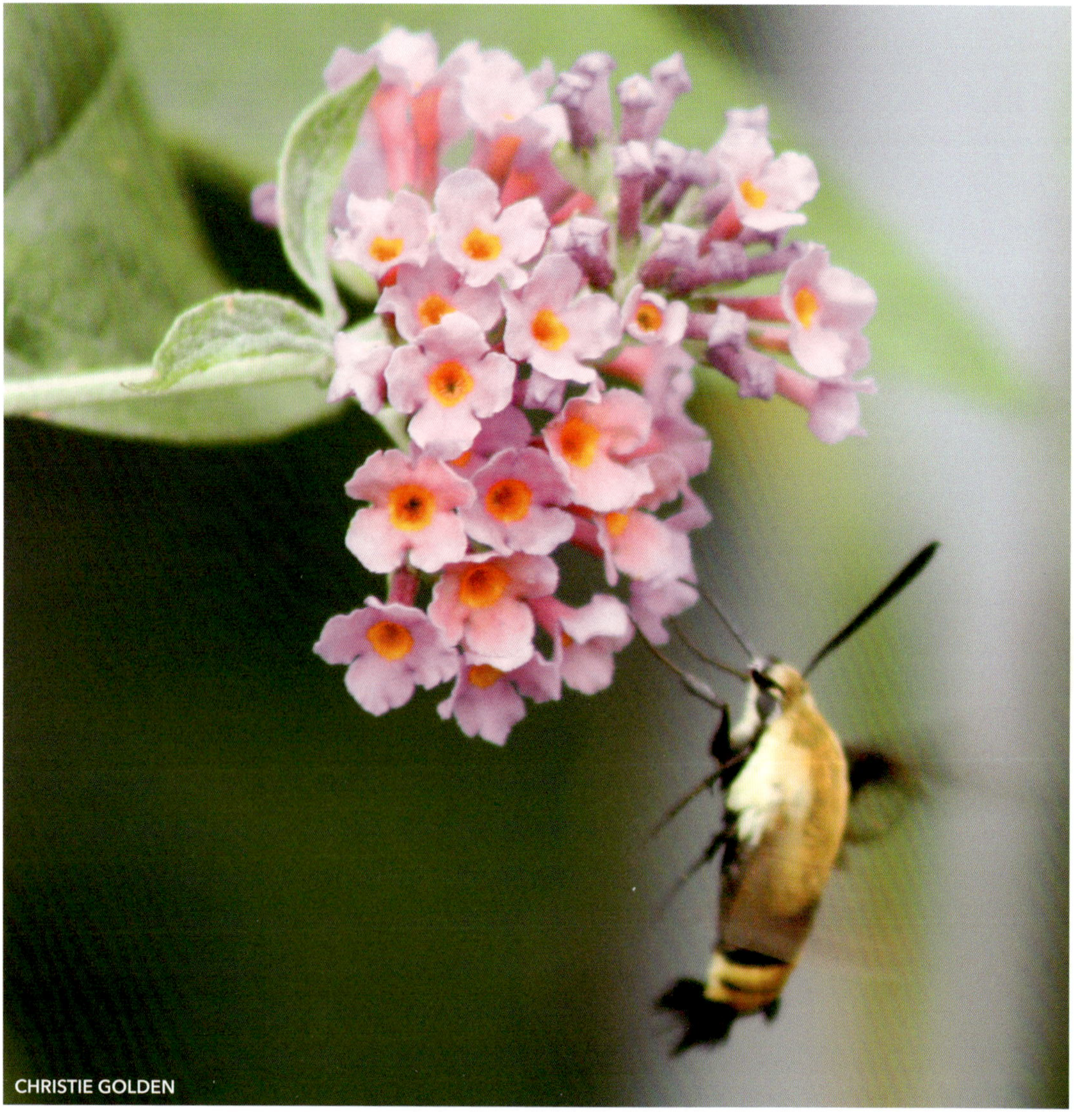

CHRISTIE GOLDEN

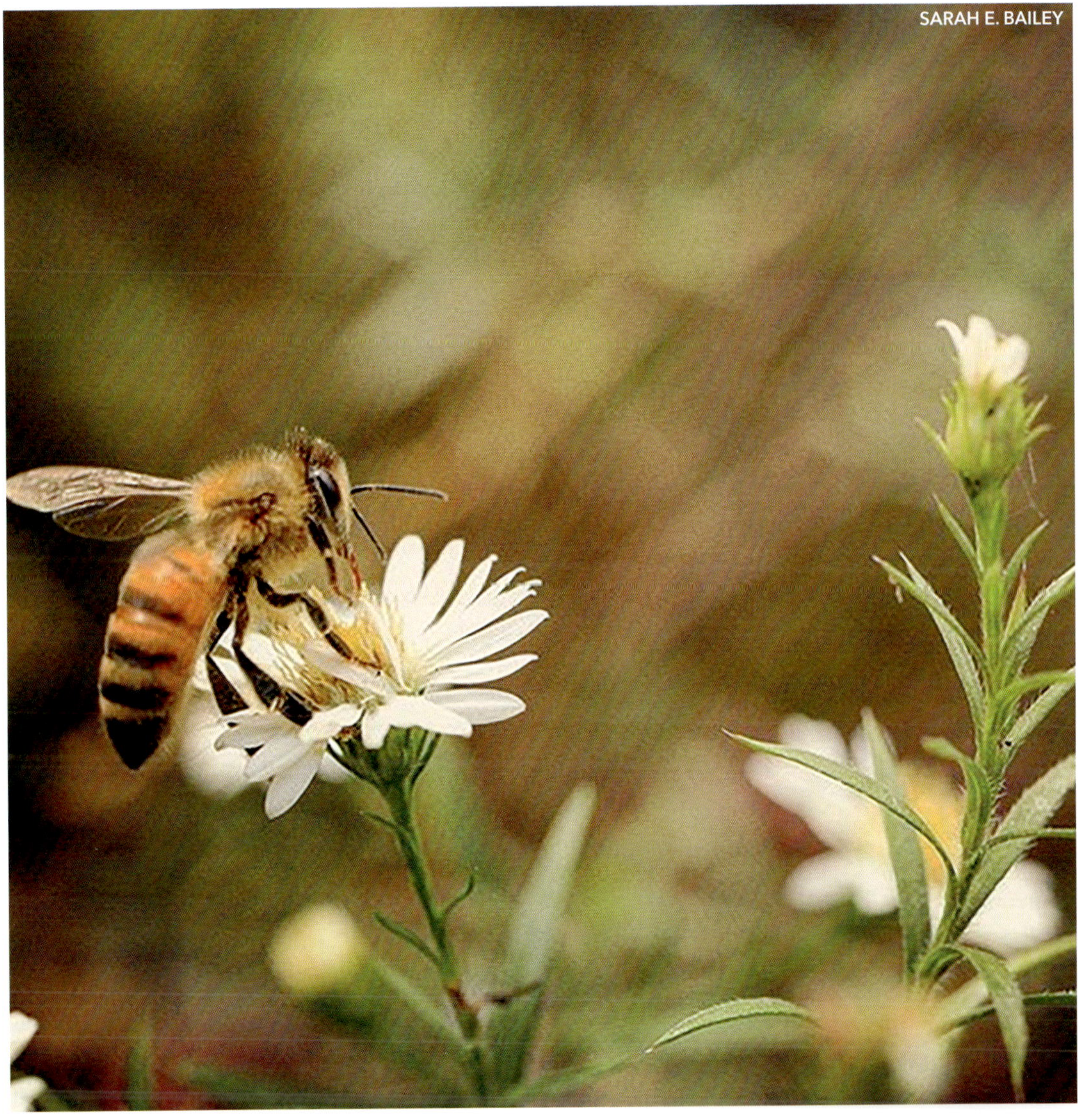
SARAH E. BAILEY

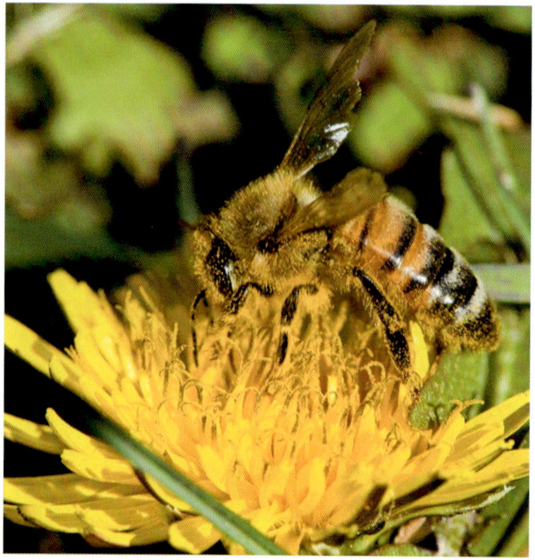

ARNOLD PARRISH

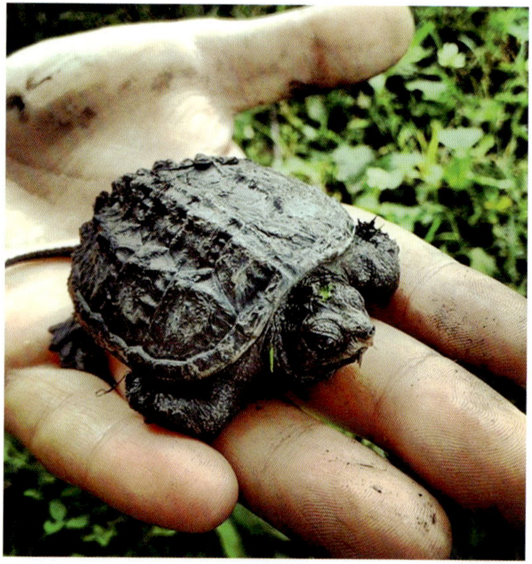

JUSTIN FRYE

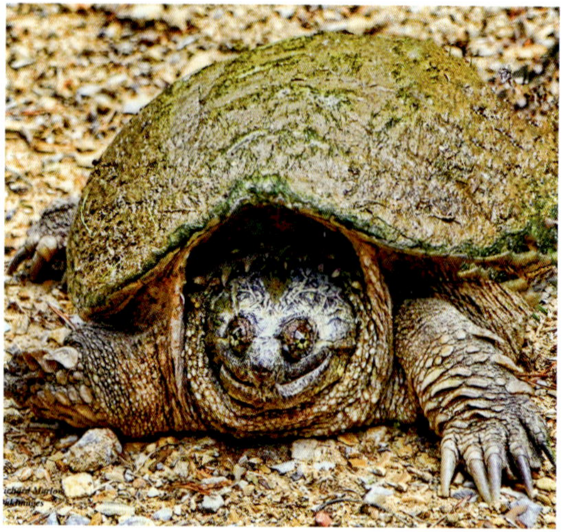

RICHARD MARLOW

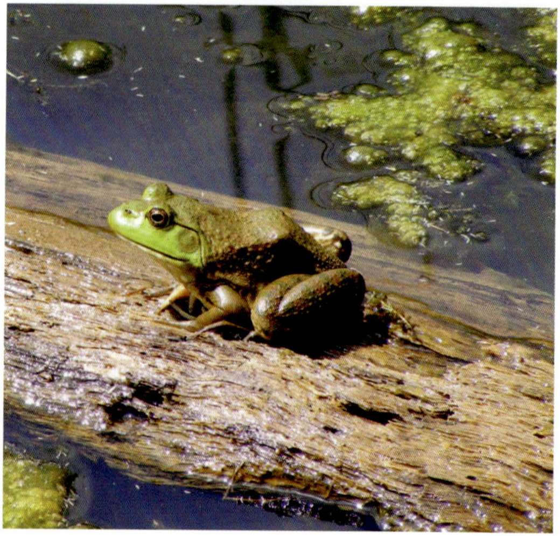

STAN WIKLE

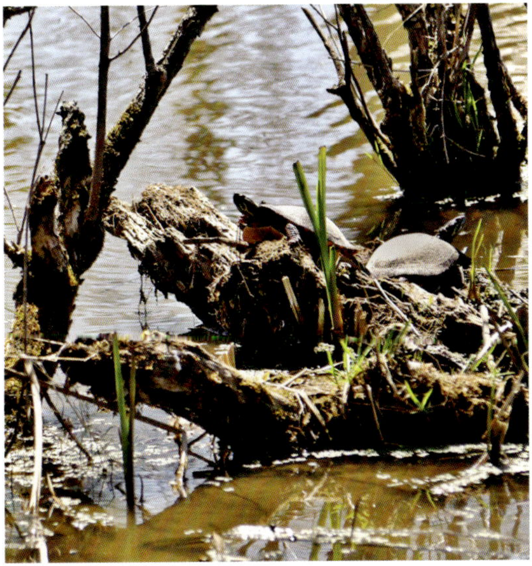

STEPHANIE CARPENTER

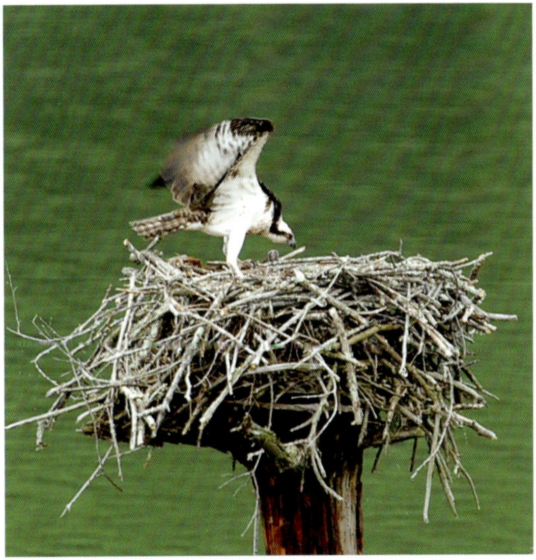

CYNTHIA MULLENS

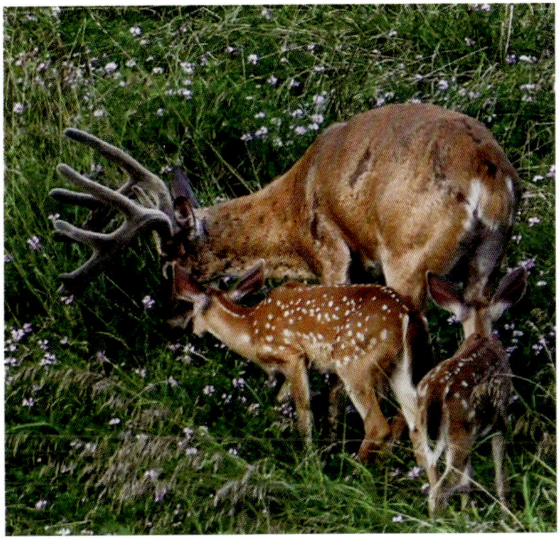

SHEILA JENKINS

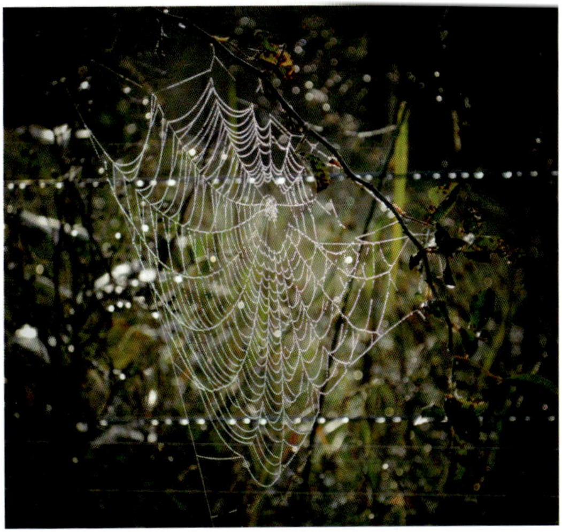

JIMMY SPENCER

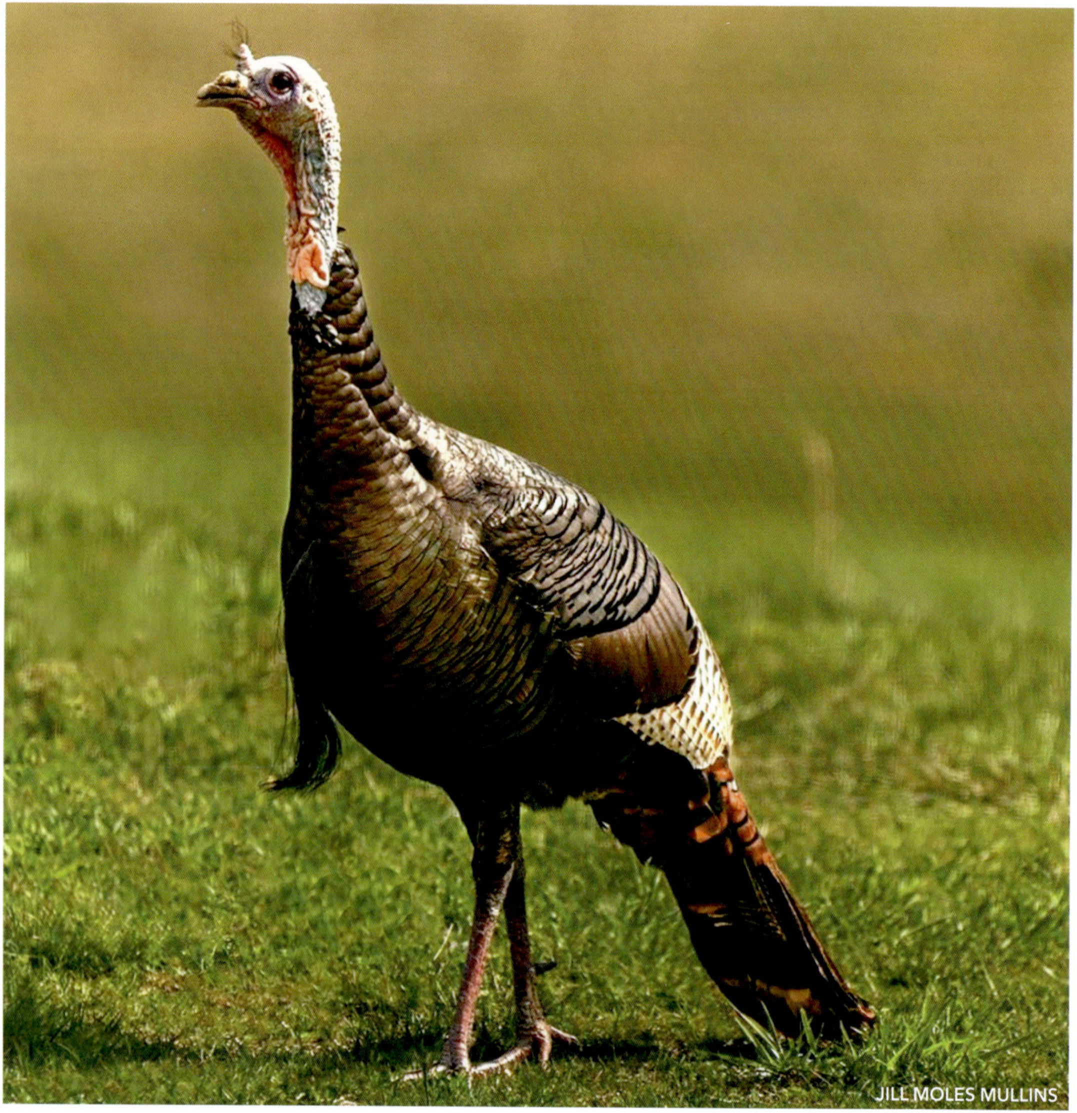
JILL MOLES MULLINS

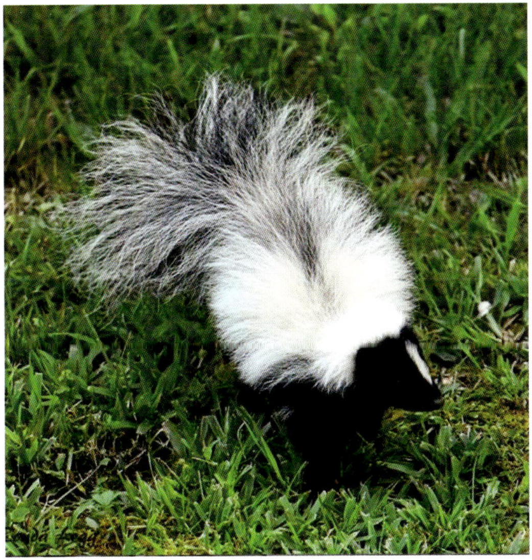

RONDA LEGG

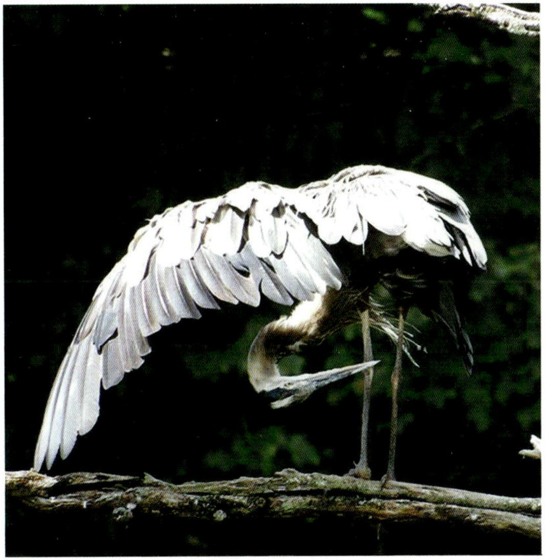

CYNTHIA MULLENS

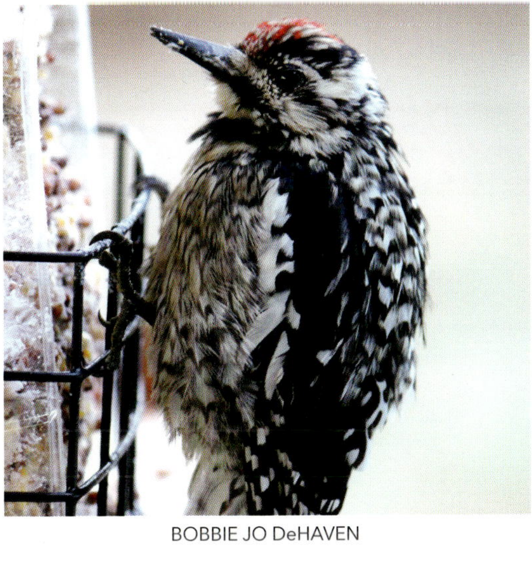

BOBBIE JO DeHAVEN

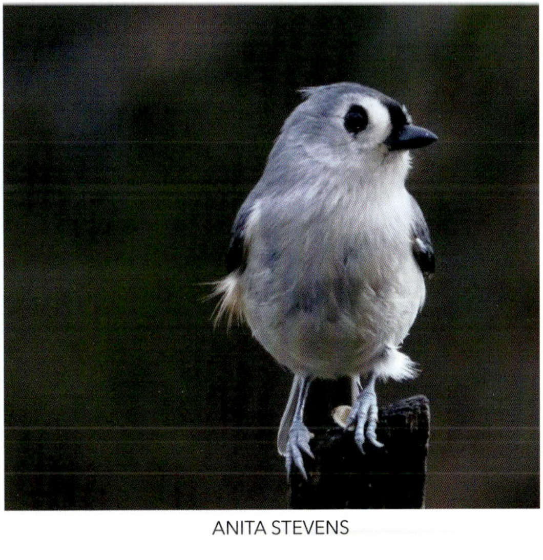

ANITA STEVENS

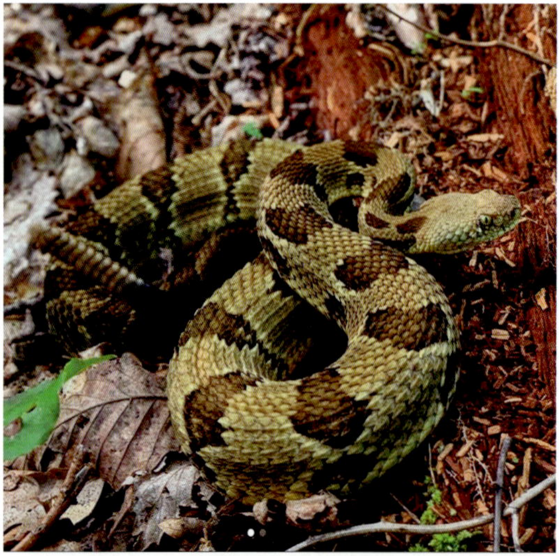

STEPHANIE BENNETT

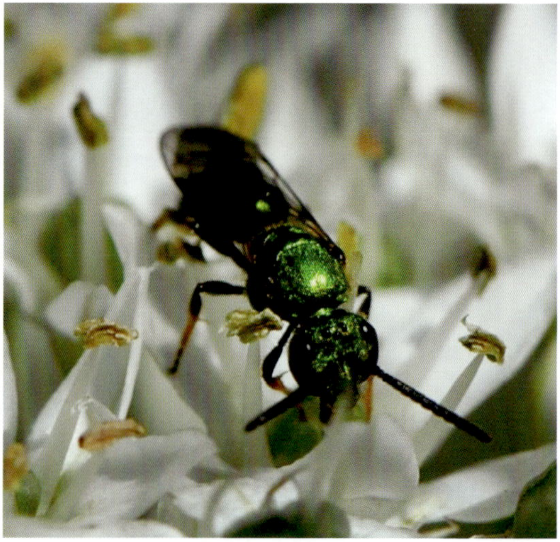

CYNTHIA MULLENS

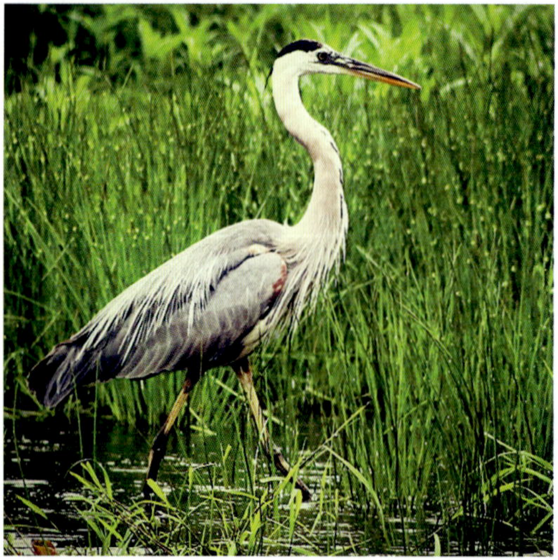

SARAH E. BAILEY

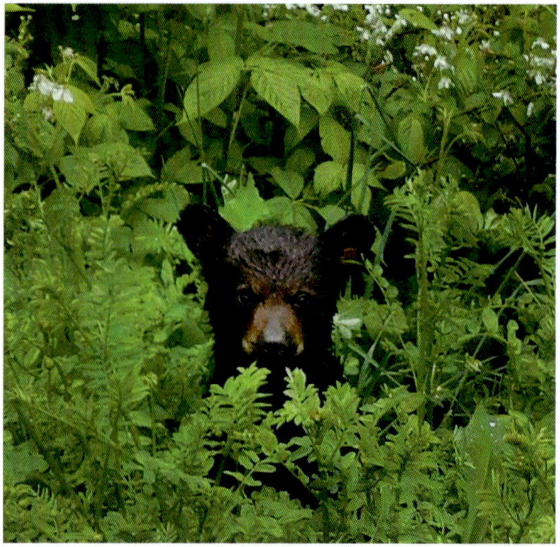

SARAH M. CARR

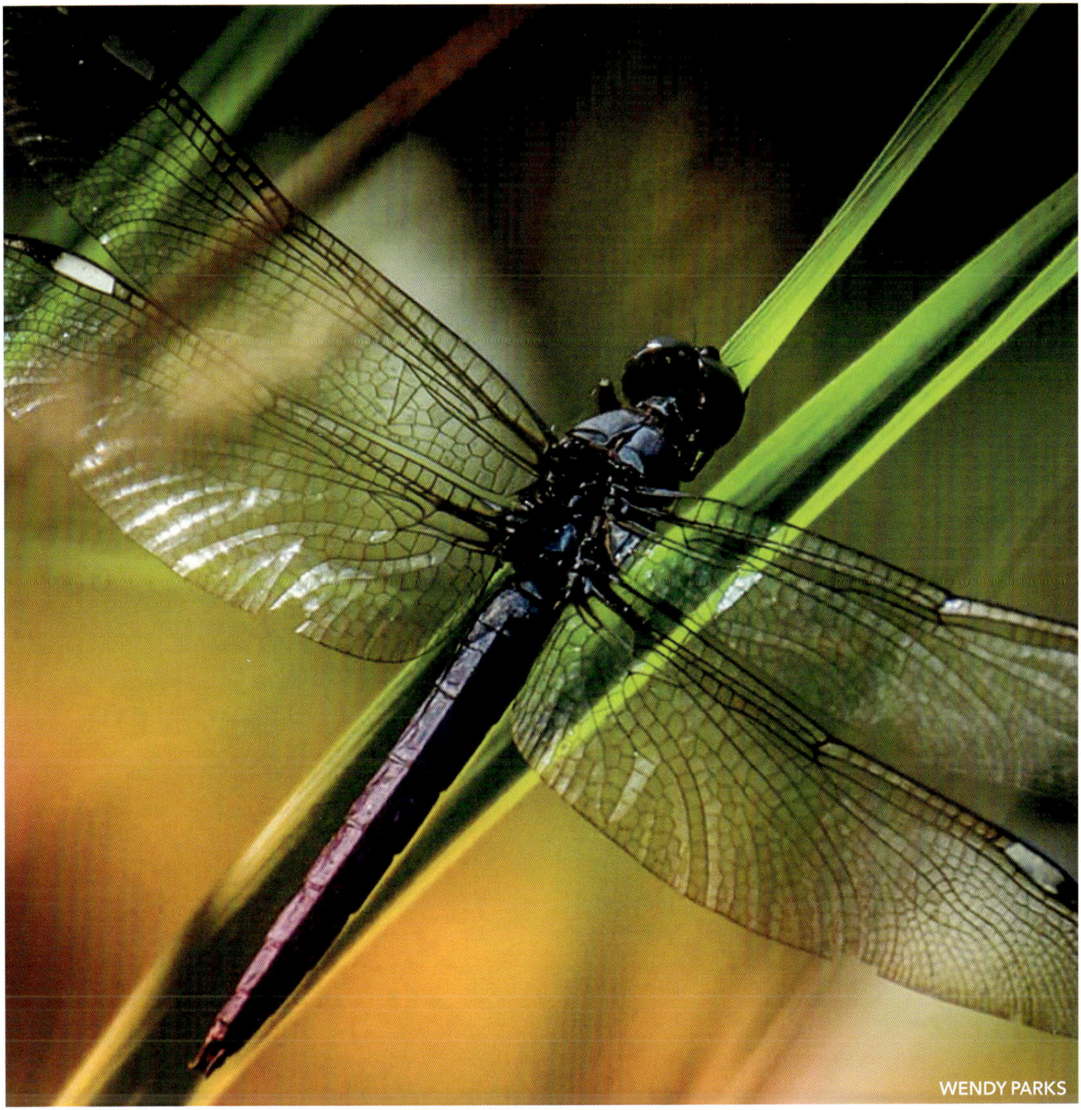

WENDY PARKS

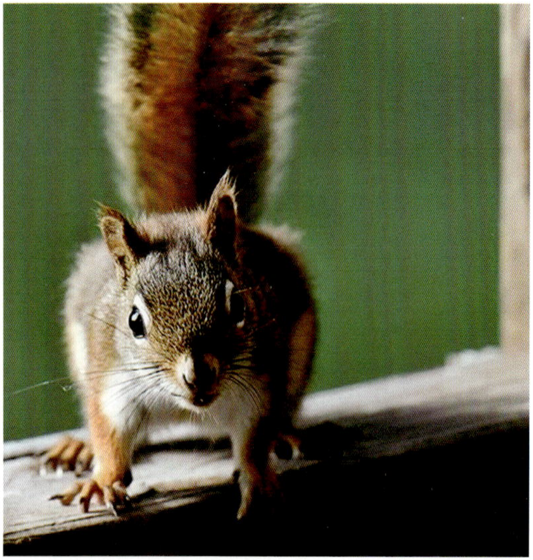

RONDA LEGG

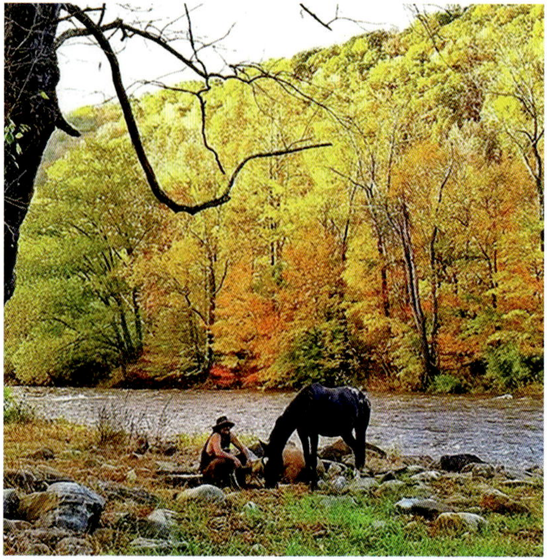

LIZ STOUT

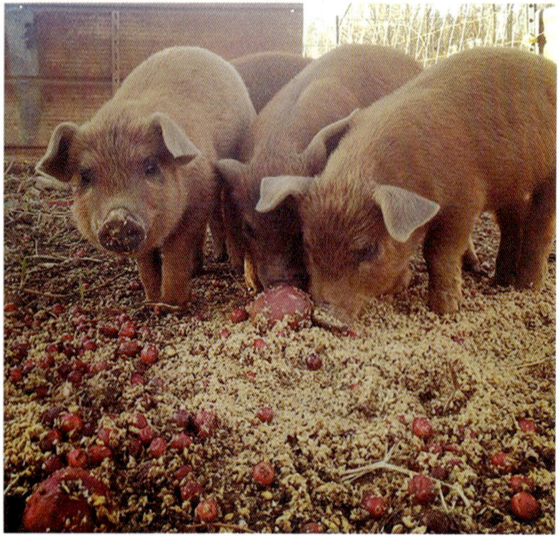

MELVILLE JOHNSON IV

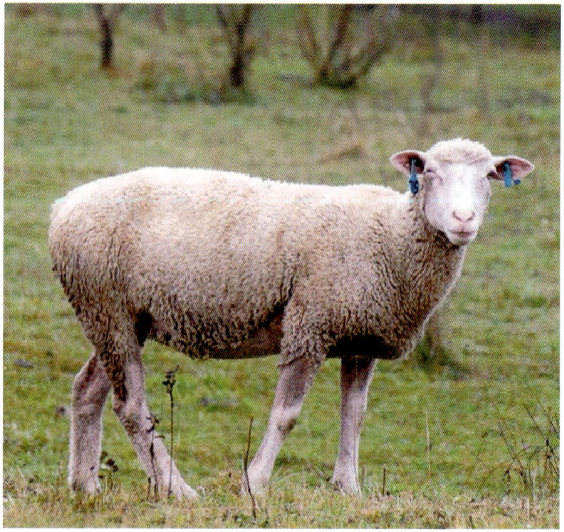

DENISE POWERS FABIAN

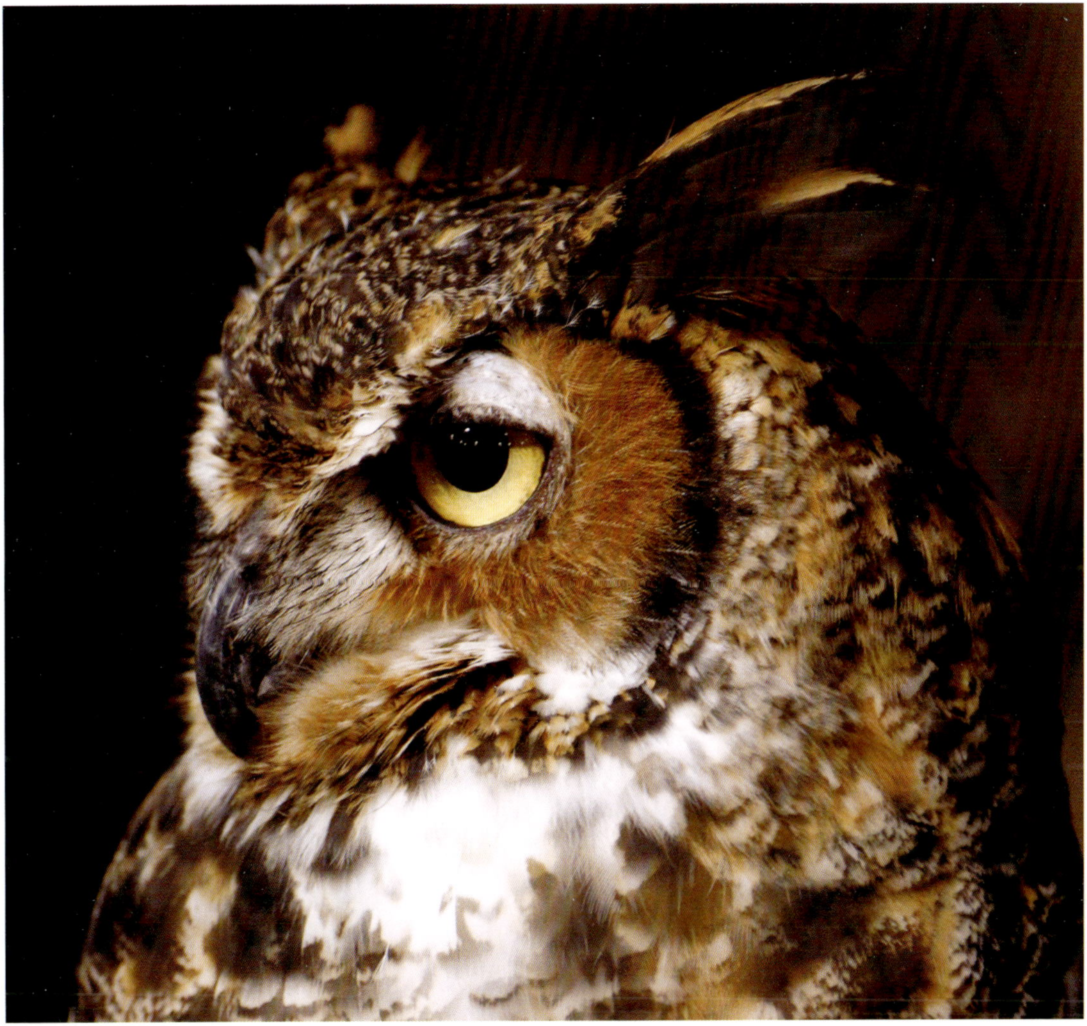

STEPHANIE CARPENTER

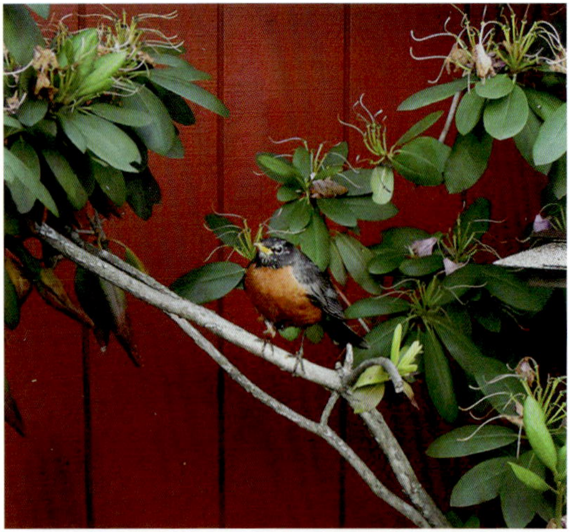

CANDY THOMPSON

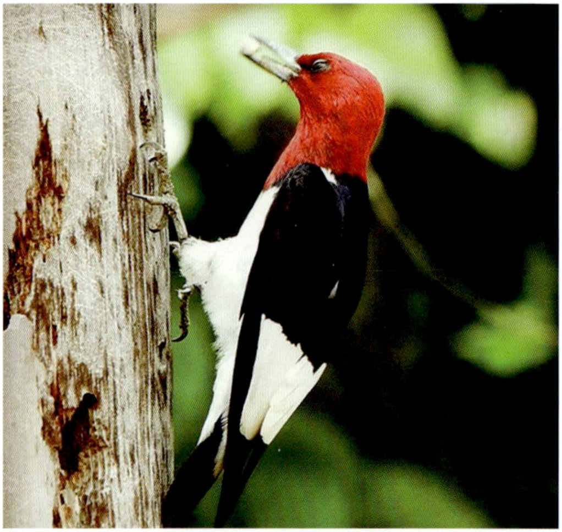

CYNTHIA MULLENS

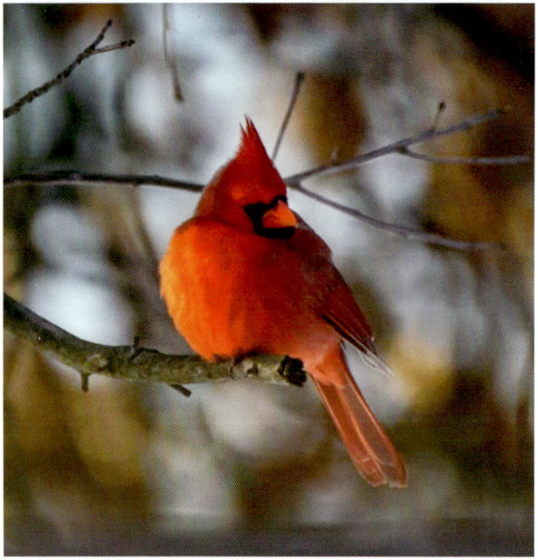

WENDY PARKS

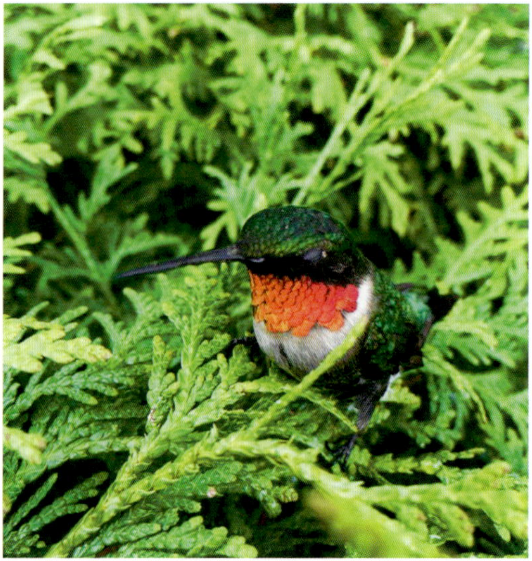

VICKY L. UNDERWOOD

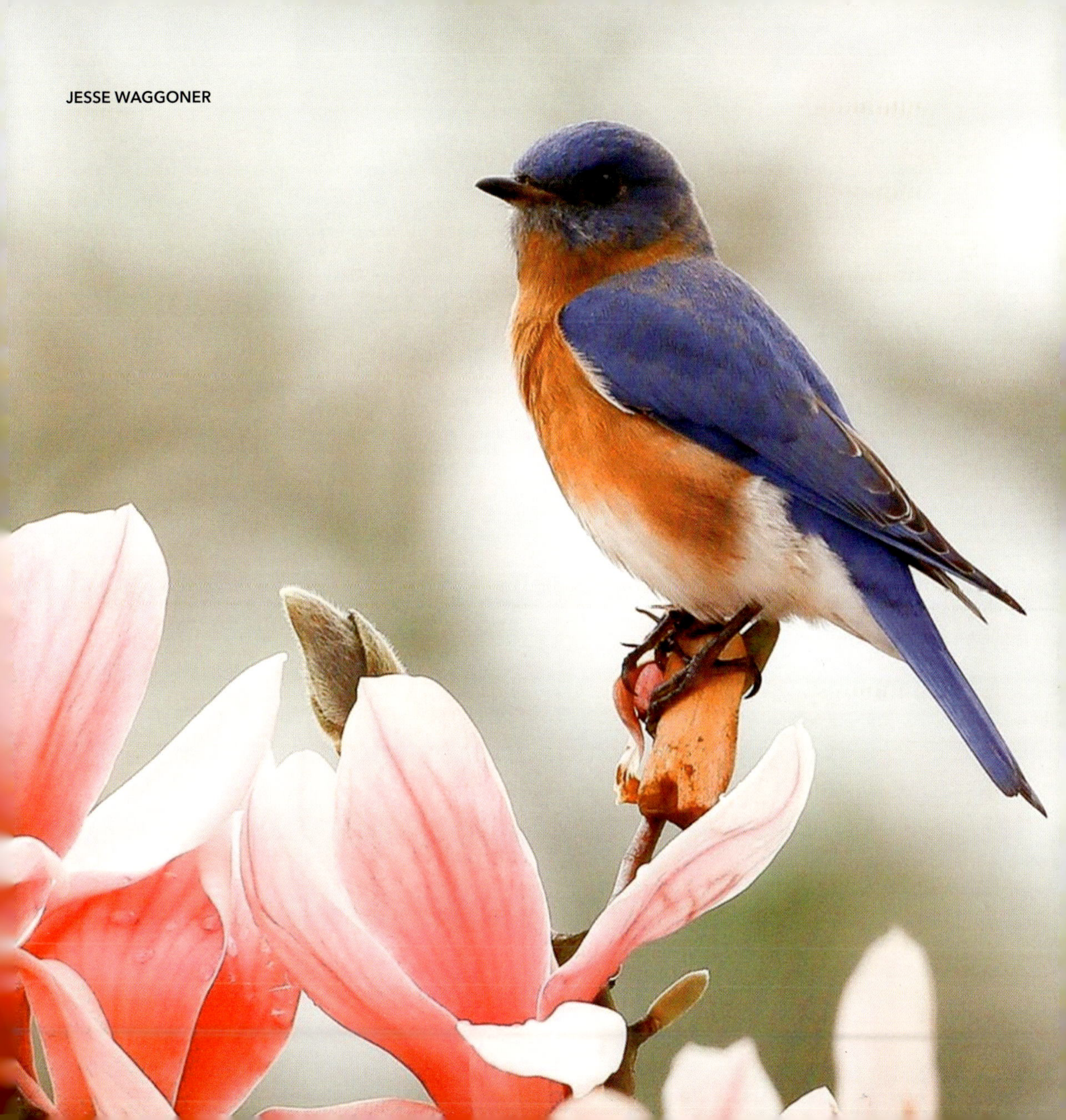
JESSE WAGGONER

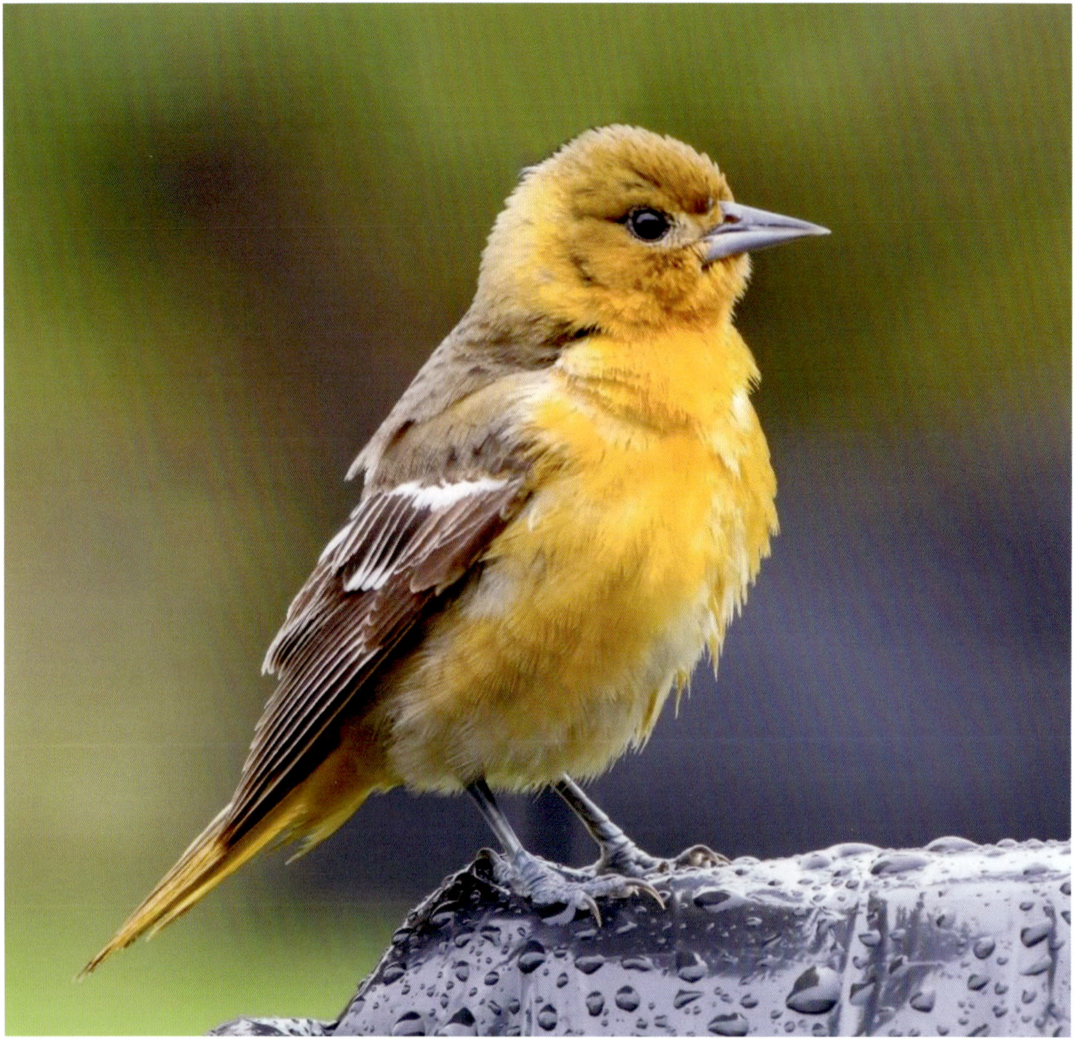

ANITA STEVENS

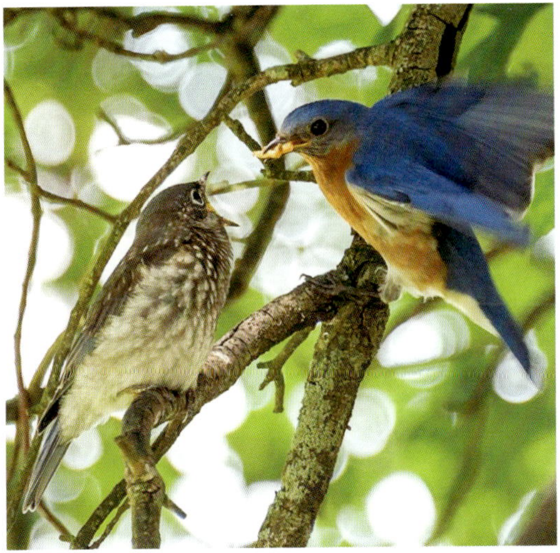

WENDY PARKS

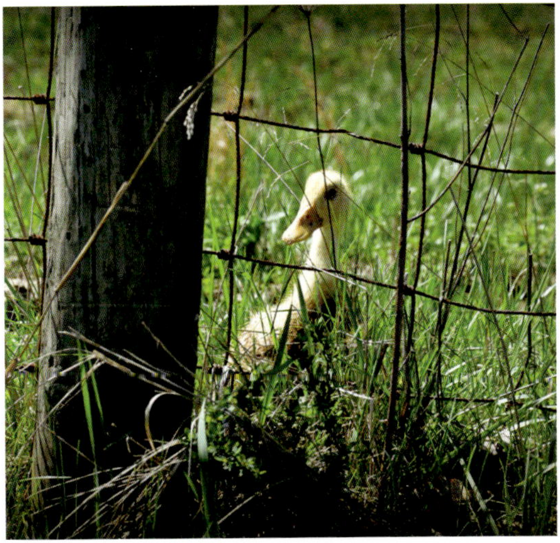

MAGGIE FISHER

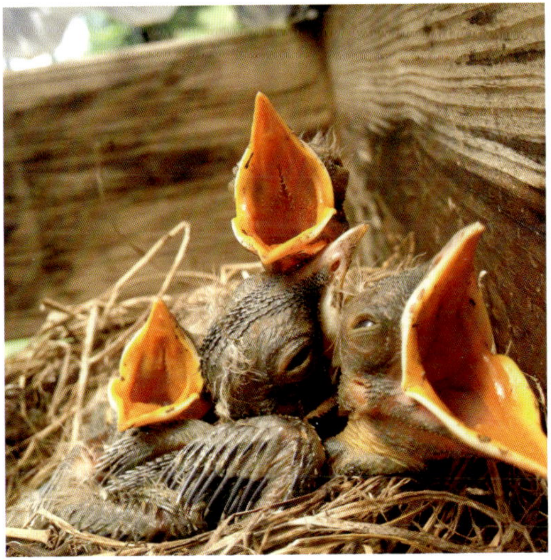

BRITTIANY BURDETTE

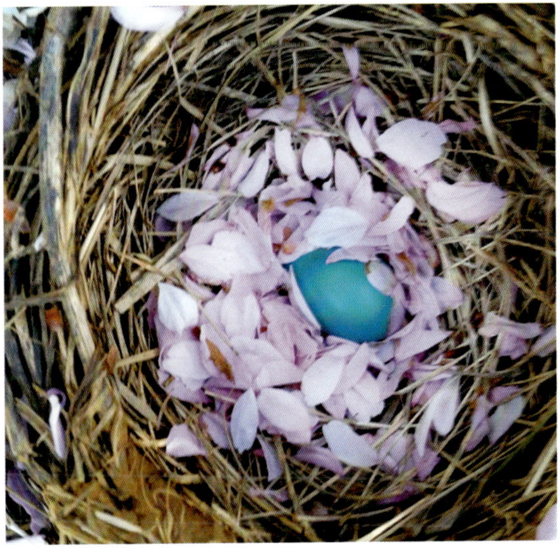

JANICE SCOTT

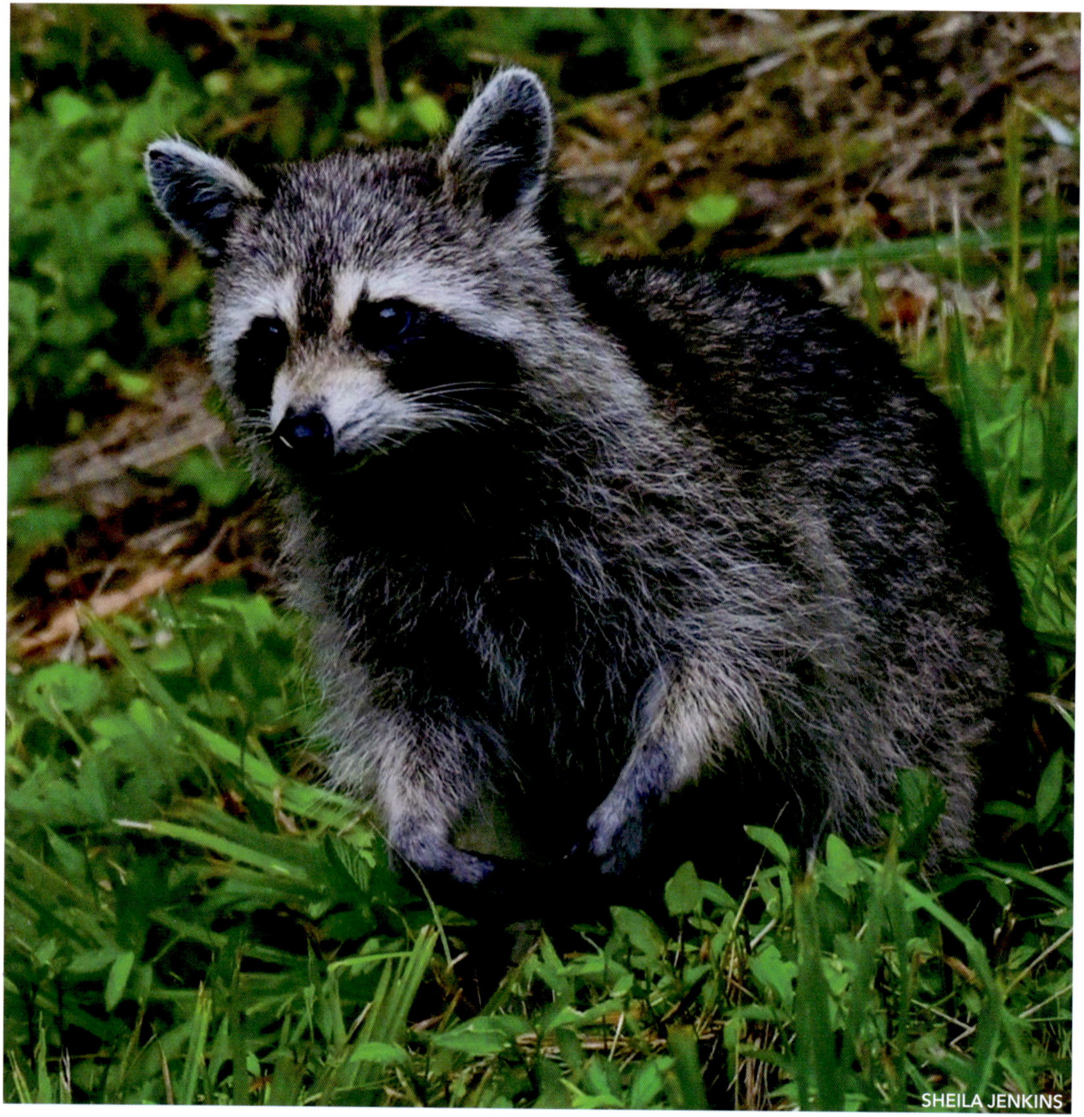
SHEILA JENKINS

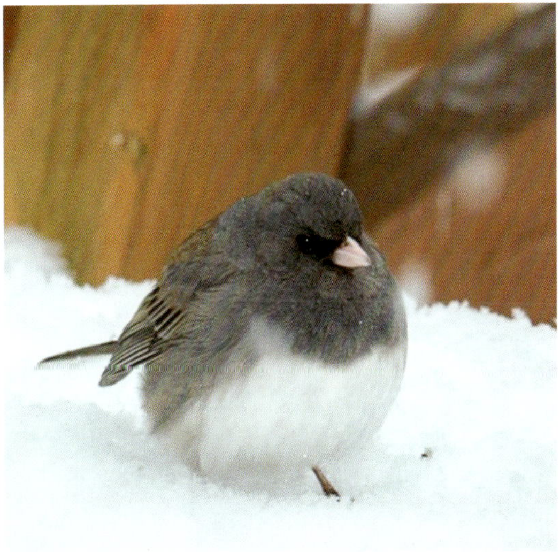

JON HOWARD

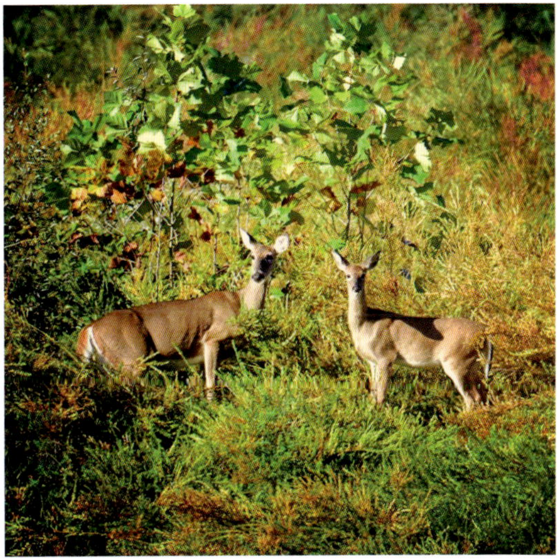

AUDRA HIXSON

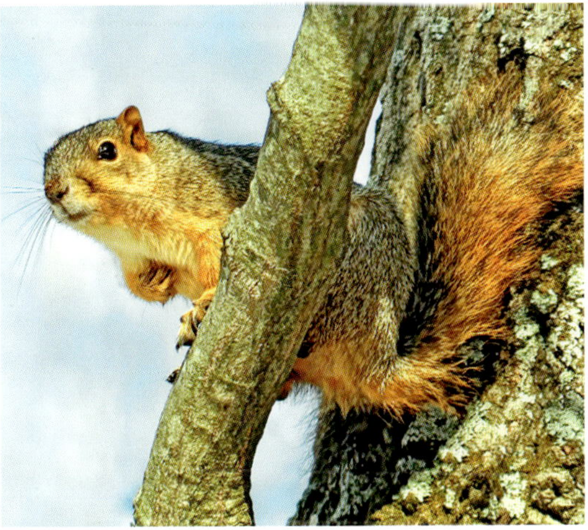

RICHARD MARLOW

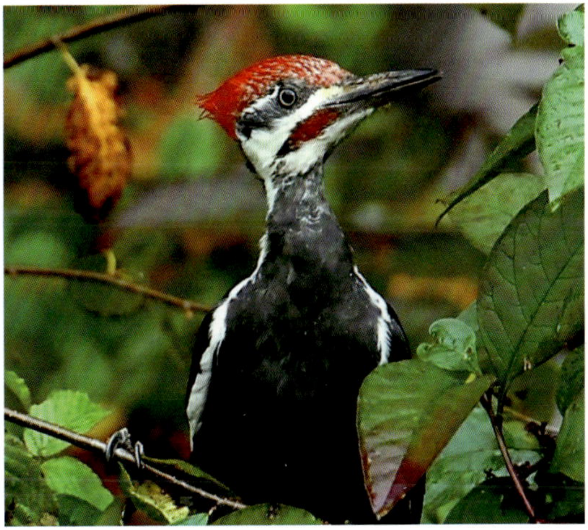

CYNTHIA MULLENS

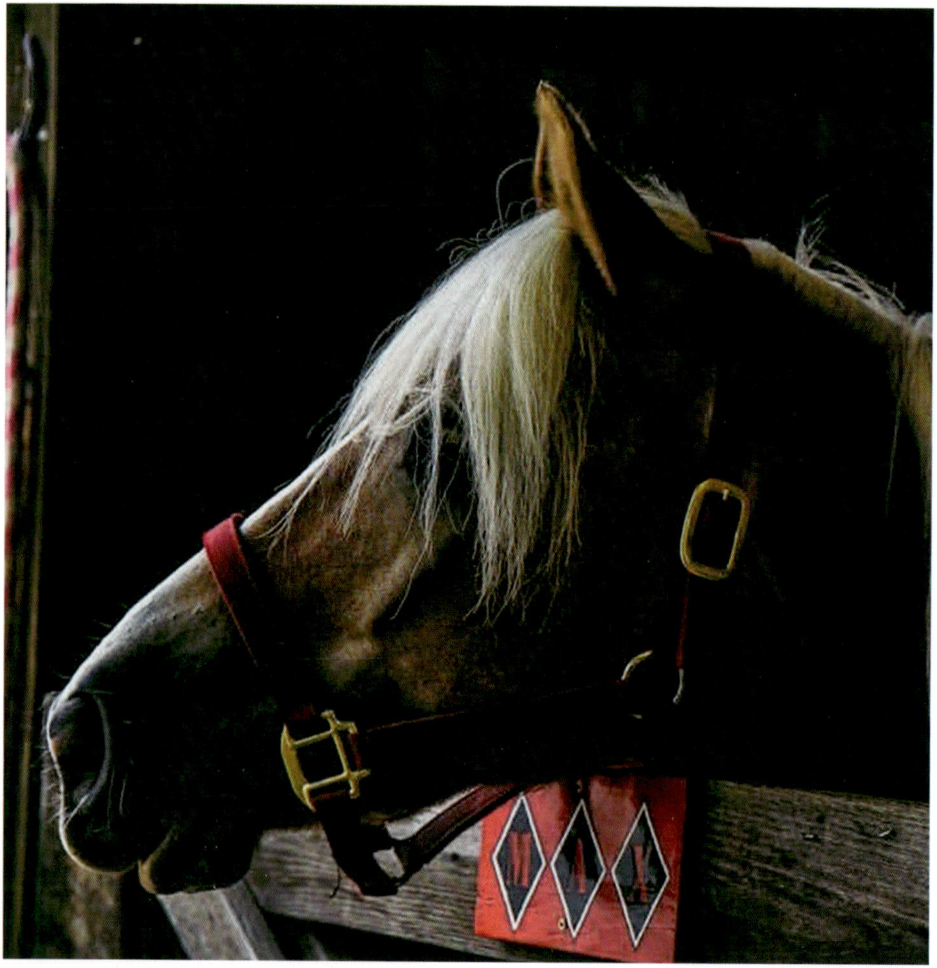

KEVIN JACK

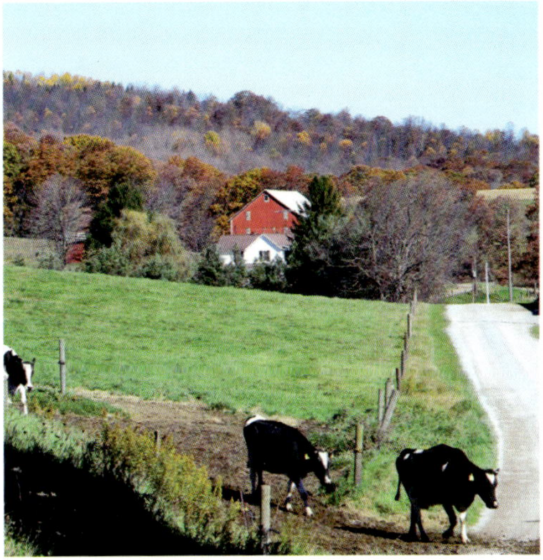

KIMBERLY FOWLER

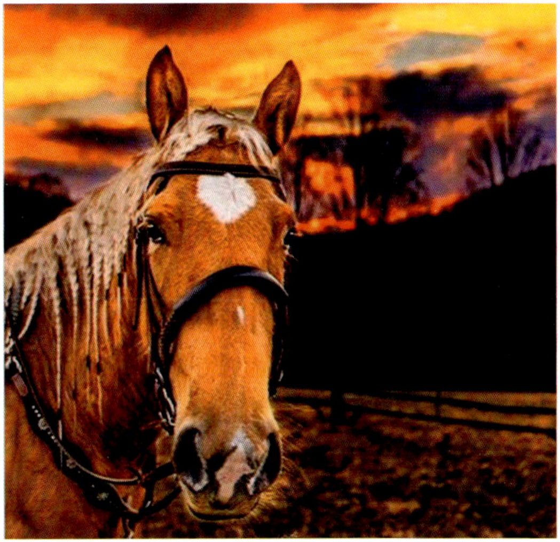

JILL MOLES MULLINS

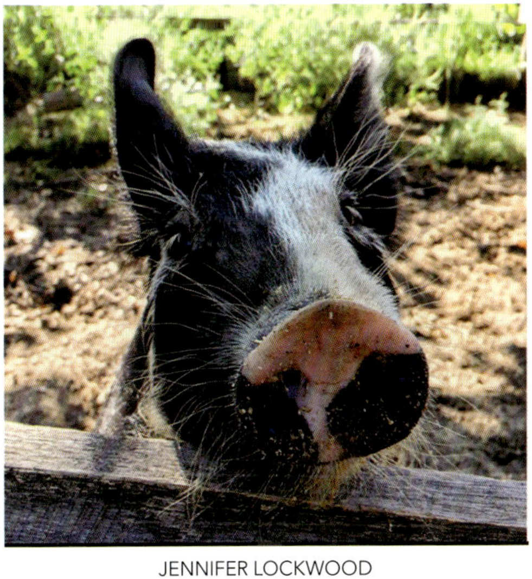

JENNIFER LOCKWOOD

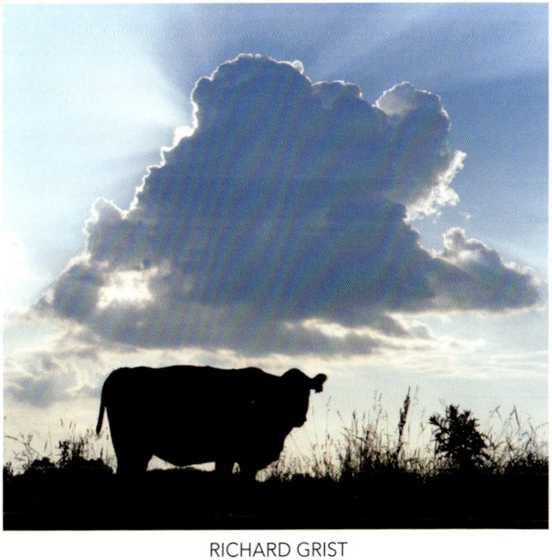

RICHARD GRIST

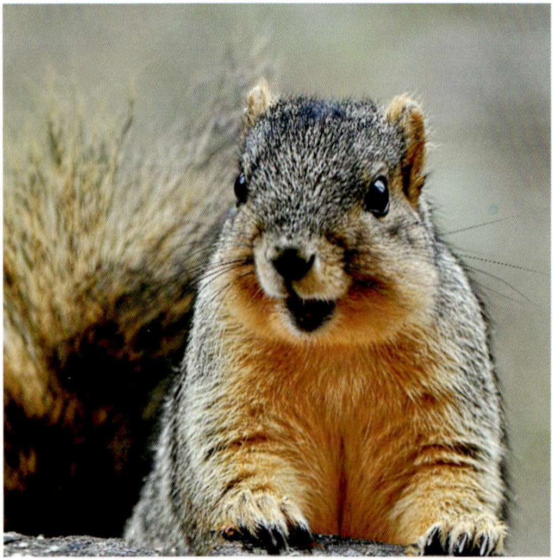
RICHARD MARLOW

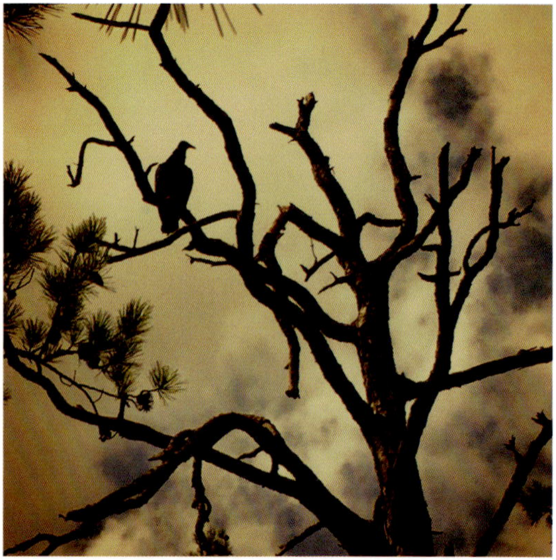
JUSTIN DYNES

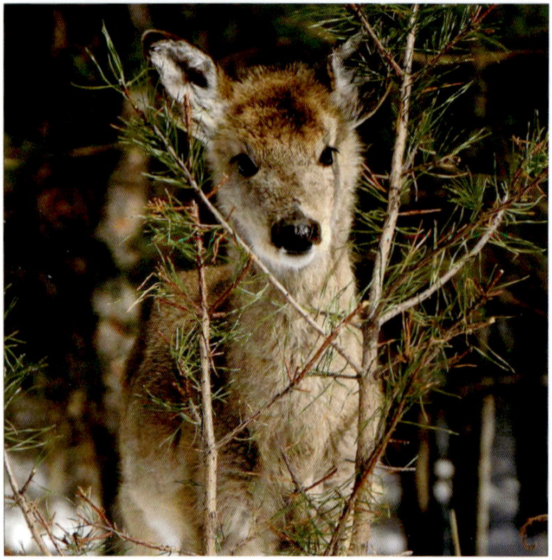
BRIAN BOYCE McCOY

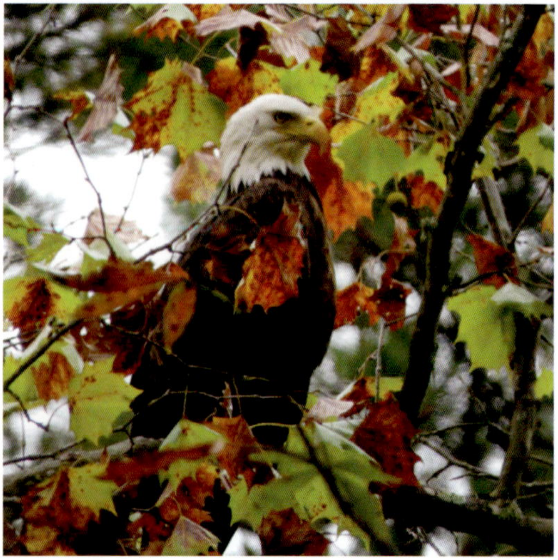
JEANNIE HANNA

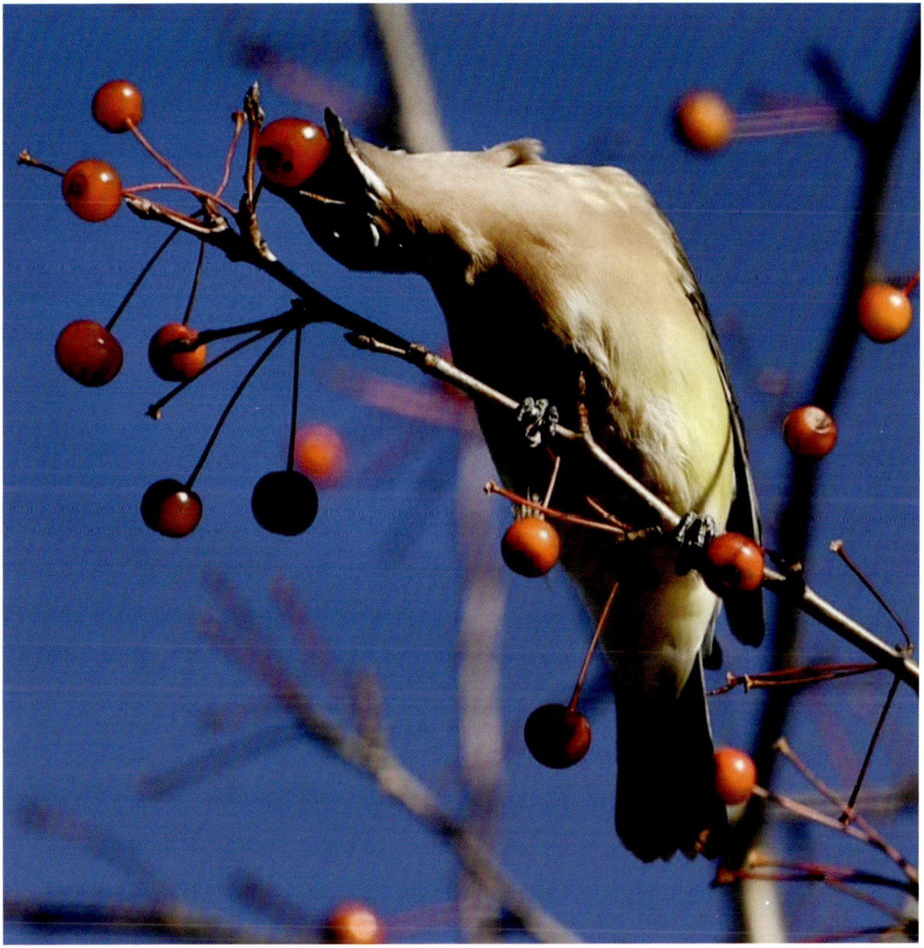

SAM SHEILS

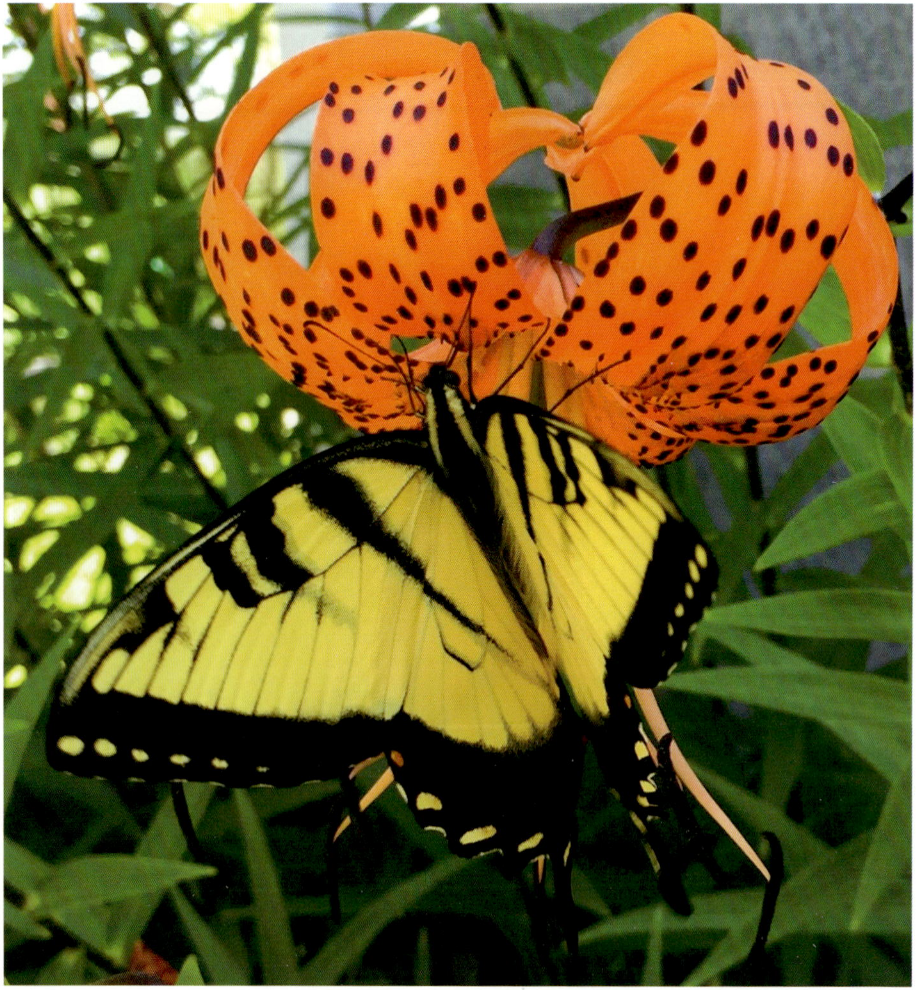

JENNIFER D. RANDOLPH

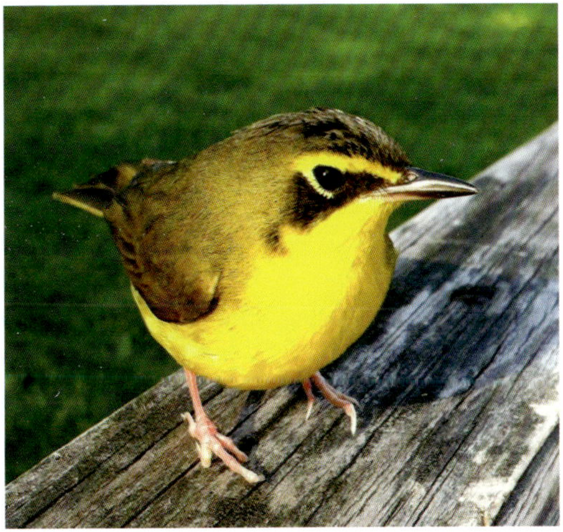

JESSICA STALNAKER

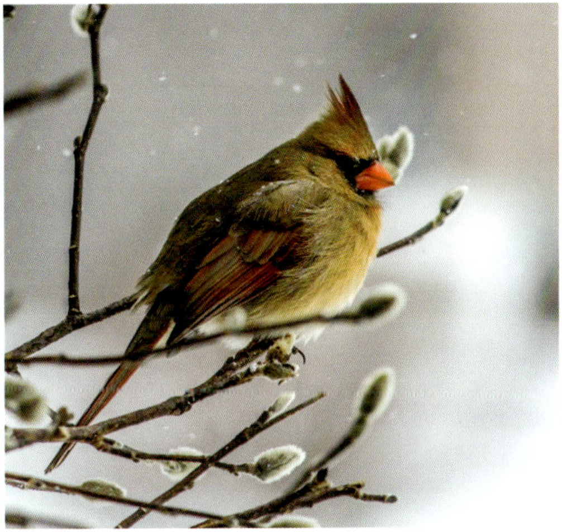

KATHY JENKINS

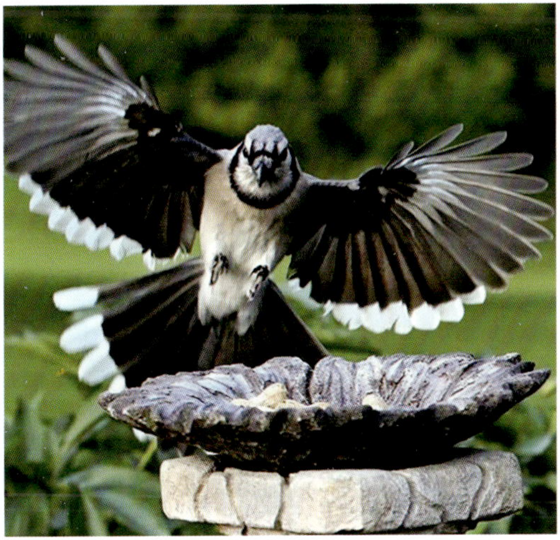

ANITA STEVENS

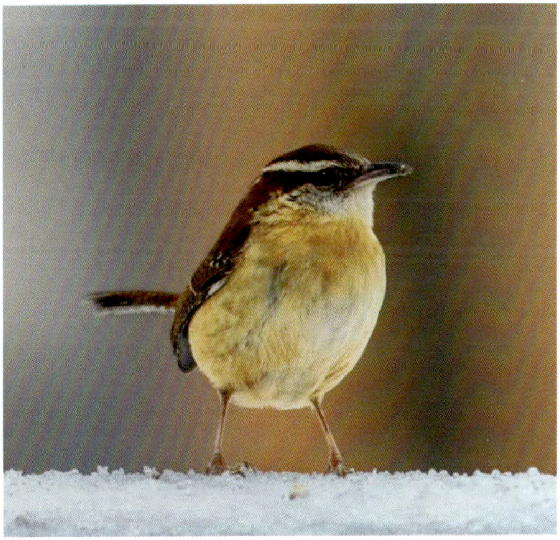

BETH SPENCER

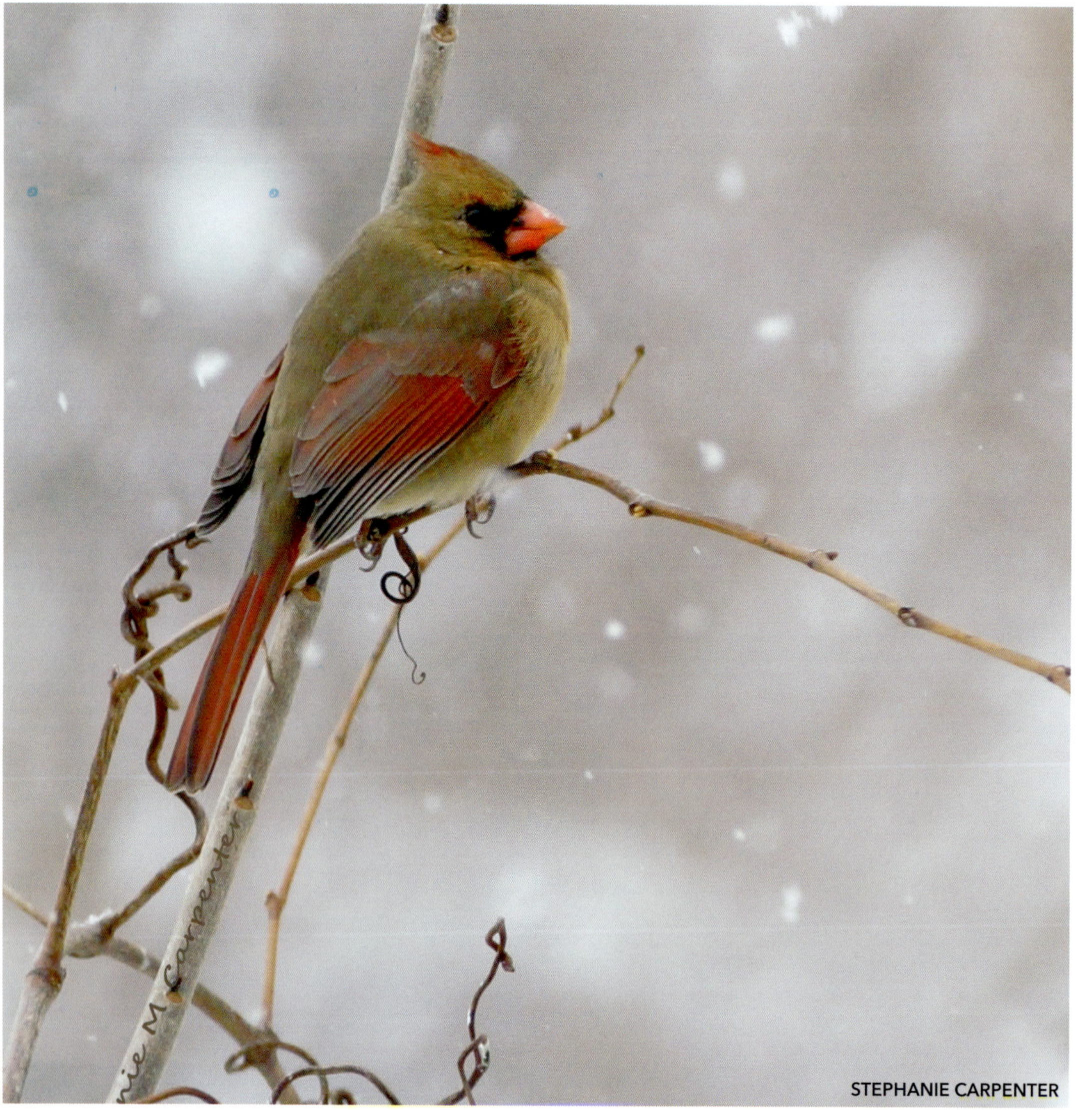

STEPHANIE CARPENTER

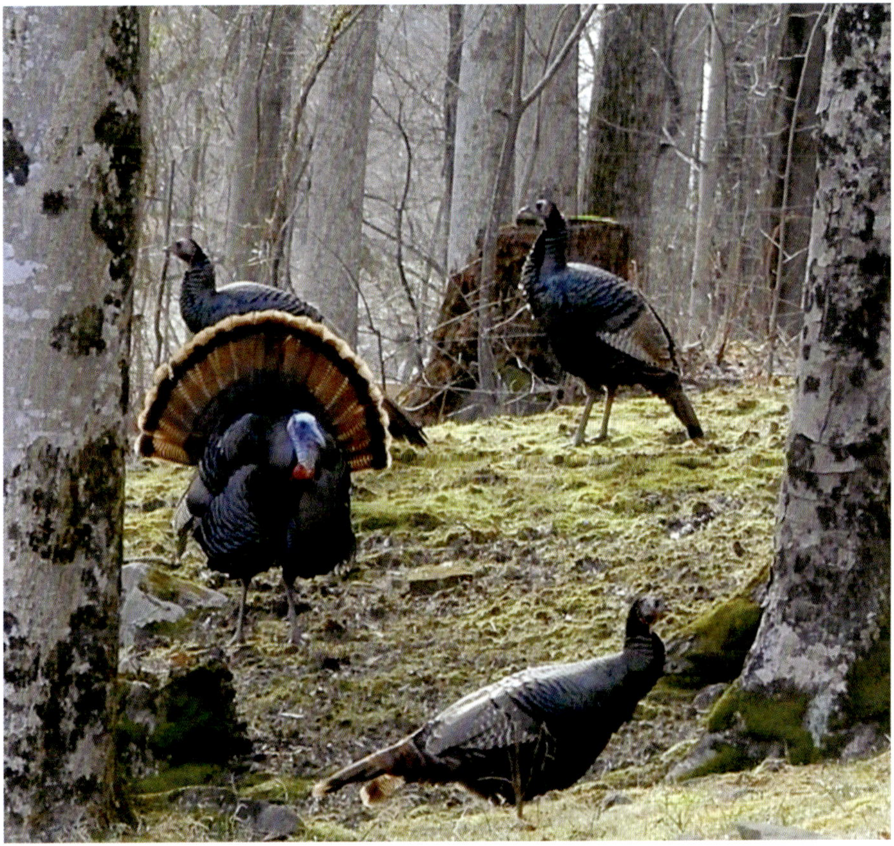

PAT DOTSON

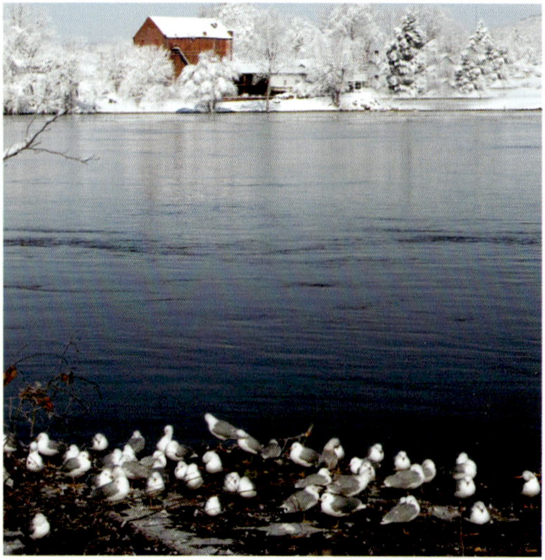

DAMON RHODES

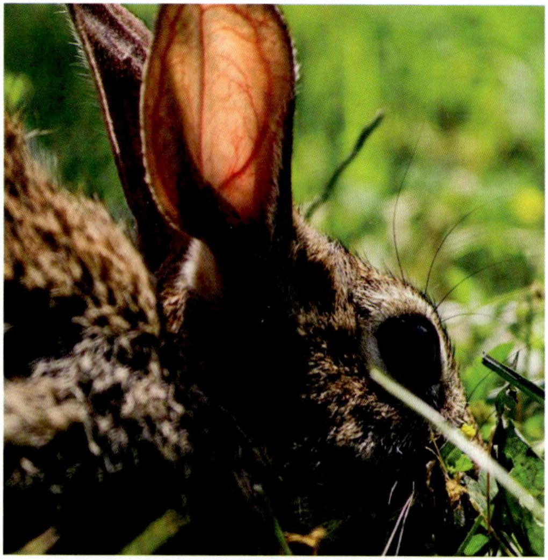

ZOE WATERS

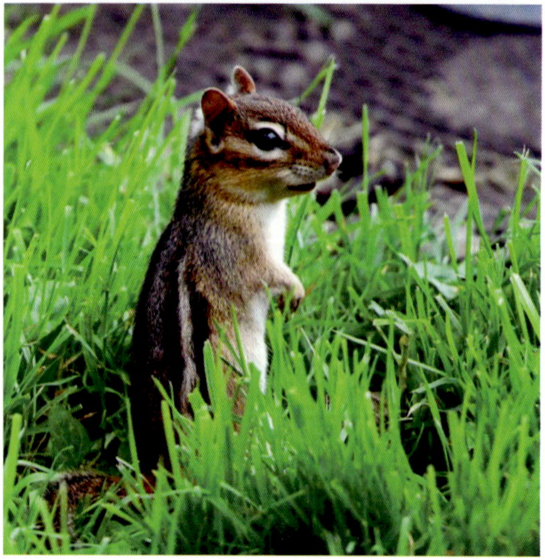

RONDA LEGG

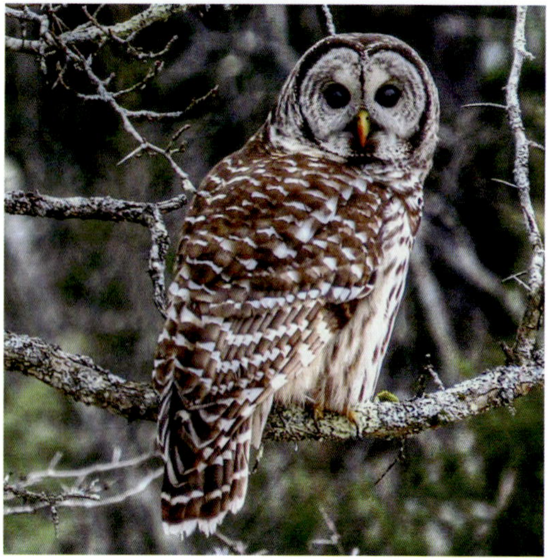

VAL CARNELL

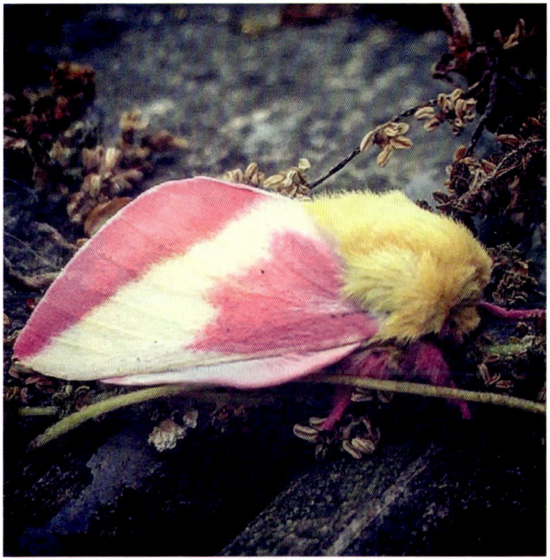
ELAINE CLARK

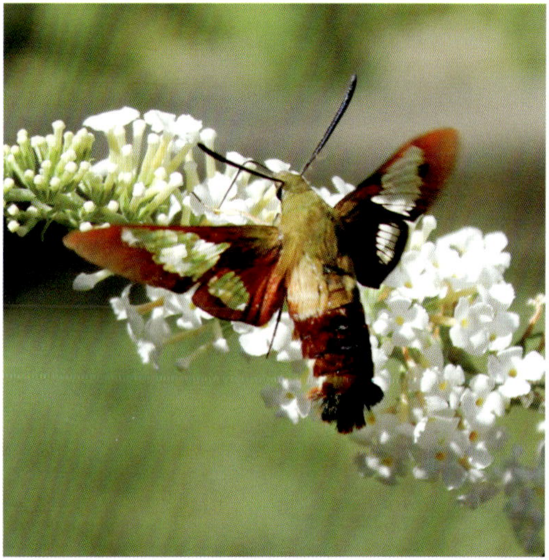
MARK REASOR

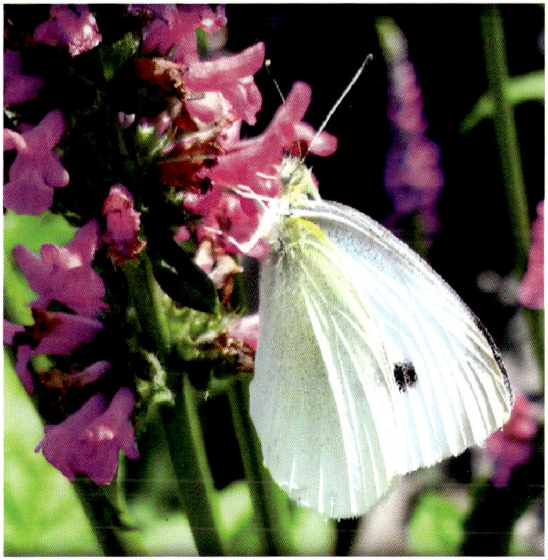
JANICE SCOTT

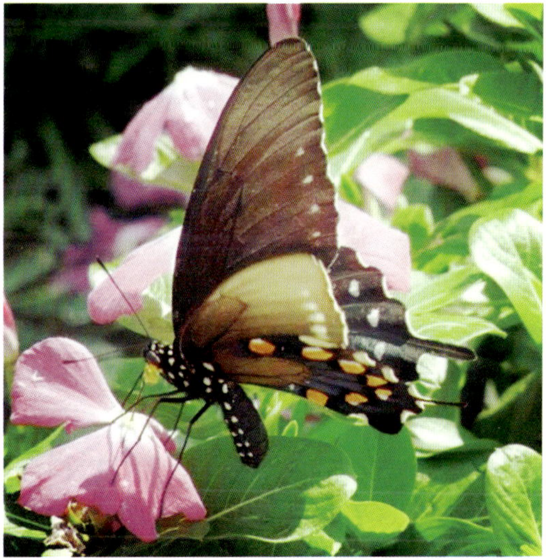
AMBER HEATH

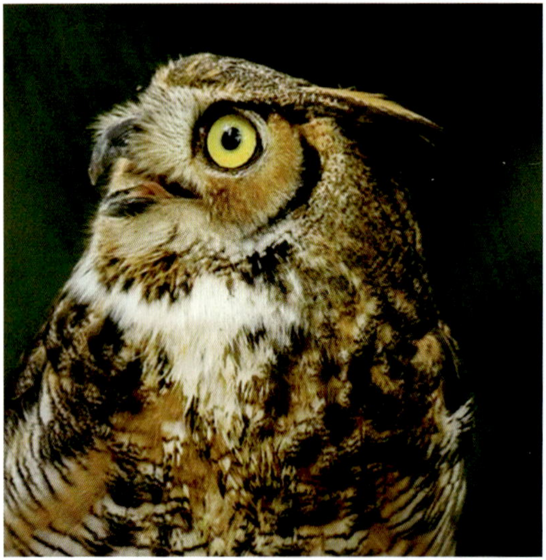

JILL MULLINS

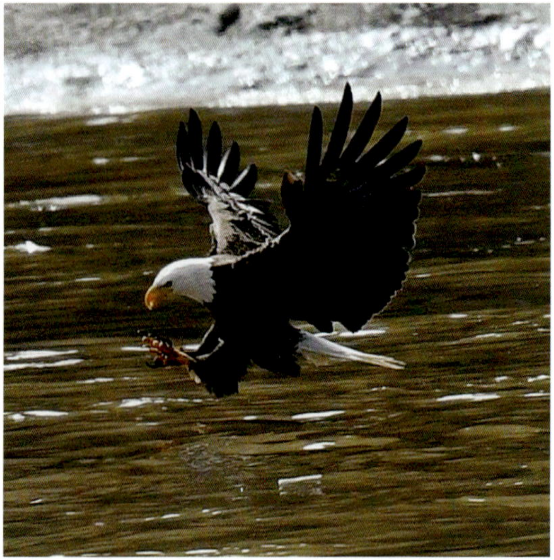

RONDA LEGG

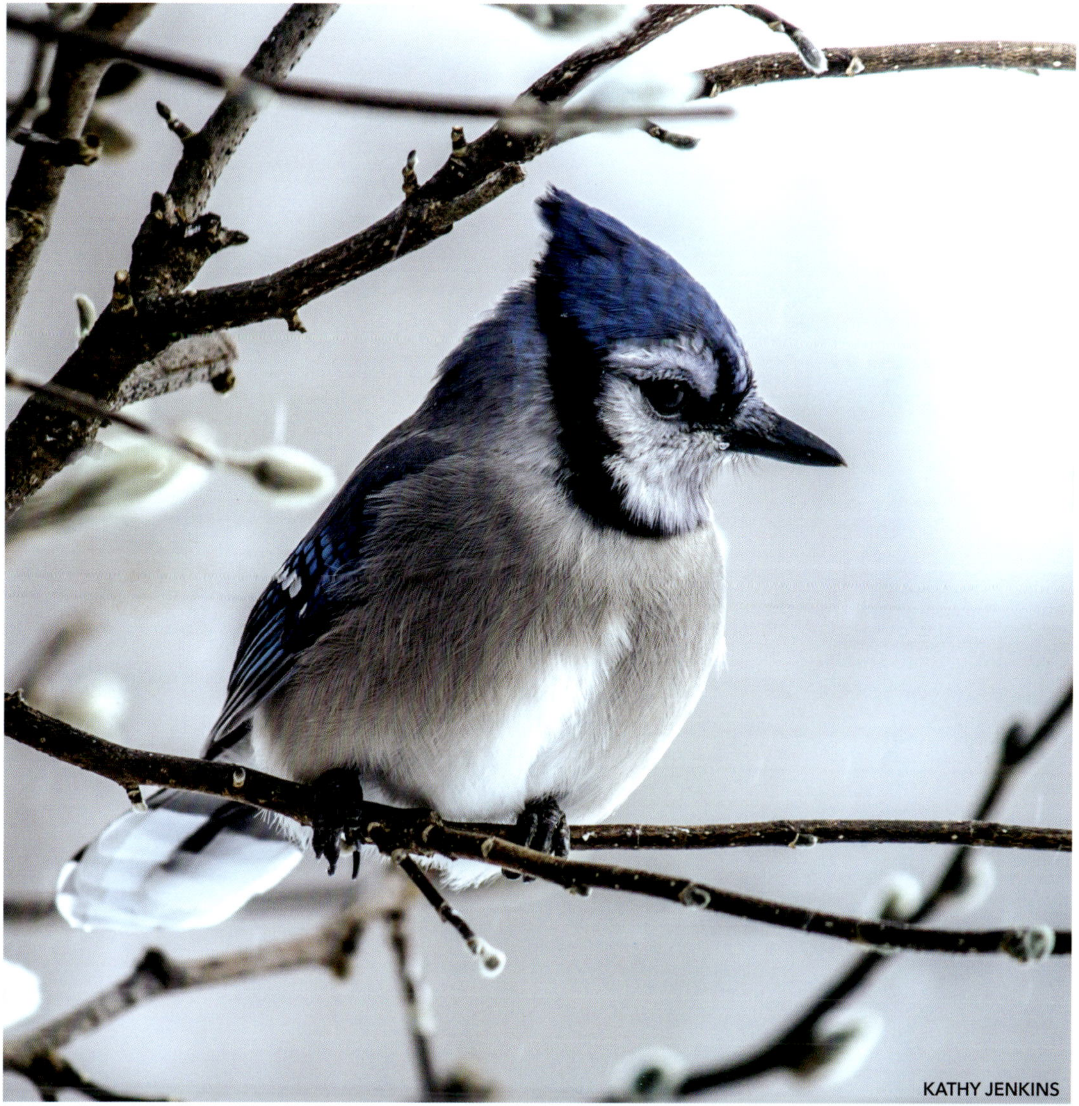
KATHY JENKINS

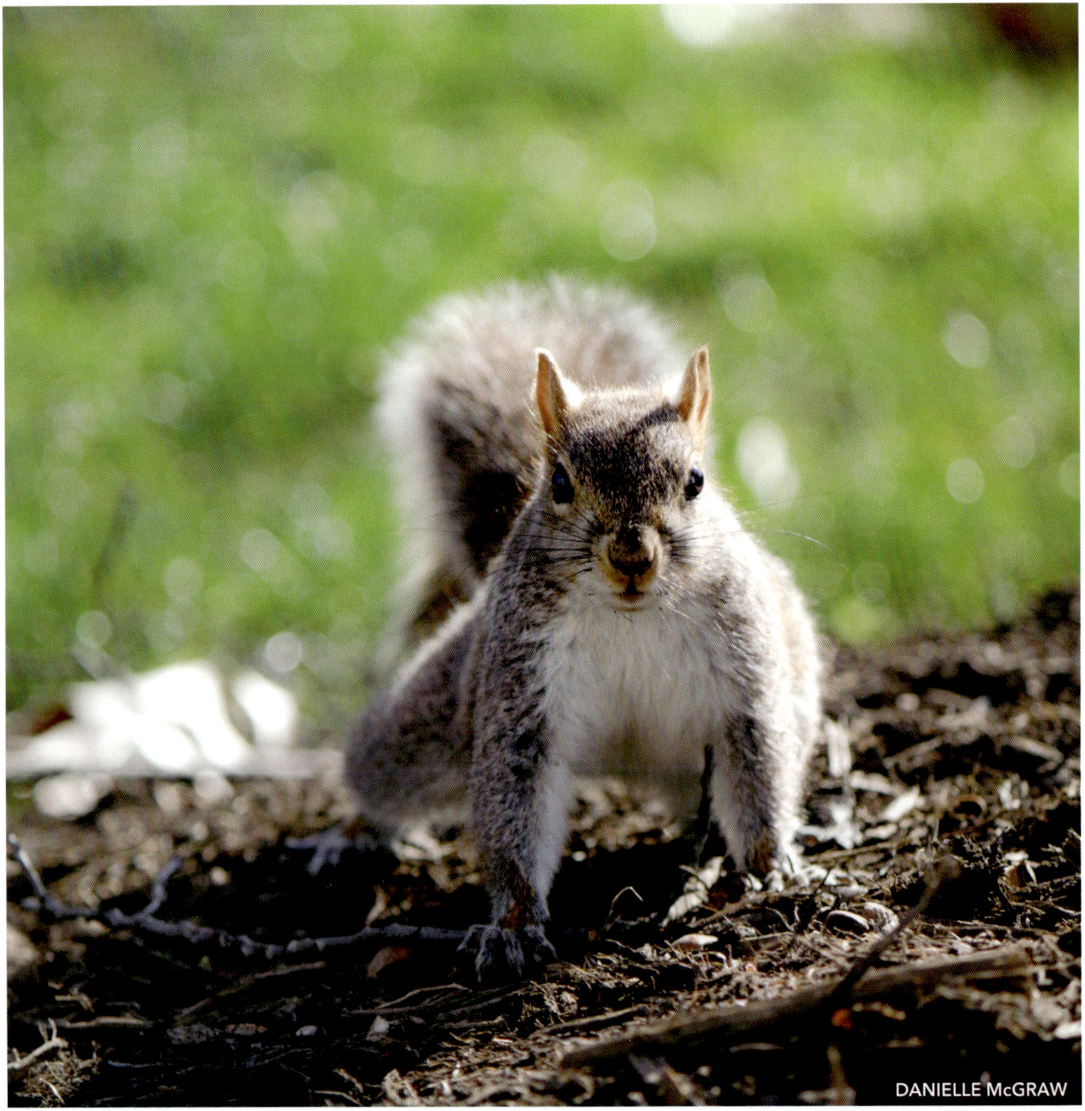
DANIELLE McGRAW

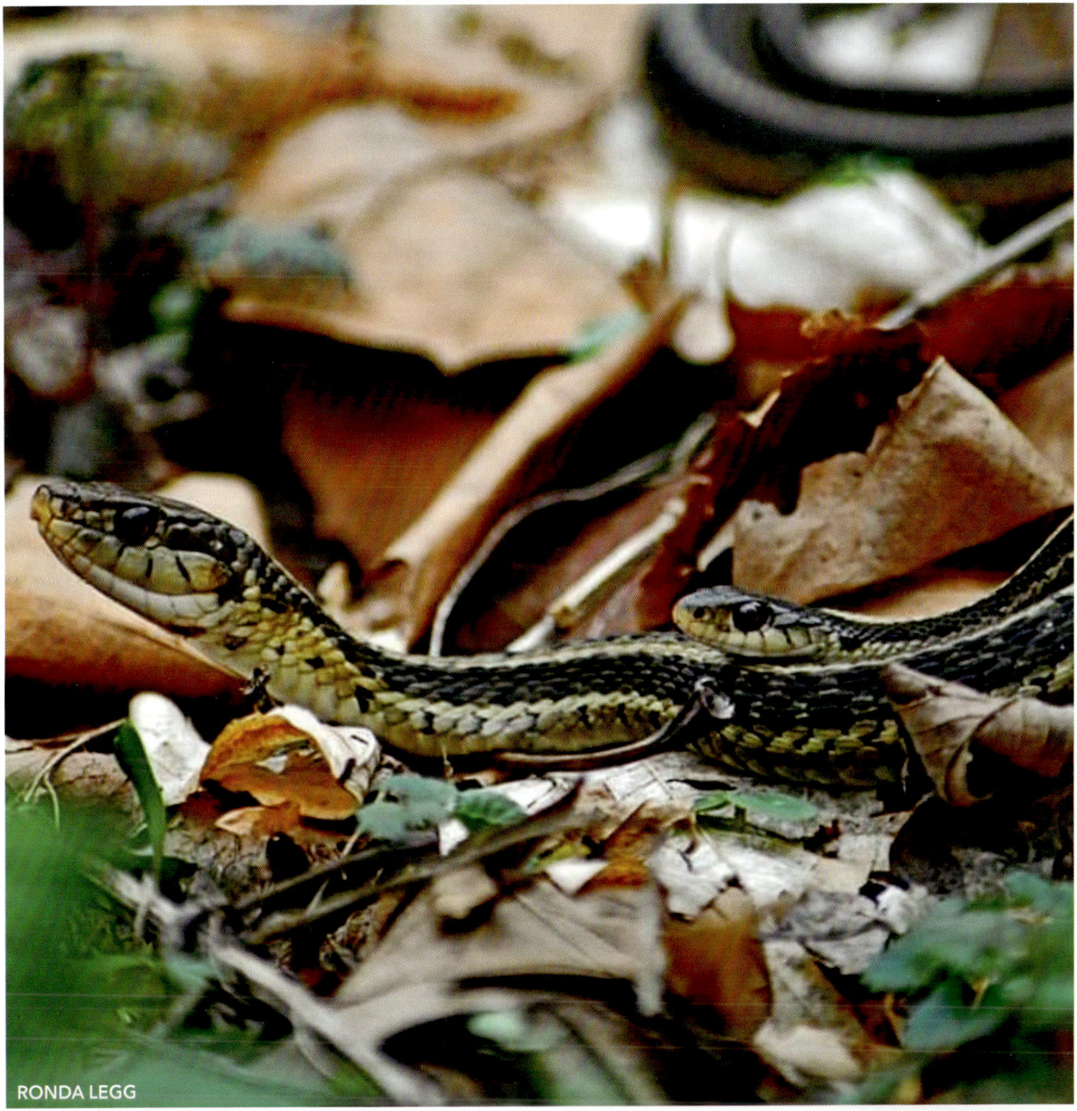
RONDA LEGG

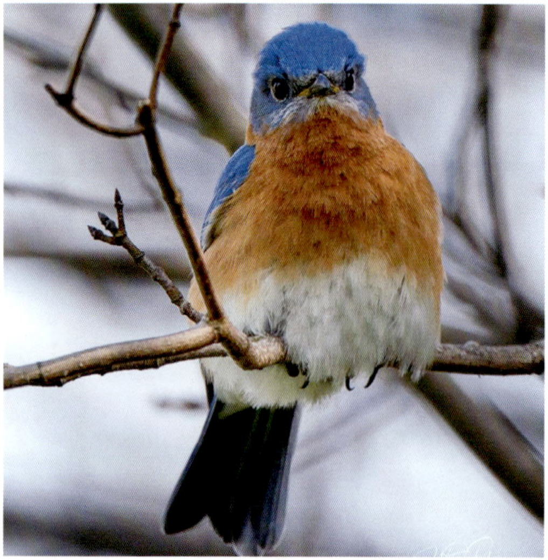

WENDY PARKS

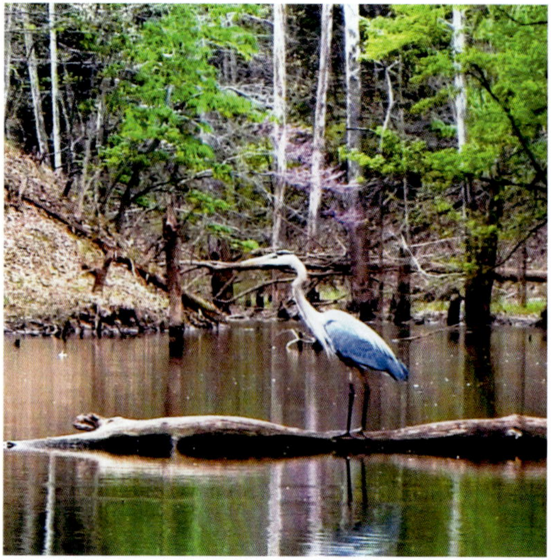

CYNTHIA MULLENS

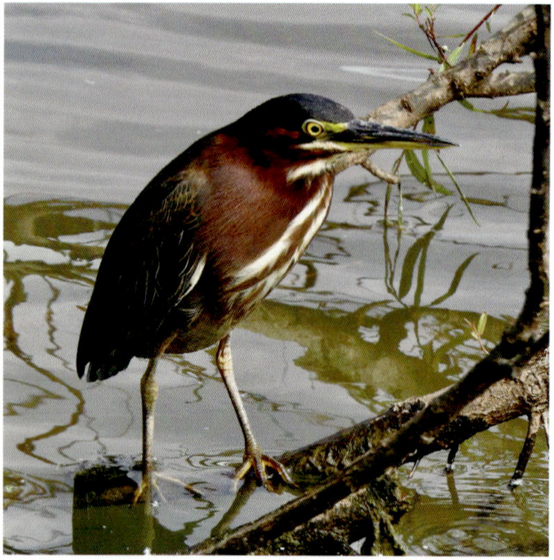

LYNN STEWART

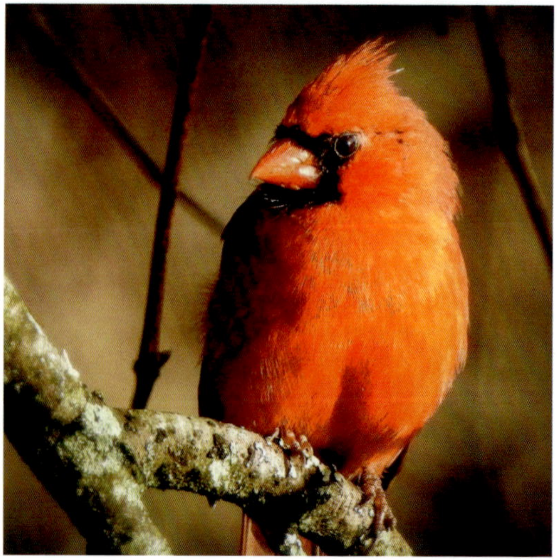

JESSE WAGGONER

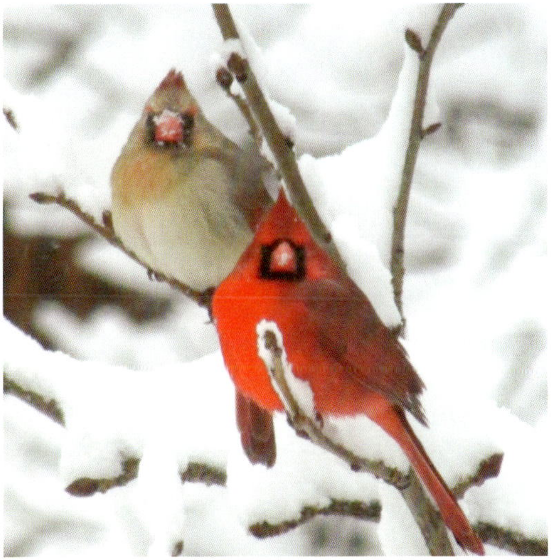

GREG BAILEY

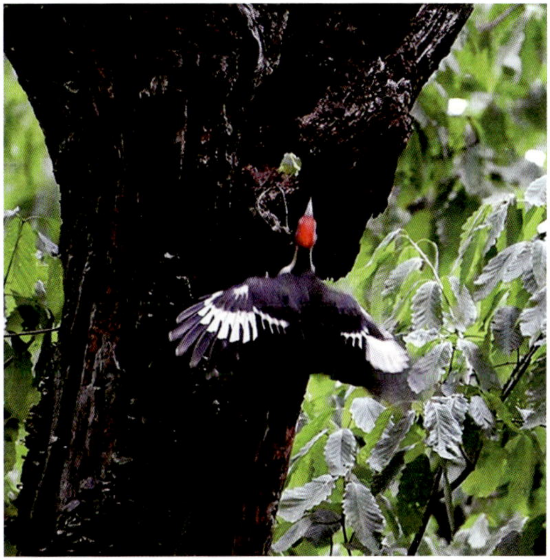

AIUDRA HIXSON

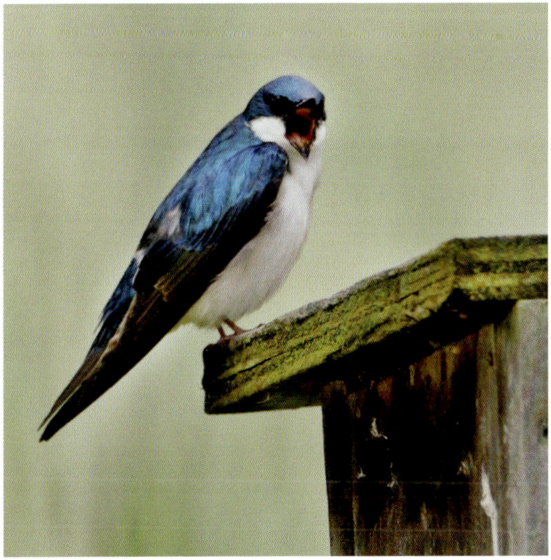

STEPHANIE CARPENTER

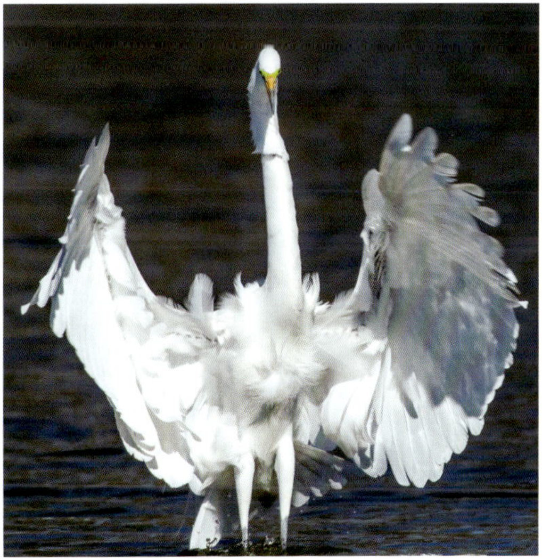

DANNY CARPENTER

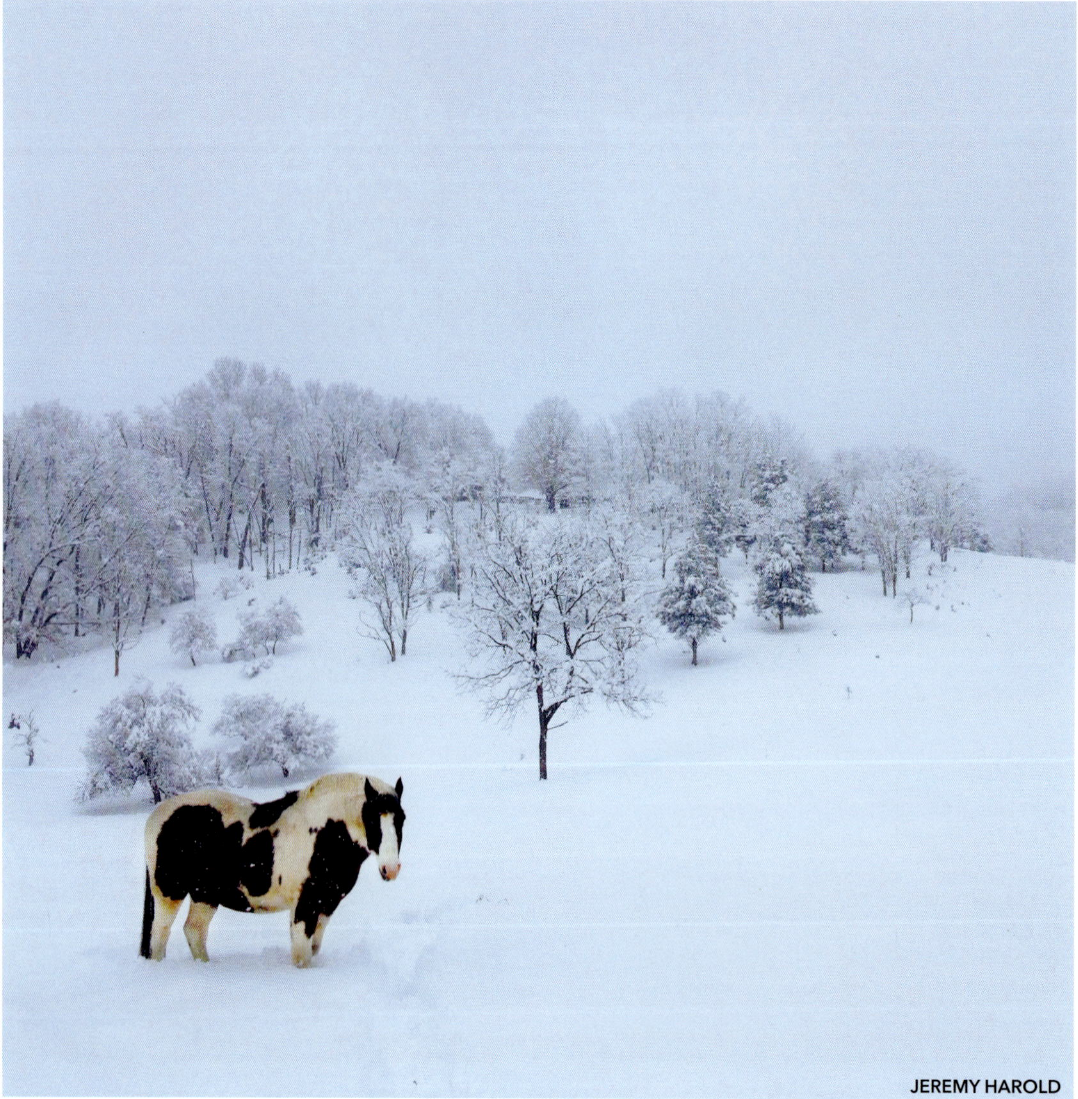

JEREMY HAROLD

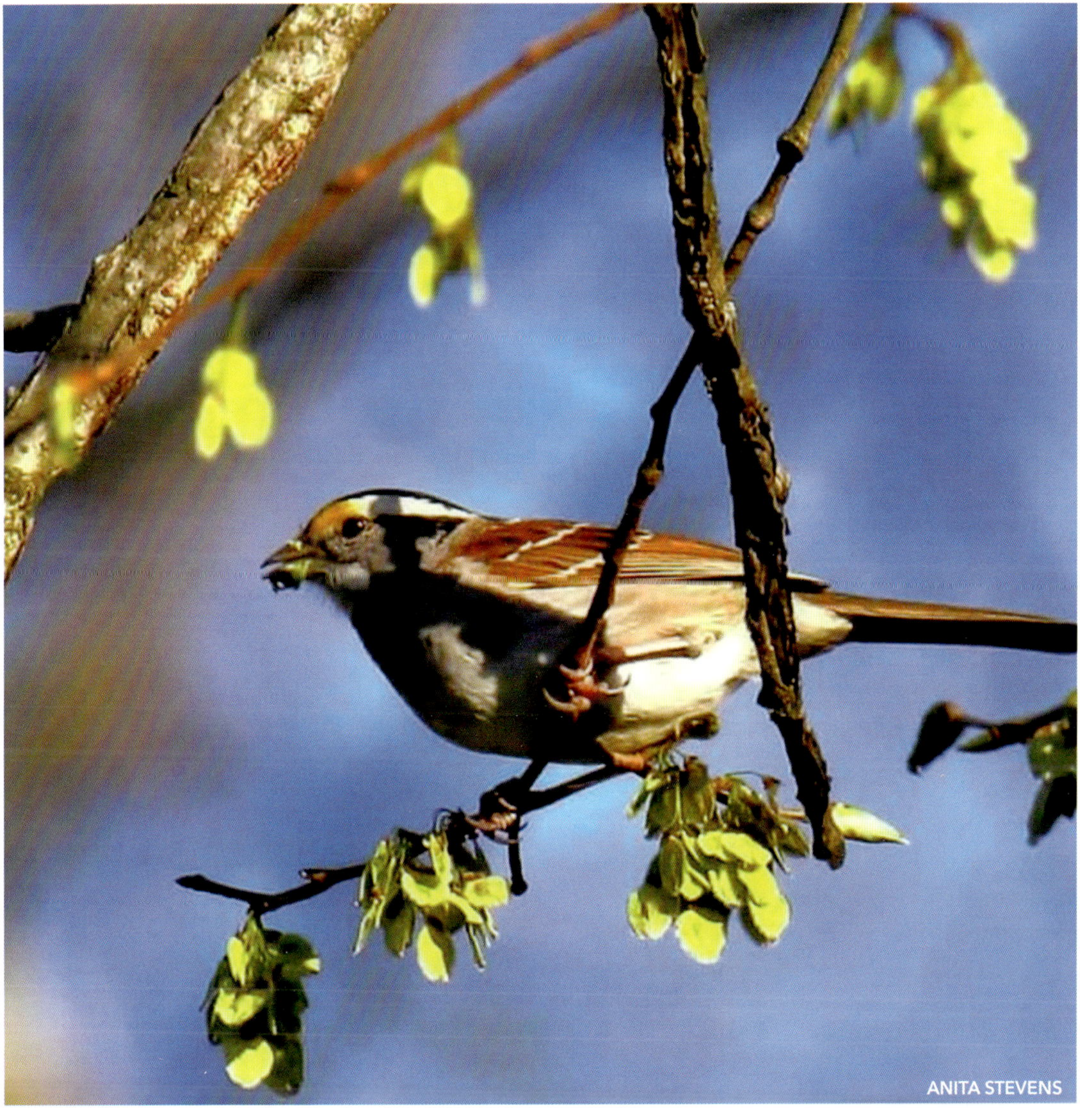
ANITA STEVENS

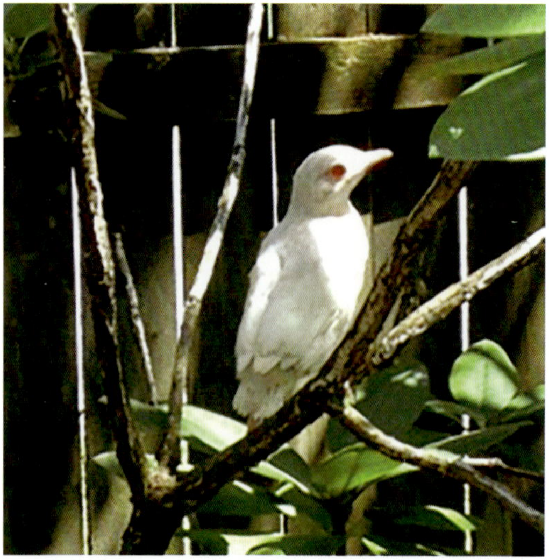

CYNDI SHAVER

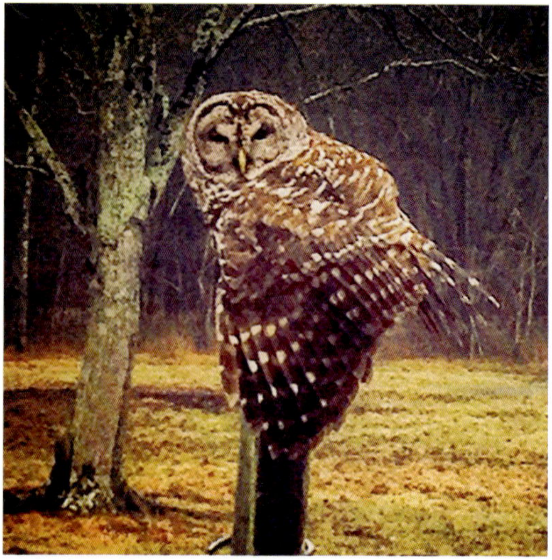

ELAINE CLARK

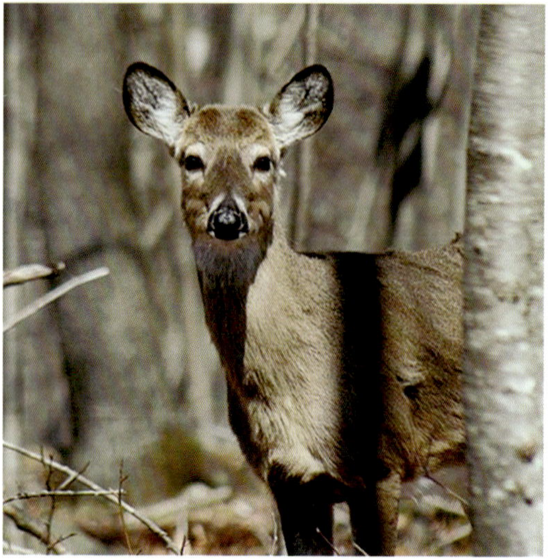

AMY DAMRON

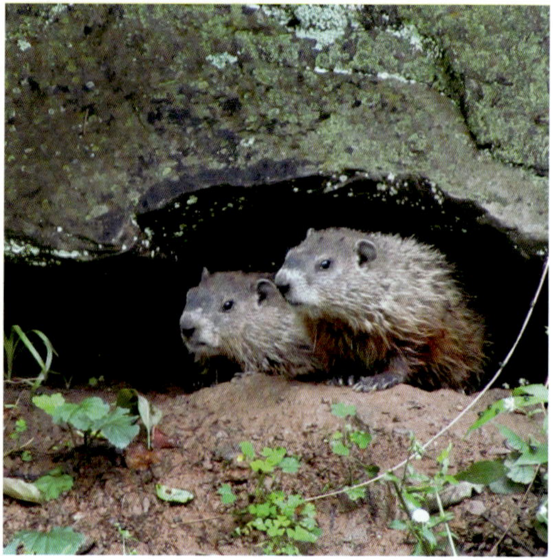

RICKY BRAGG

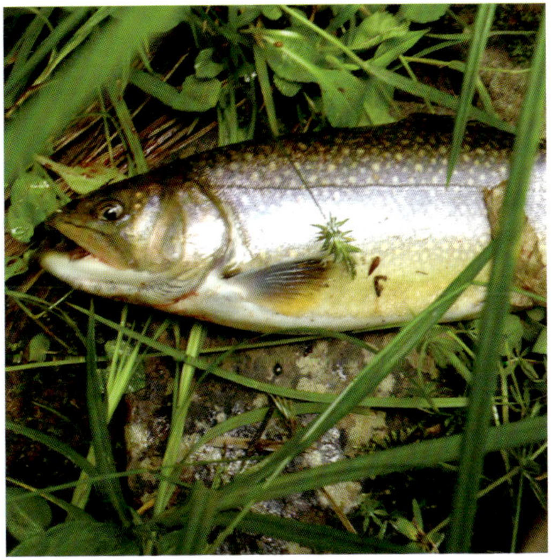

MICHAEL ROLES

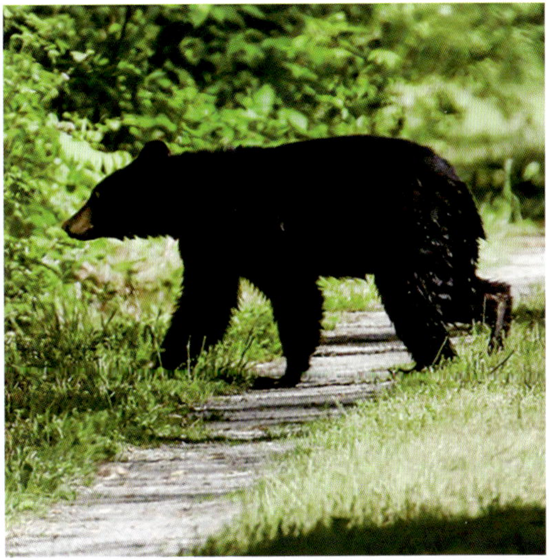

BRENT SCHNUPP

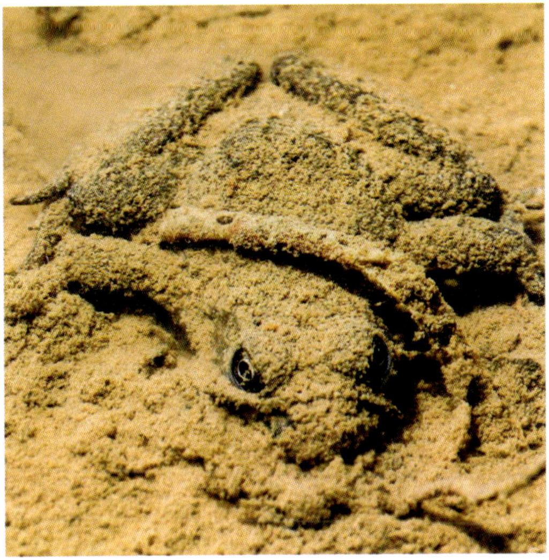

SHEILA JENKINS

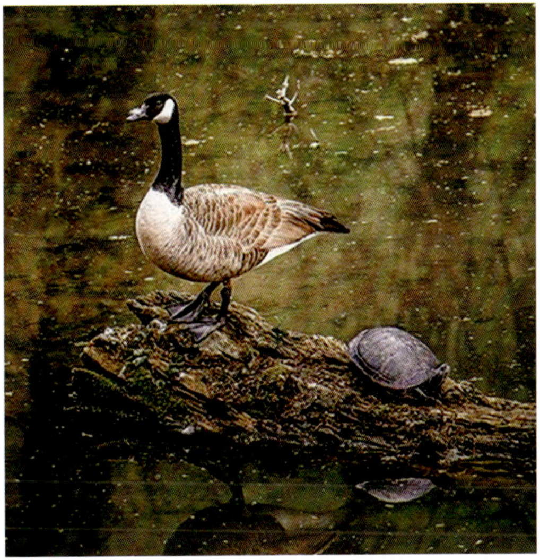

CINDI DUNN

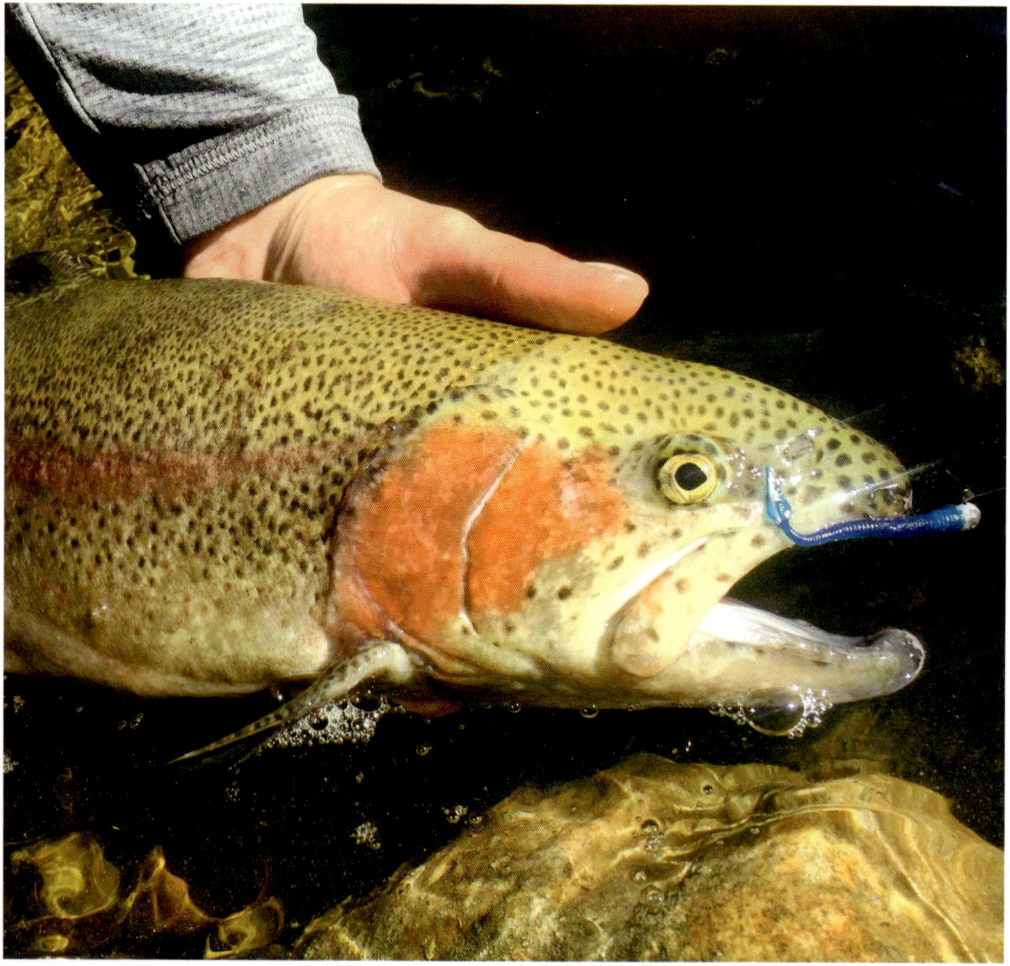

FRANKLIN SMITH

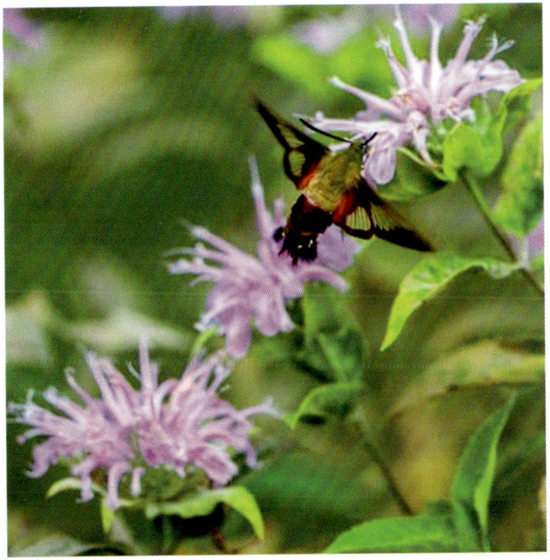

BETH SPENCER

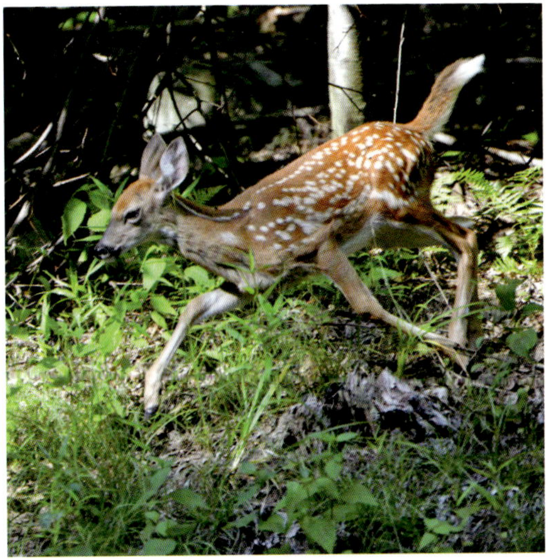

KIMBERLY FOWLER

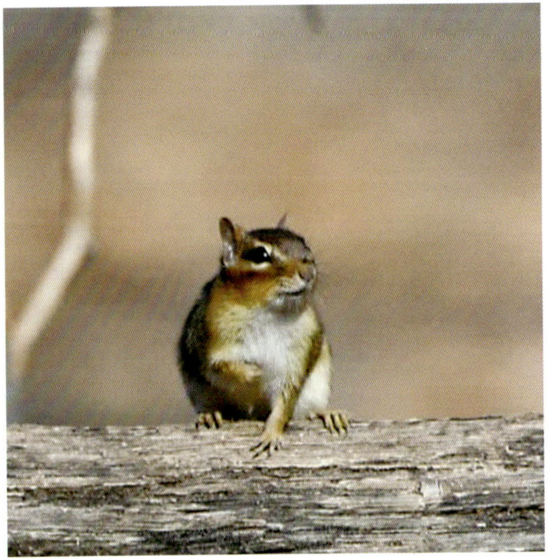

SAM SHEILS

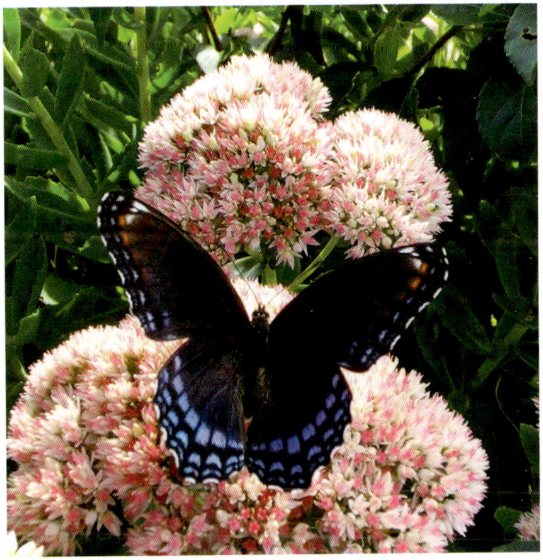

KAY NESSLEROTTE

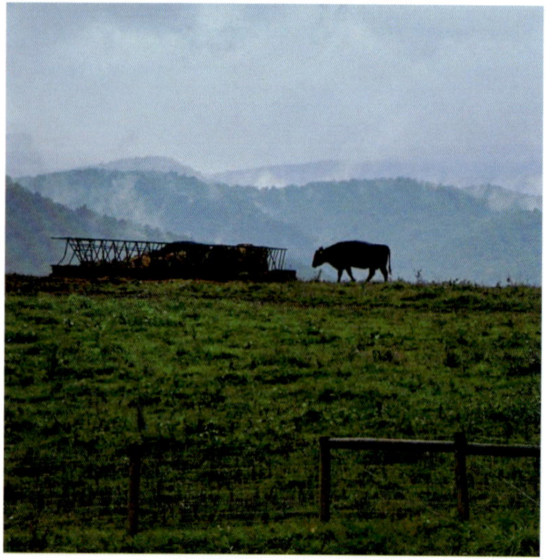

KENDALL BRUMBAUGH

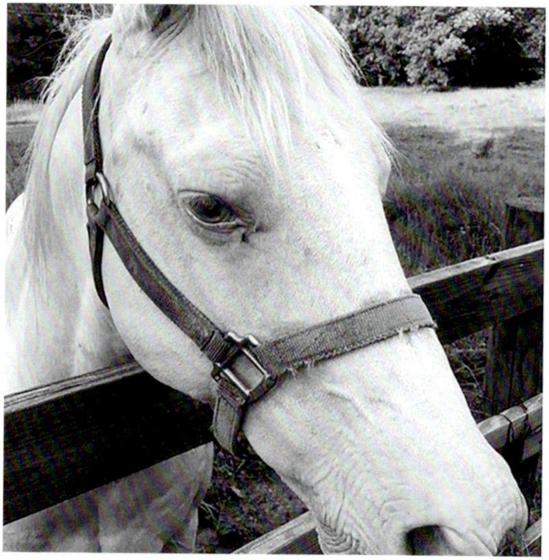

AMBER MESSICK

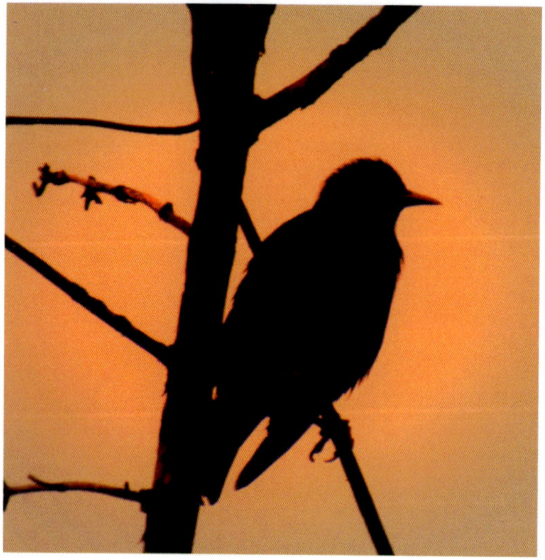

BROWN NICHOLS II

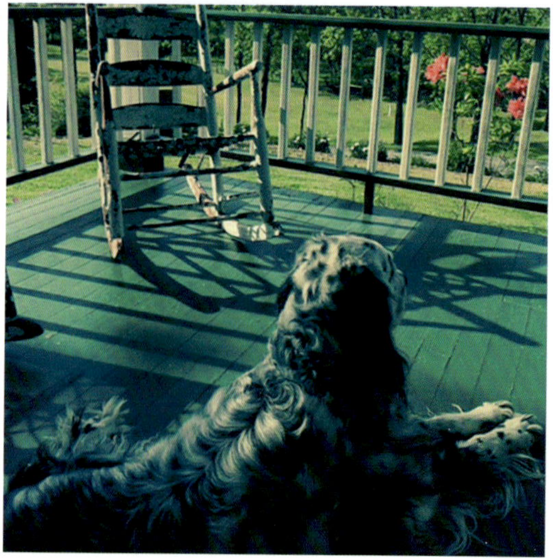

DEBRA A. WASSUM

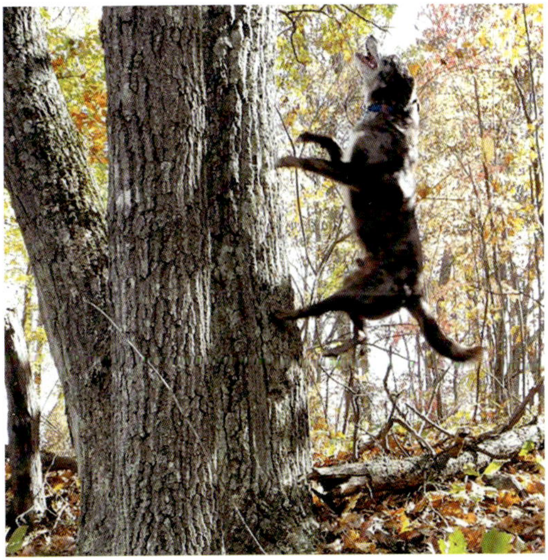

ELAINE WYKLE

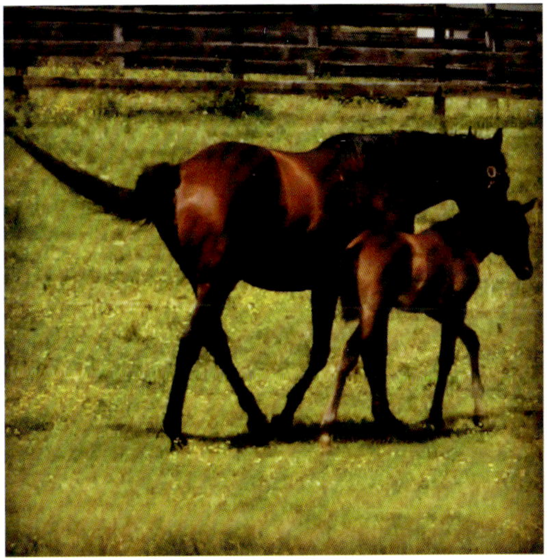

JANICE SCOTT

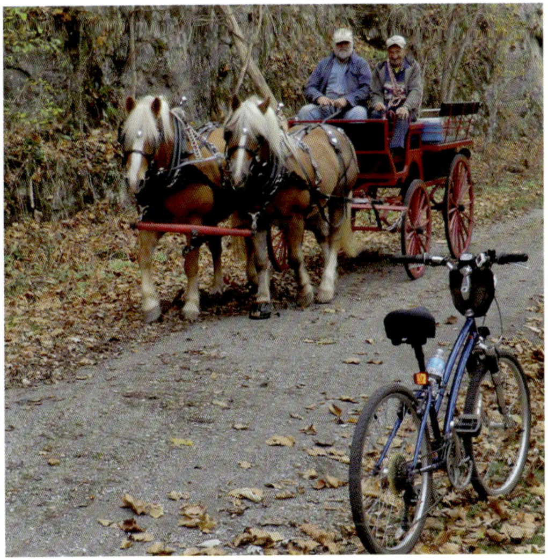

CORALETTA HOUCK

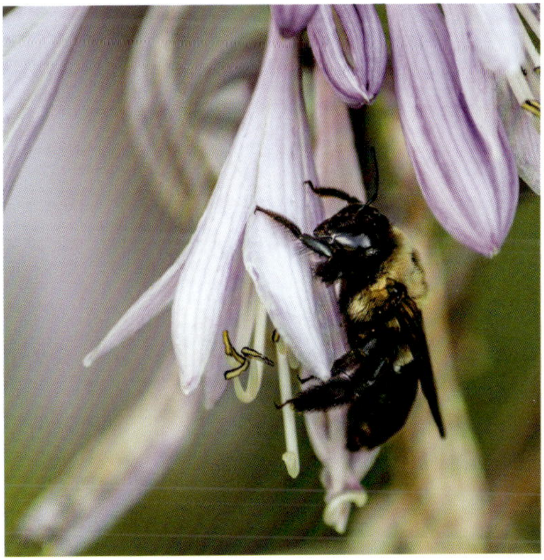

KATHY JENKINS

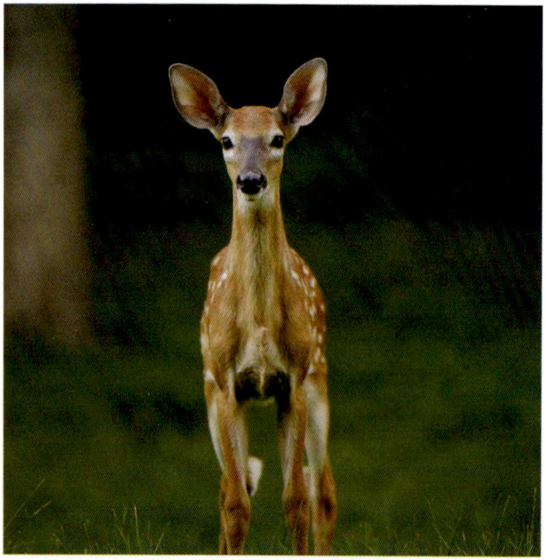

LORI COUNTS-SMITH

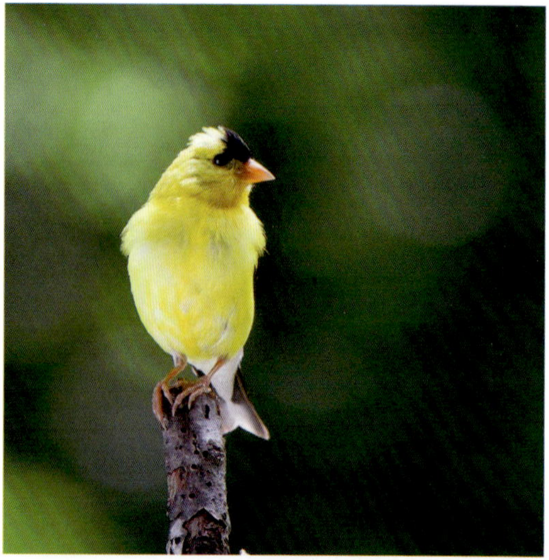

JON HOWARD

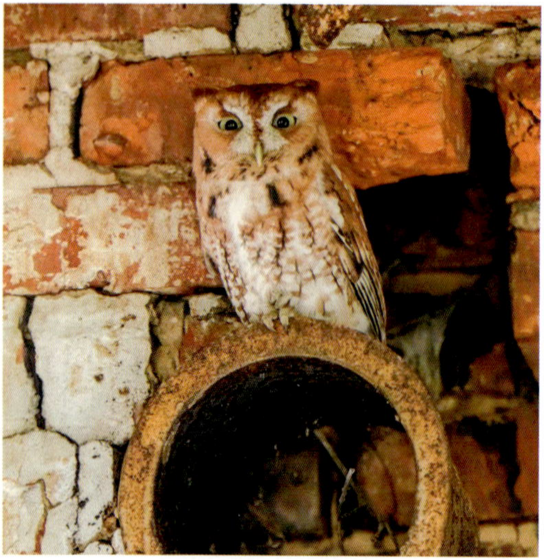

BRENT SCHNUPP

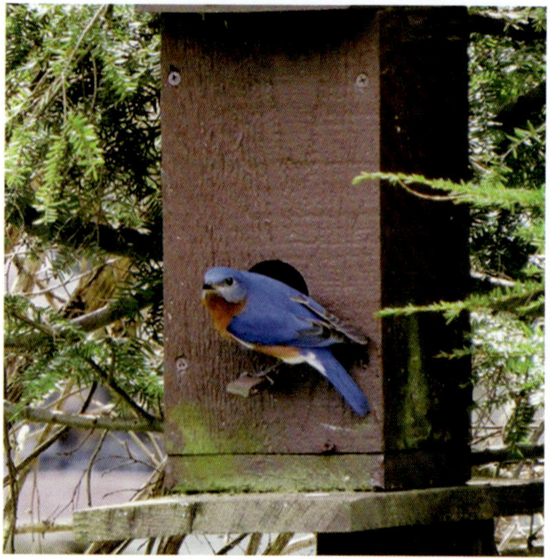

CANDY THOMPSON

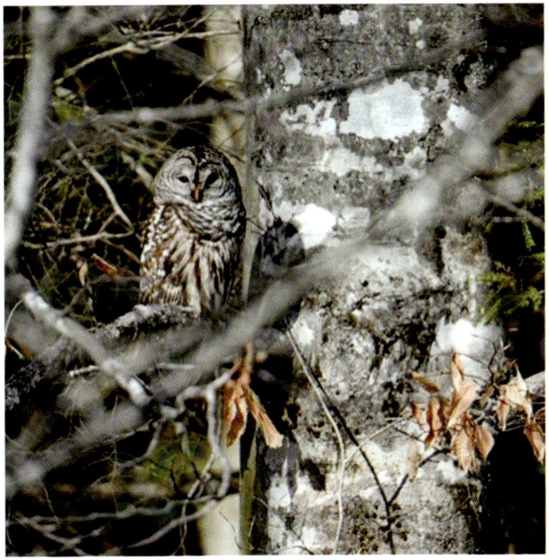

RONDA LEGG

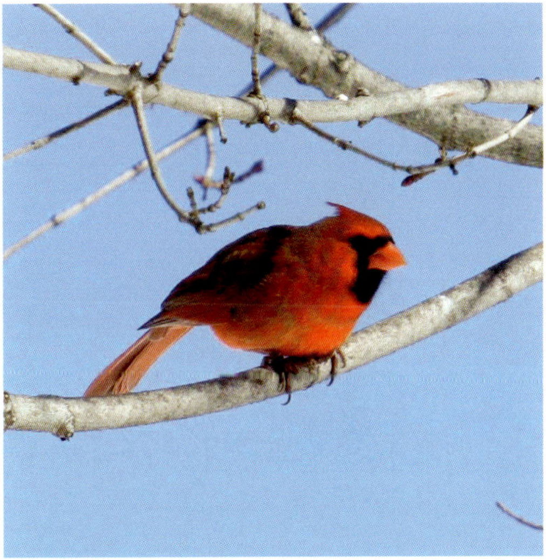

CANDY THOMPSON

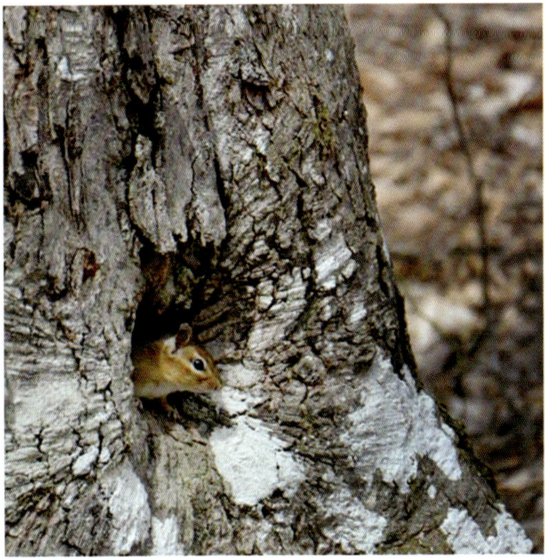

MELANIE HAYSLETTE-MOSES

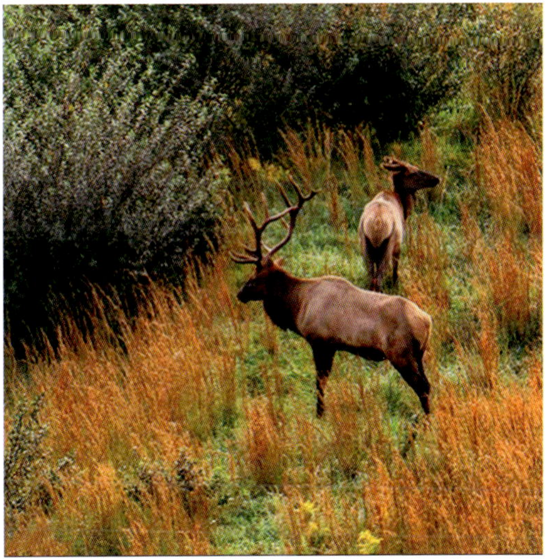

JILL MOLES MULLINS

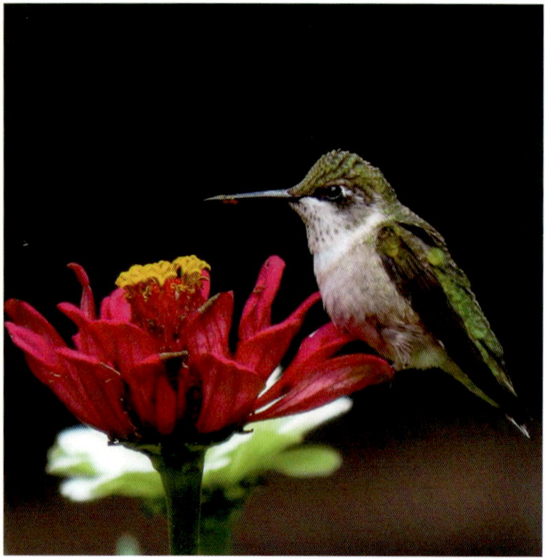

SARAH E. BAILEY

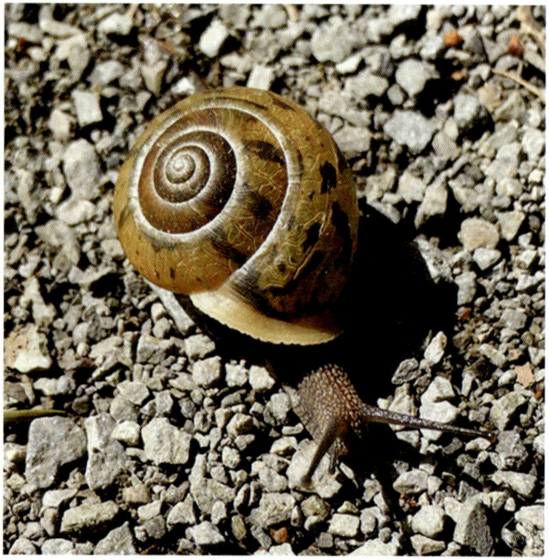

LORI TURNER

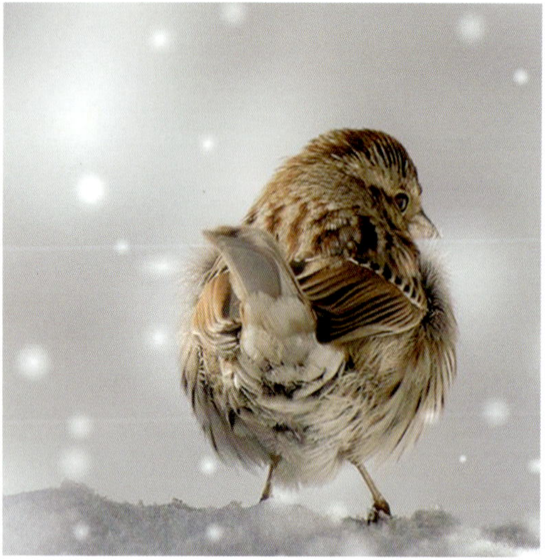

WENDY PARKS

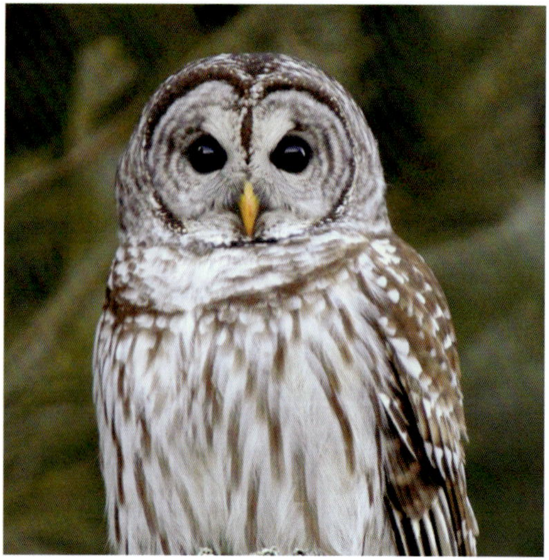

MICHAEL PUFFENBARGER

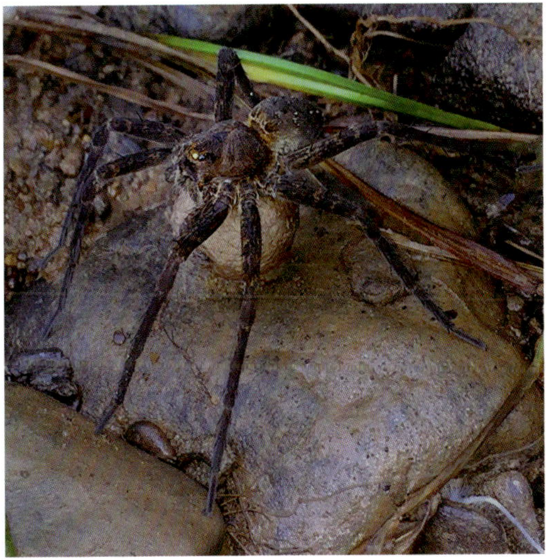

JEREMY M. ALBERTS

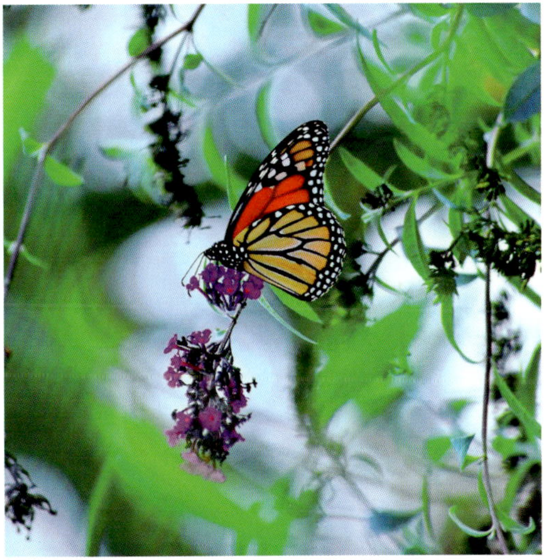

VANESSA HOCHARD

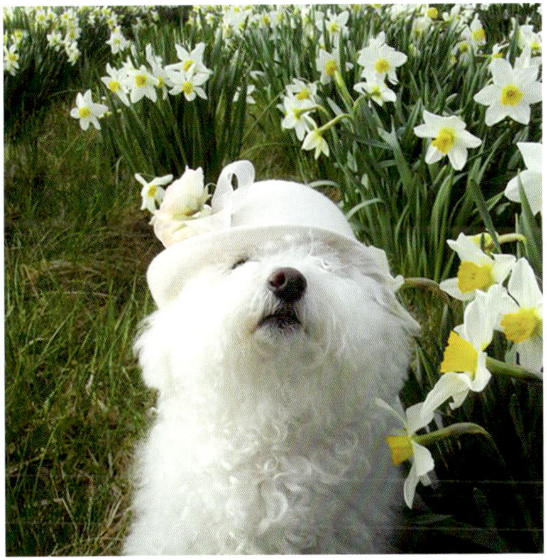

SHARON KAY CARPER

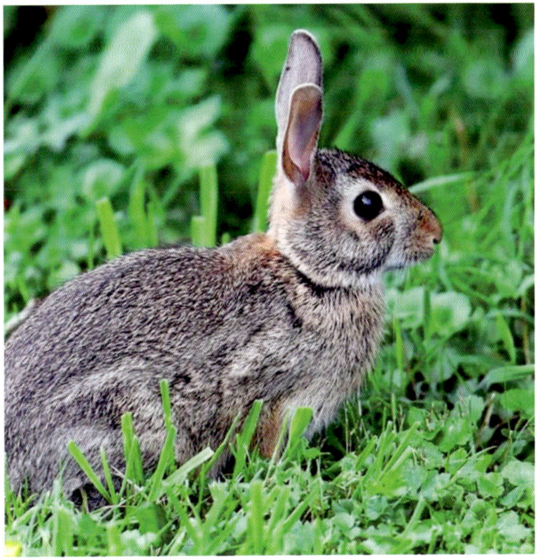

RONDA LEGG

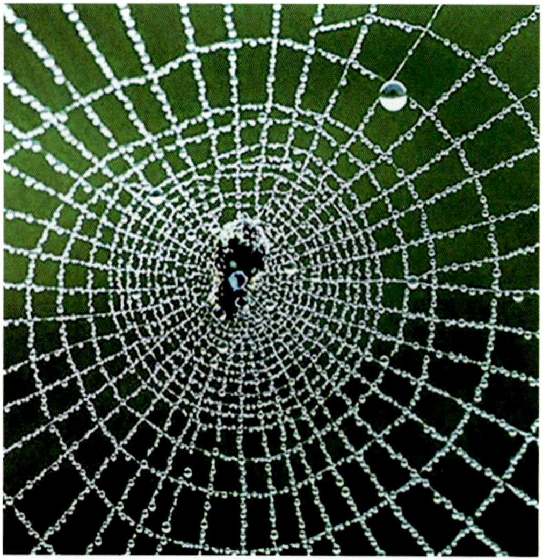
SARAH E. BAILEY

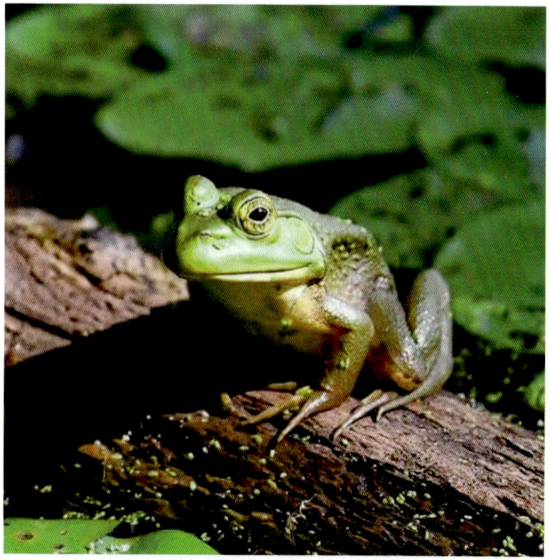
RONDA LEGG

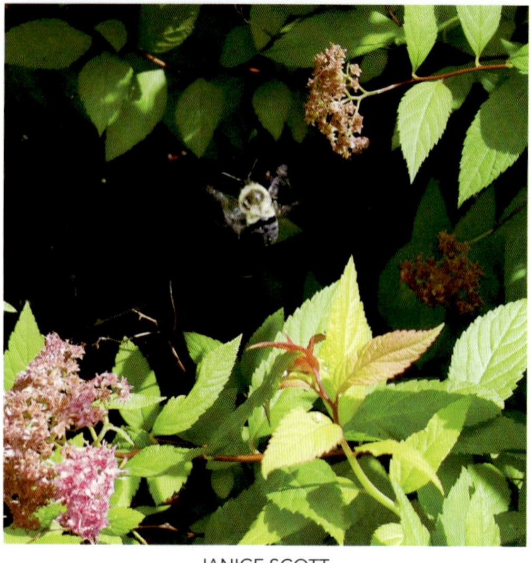
JANICE SCOTT

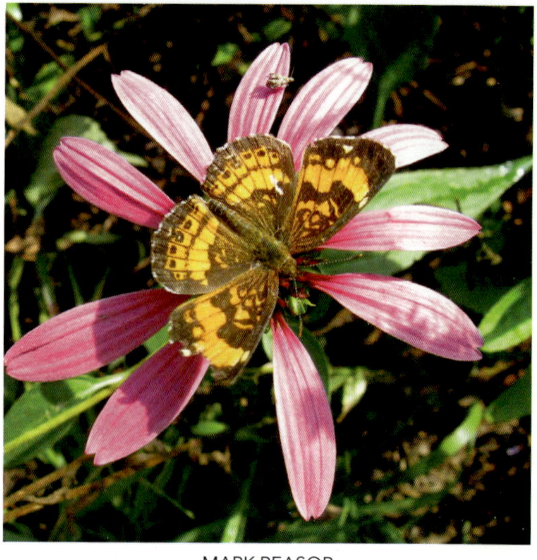
MARK REASOR

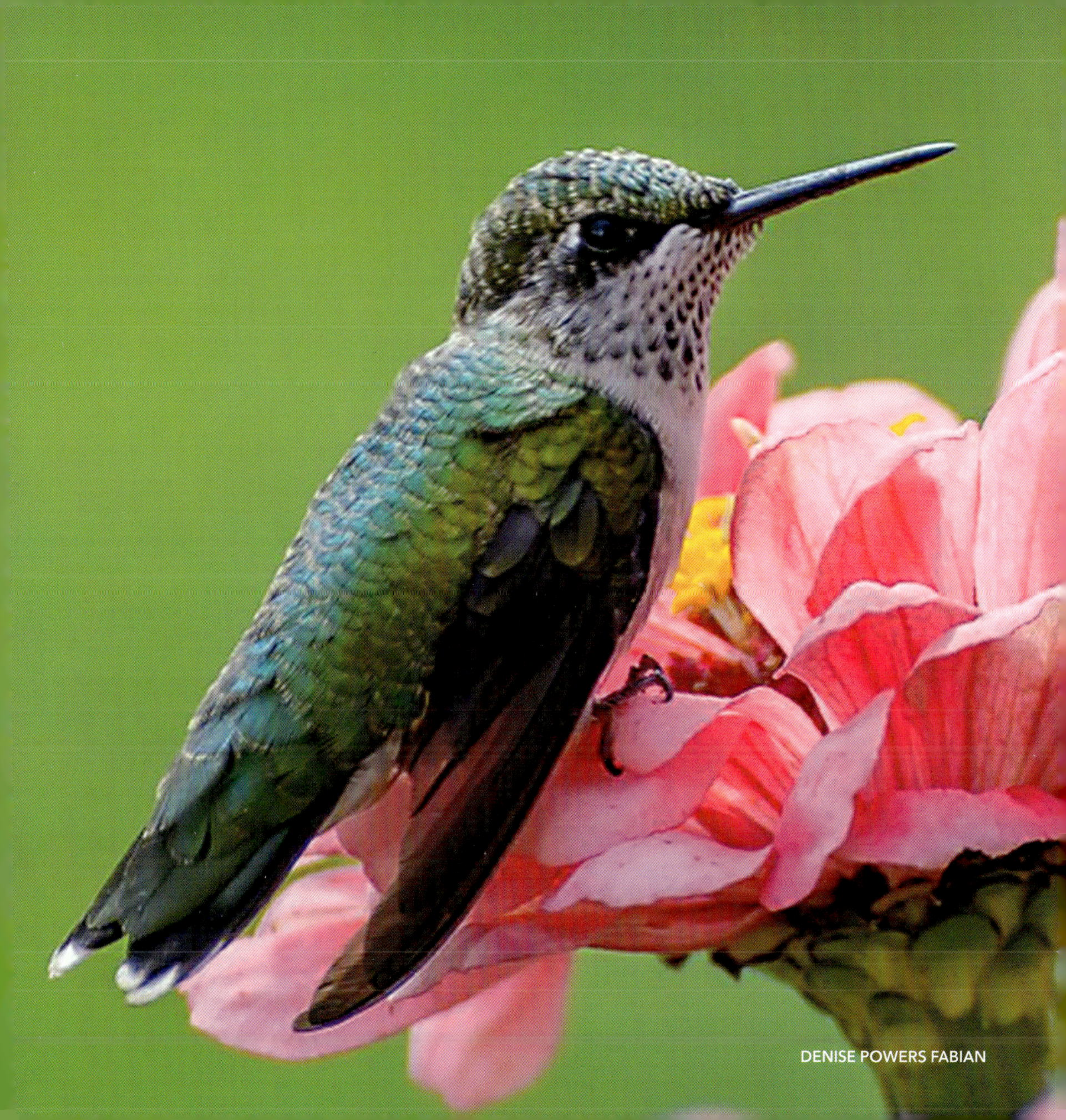
DENISE POWERS FABIAN

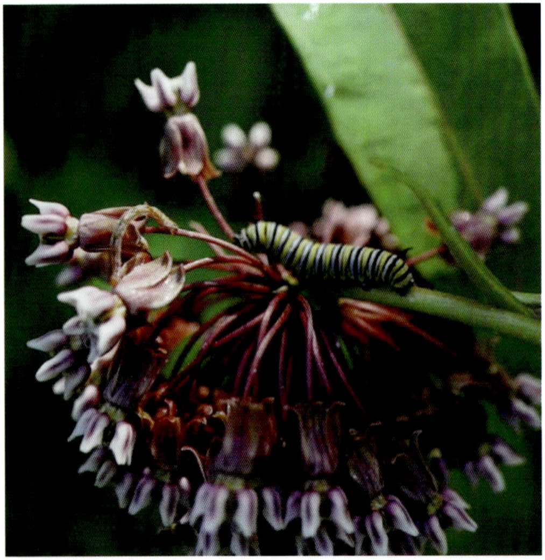

JULIE RATLIFF

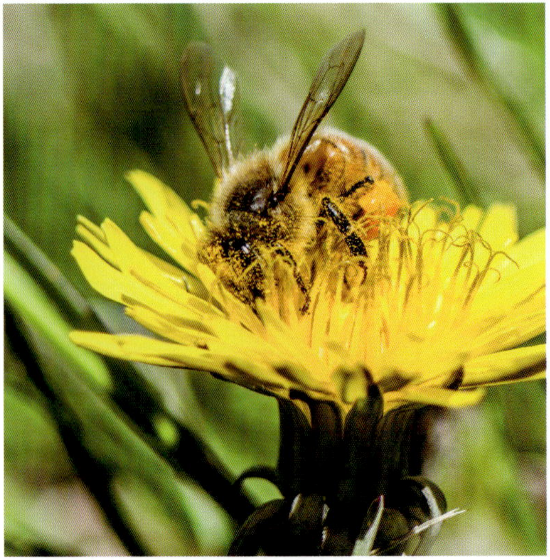

KATHY JENKINS

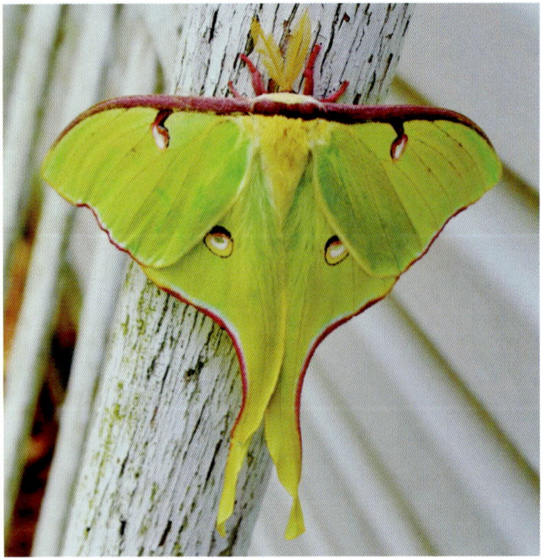

ELAINE CLARK

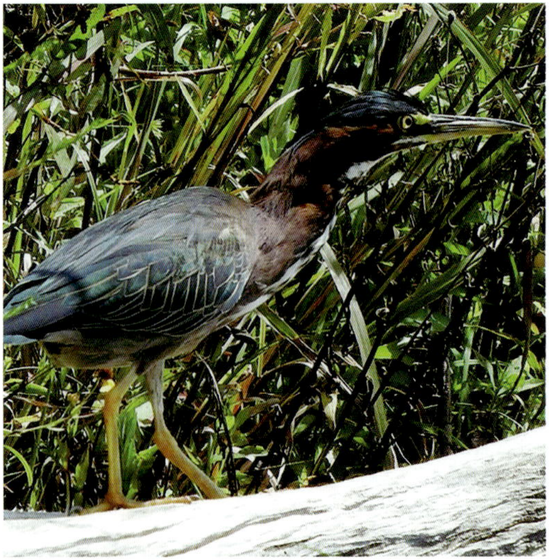

CYNTHIA MULLENS

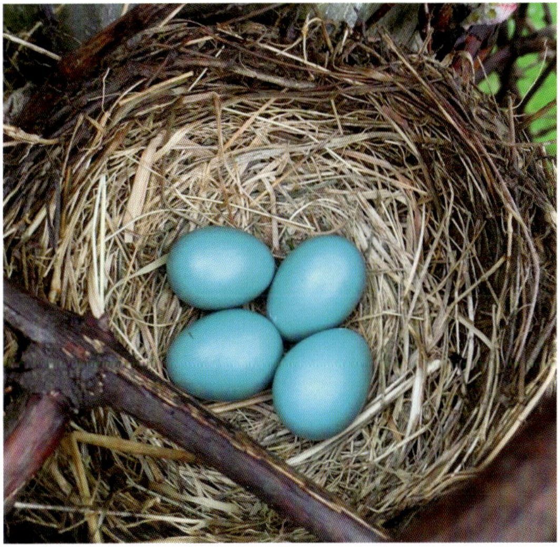

LORI TURNER

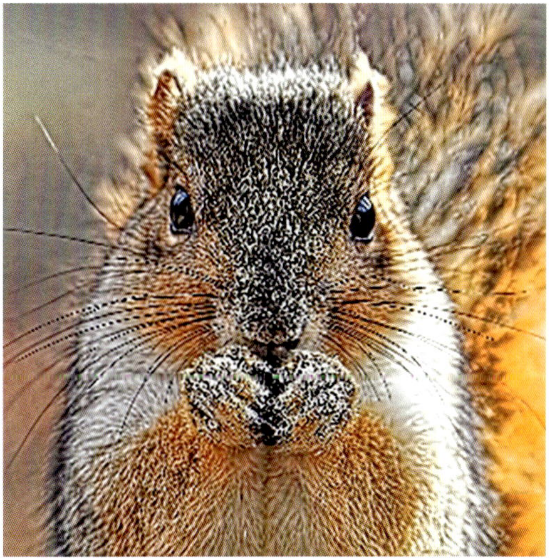

RICHARD MARLOW

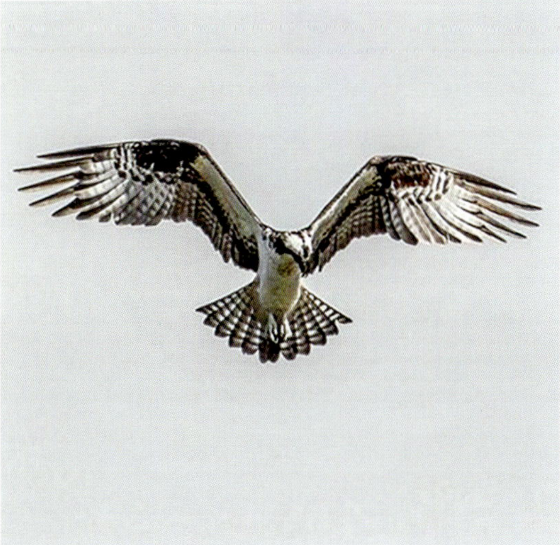

SARAH E. BAILEY

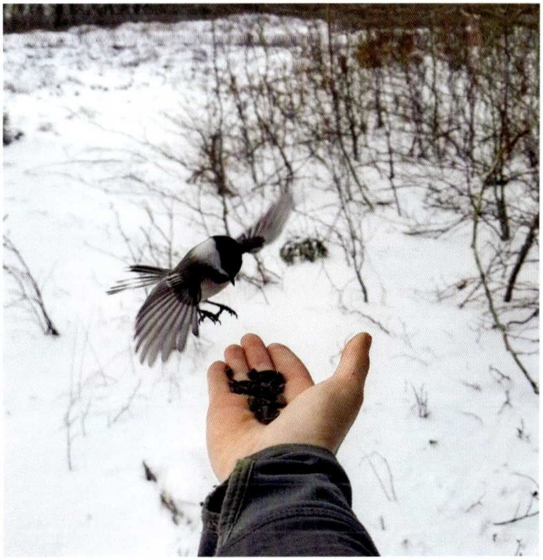

LIZ STOUT

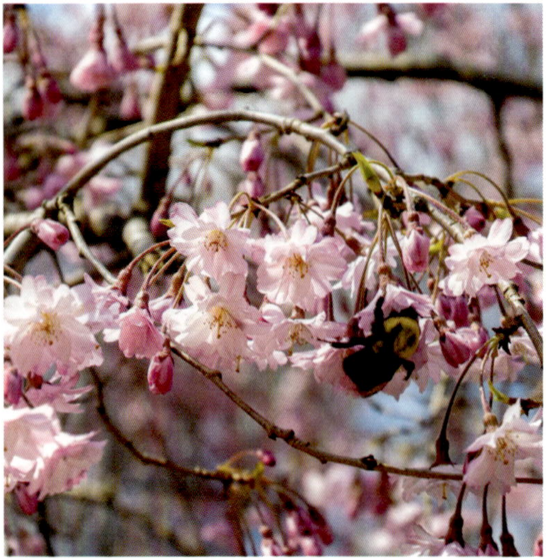

SHEILA JENKINS

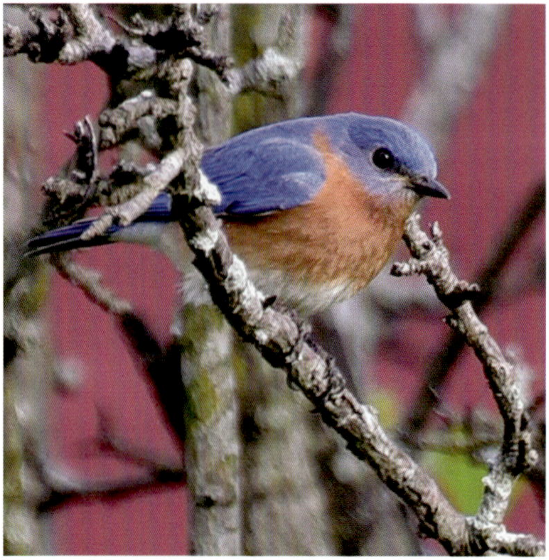

WENDY PARKS

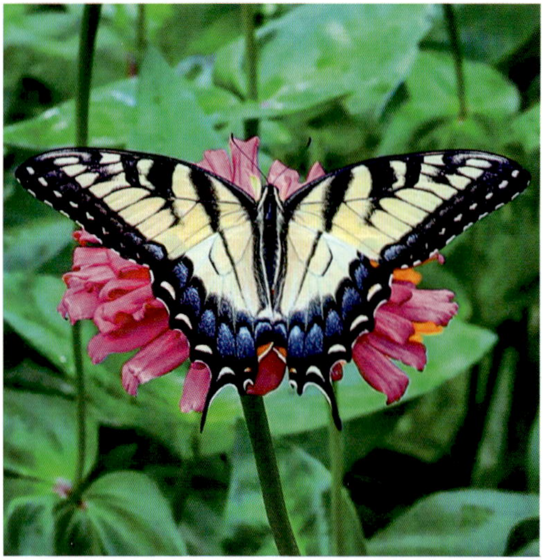

SARAH E. BAILEY

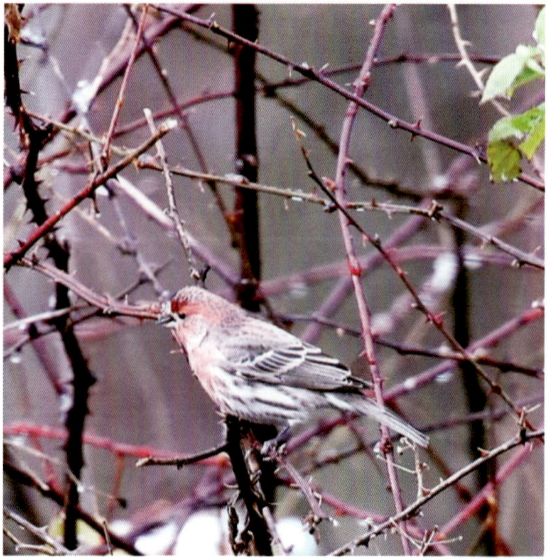

CYNTHIA MULLENS

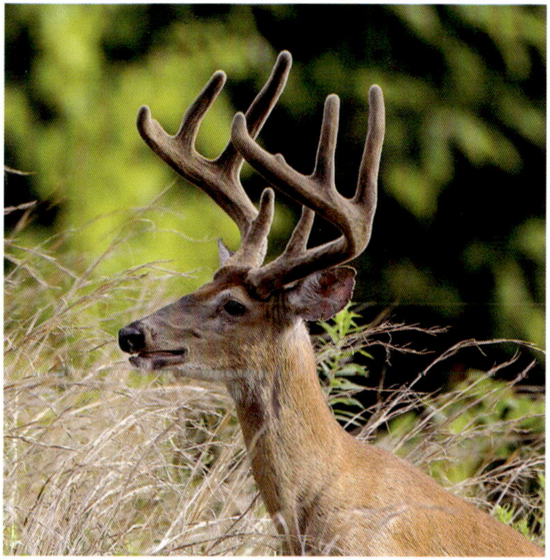

JOSH SIMONS

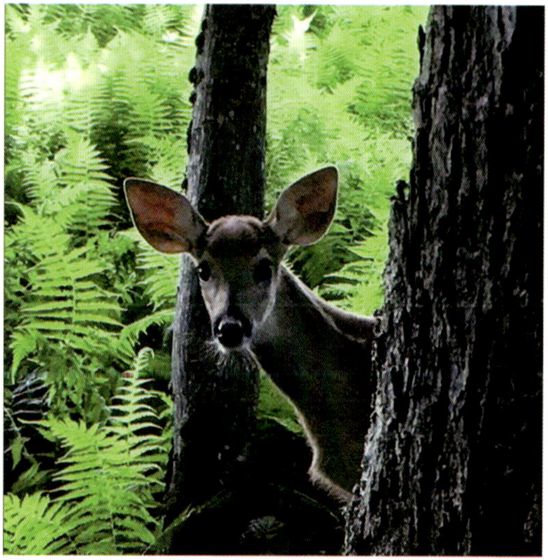

LORI TURNER

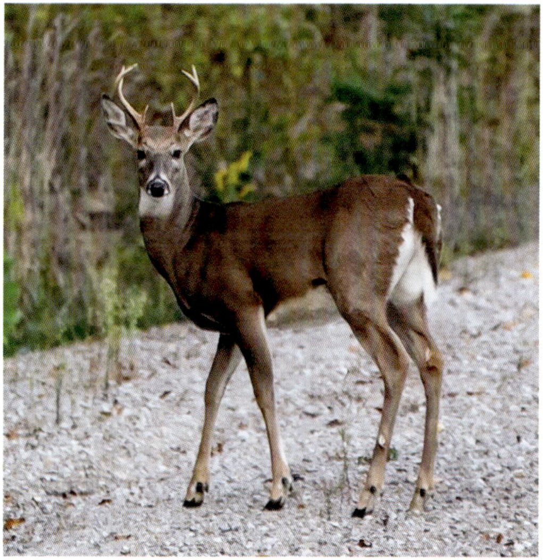

WENDY PARKS

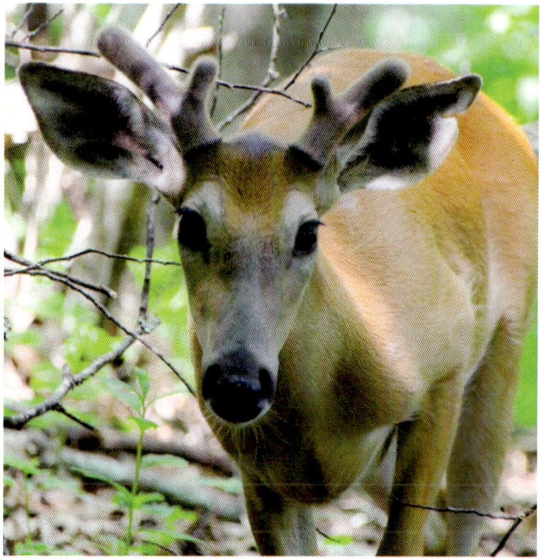

JESSE WAGGONER

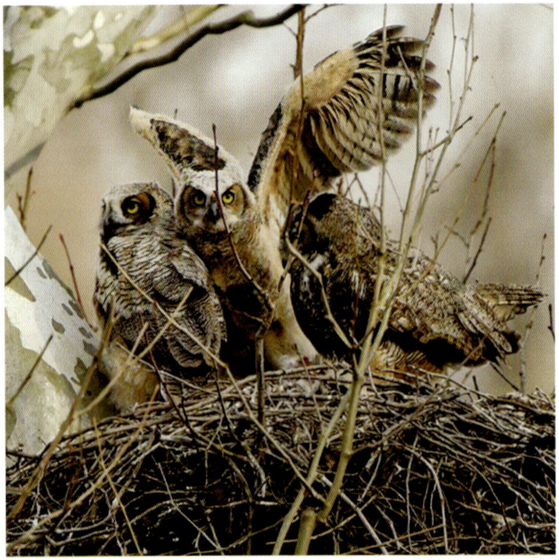

BRENT SCHNUPP

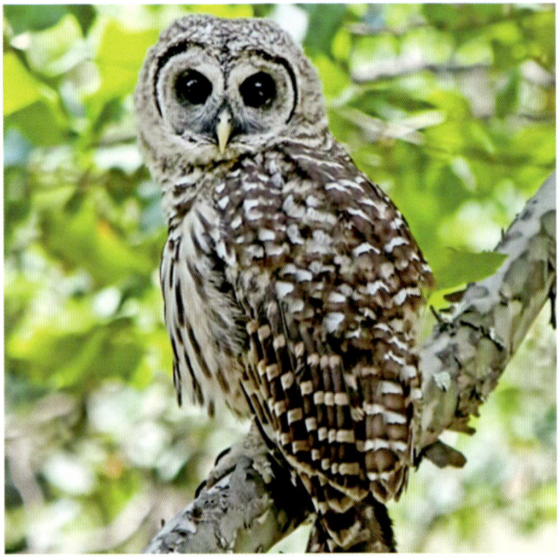

RICHARD MARLOW

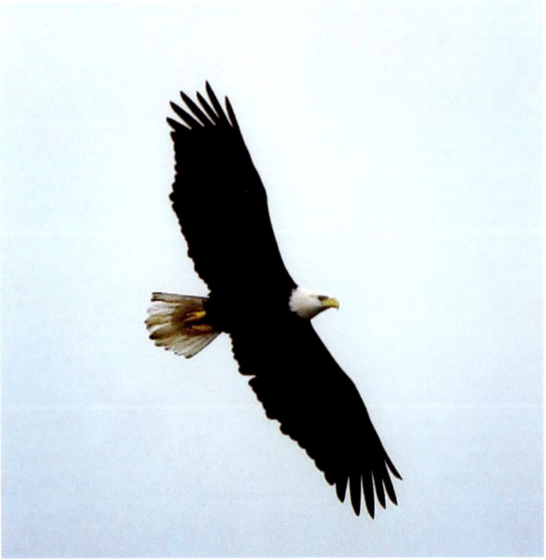

RONDA LEGG

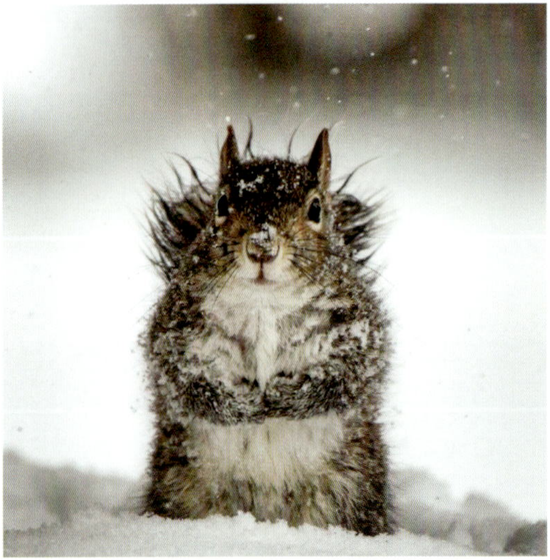

KEVIN JACK

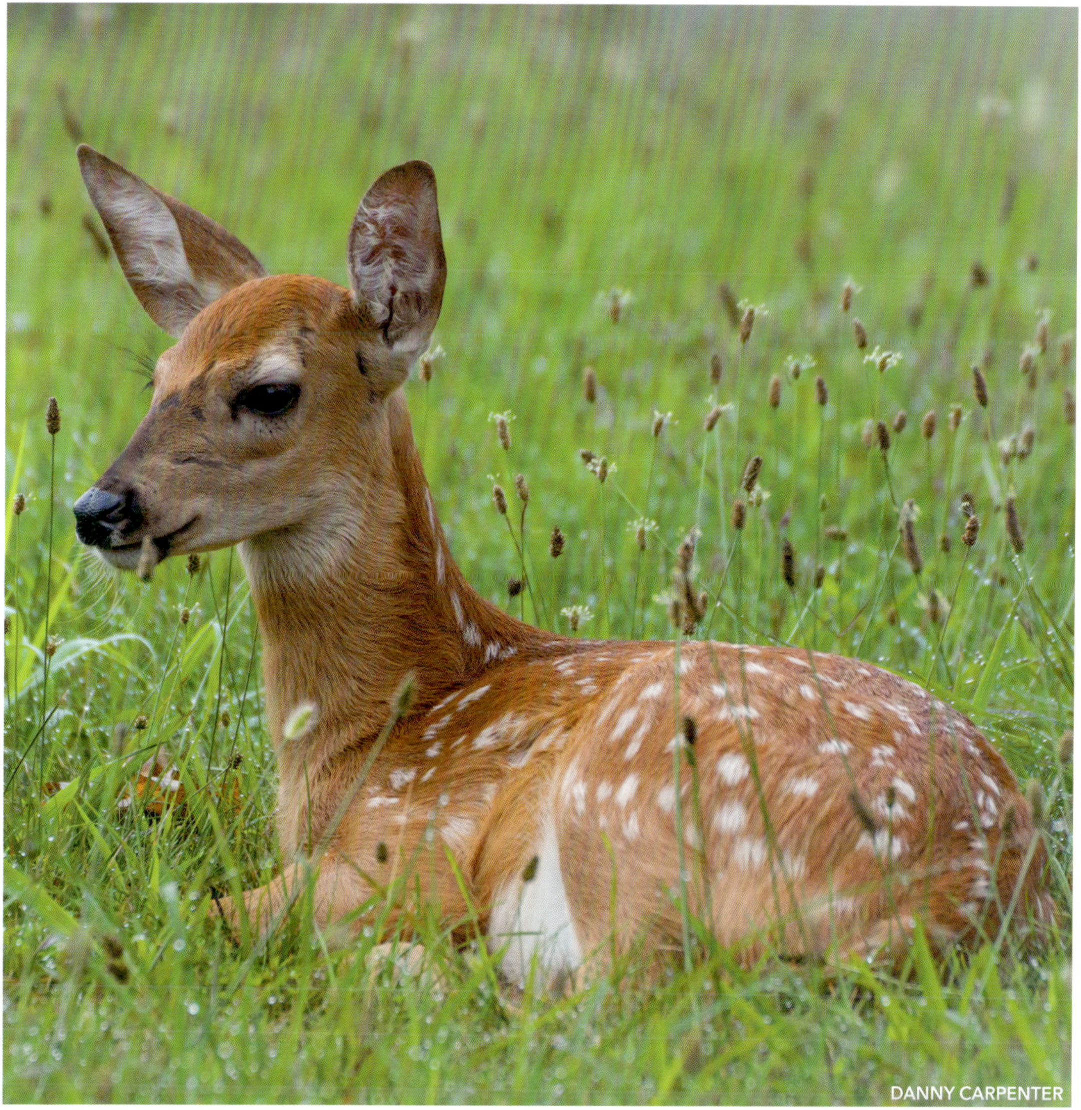
DANNY CARPENTER

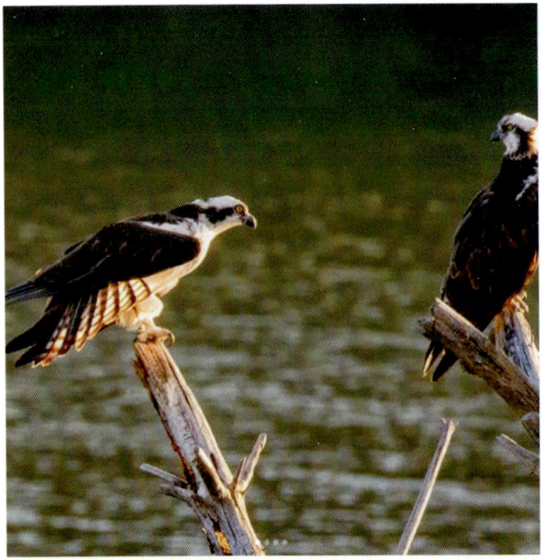

CHARMAGNE AYOTTE

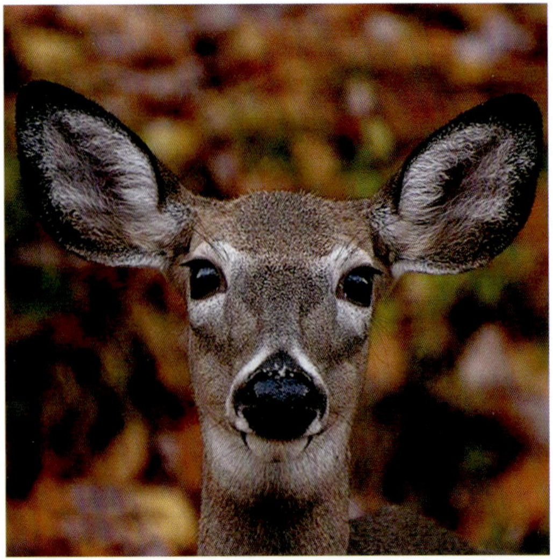

DENISE POWERS FABIAN

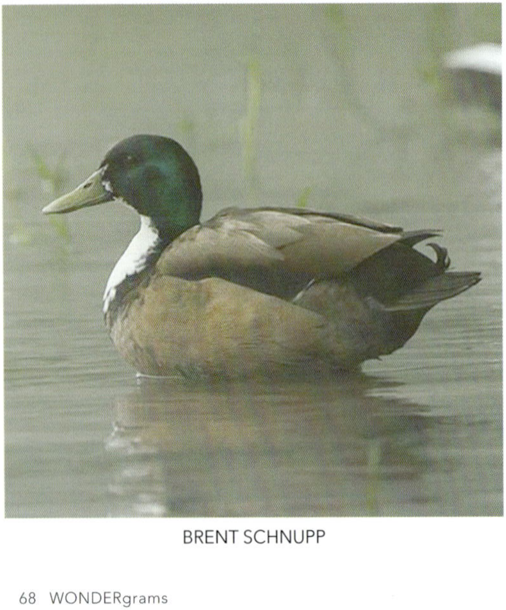

BRENT SCHNUPP

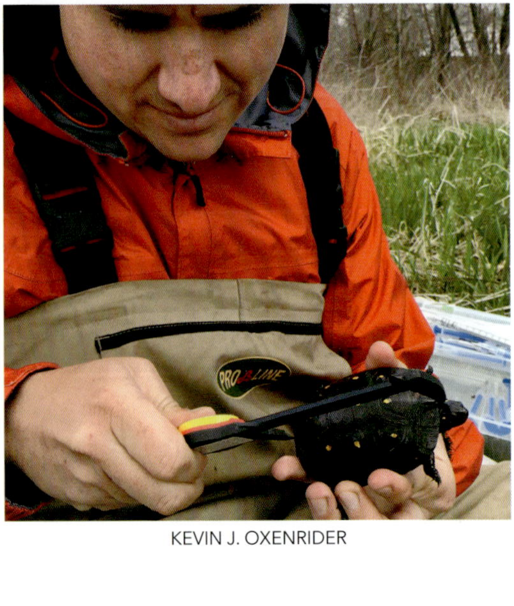

KEVIN J. OXENRIDER

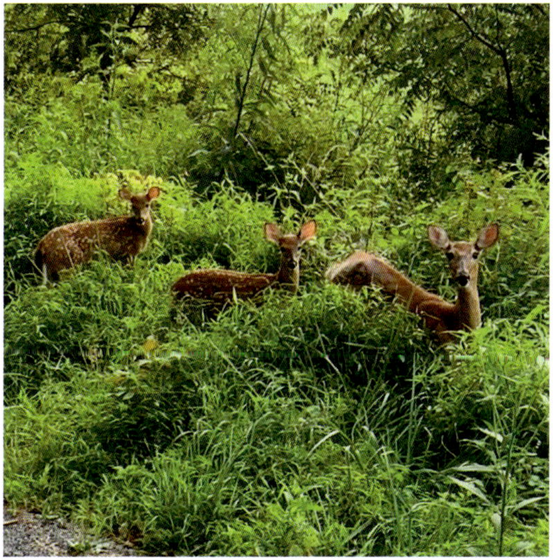

LORI TURNER

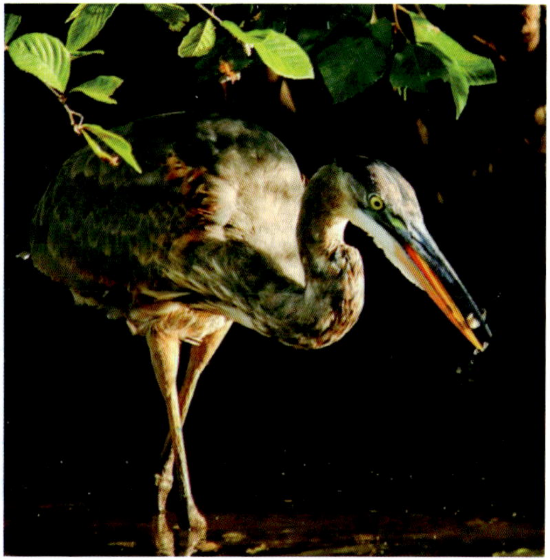

SARAH E. BAILEY

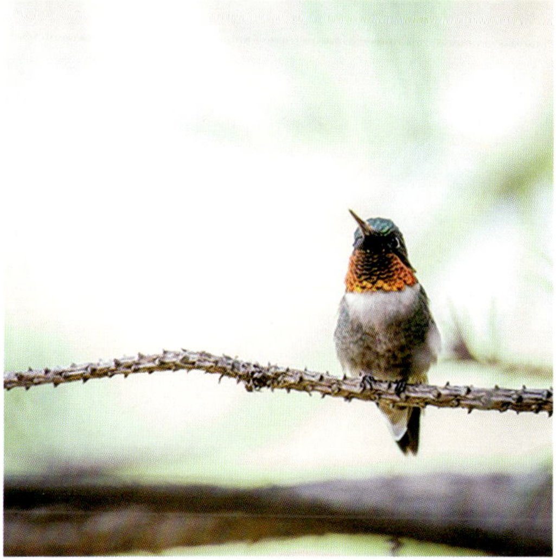

JON HOWARD

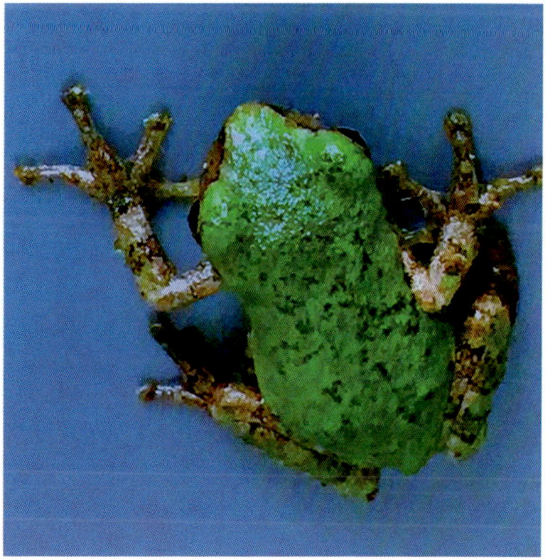

WESLEY PHILP

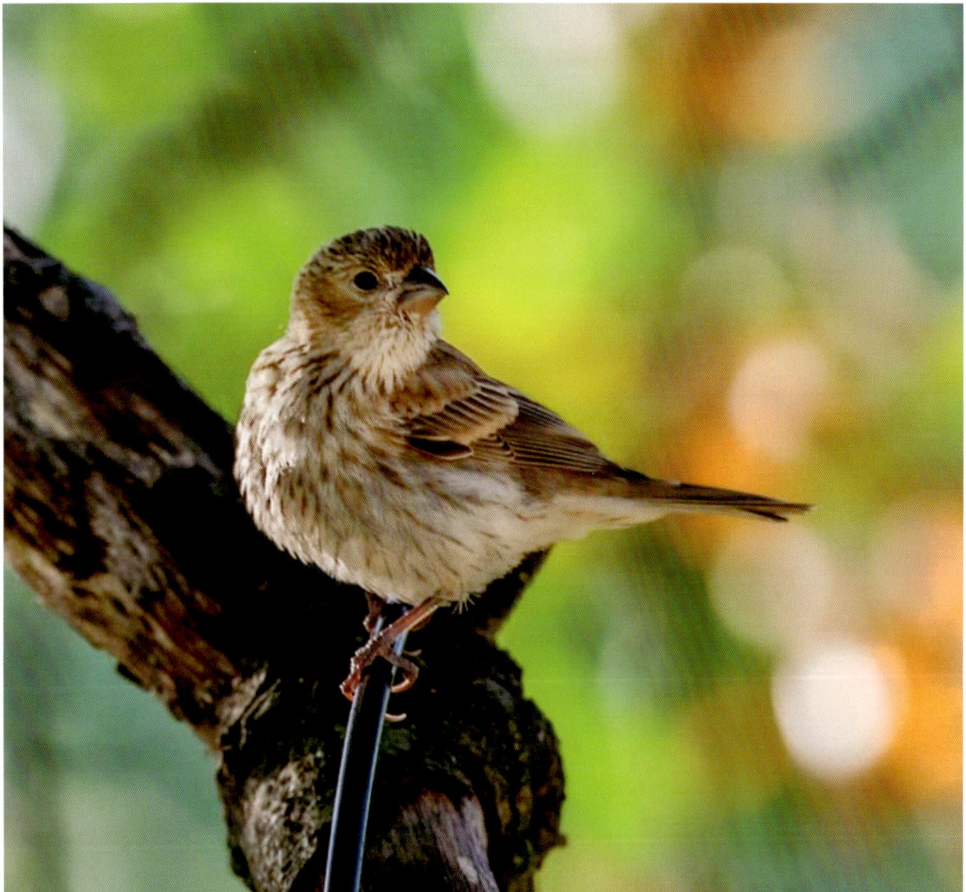

WENDY PARKS

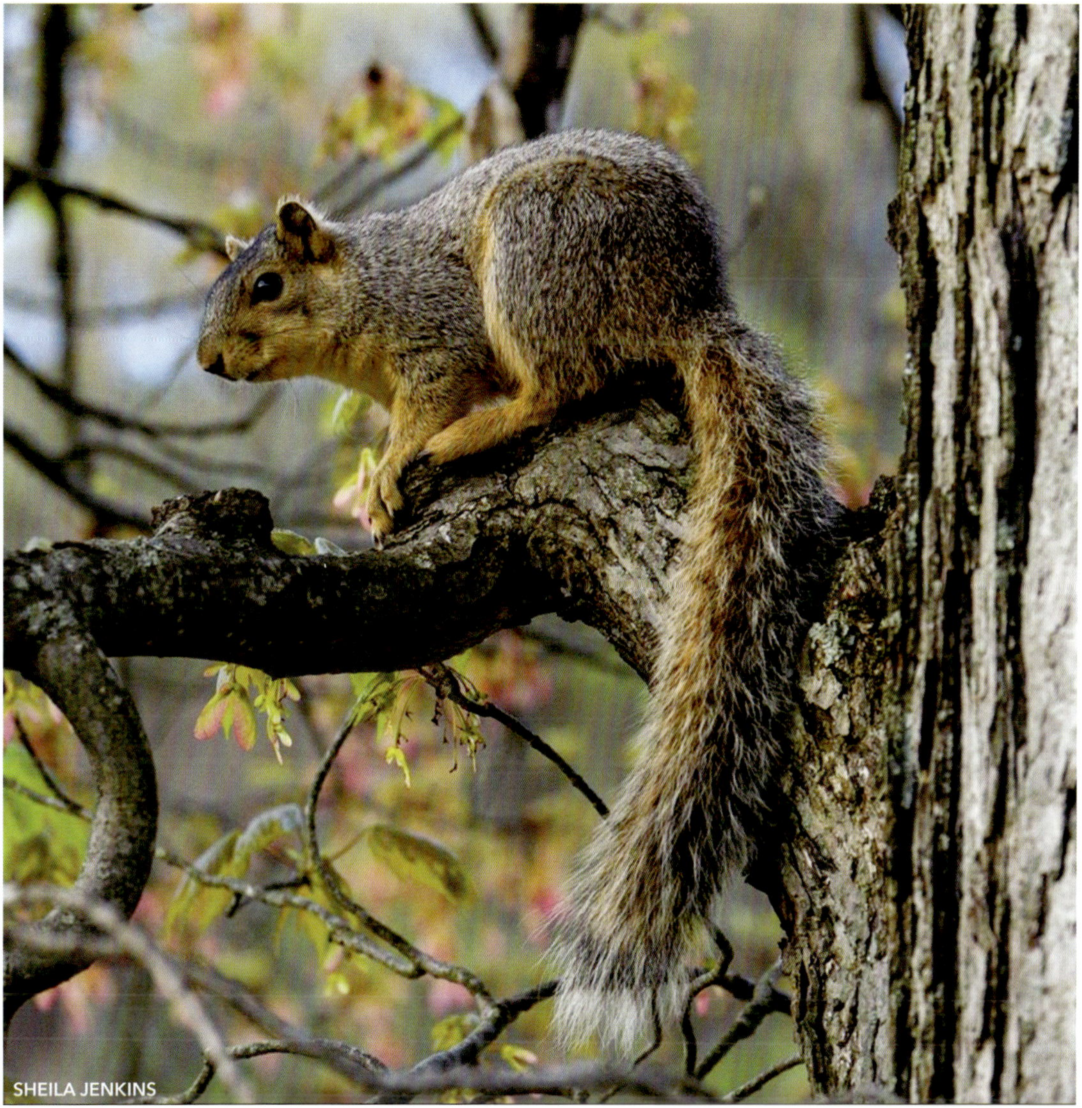
SHEILA JENKINS

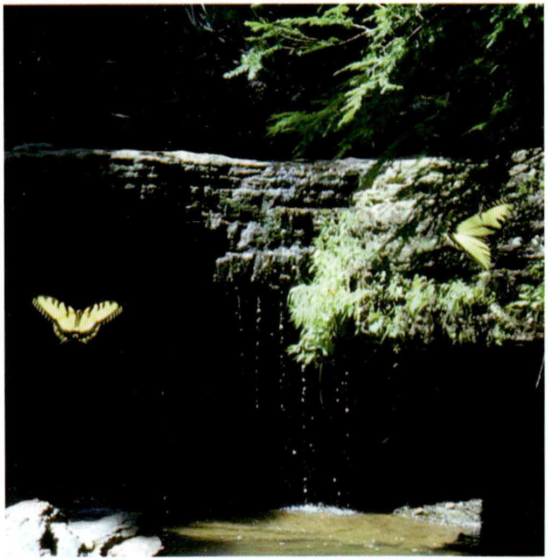
BO ANTHONY LAMBERT

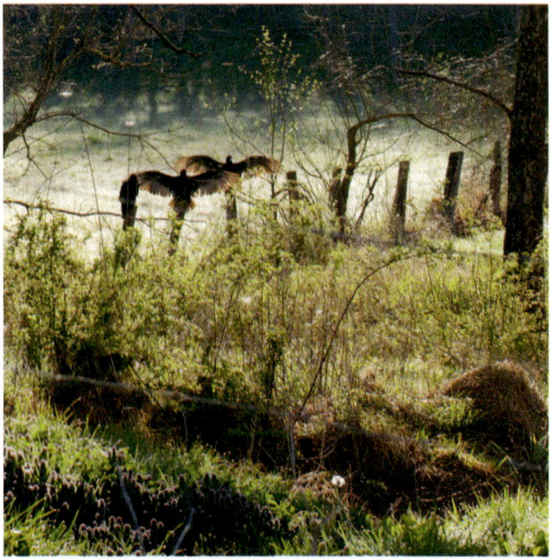
MAGGIE FISHER

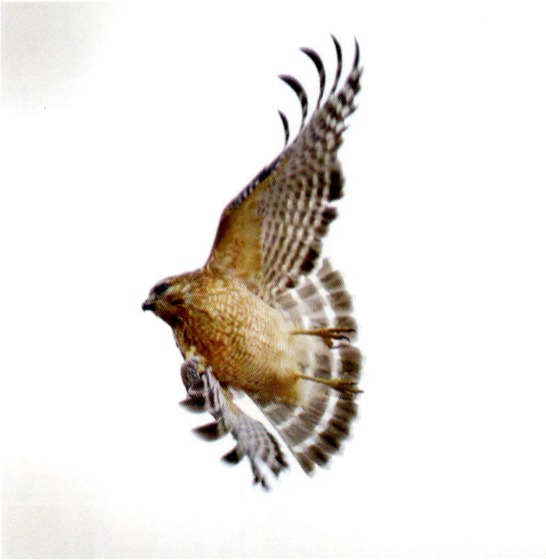
DANNY CARPENTER

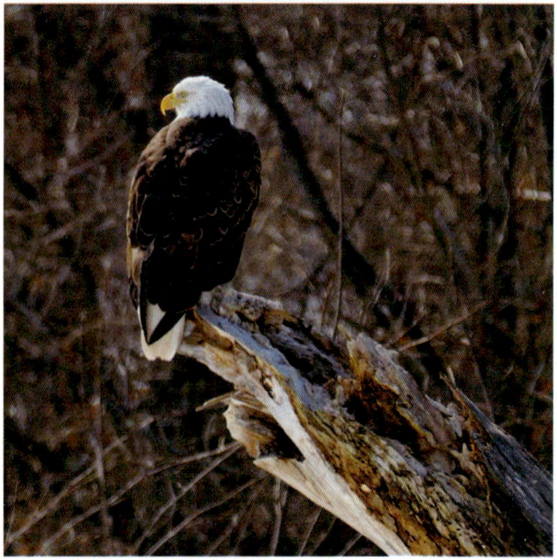
STEPHANIE CARPENTER

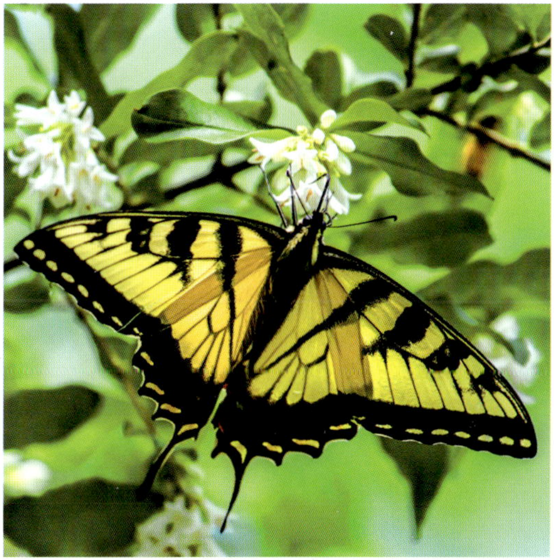

KATHY JENKINS

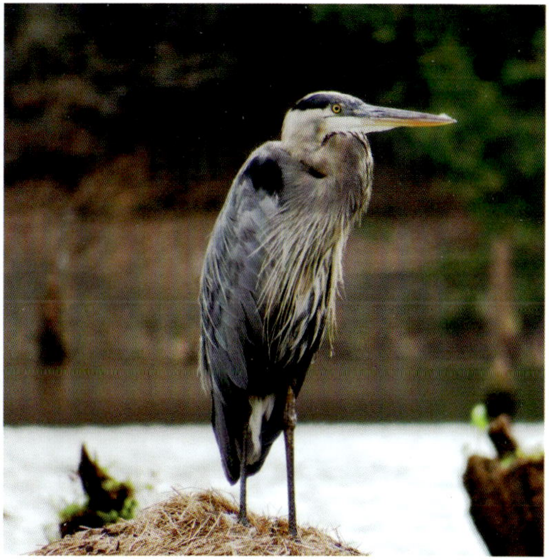

CYNTHIA MULLENS

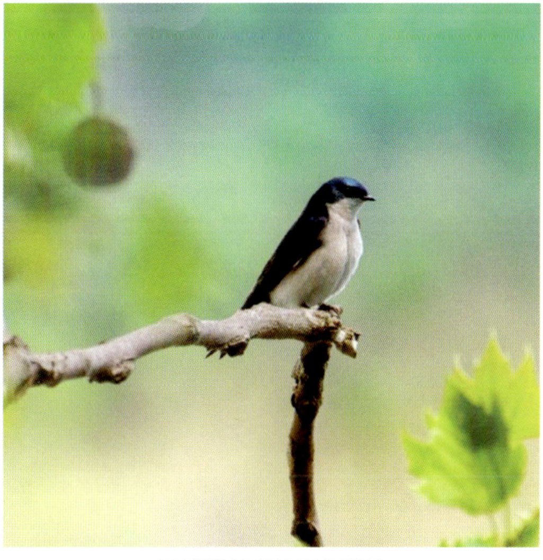

DENISE POWERS FABIAN

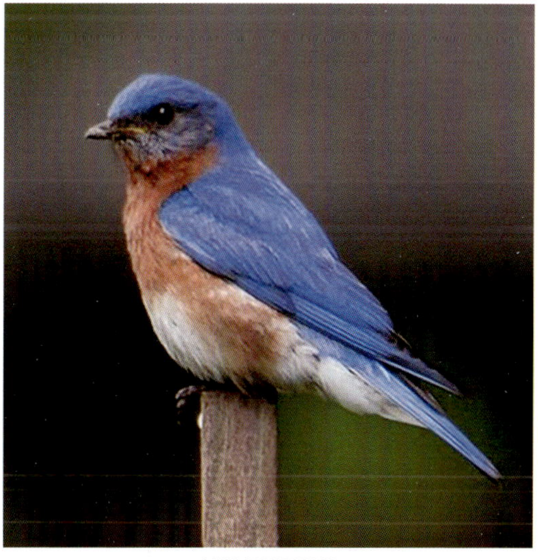

WENDY PARKS

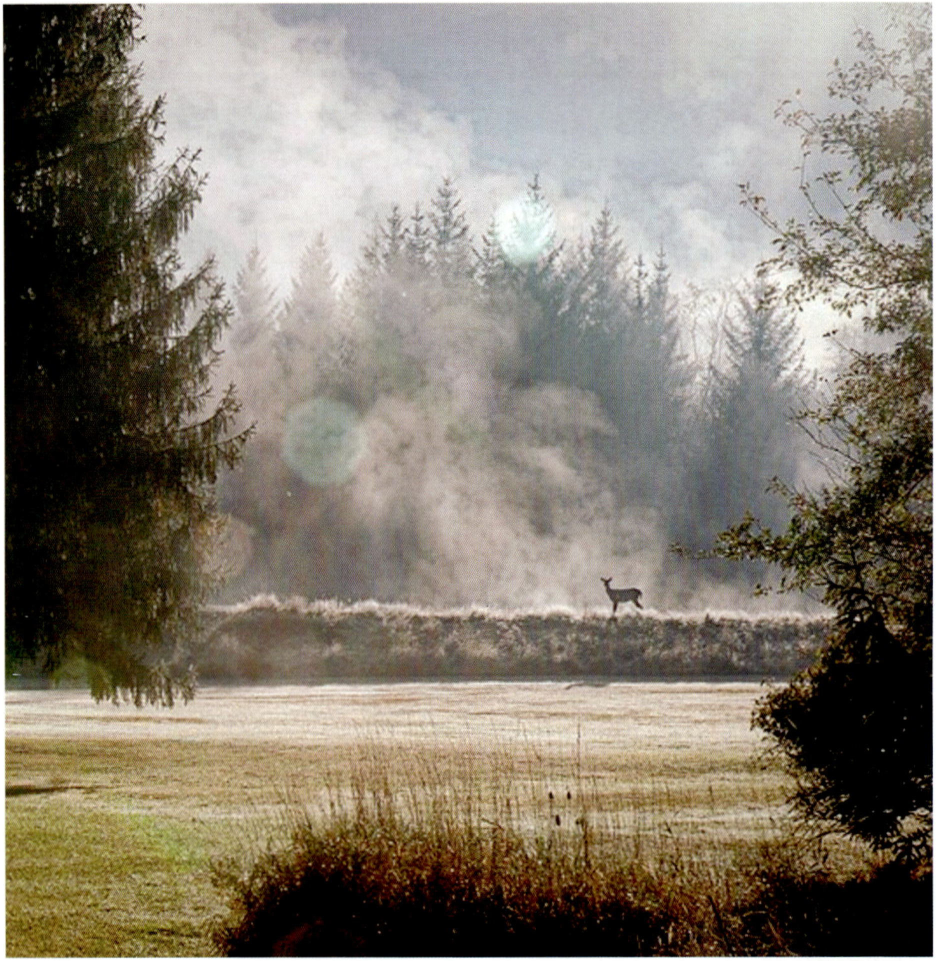

DENISE POWERS FABIAN

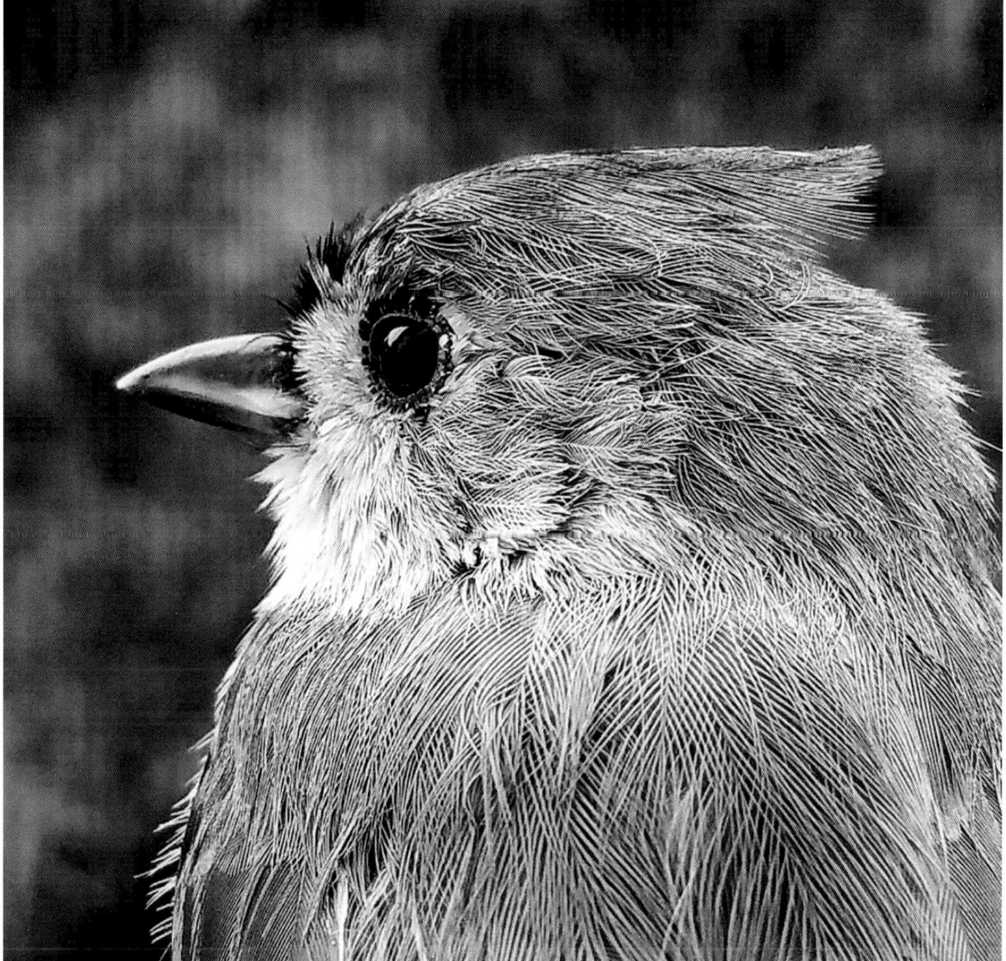

JESSE WAGGONER

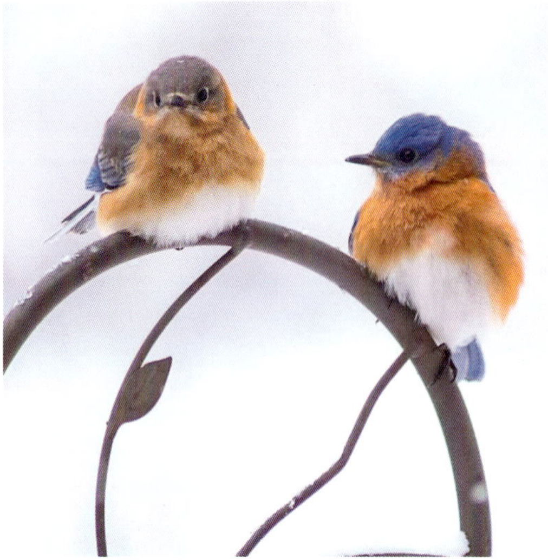

SARAH E. BAILEY

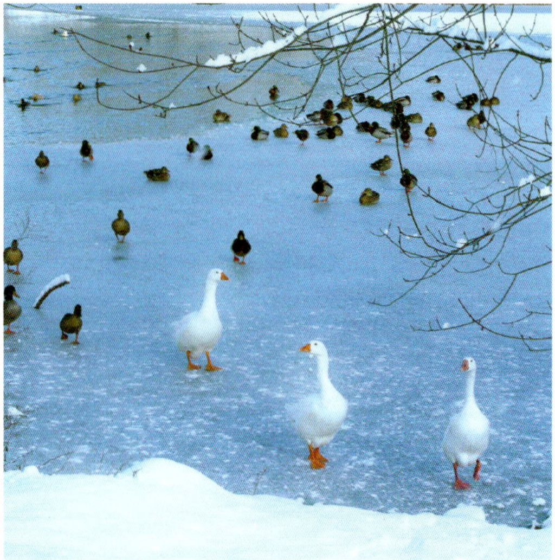

LAURA MOUL

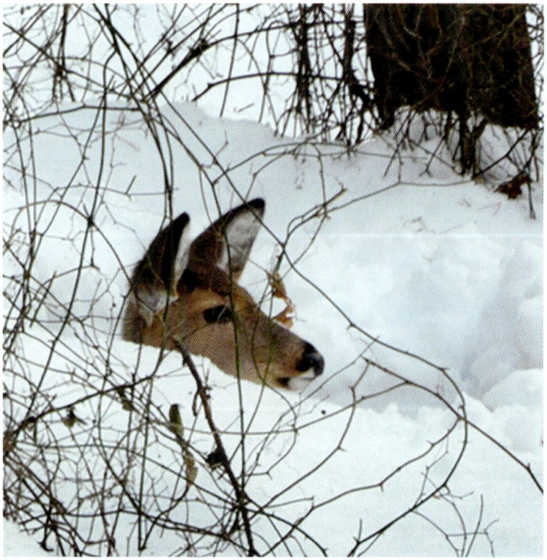

JOHNNIE C. WALTER

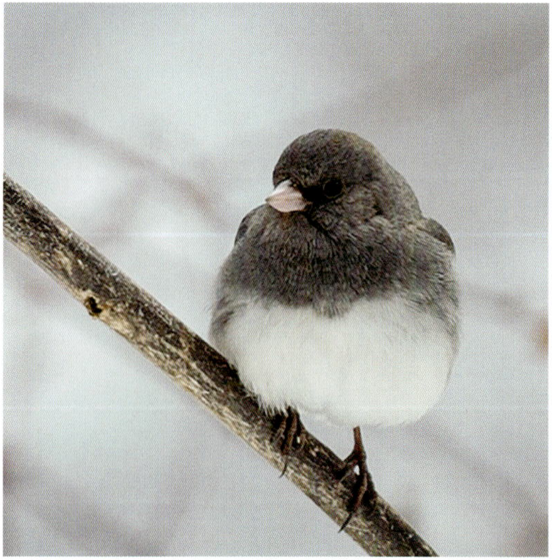

JON HOWARD

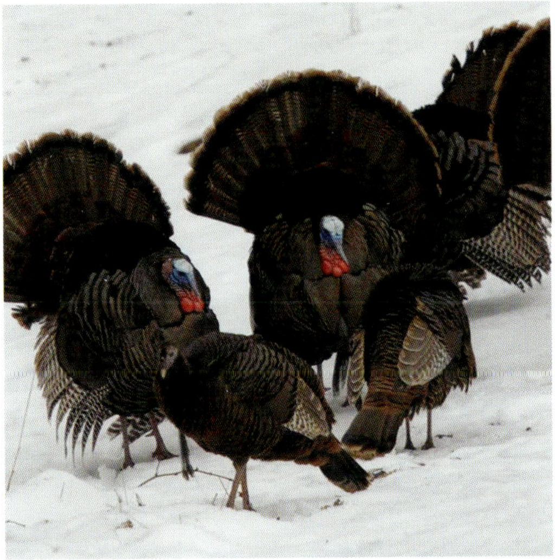

CYNTHIA MULLENS

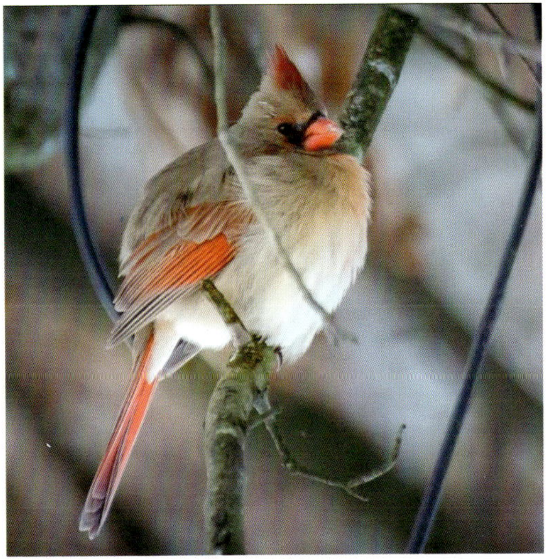

WENDY PARKS

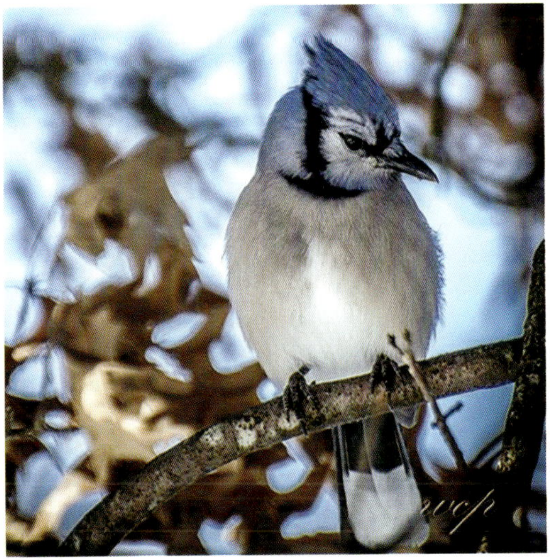

WENDY CLARK

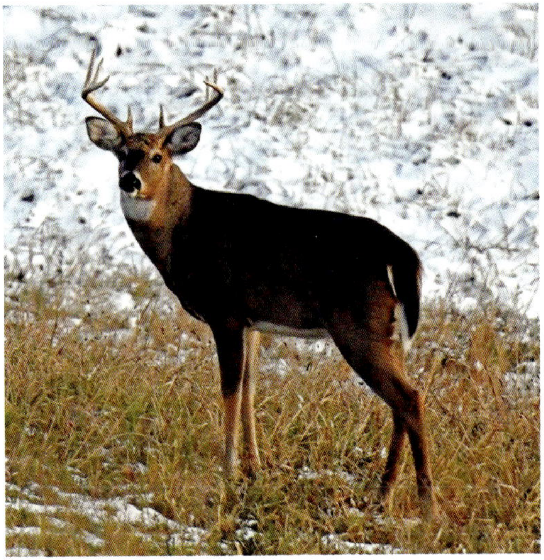

RONDA LEGG

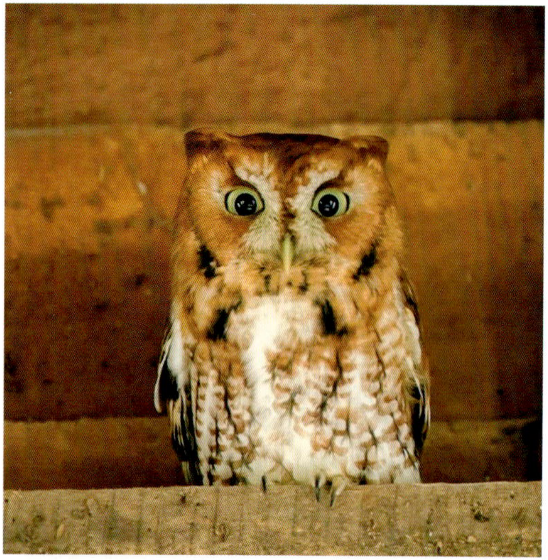

BRENT SCHNUPP

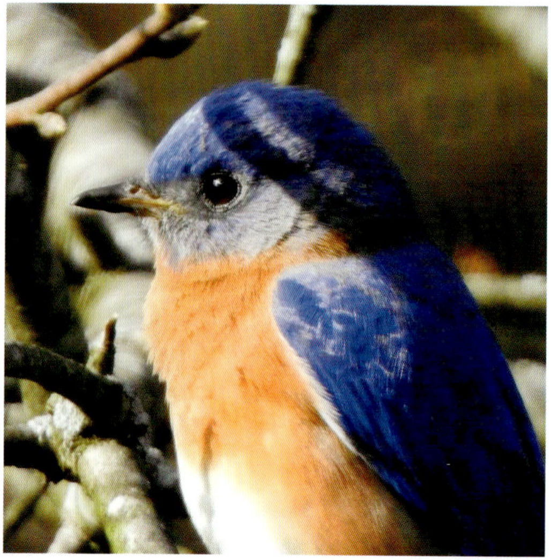

JESSE WAGGONER

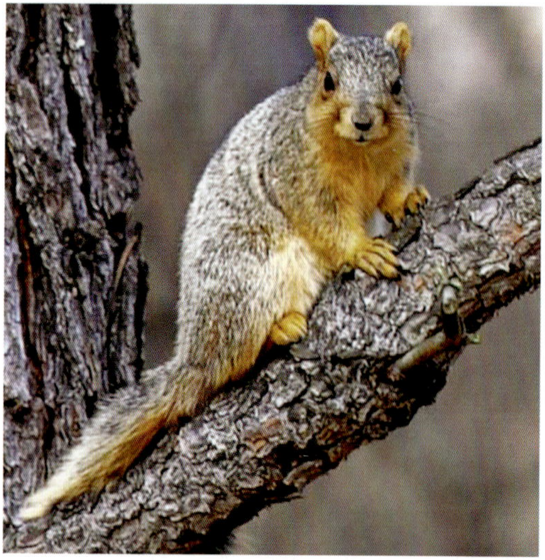

ARNOLD PARRISH

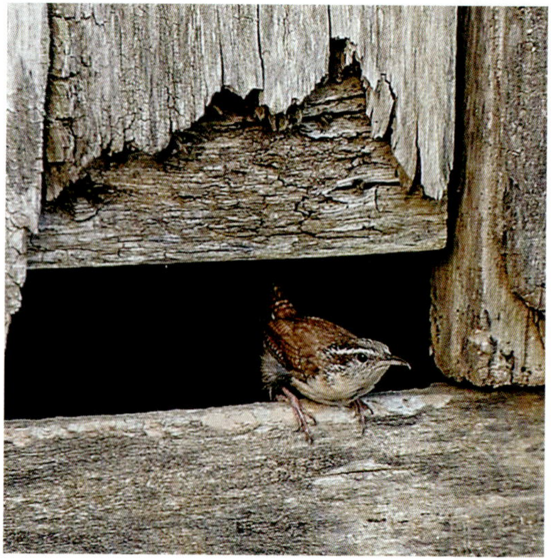

DENISE POWERS FABIAN

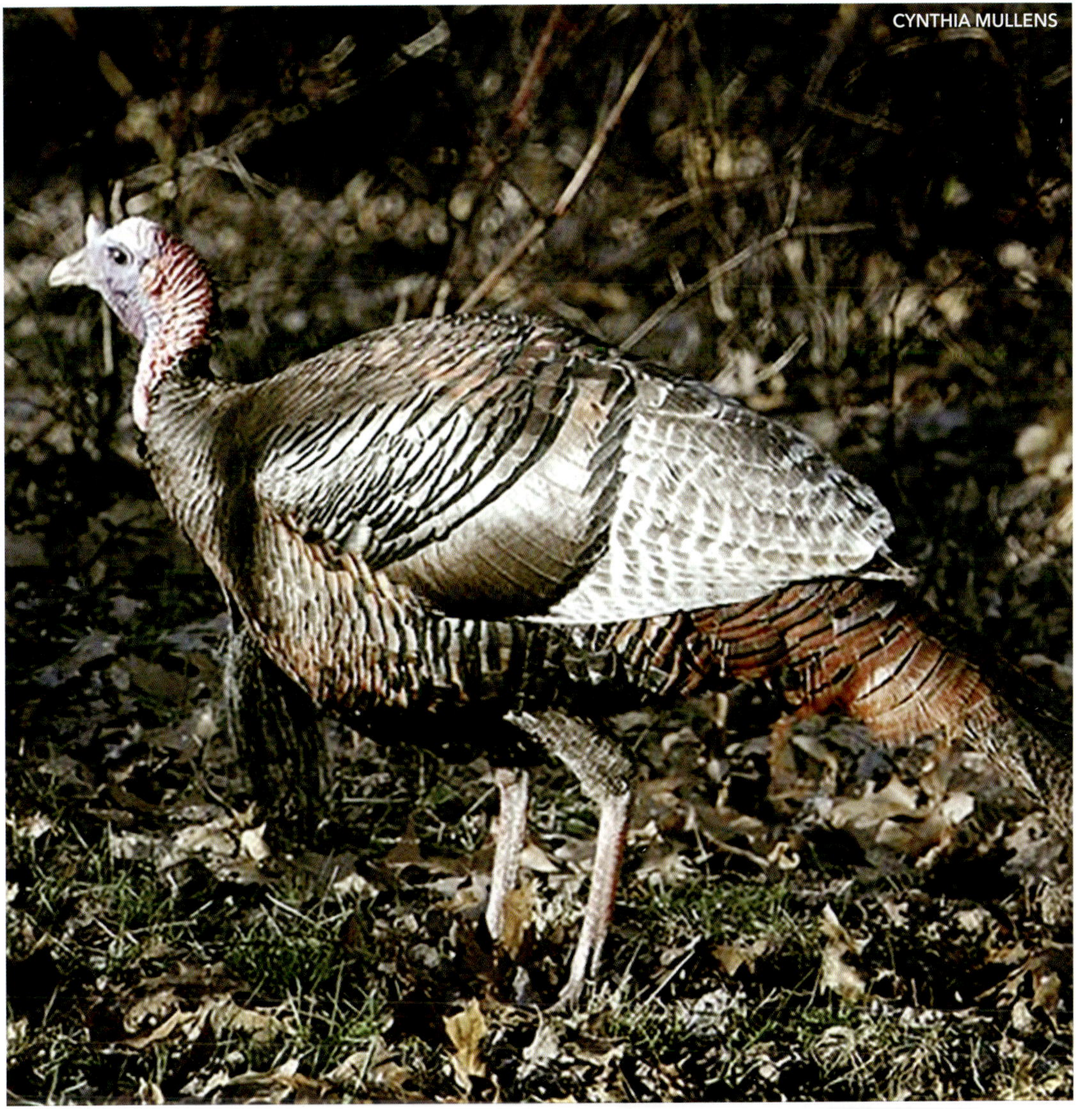
CYNTHIA MULLENS

flora

Earth laughs in flowers.

- RALPH WALDO EMERSON

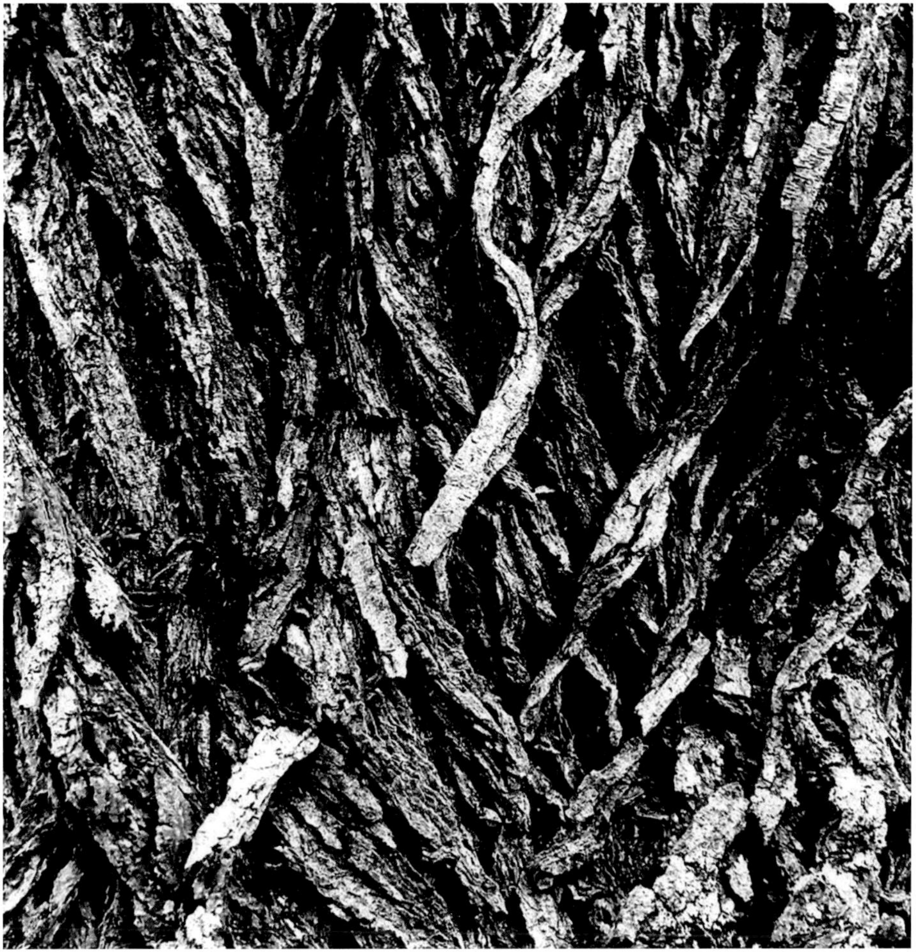

WESLEY PHILP

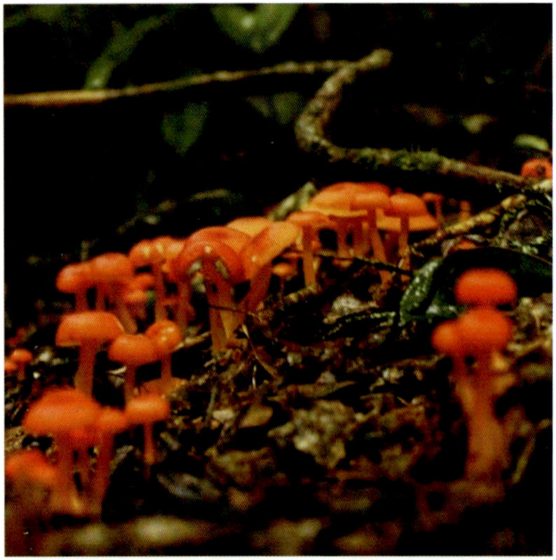

JEREMY CUTLIP

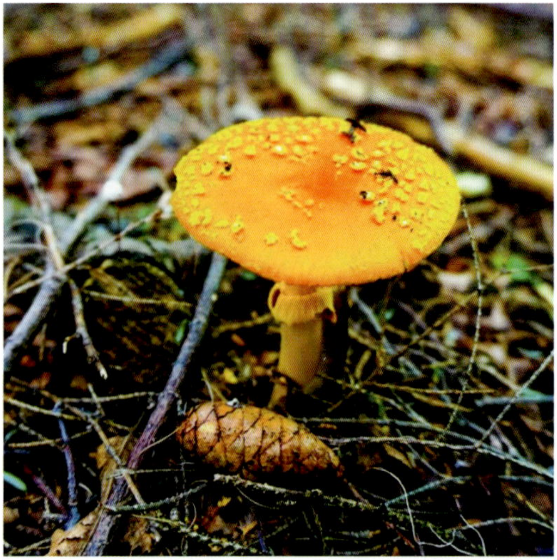

LEAH BOWES

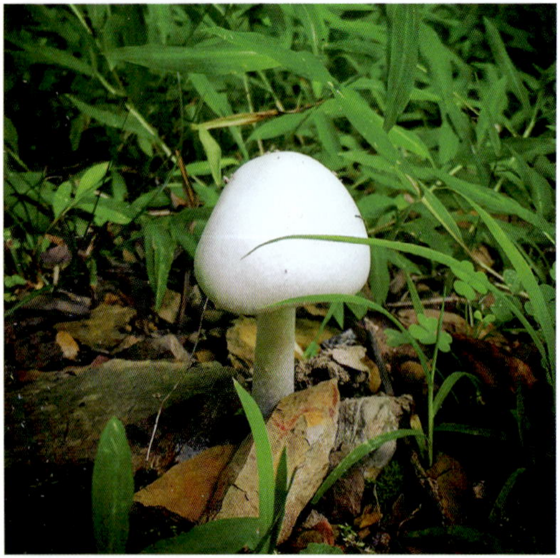

ELAINE CLARK

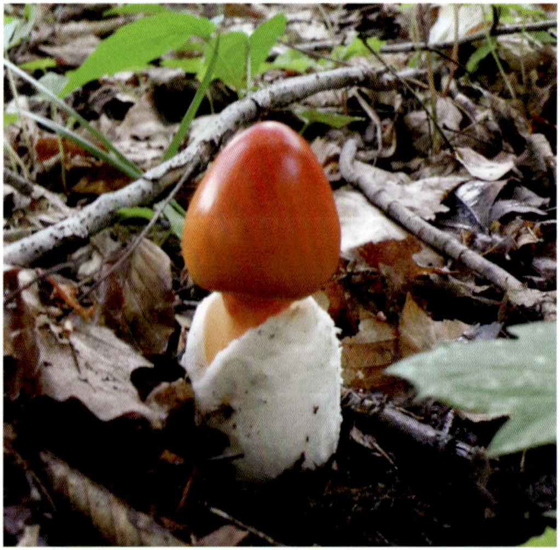

ARNOLD PARRISH

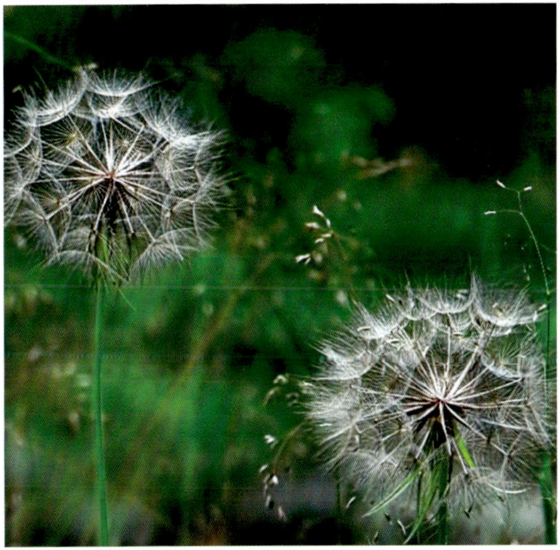

RICHARD MARLOW

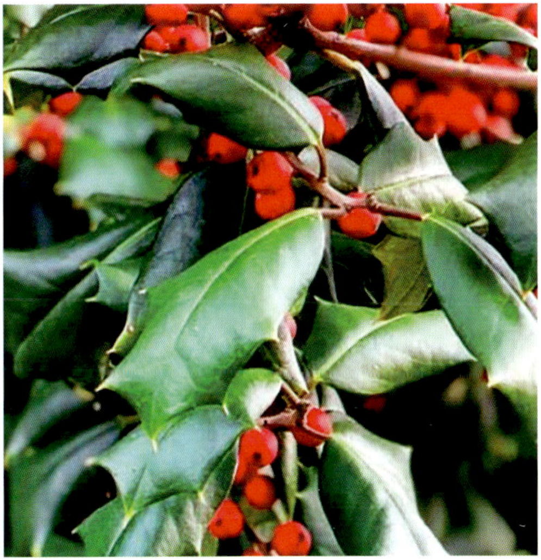

WESLEY PHILP

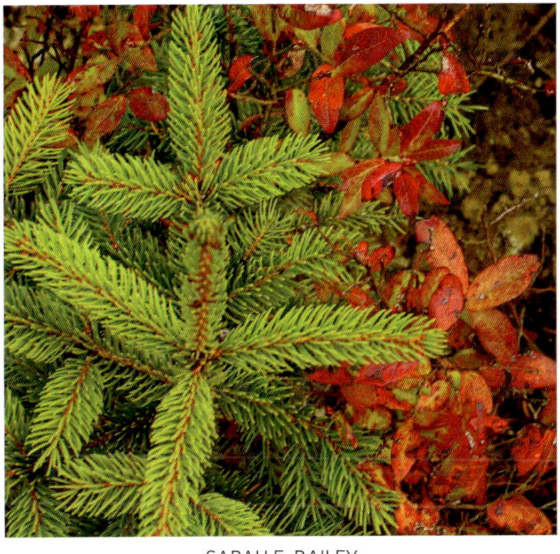

SARAH E. BAILEY

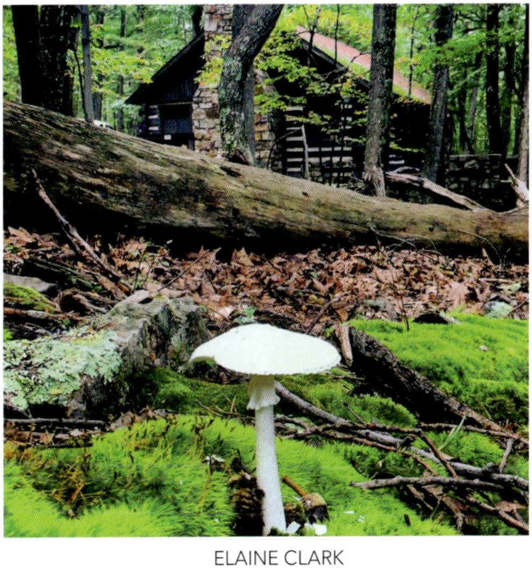

ELAINE CLARK

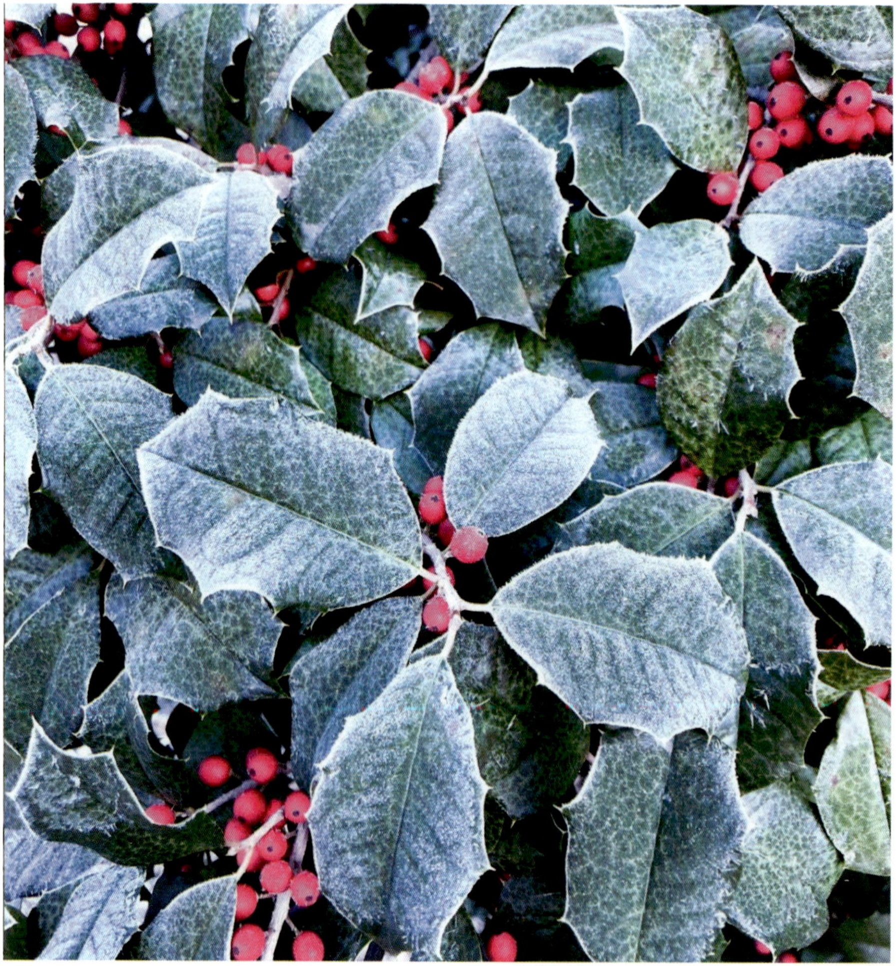

WES PHILP

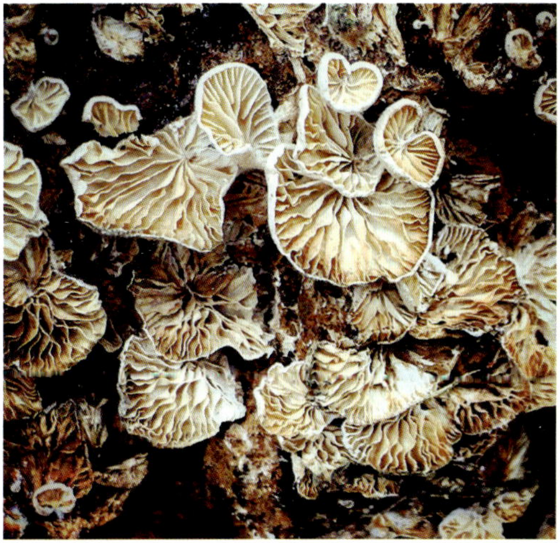

ELAINE CLARK

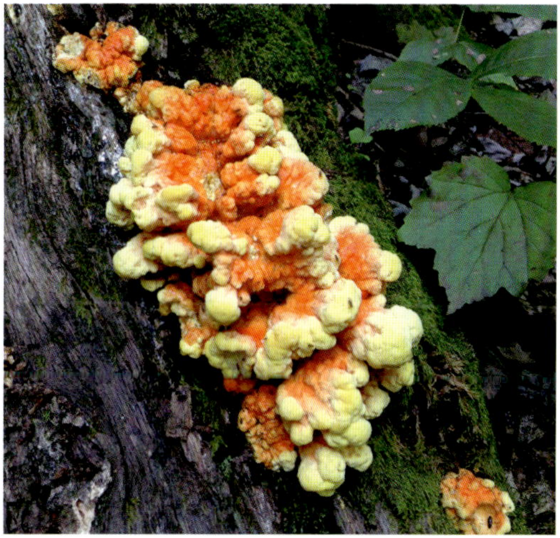

MARK REASOR

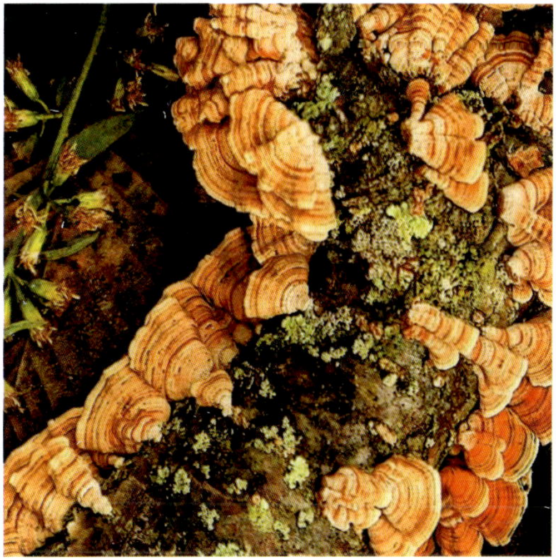

BETH SPENCER

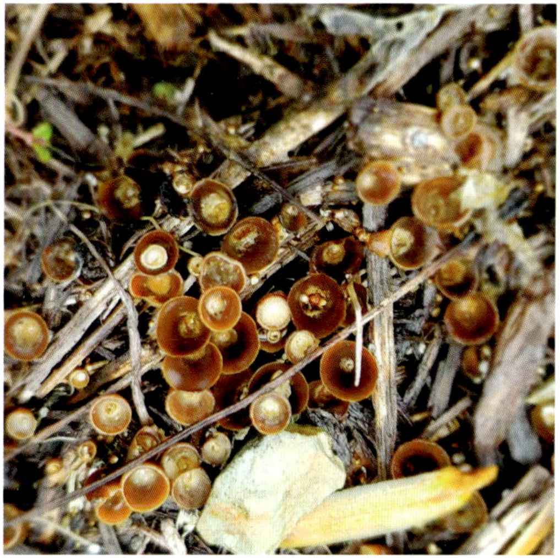

CYNTHIA MULLENS

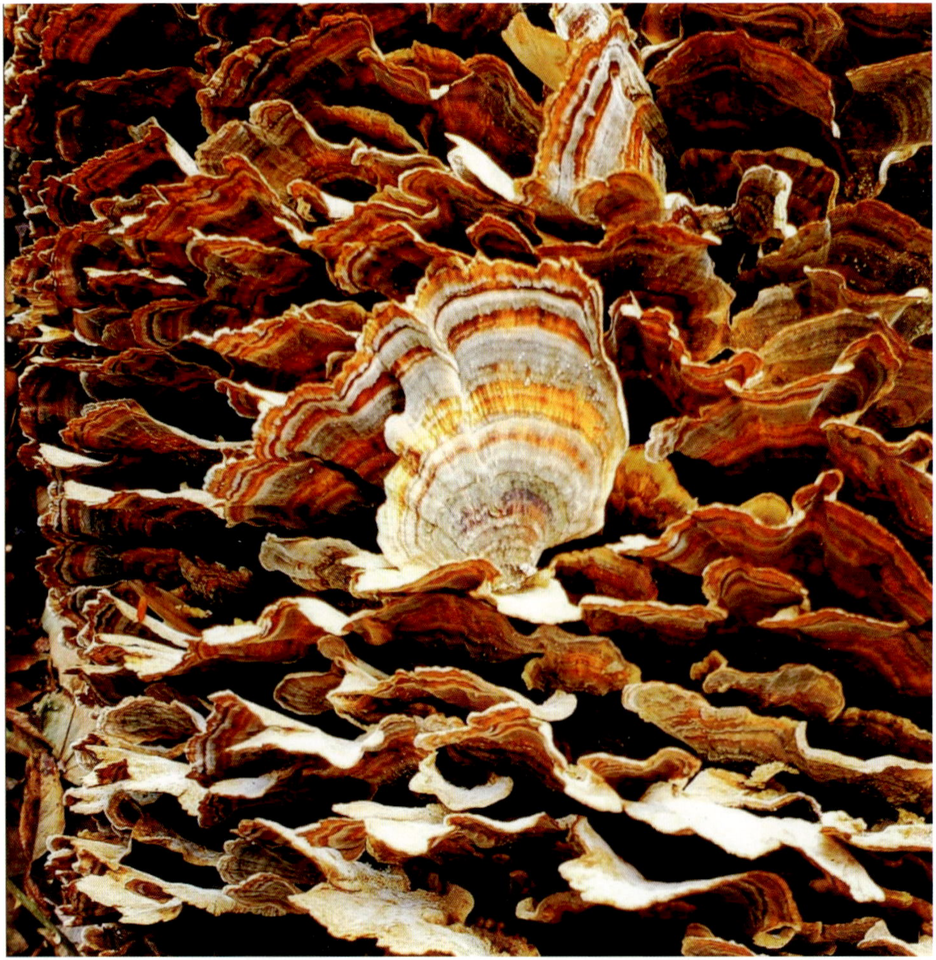

CYNTHIA MULLENS

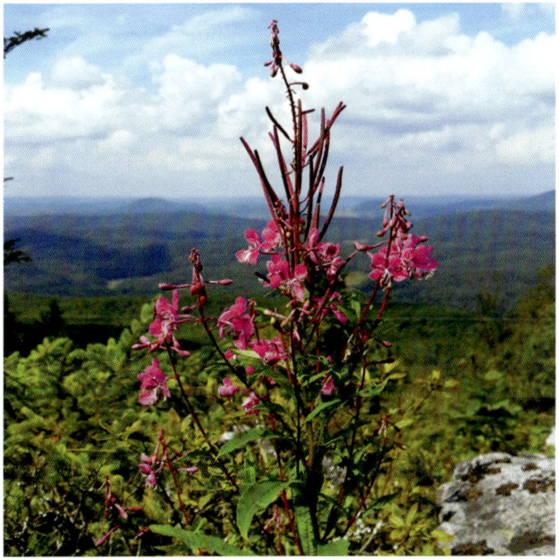

RYAN LOGUE

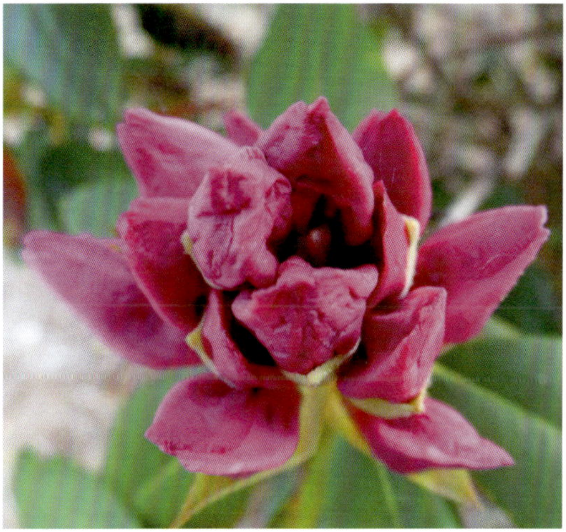

MARK HESLEP

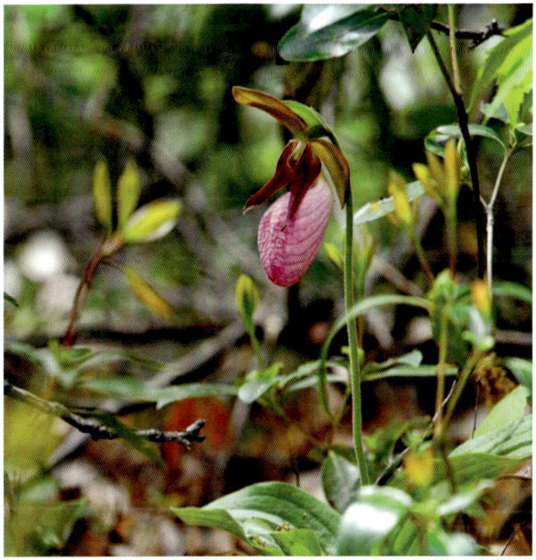

RONDA LEGG

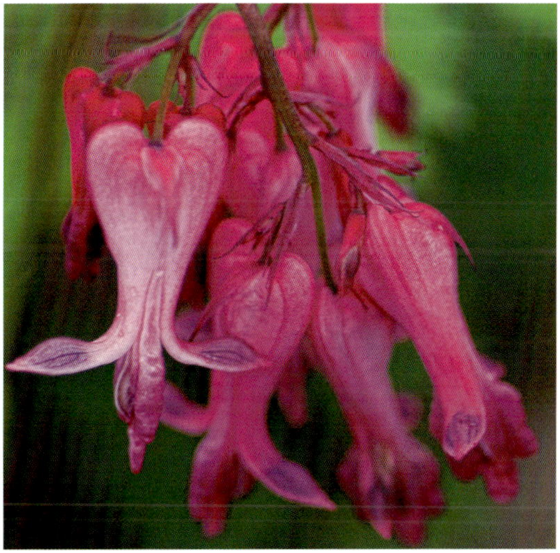

LAURA MOUL

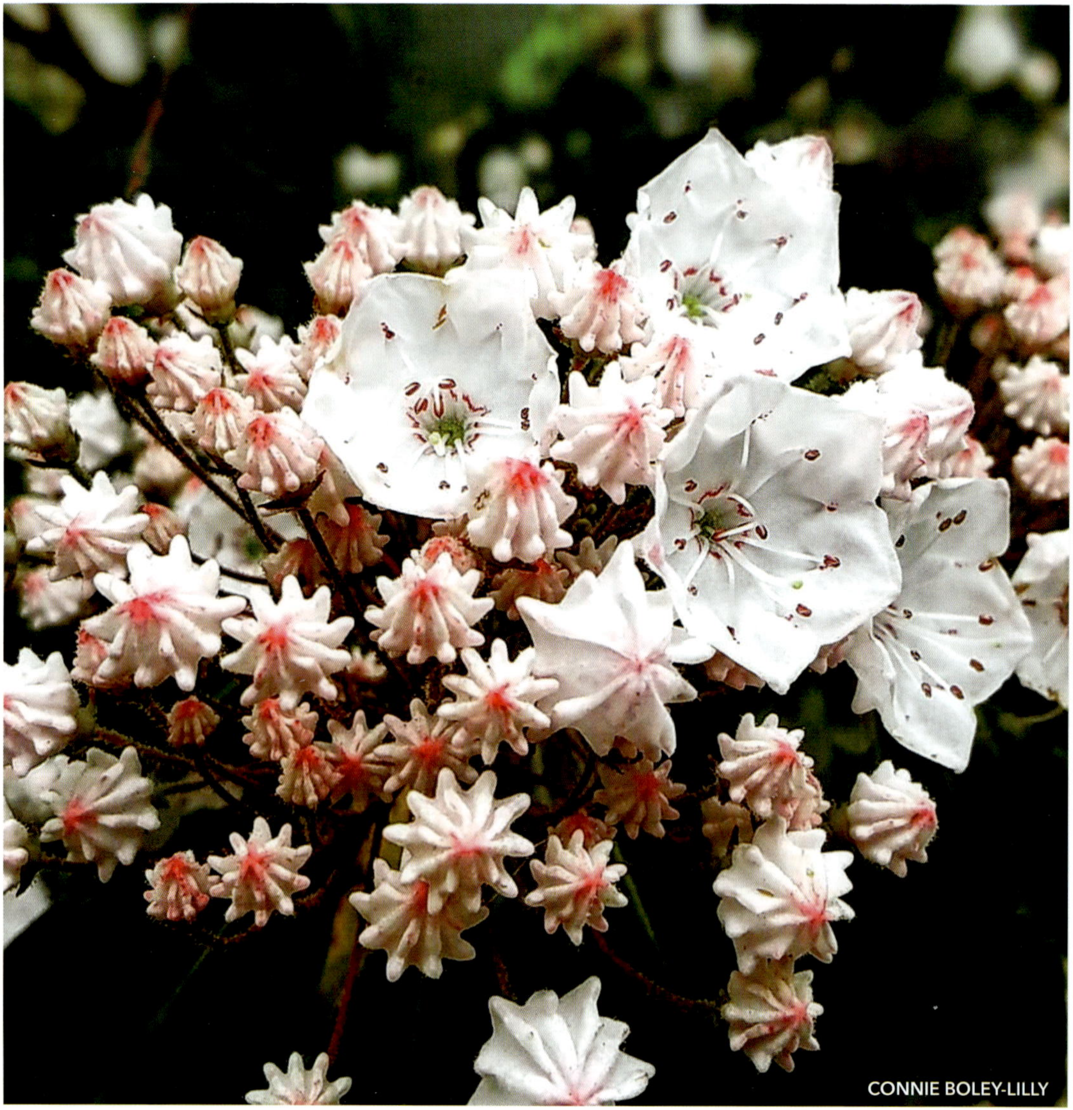
CONNIE BOLEY-LILLY

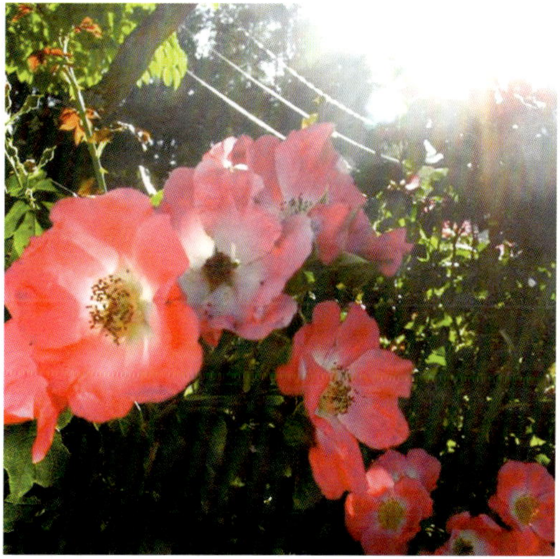

CANDY THOMPSON

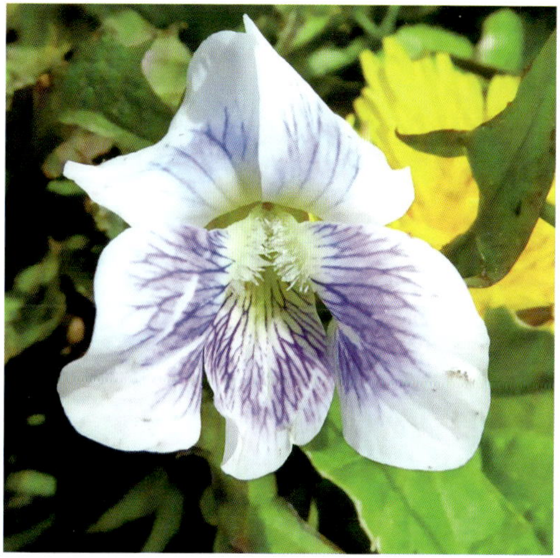

VANESSA HOCHARD

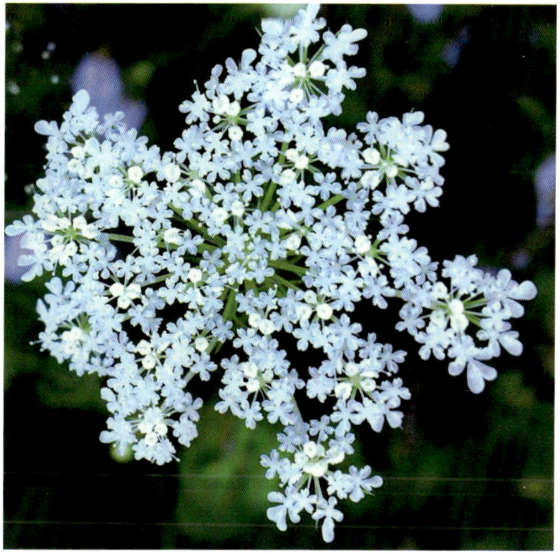

WESLEY PHILP

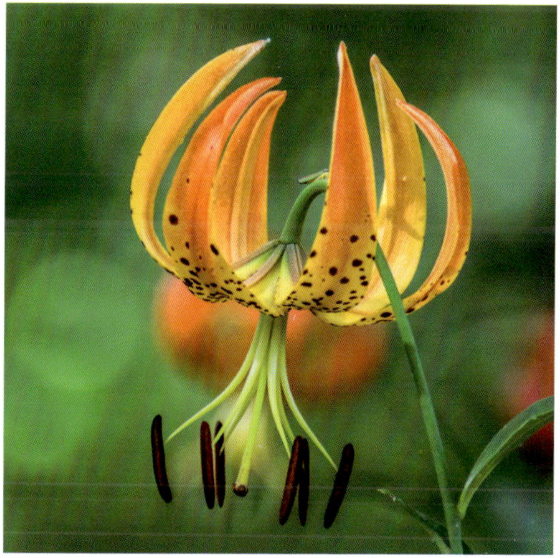

KATHY JENKINS

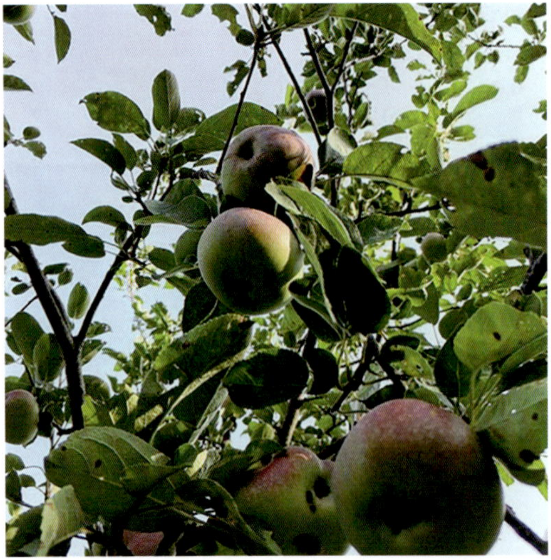

JENNIFER LOCKWOOD

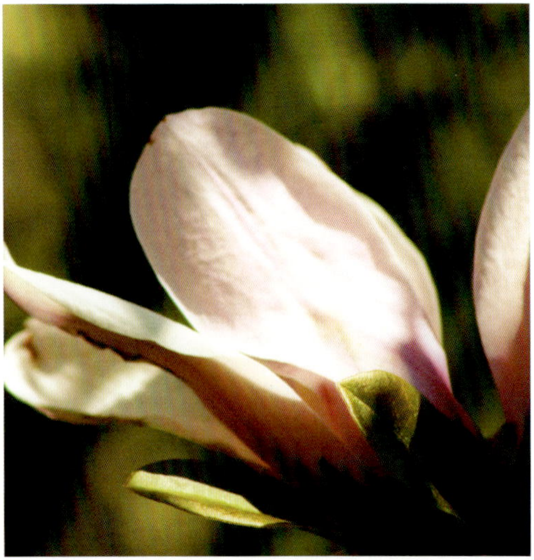

CHRISTIE GOLDEN

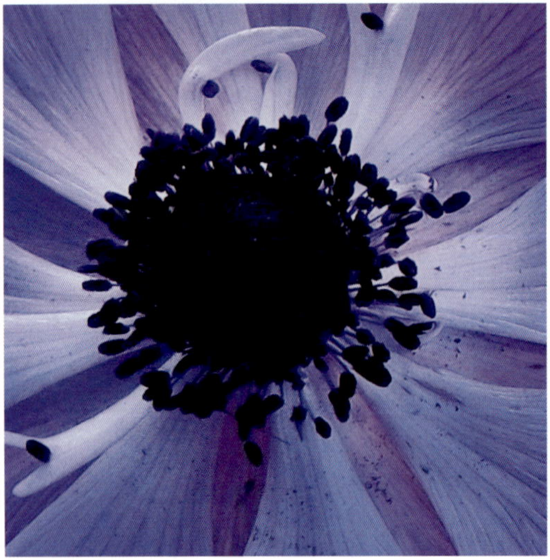

MARY K. YOUNGBLOOD

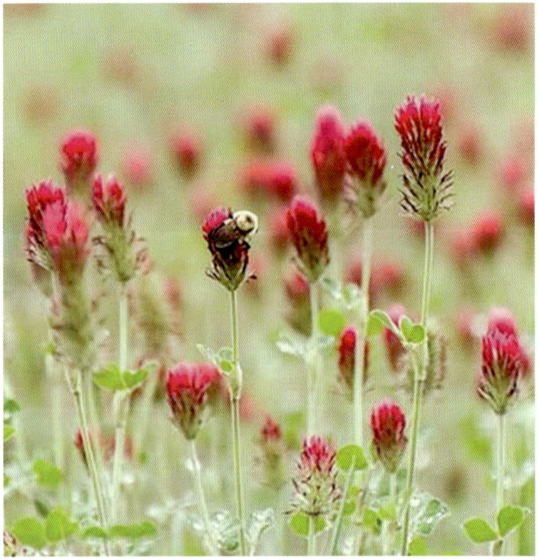

DENISE POWERS FABIAN

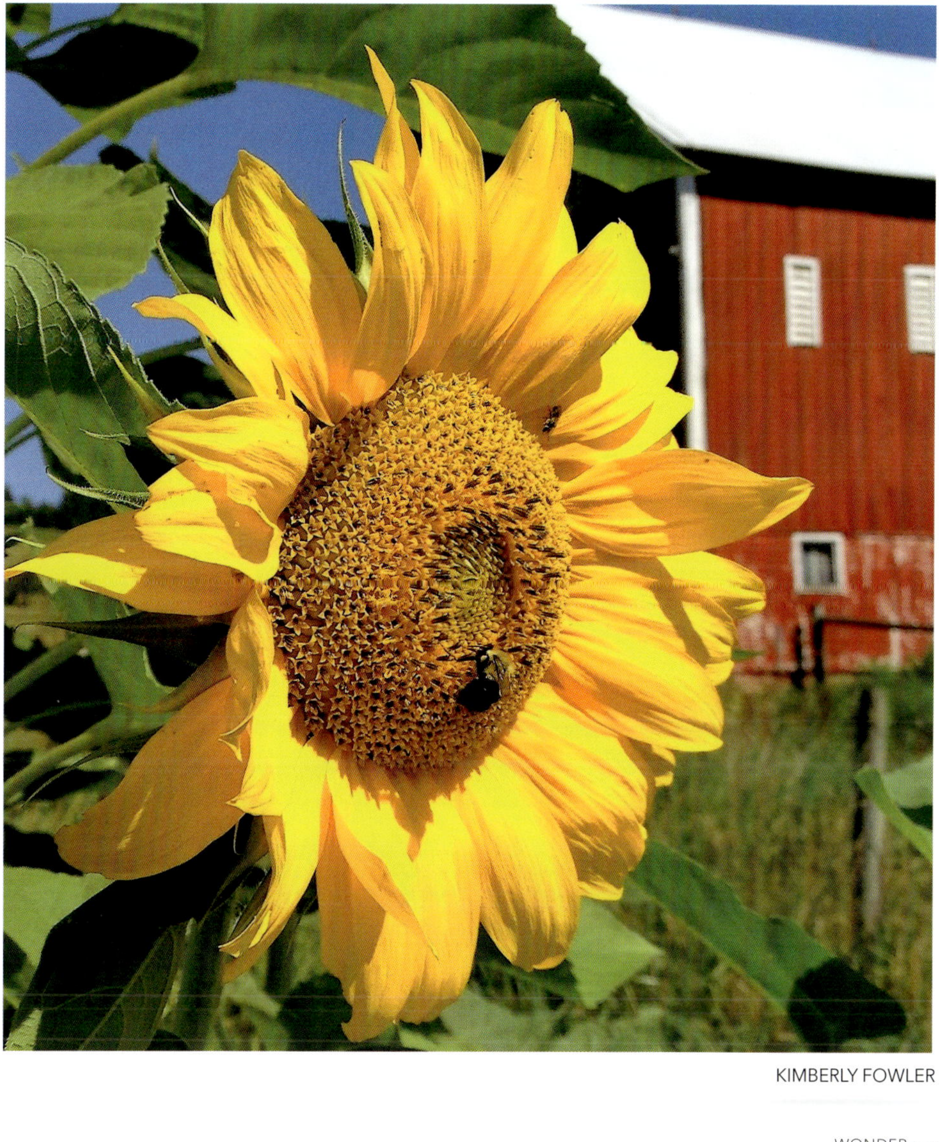

KIMBERLY FOWLER

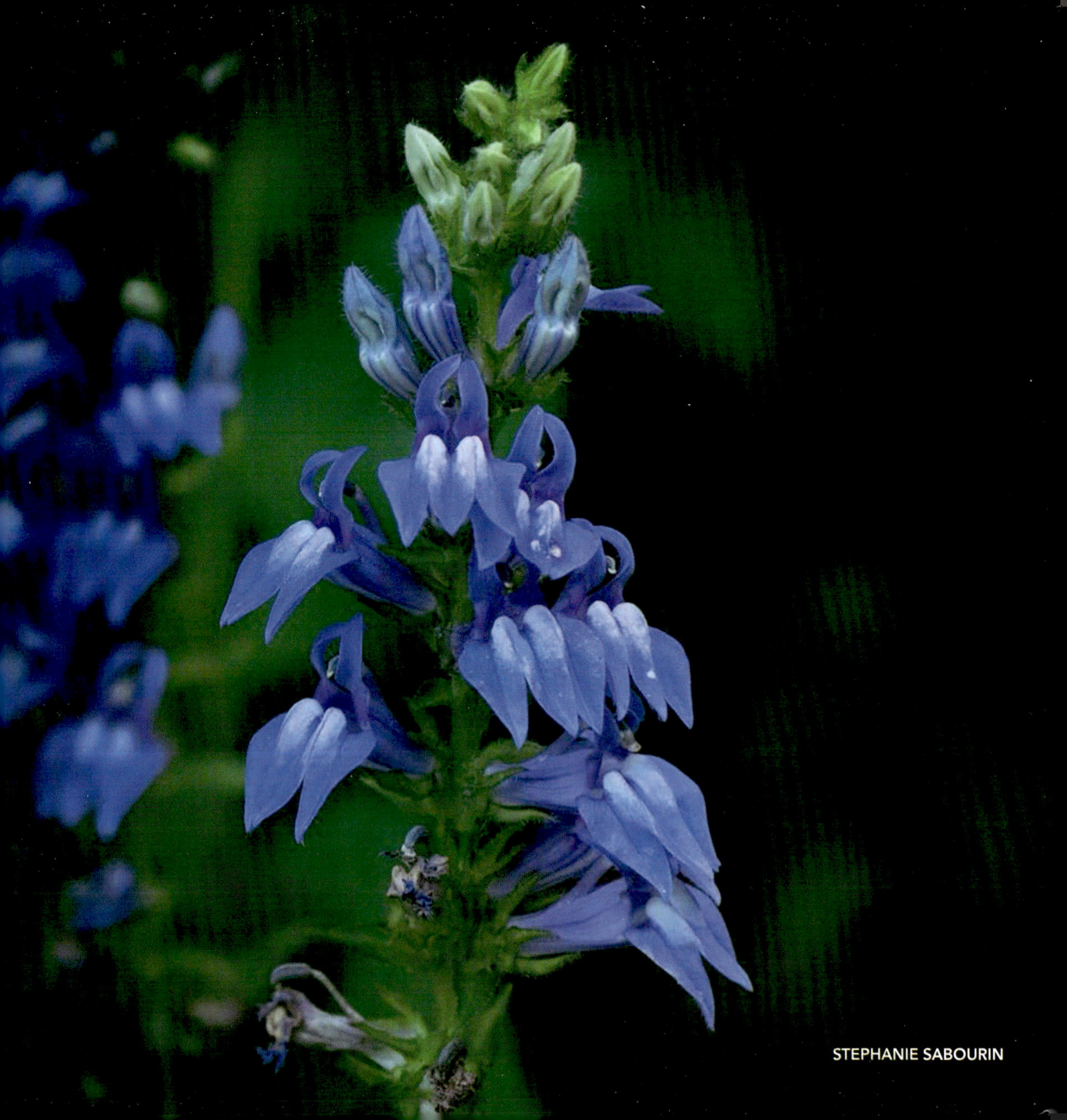
STEPHANIE SABOURIN

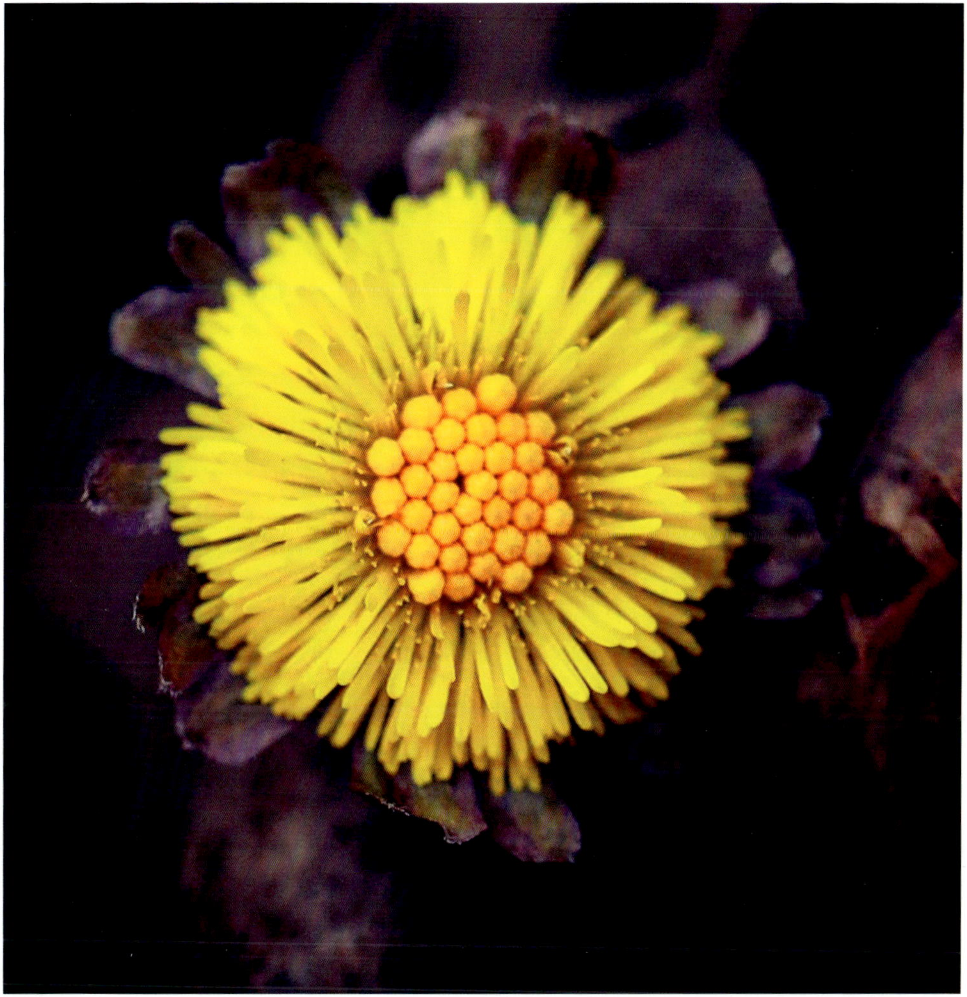

SARAH E. BAILEY

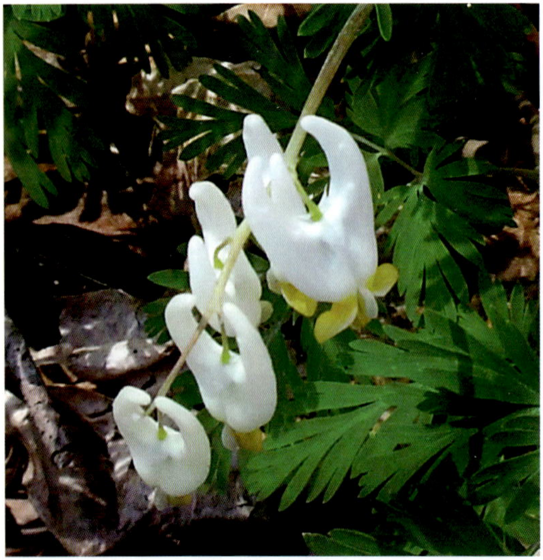

SARAH E. BAILEY

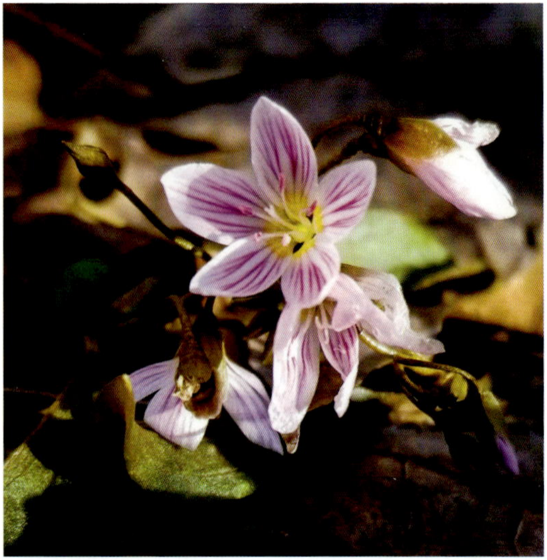

BETH SPENCER

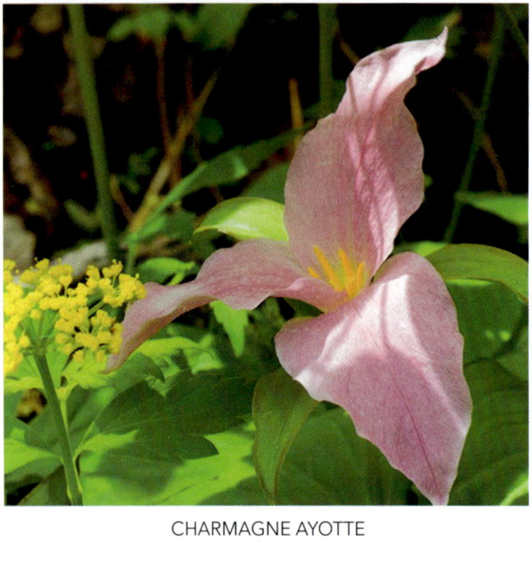

CHARMAGNE AYOTTE

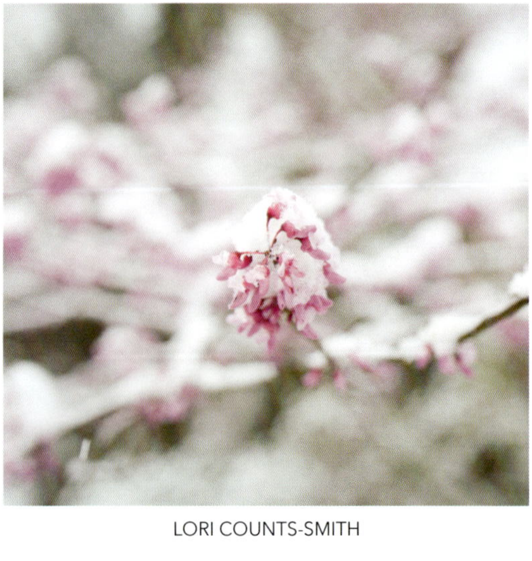

LORI COUNTS-SMITH

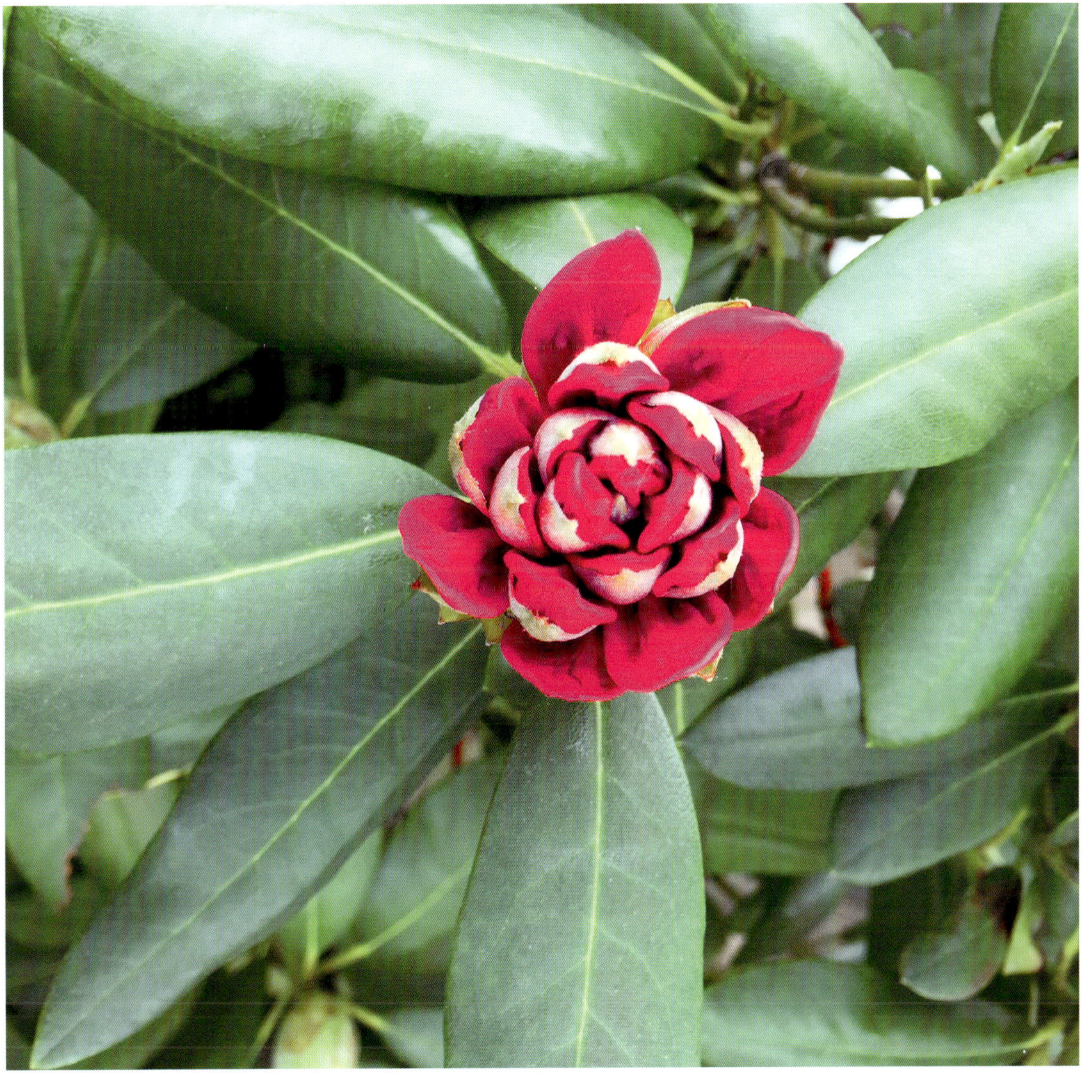

JENNIFER D. RANDOLPH

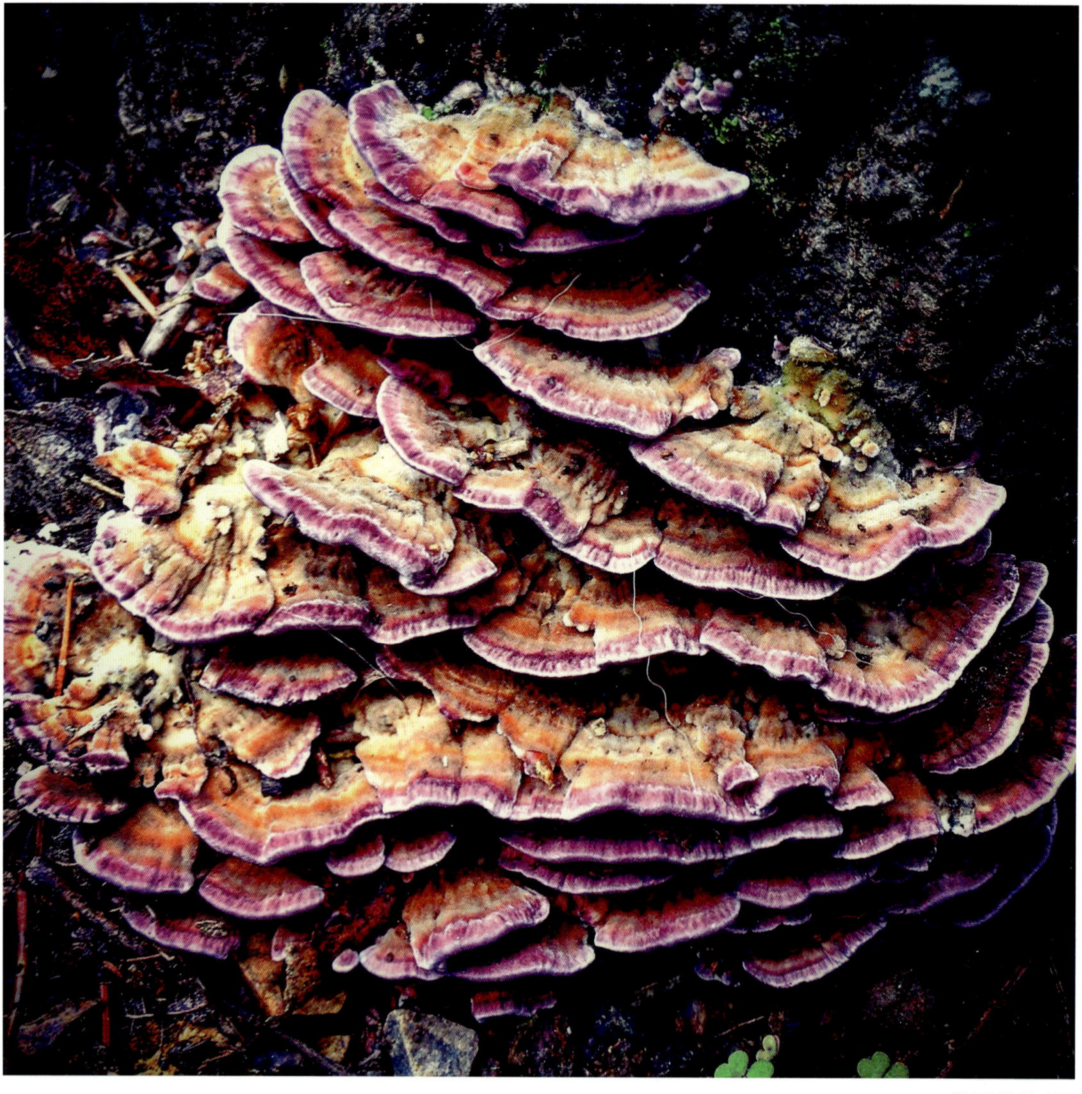

ELAINE CLARK

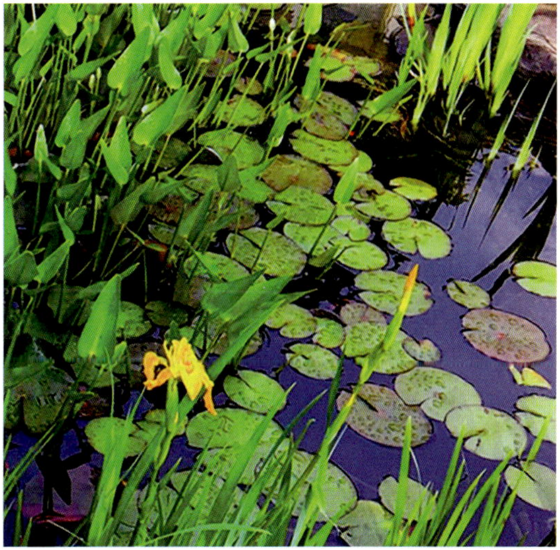
WESLEY PHILP

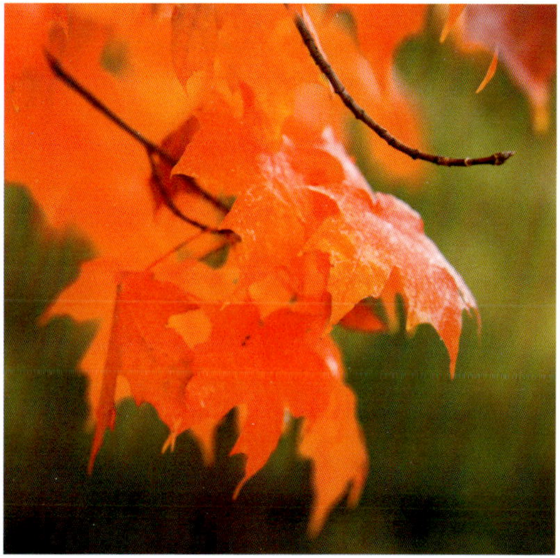
LORI COUNTS-SMITH

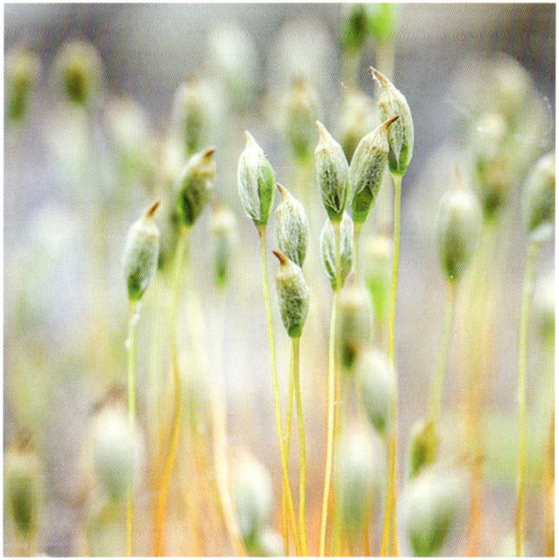
JON HOWARD

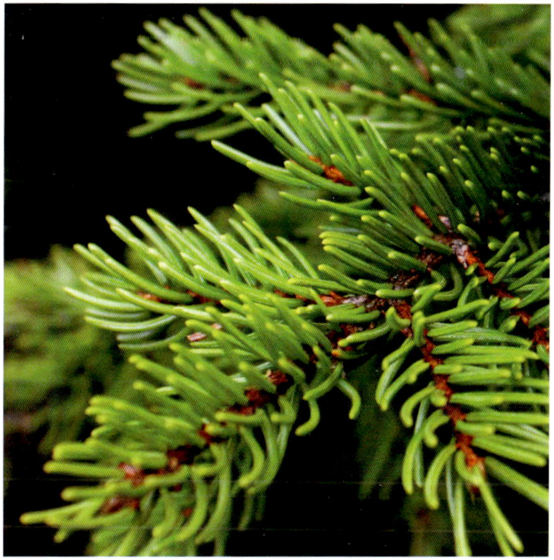
JUSTIN DYNES

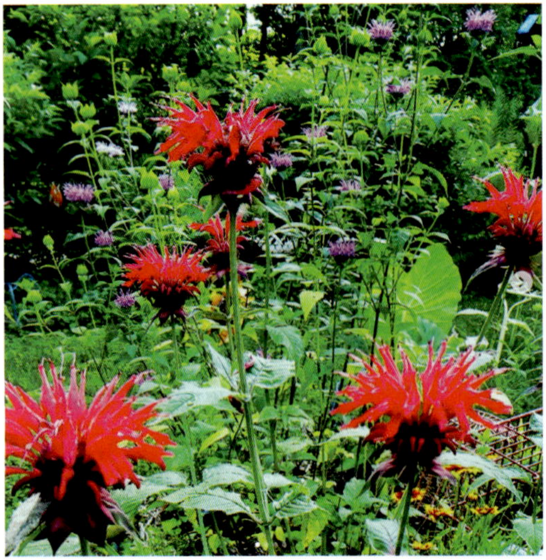
CYNTHIA MULLENS

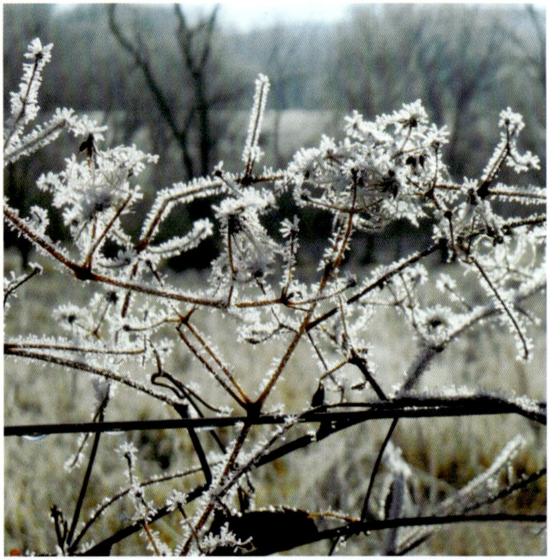
JIMMY SPENCER

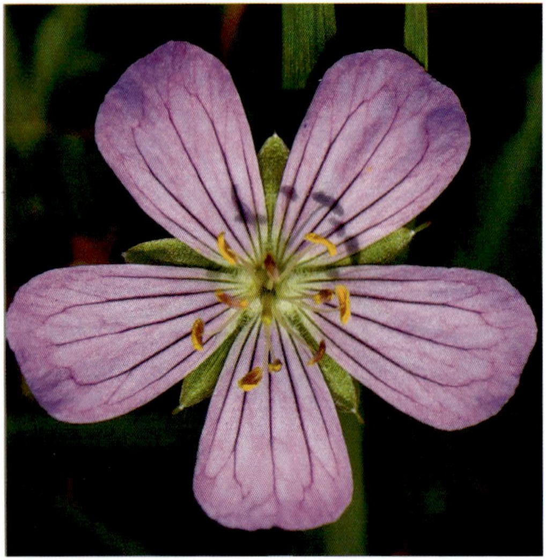
SARAH E. BAILEY

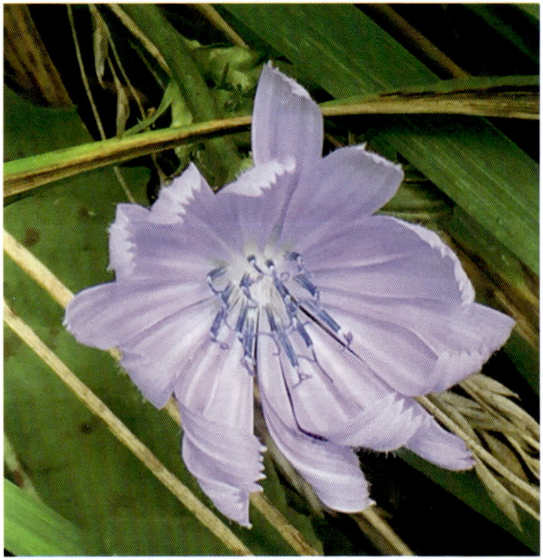
LISA HALE

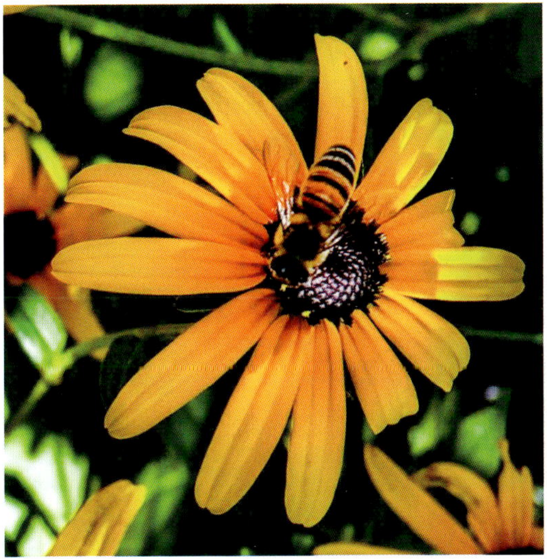

WESLEY PHILP

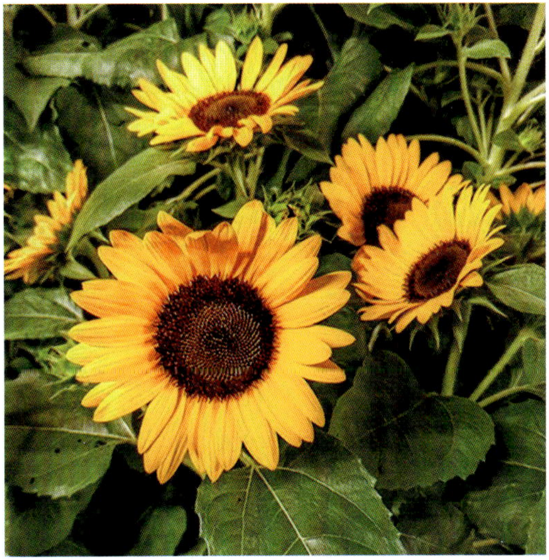

EMILEE GREATHOUSE

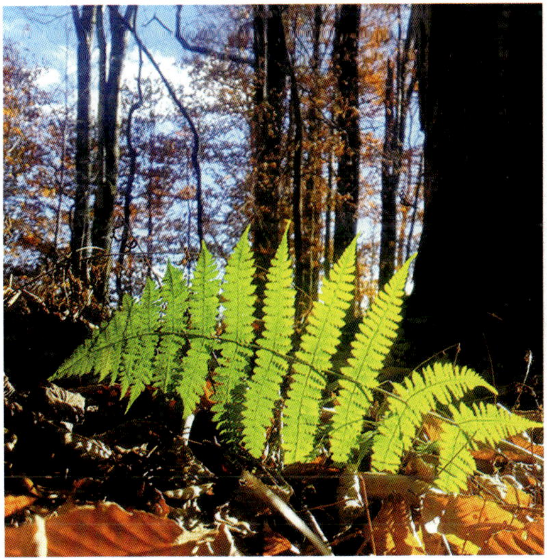

LIZ STOUT

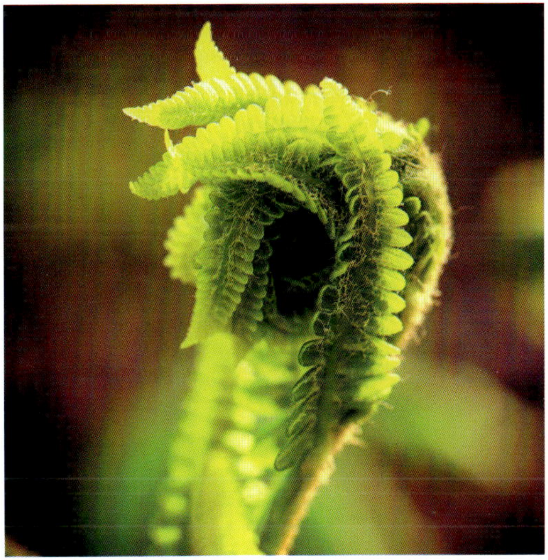

SARAH E. BAILEY

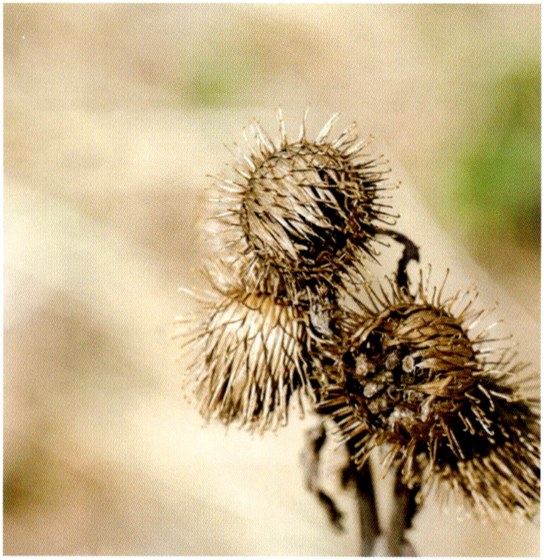

JON HOWARD

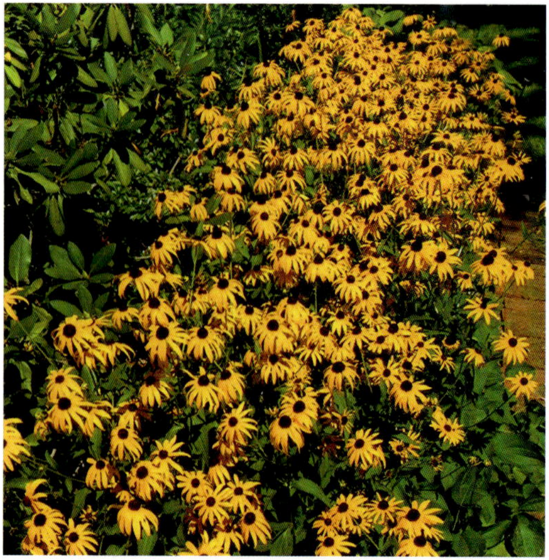

MARK REASOR

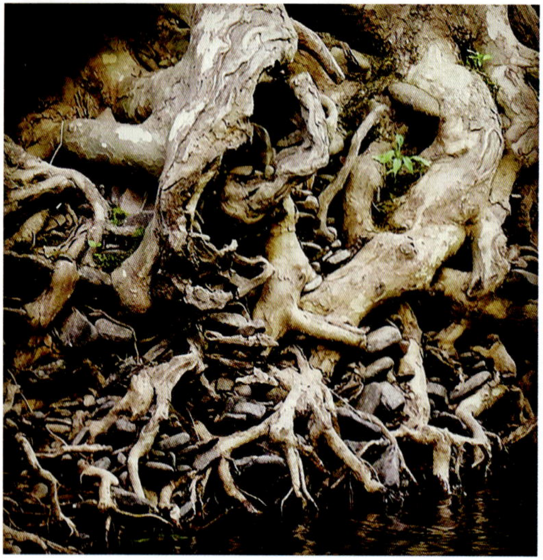

CYNTHIA MULLENS

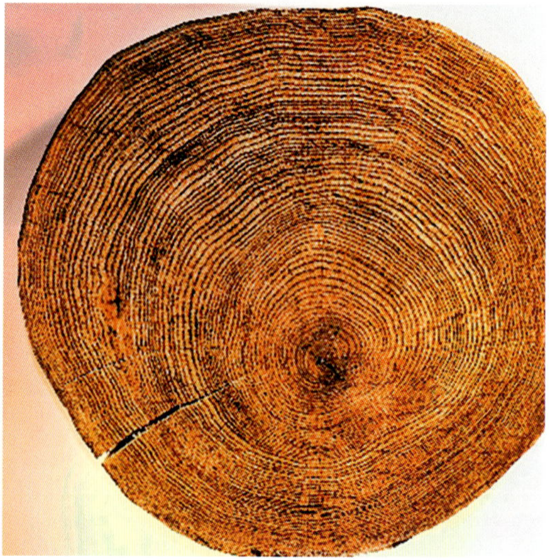

RICHARD MARLOW

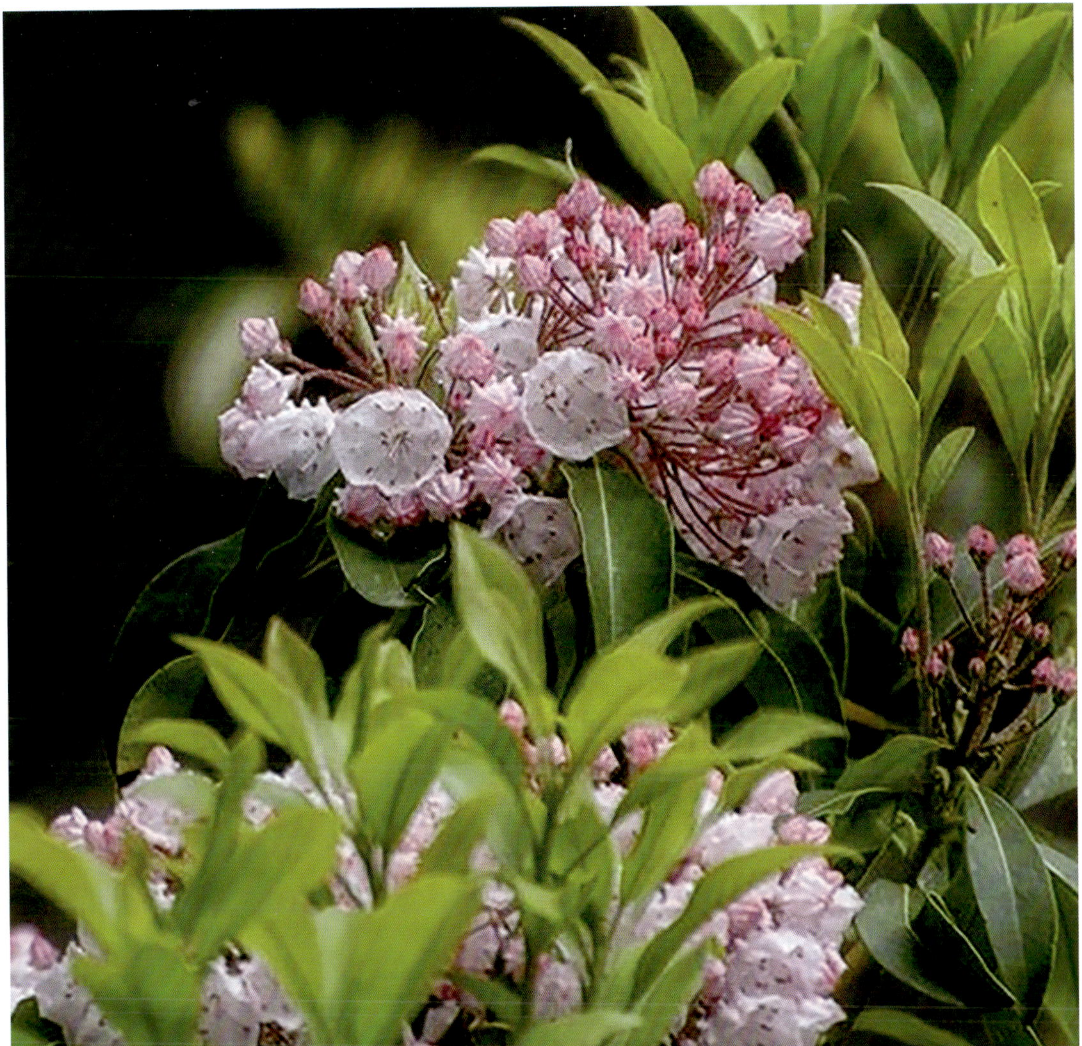

DENISE POWERS-FABIAN

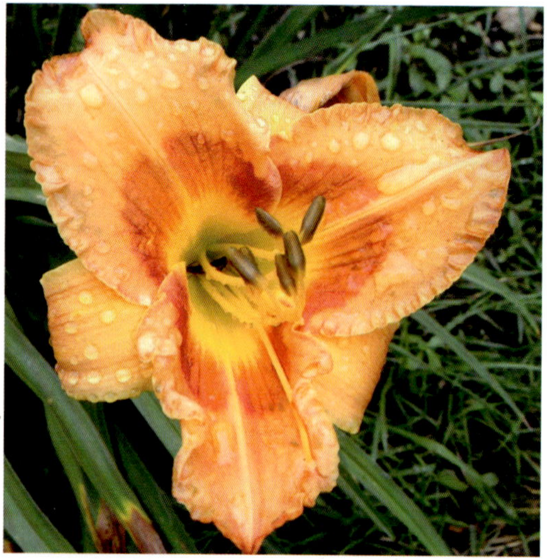

MARK REASOR

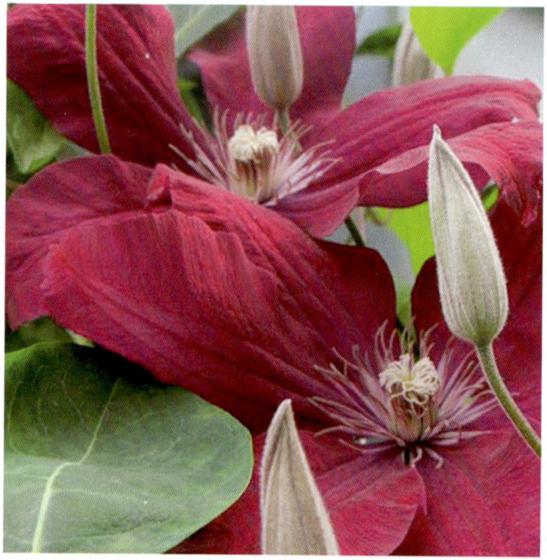

AMY HYPES GRANTHAM

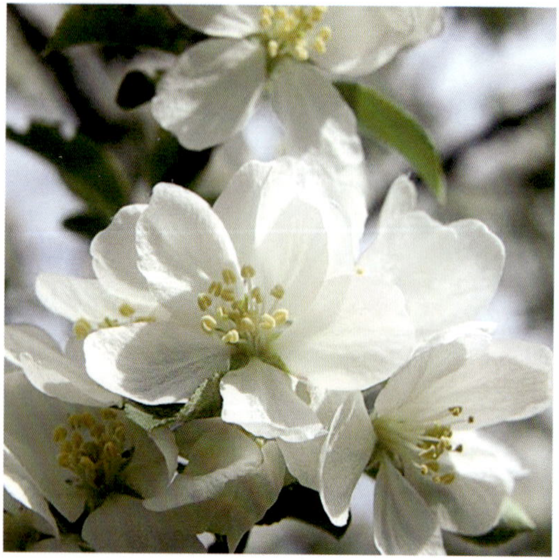

CARLETTA JOHNSTON

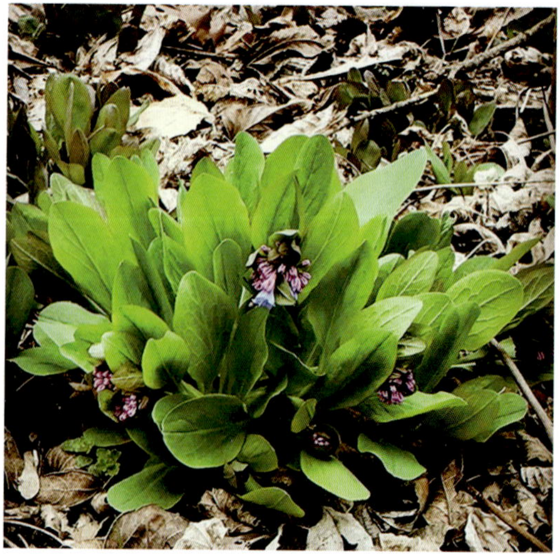

CINDI DUNN

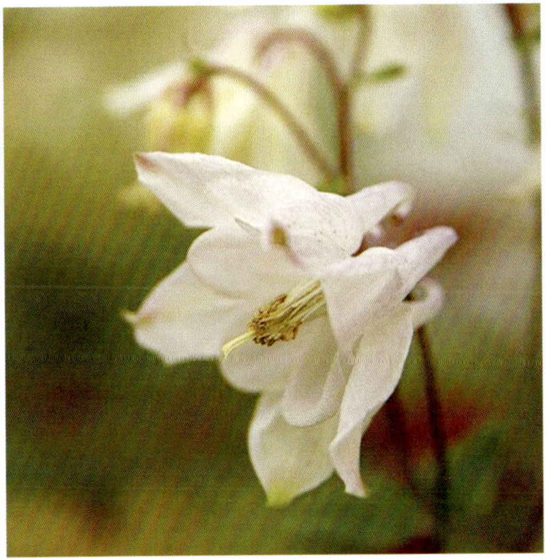

DENISE POWERS FABIAN

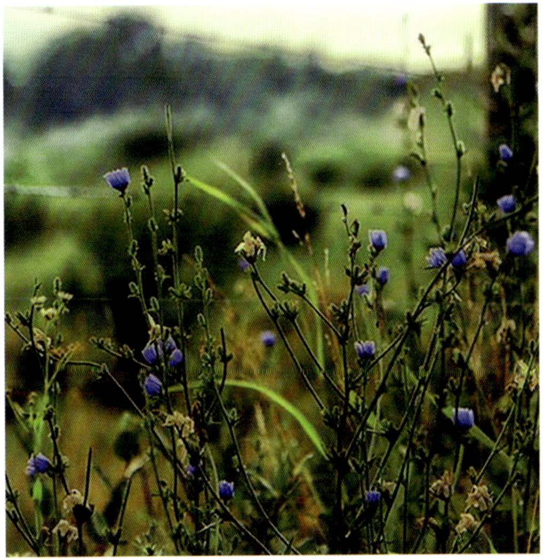

WENDY PARKS

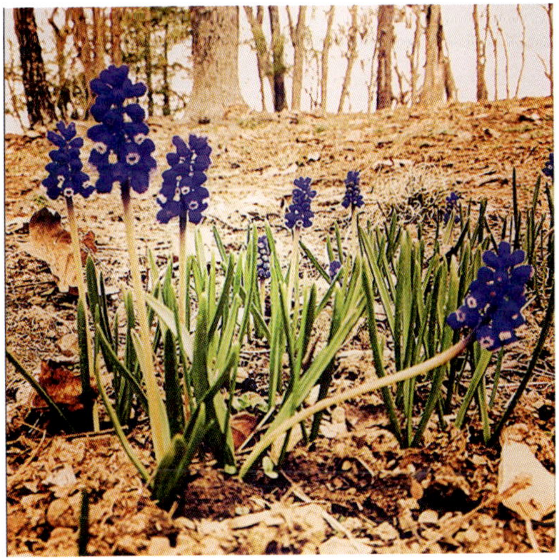

ELAINE CLARK

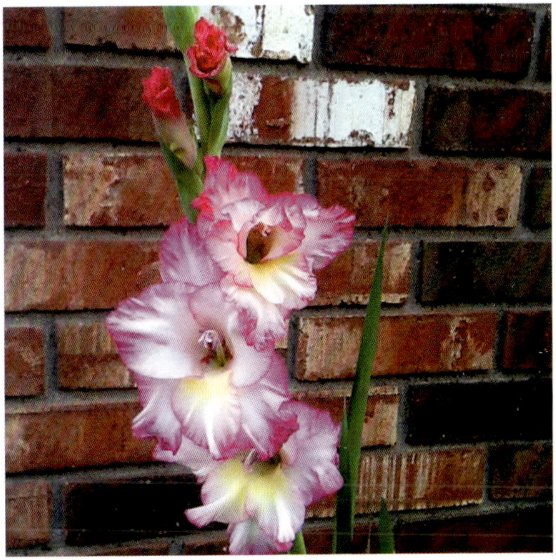

LEONARD BOSTON

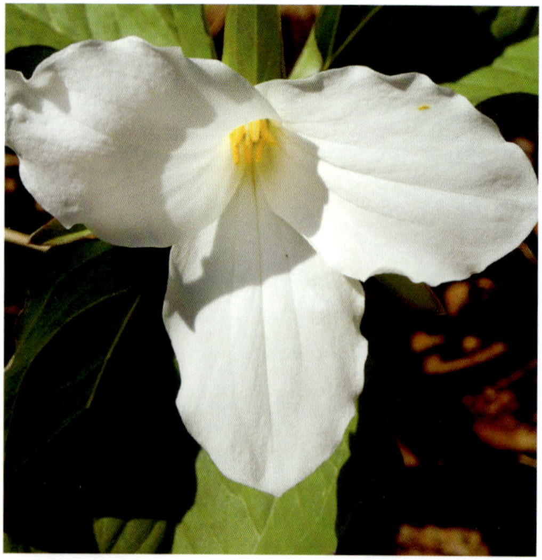

MARK REASOR

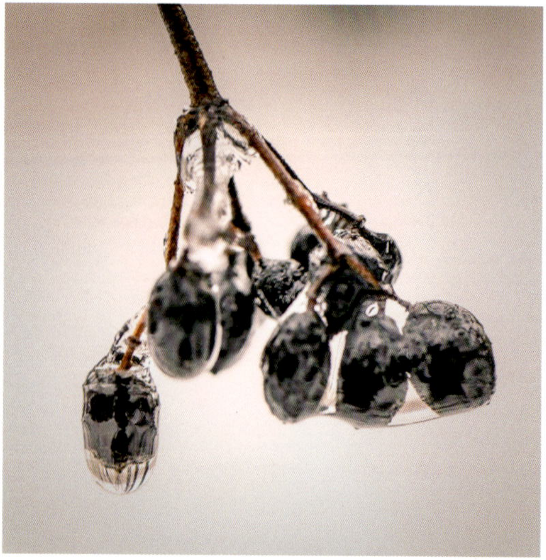

JON HOWARD

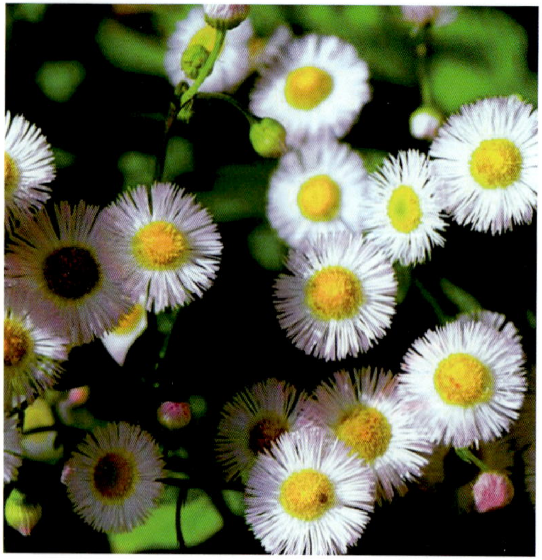

WES PHILP

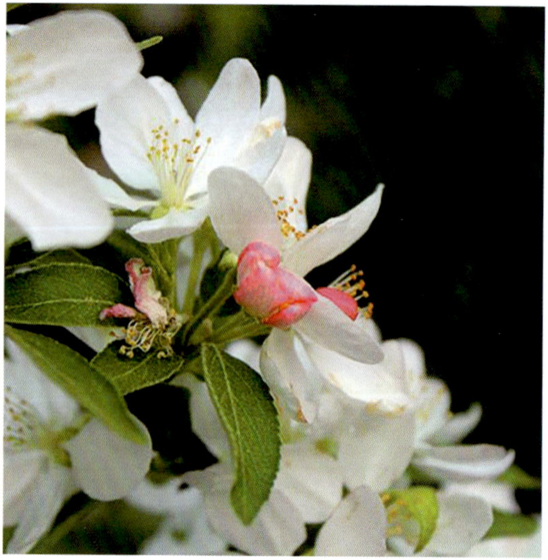

SHARON KAY CARPER

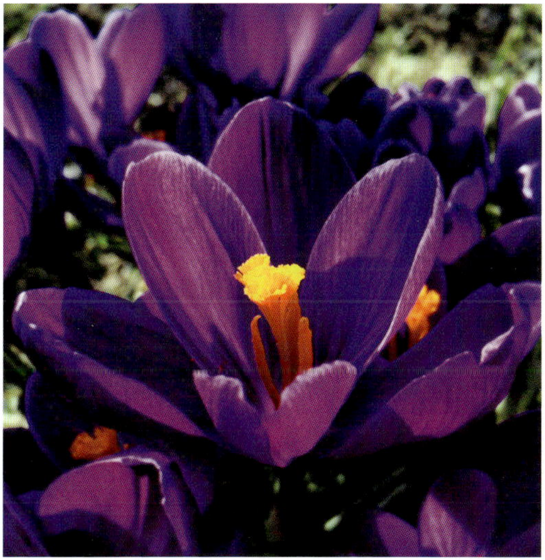

JESSICA STALNAKER

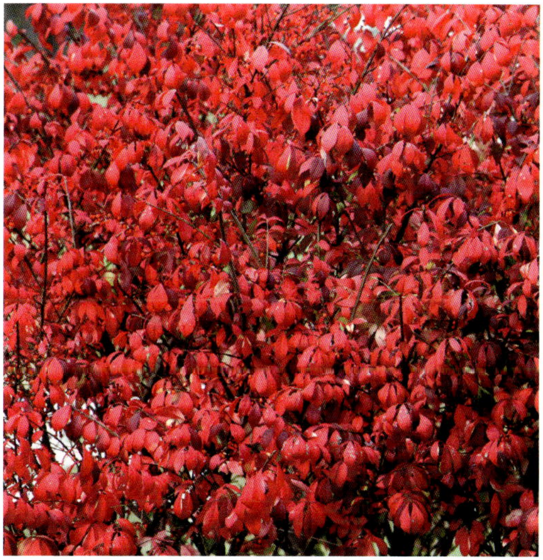

JUDITH ANN BOSTON

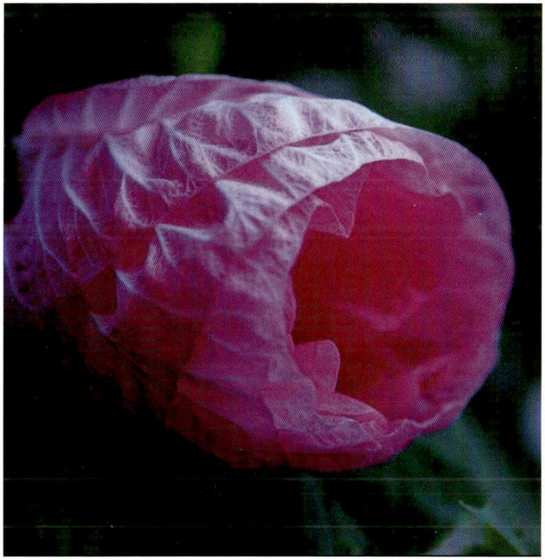

WESLEY PHILP

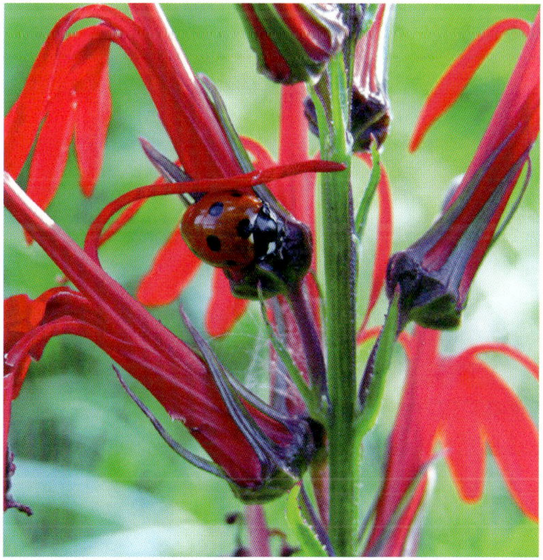

ARNOLD PARRISH

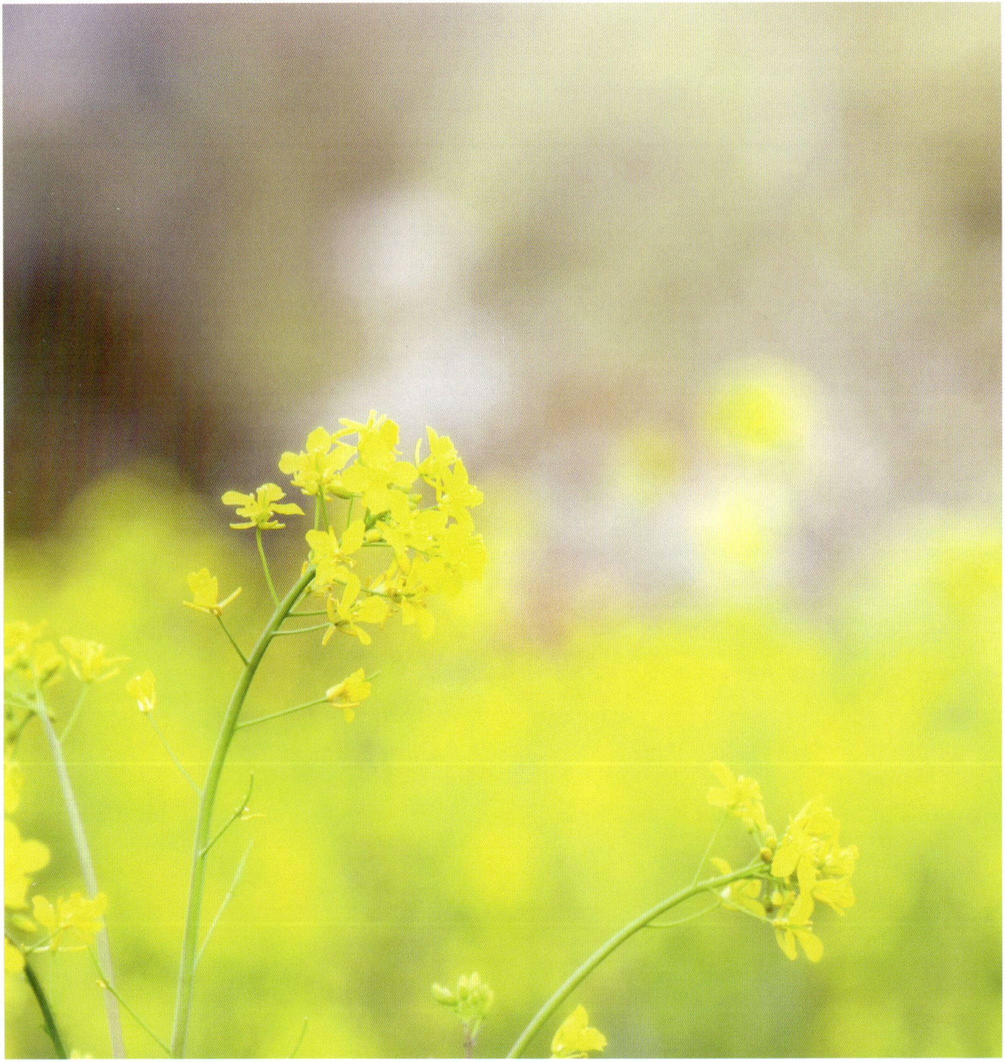

TONYA NESSELRODT

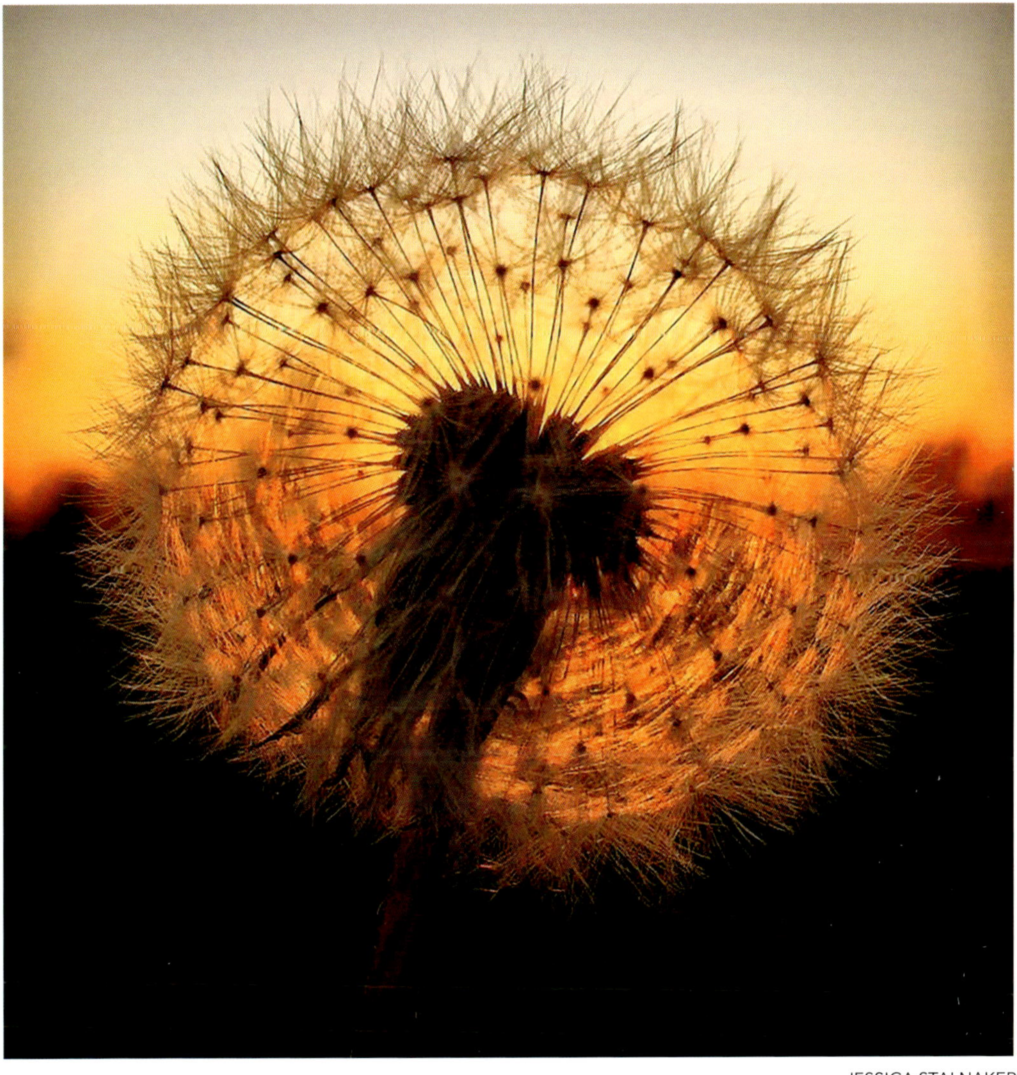

JESSICA STALNAKER

sunrise & sunset

How glorious a greeting the sun gives the mountains!

- JOHN MUIR

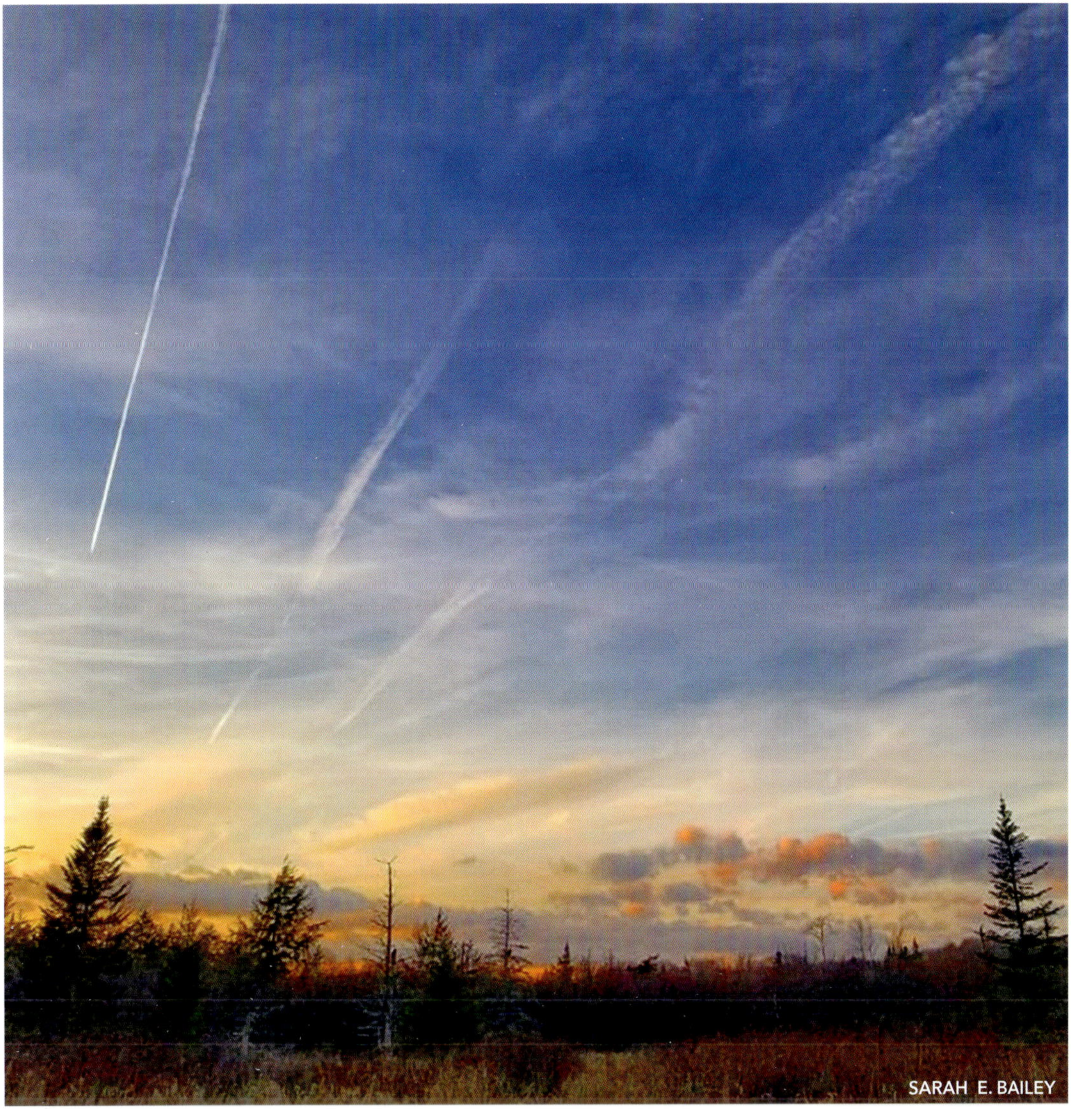
SARAH E. BAILEY

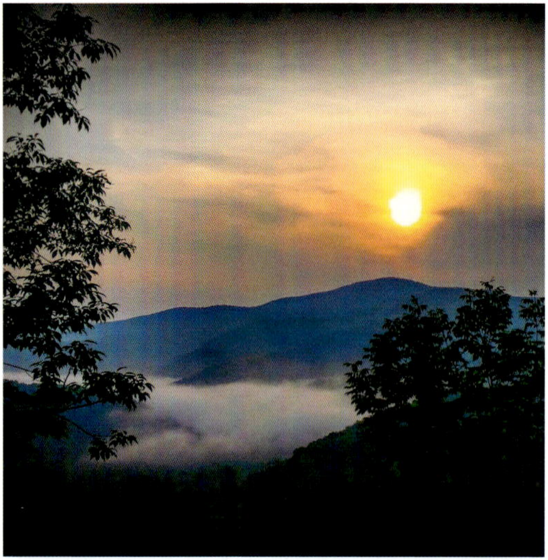

TARA L. CHAMBERS

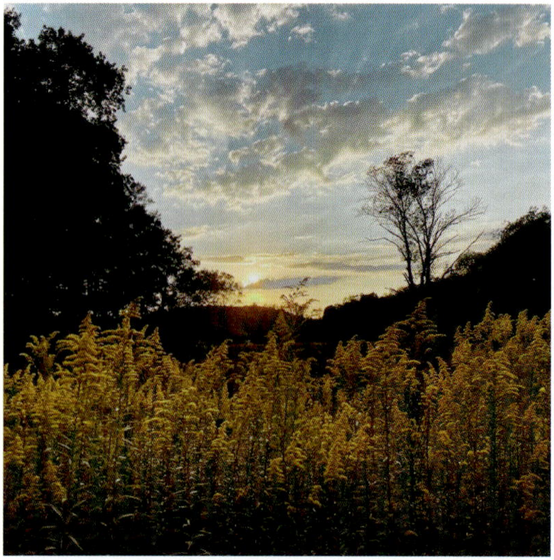

HUNTER BAUER

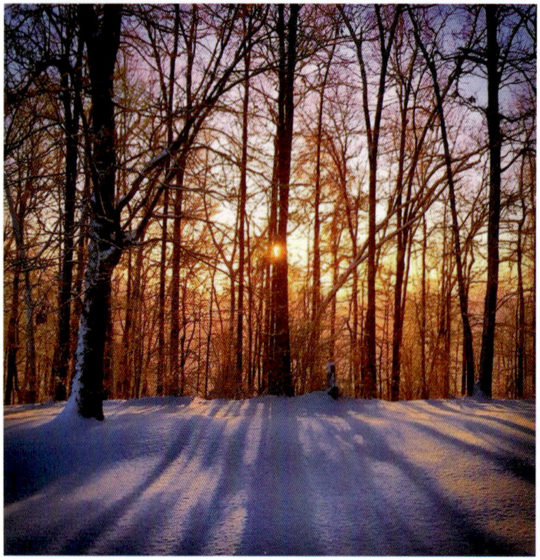

JESSICA STALNAKER

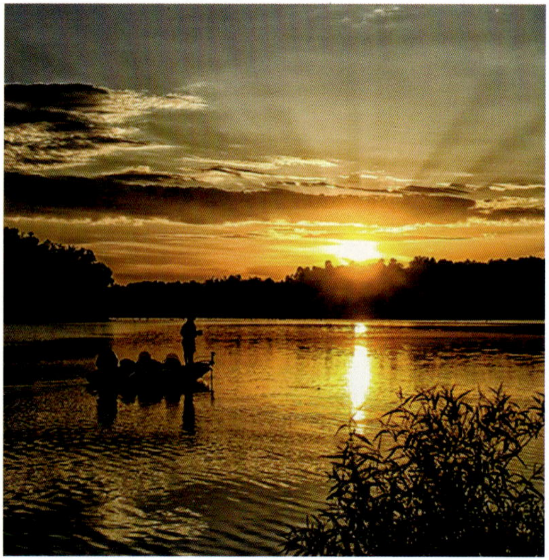

KEVIN JACK

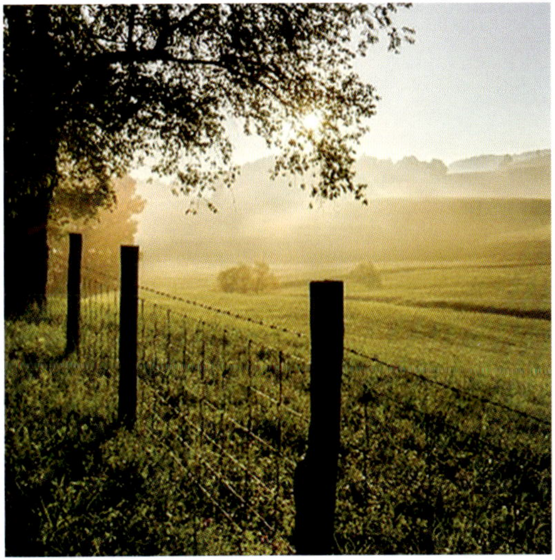

KEVIN FRICK

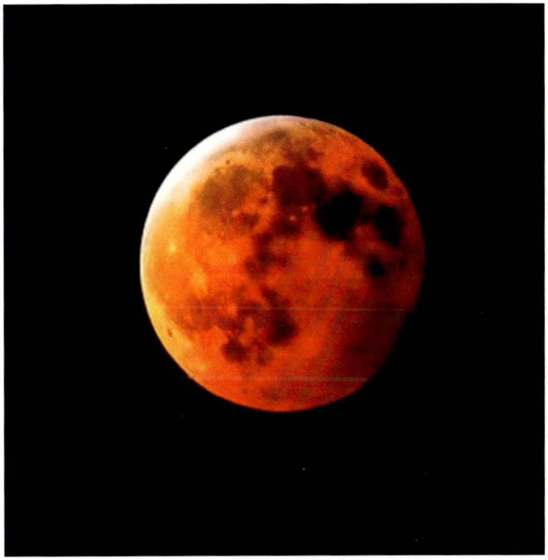

JILL MOLES MULLINS

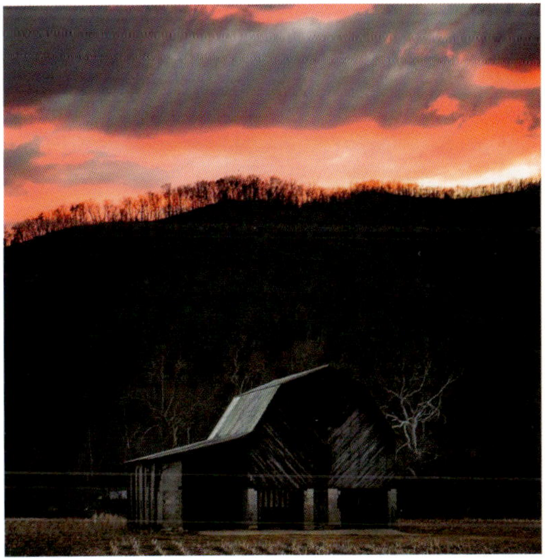

NICOLE VIEWS

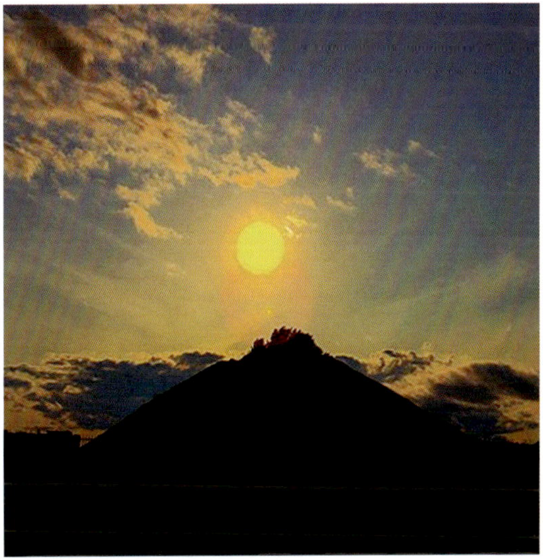

WESLEY PHILP

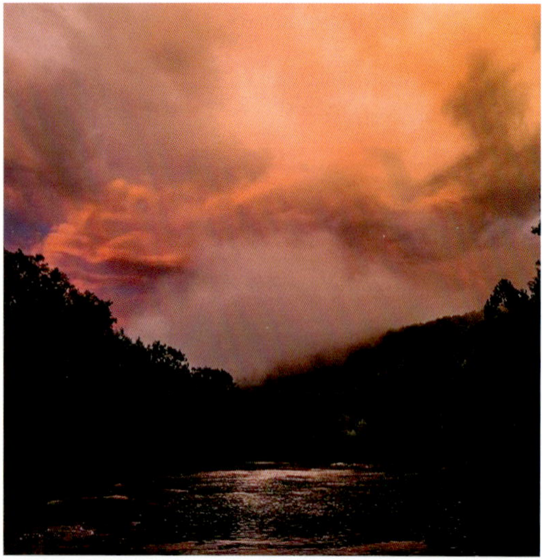

NICOLE VIEWS

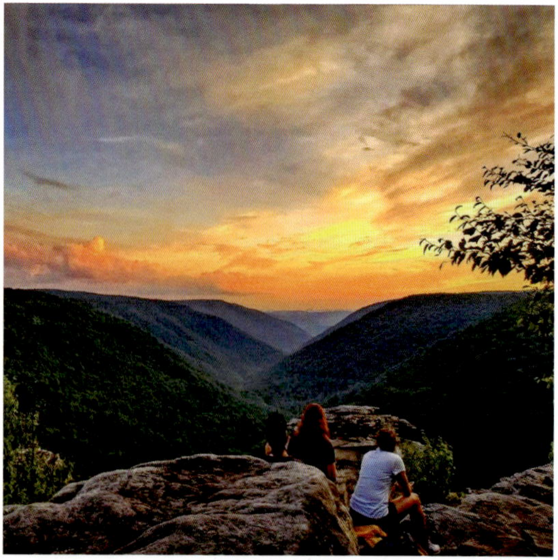

KEVIN GROSE

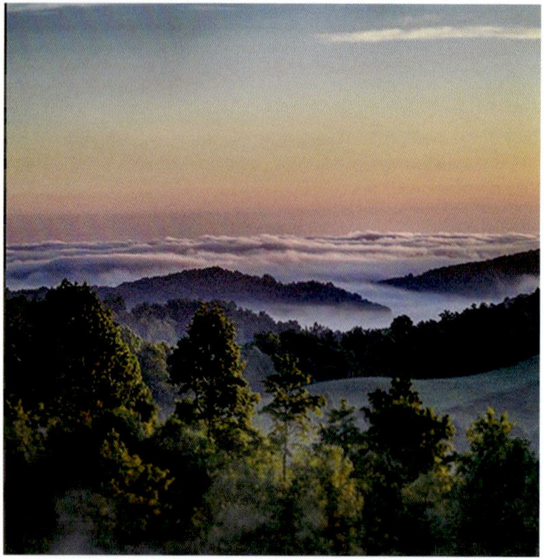

JESSICA STALNAKER

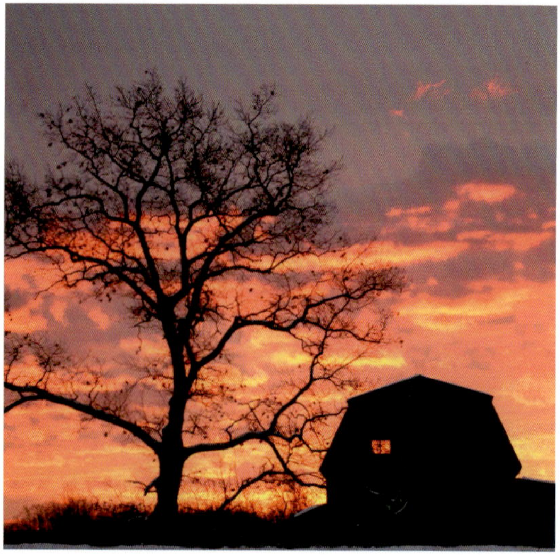

JEFFERY ALMOND

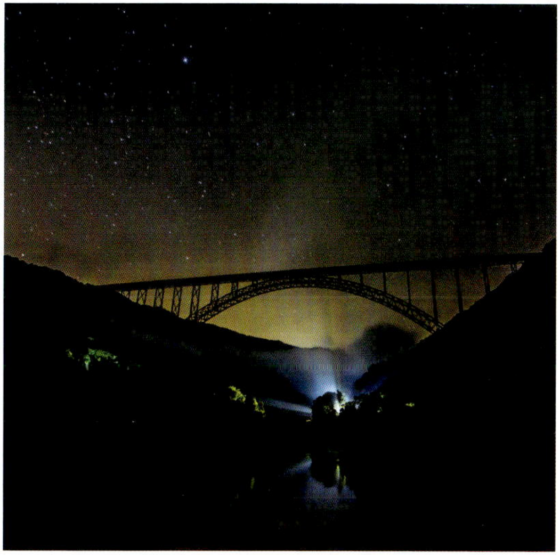

MELVIN HARTLEY

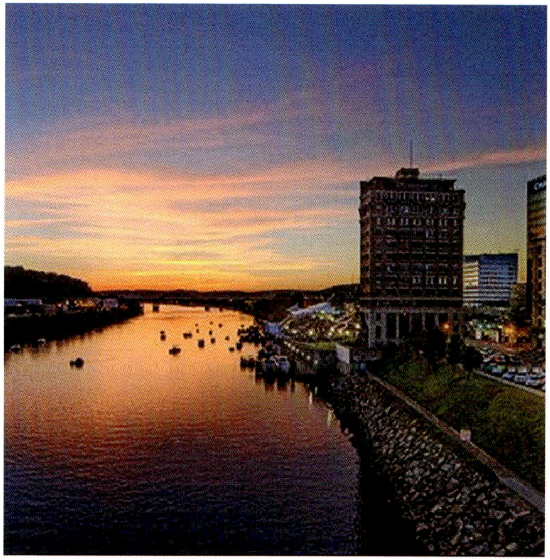

TOM DEAN

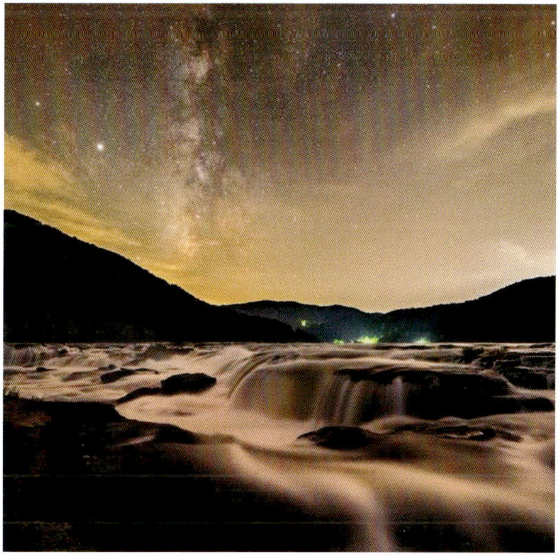

JESSE THORNTON

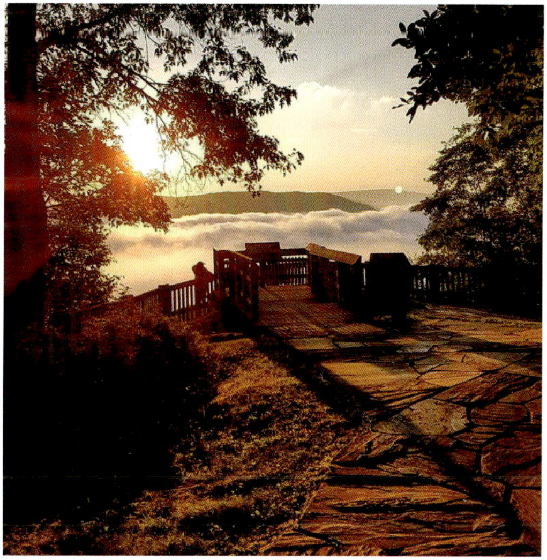

CONNIE BOLEY-LILLY

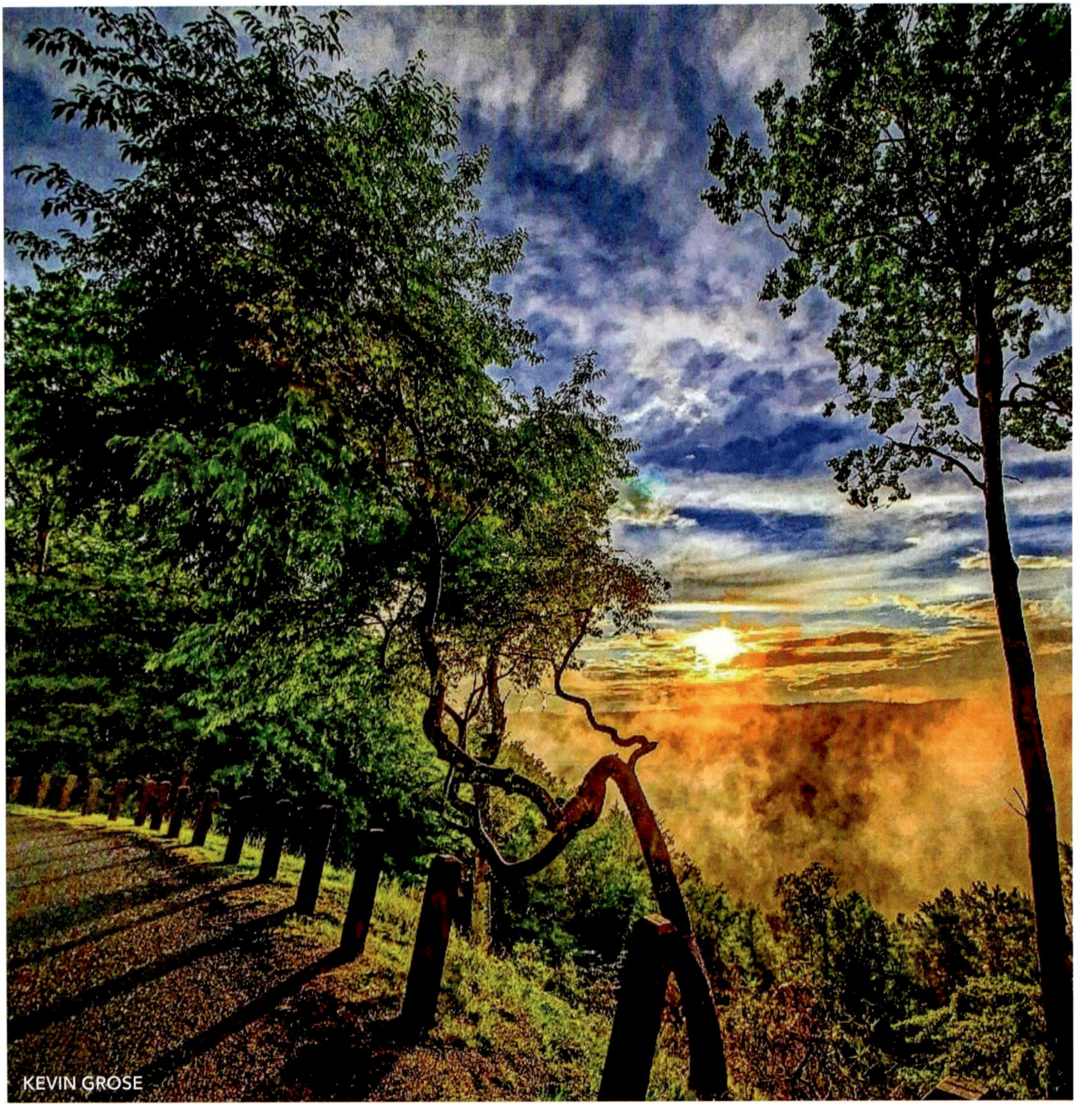
KEVIN GROSE

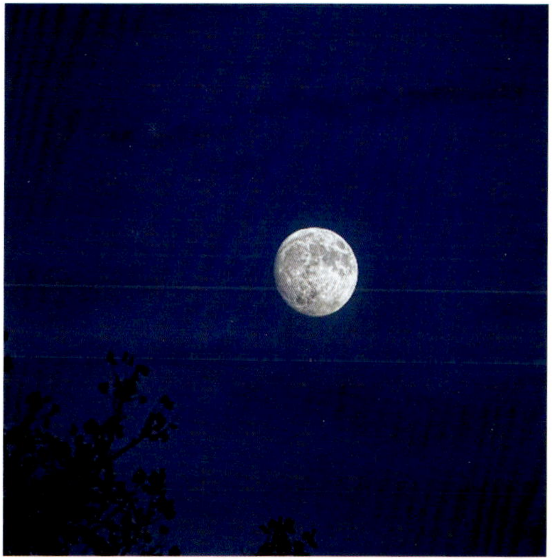
RICHARD MARLOW

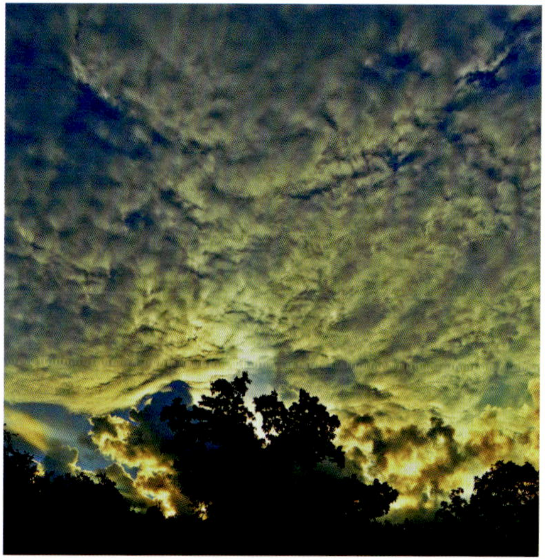
OTIS CAMPBELL

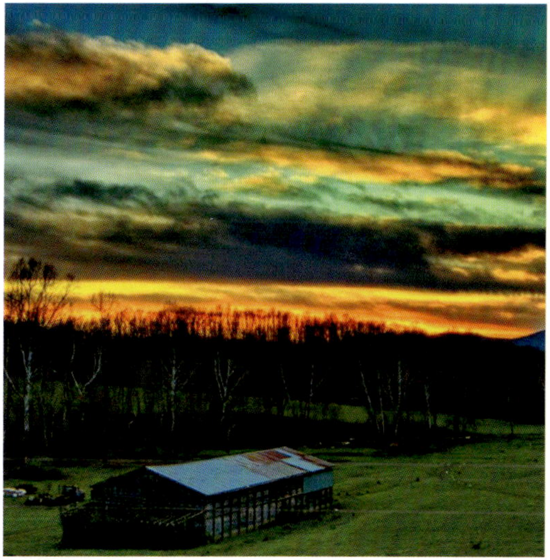
ERIC BRIUMBAUGH

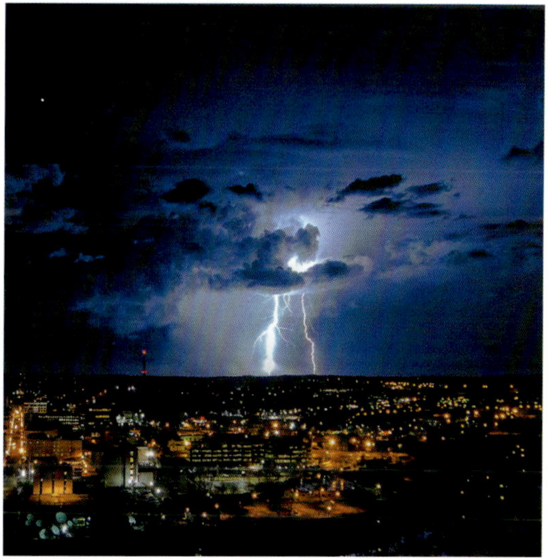
DANNY CARPENTER

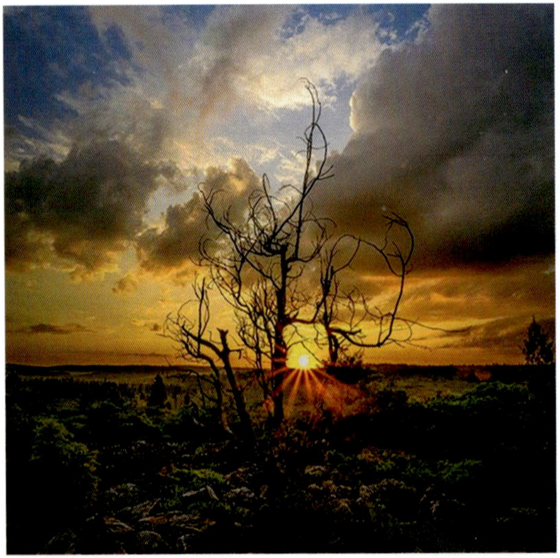

TOM DEAN

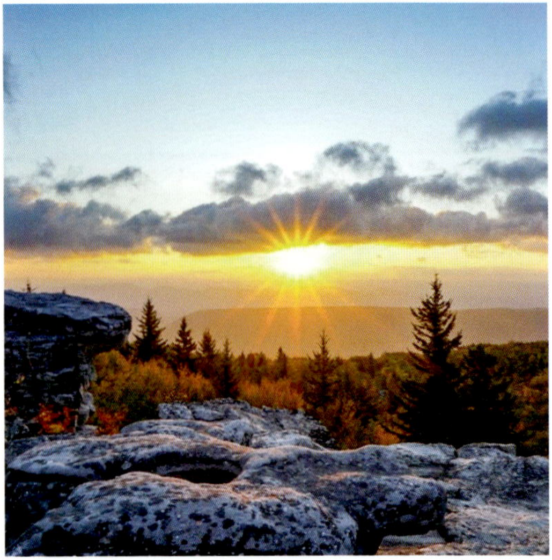

LEAH BOWES

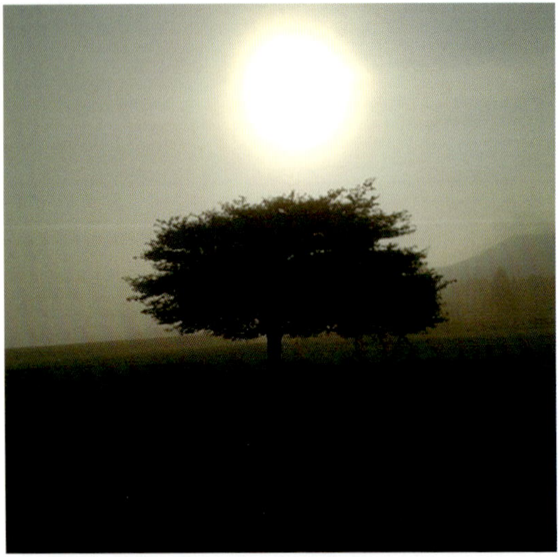

GEORGE MILLER

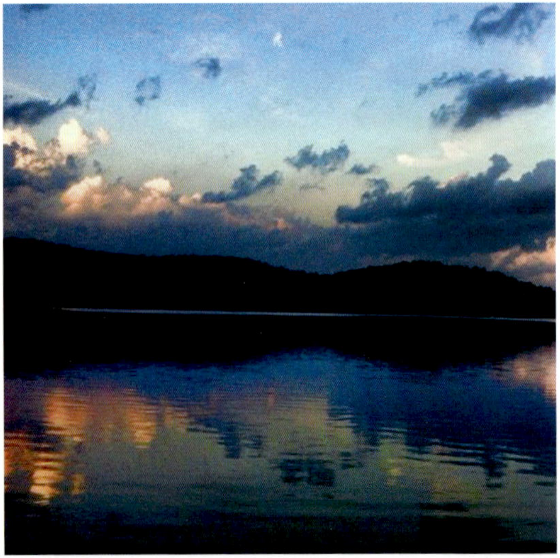

PAULA COLEMAN

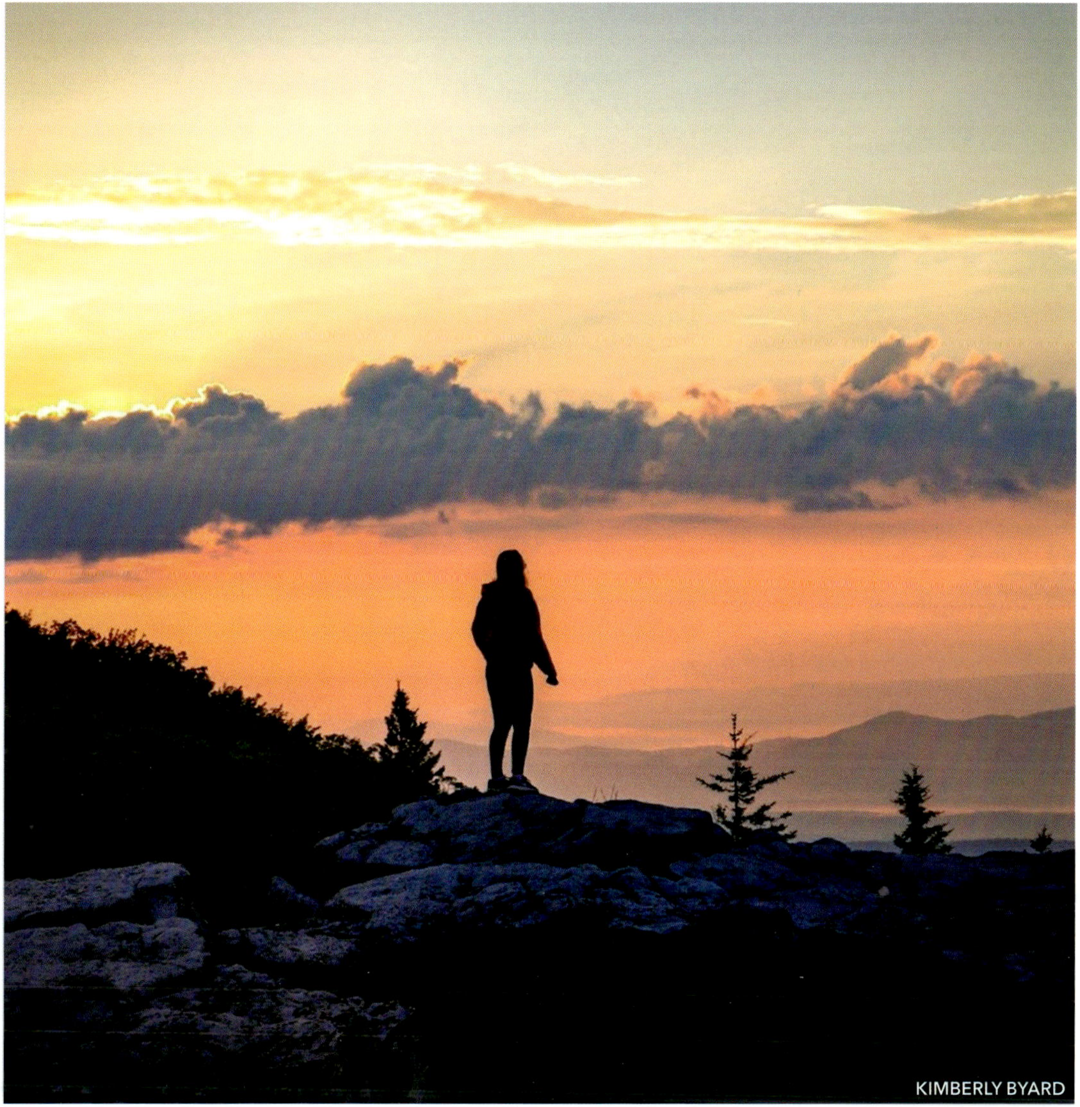
KIMBERLY BYARD

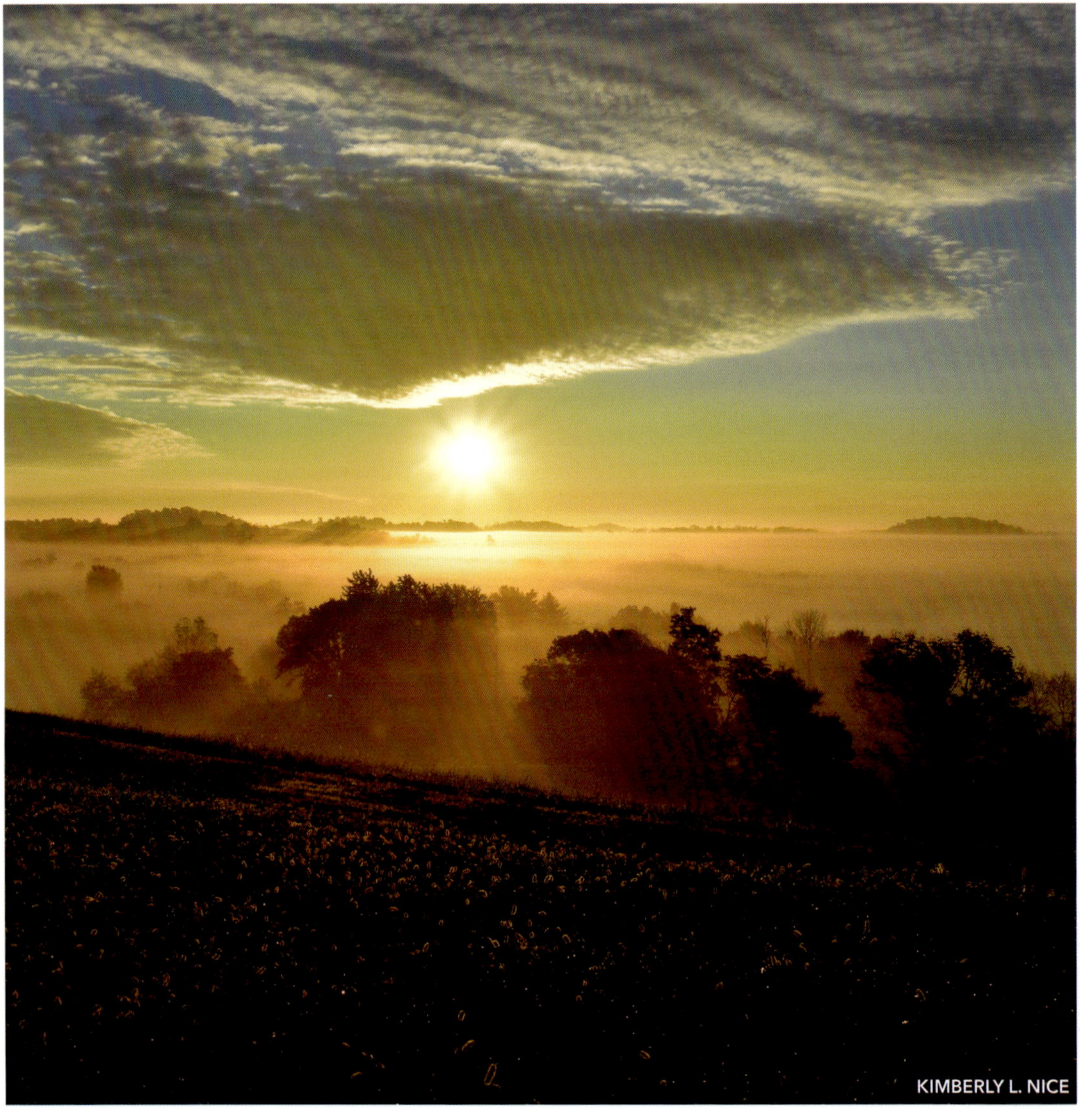
KIMBERLY L. NICE

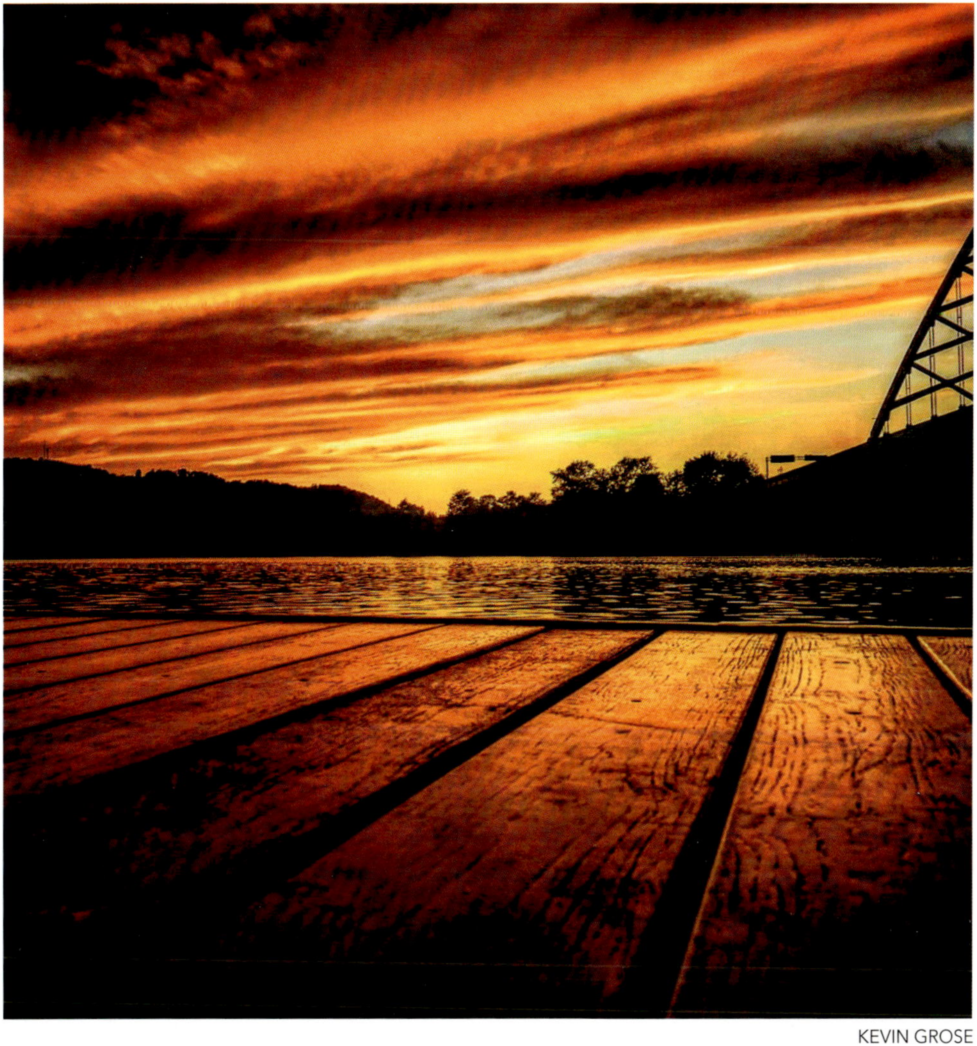

KEVIN GROSE

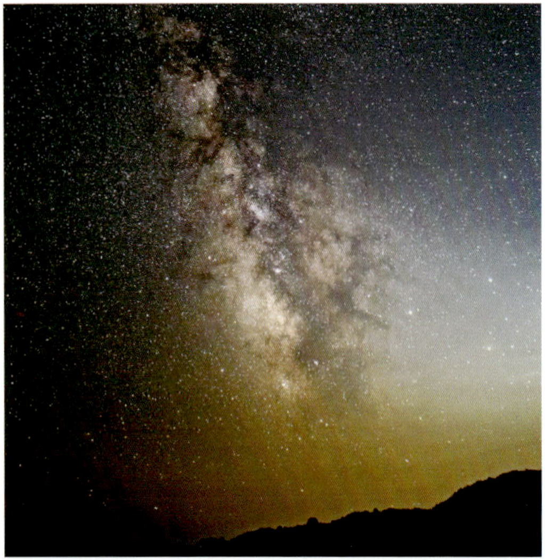

JOGUES R. PRANDONI

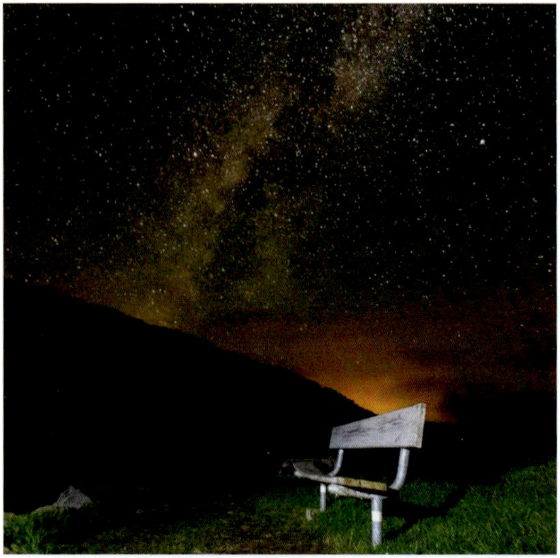

TOM DEAN

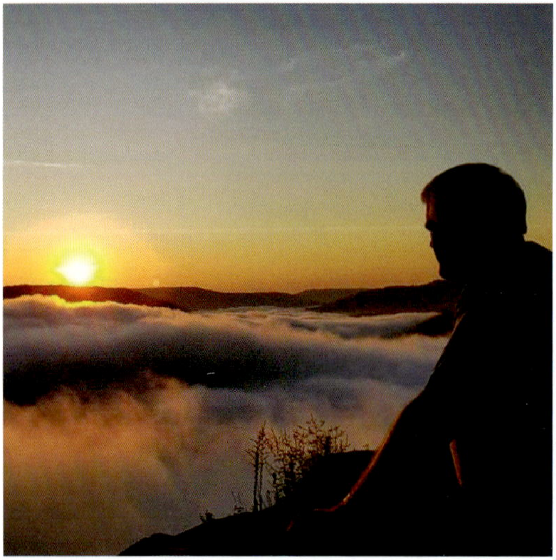

CONNIE BOLEY-LILLY

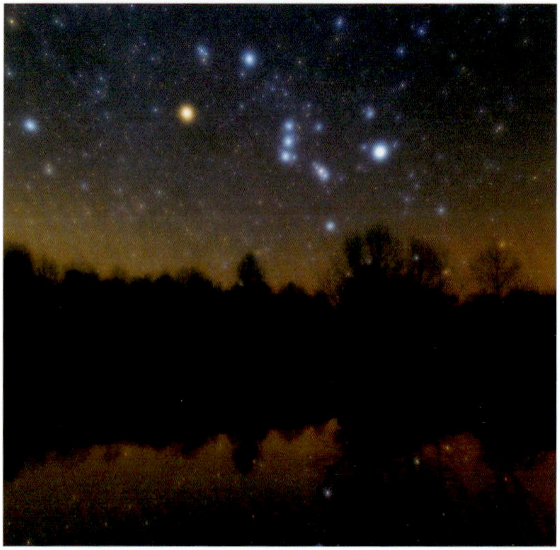

BRIAN OTTUM

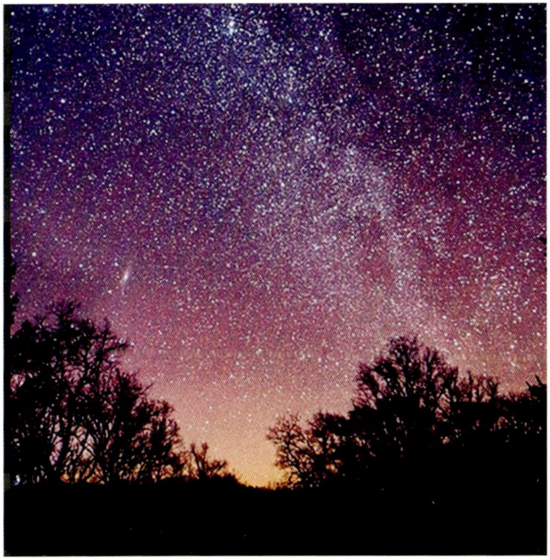

SARAH E. BAILEY

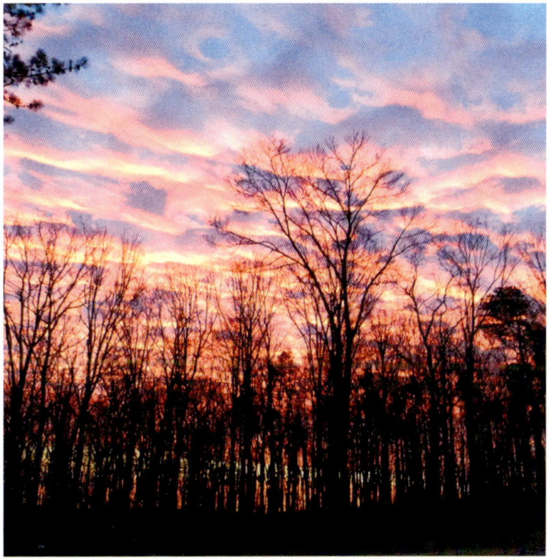

TERESA YOST

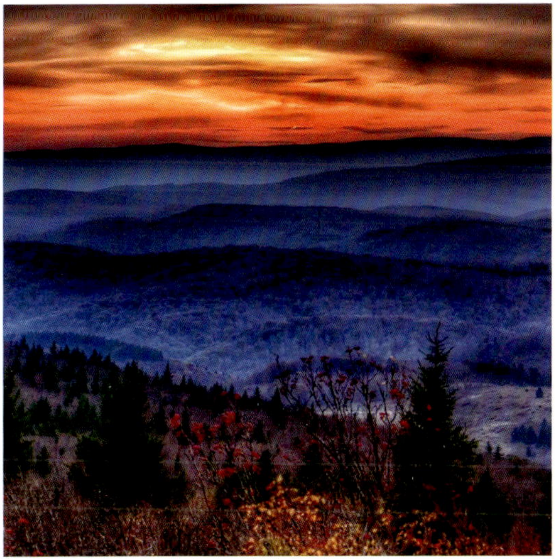

WENDY PARKS

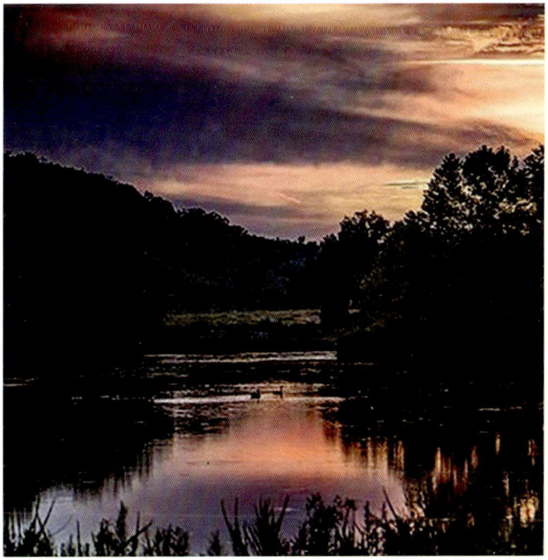

KEVIN JACK

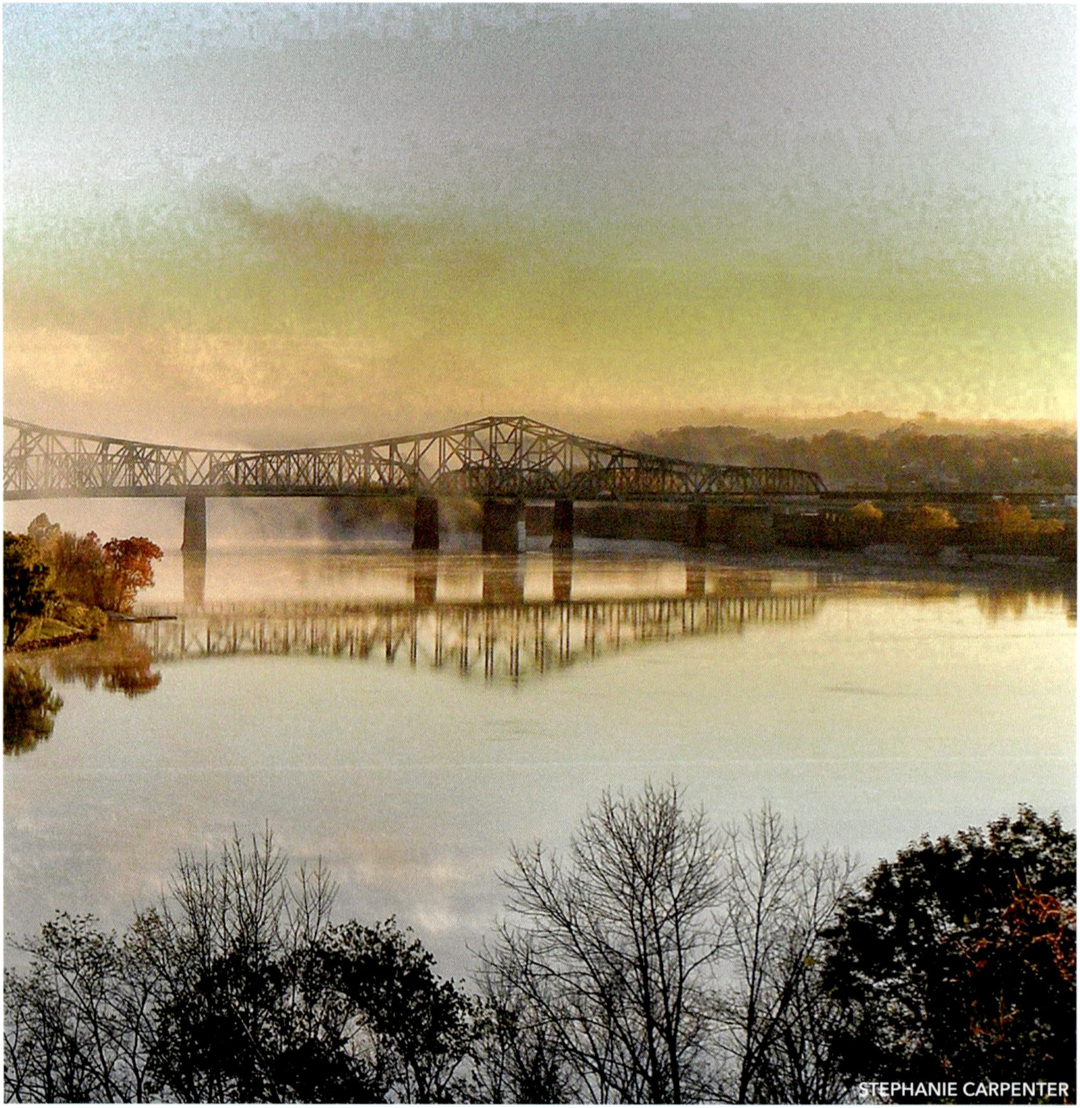
STEPHANIE CARPENTER

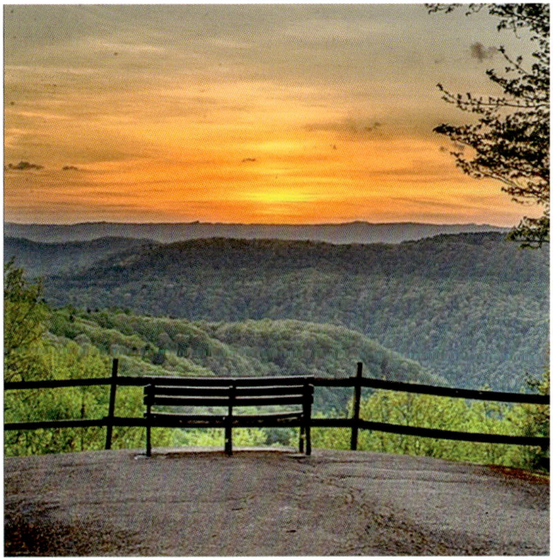

DENISE POWERS FABIAN

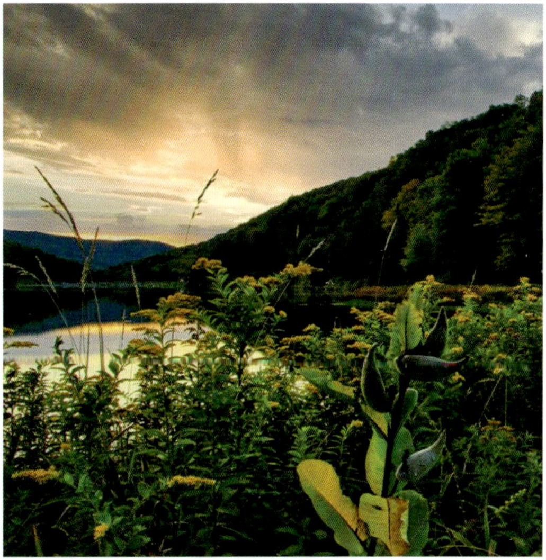

KENDALL BRUMBAUGH

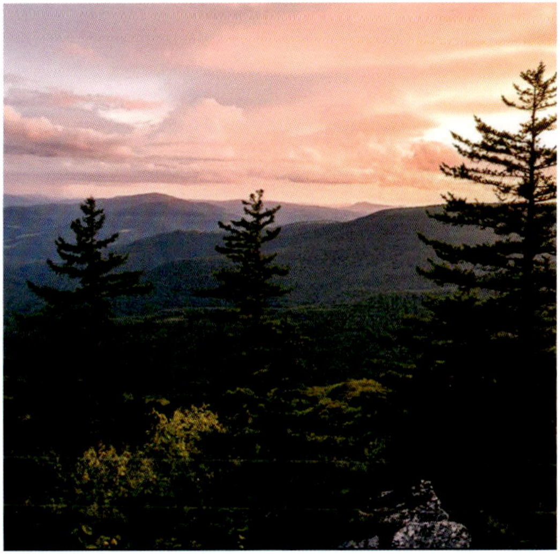

LIZ STOUT

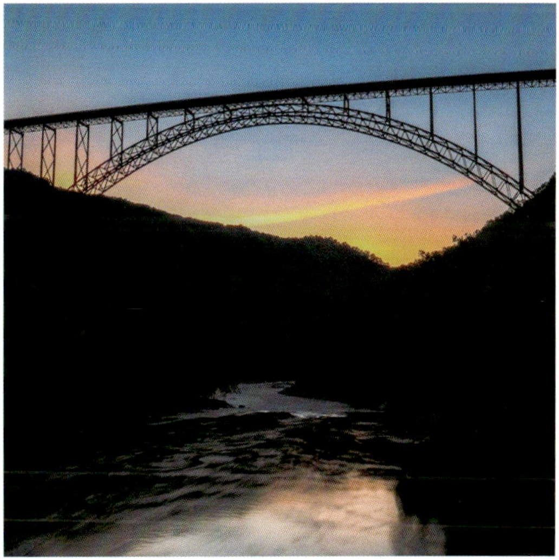

NICOLE VIEWS

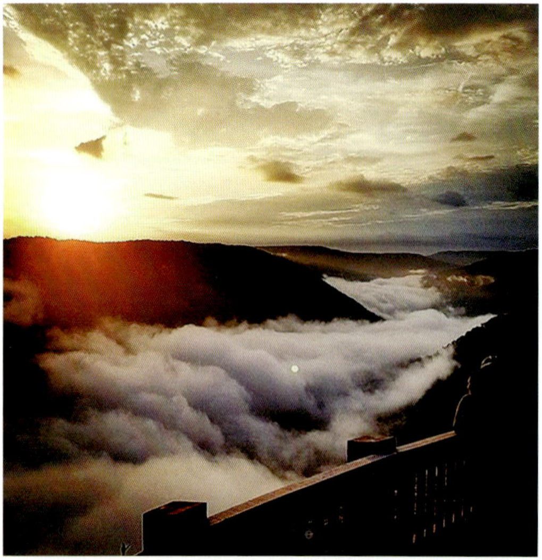

CONNIE BOLEY-LILLY

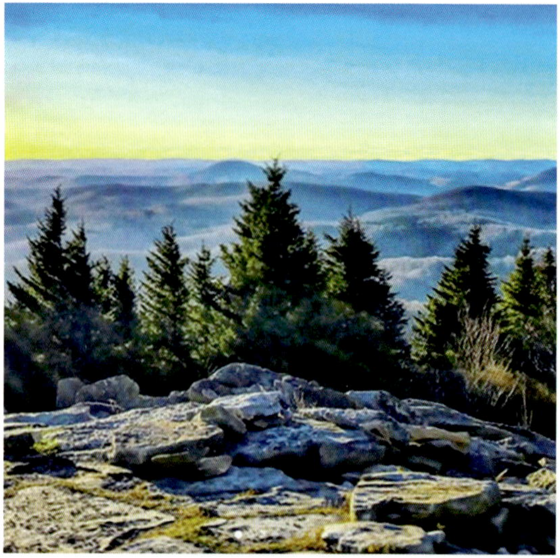

JESSICA STALNAKER

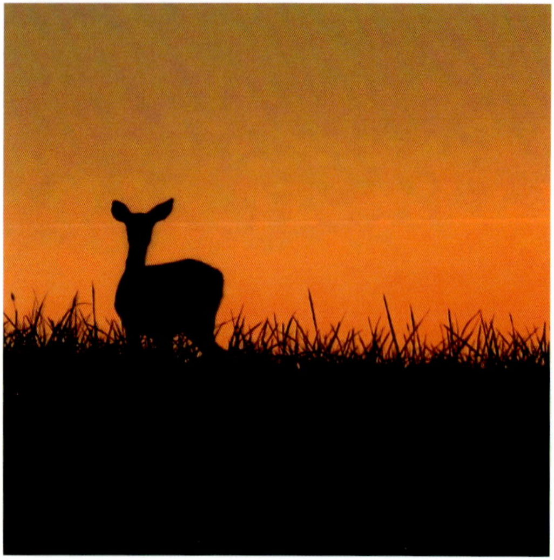

STAN WILKE

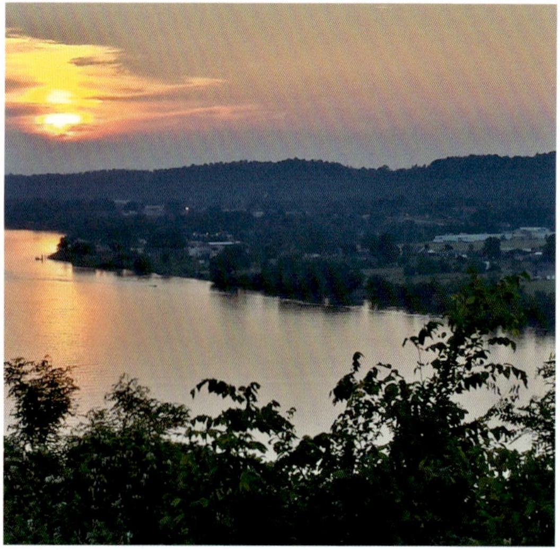

STEPHANIE CARPENTER

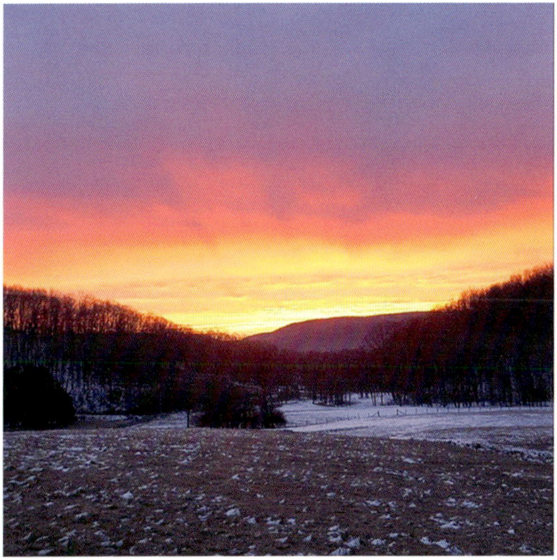

CANDY THOMPSON

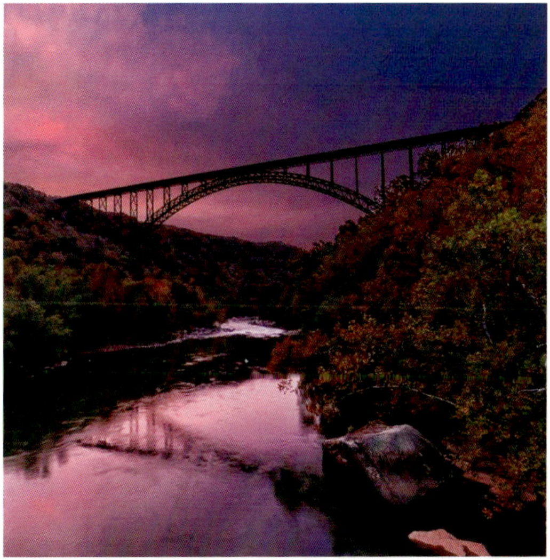

JILL MOLES MULLINS

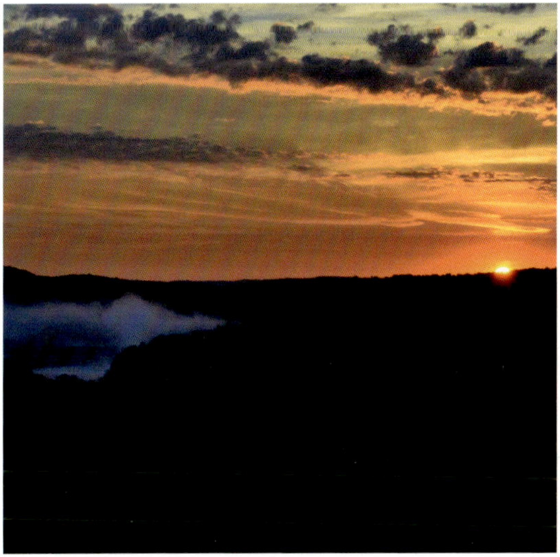

CHERYL KESNER

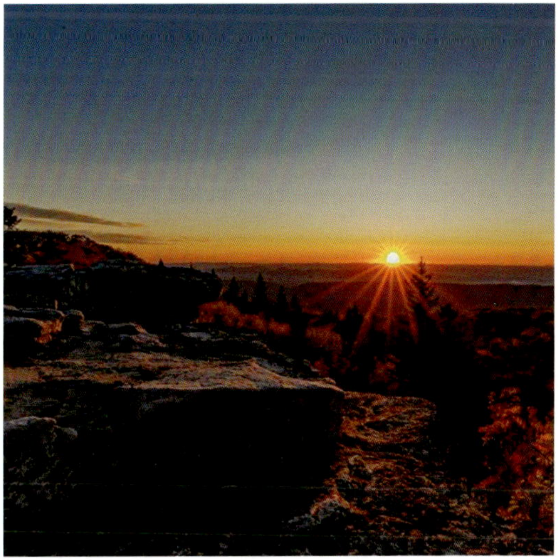

BRENT SCHNUPP

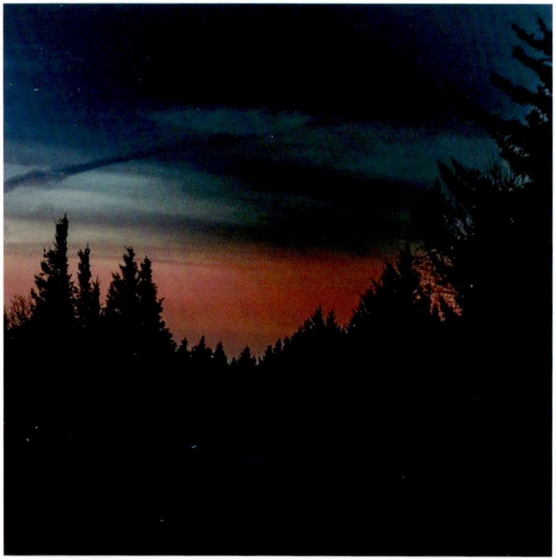

WENDY PARKS

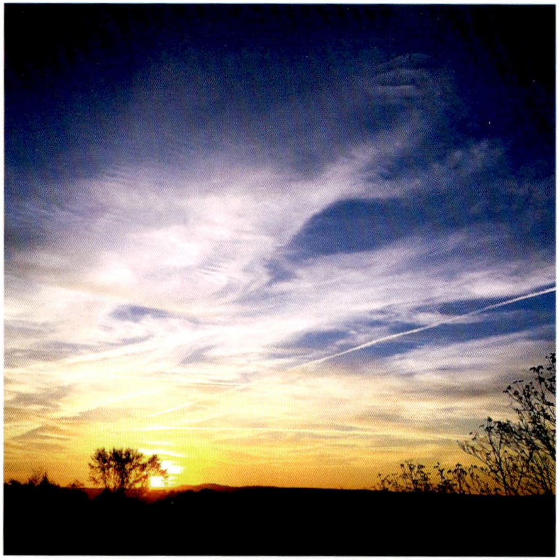

PAULA COLEMAN

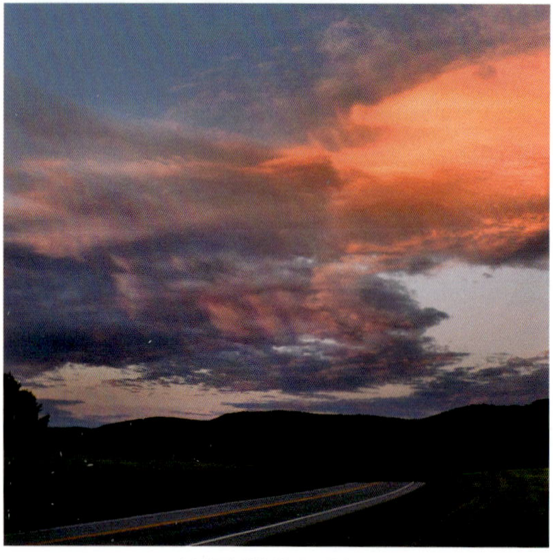

MATTHEW S. MARSH

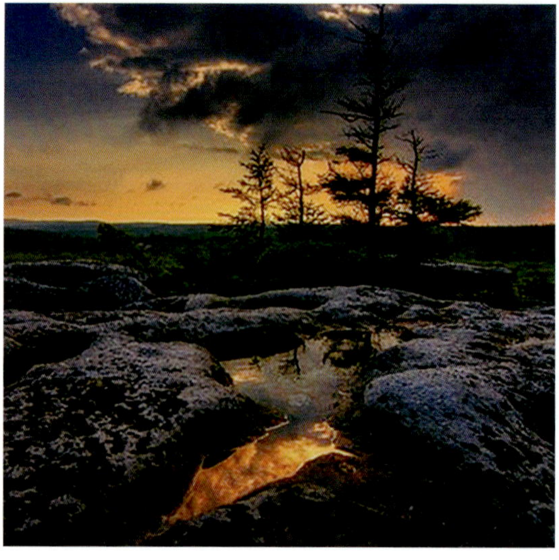

TOM DEAN

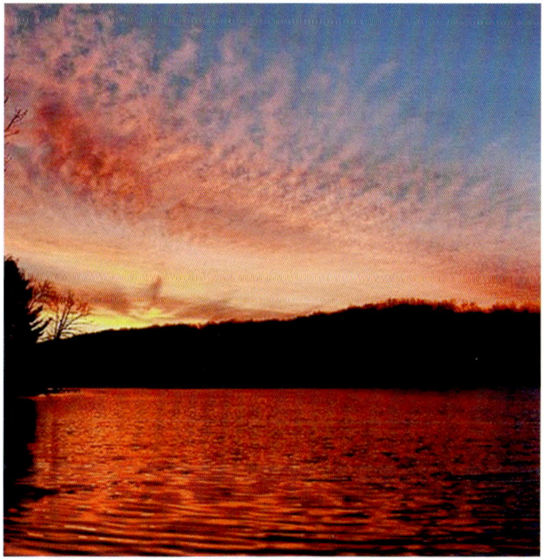

SARAH E. BAILEY

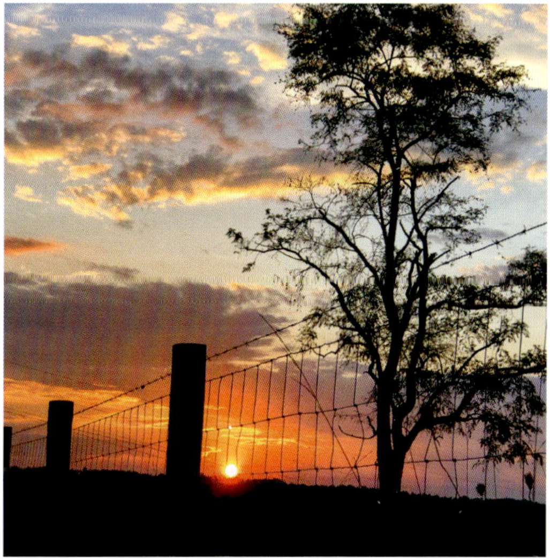

LYNN STEWART

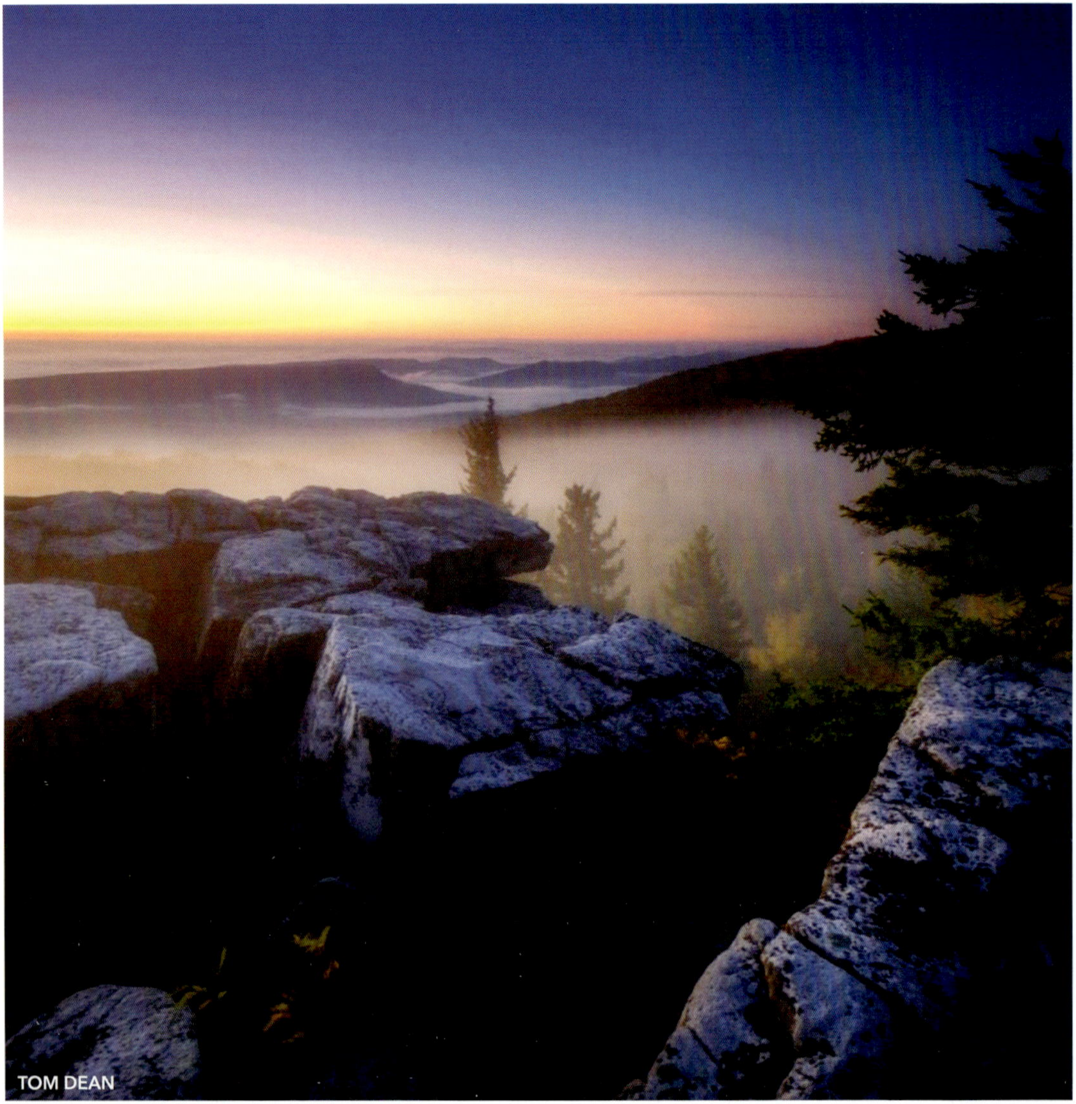
TOM DEAN

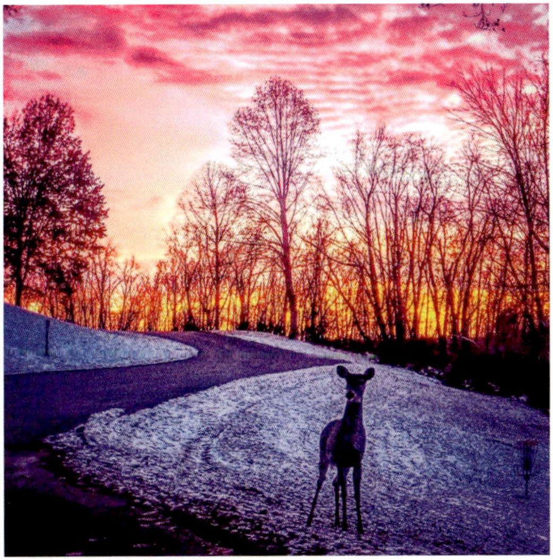

KEVIN GROSE

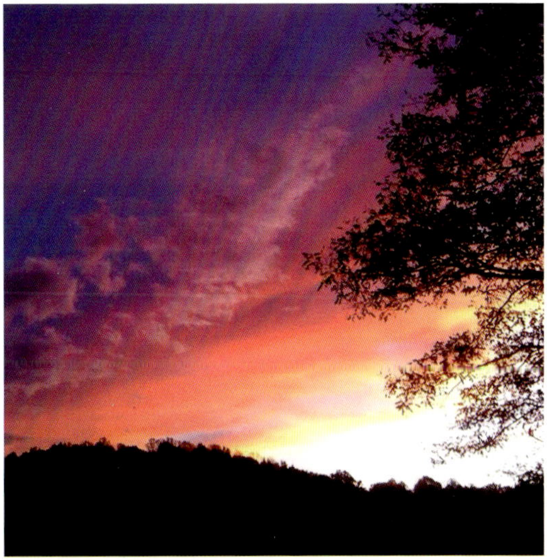

PAULA COLEMAN

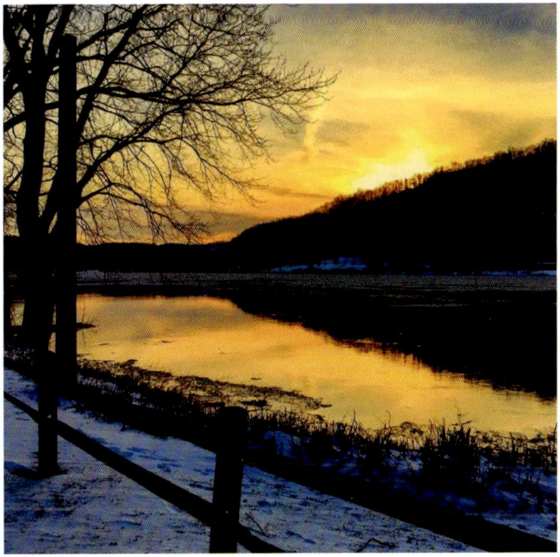

WESLEY PHILP

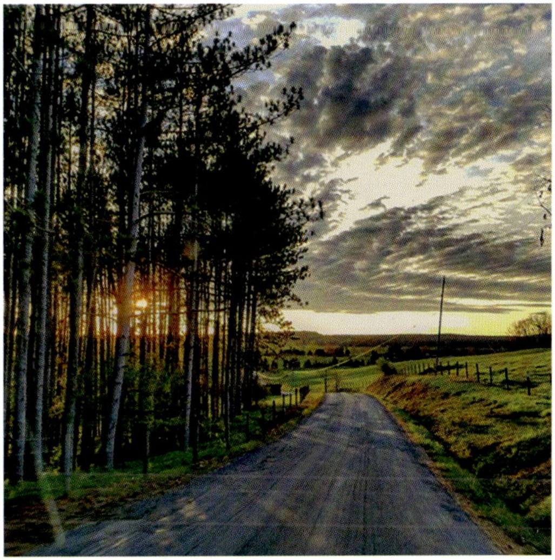

SARAH E. BAILEY

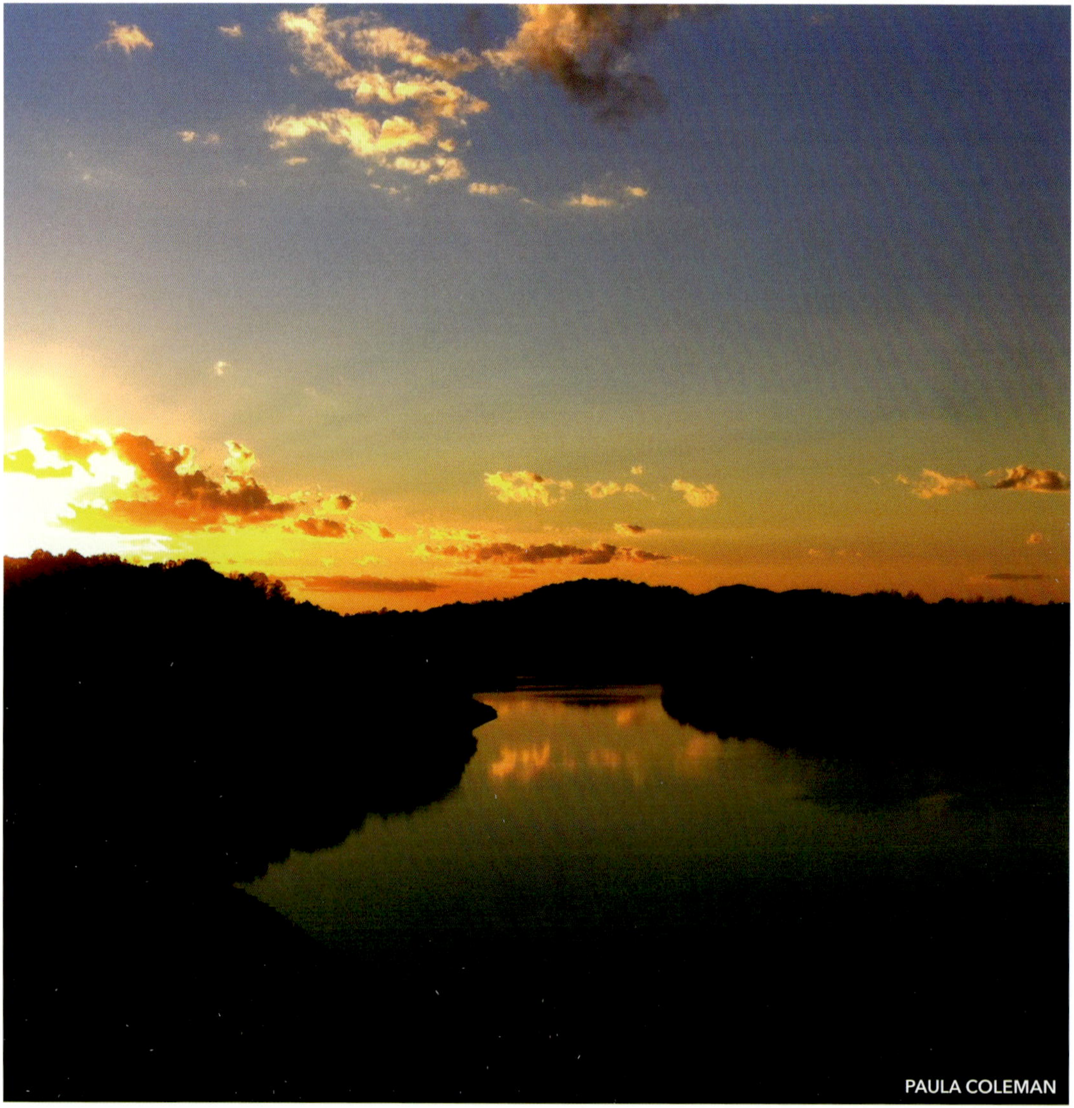
PAULA COLEMAN

water

**Thousands have lived without love,
not one without water.**

– W. H. AUDEN

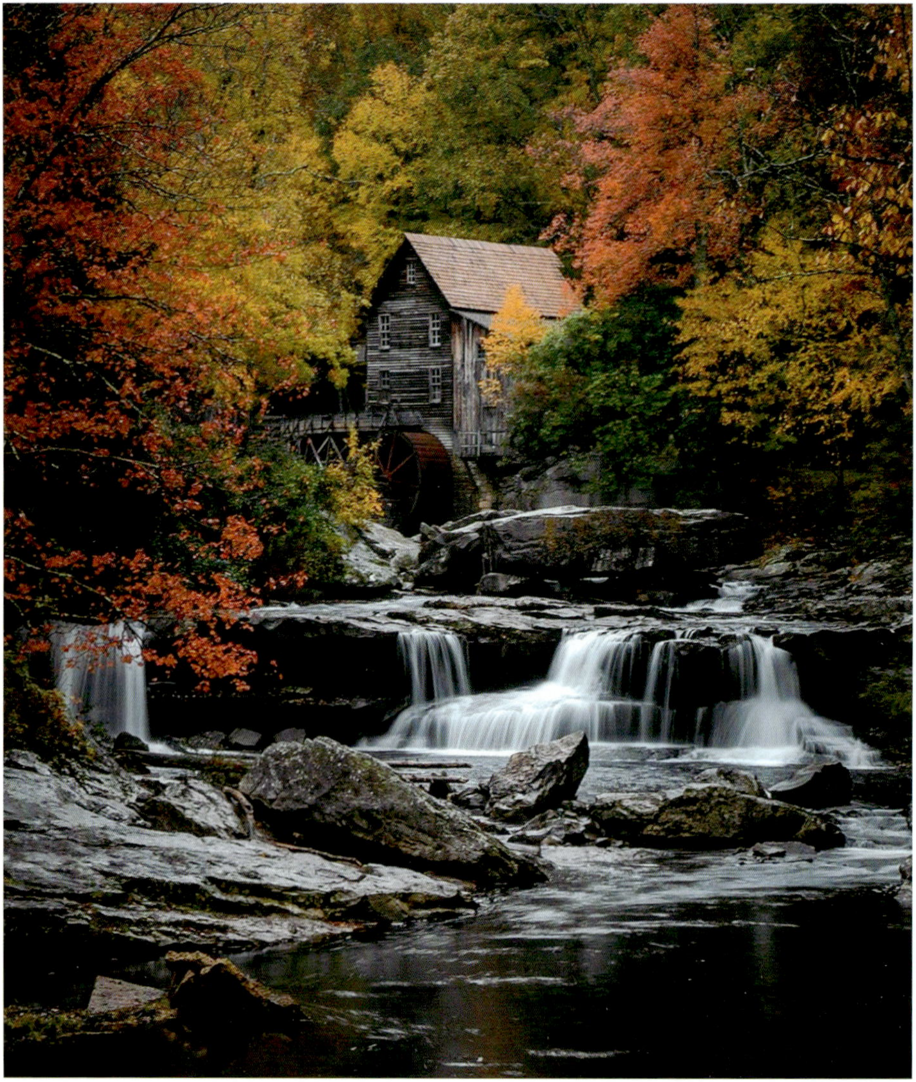

NICOLE VIEWS

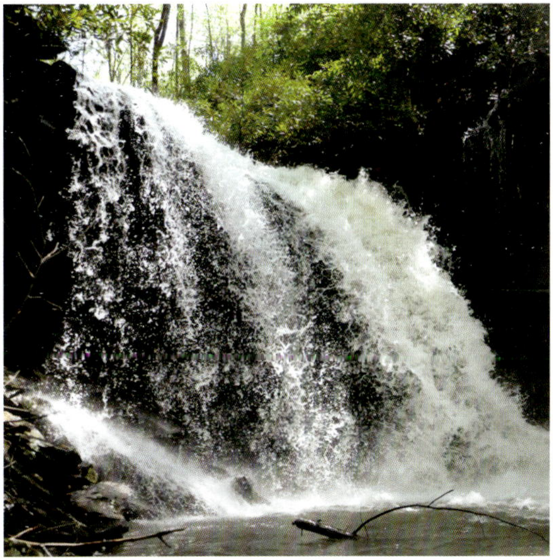

MAGGIE FISHER

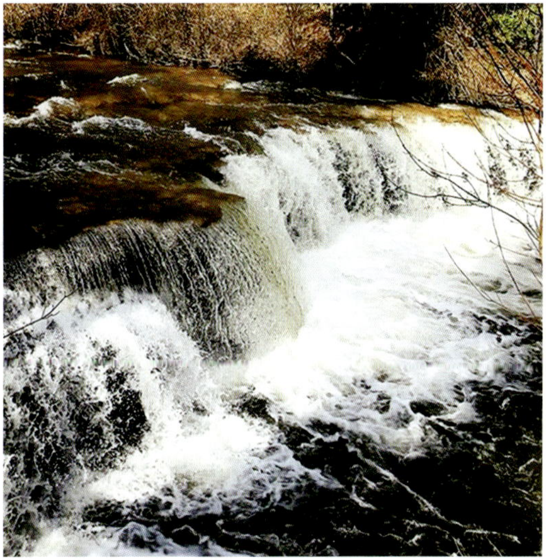

AMBER MESSICK

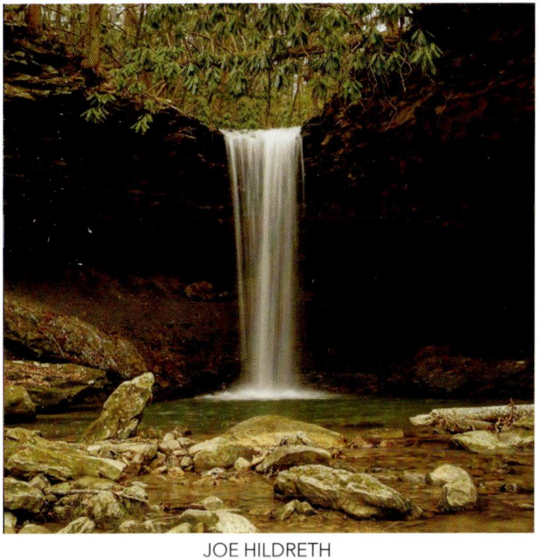

JOE HILDRETH

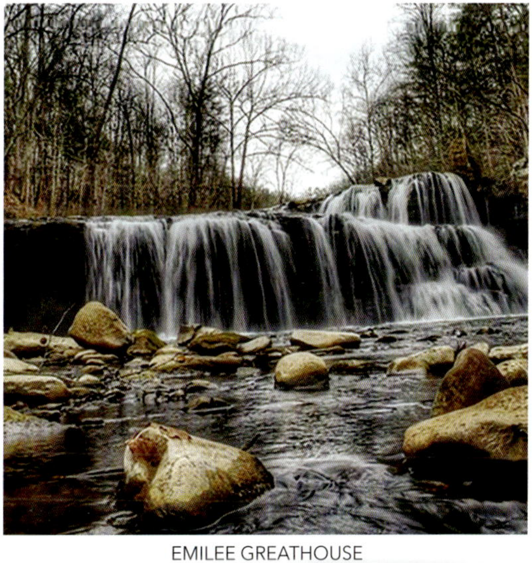

EMILEE GREATHOUSE

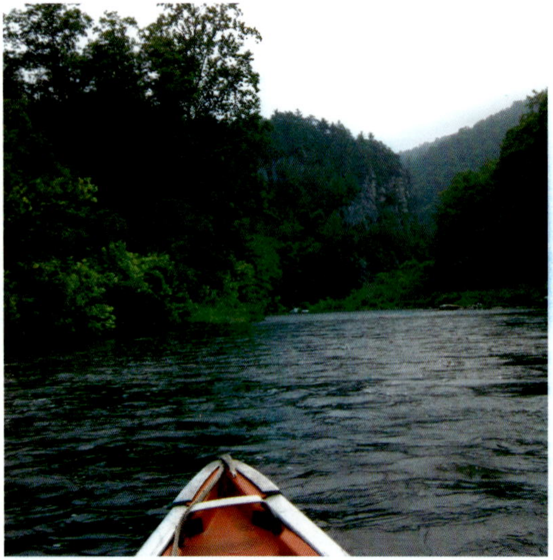

TESSA YOST

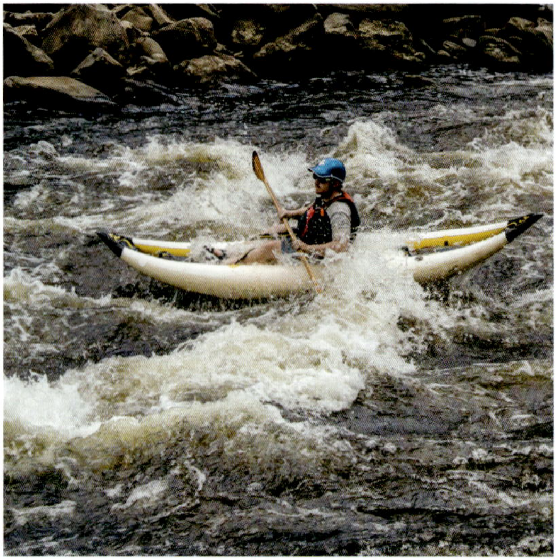

KATHY JENKINS

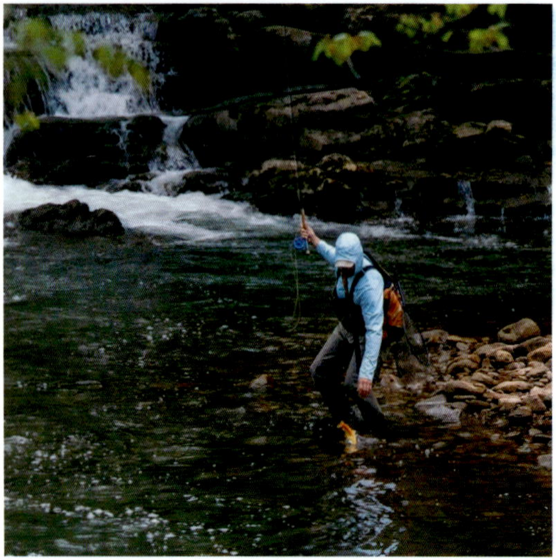

WENDY PARKS

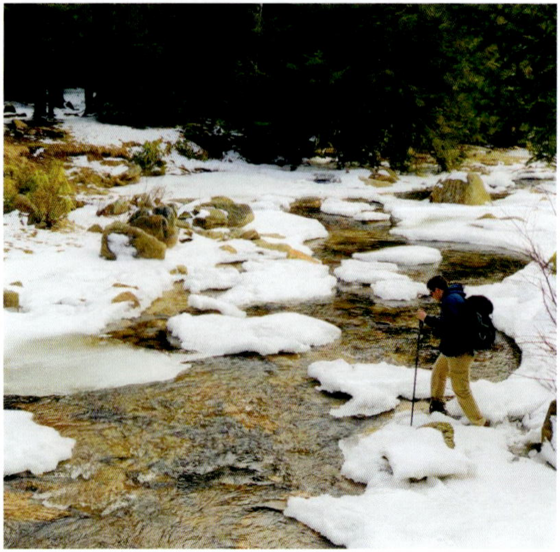

BRIAN BOYCE McCOY

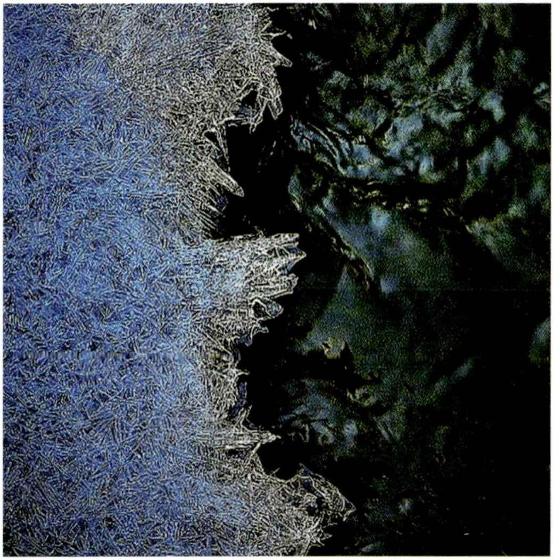

ELAINE CLARK

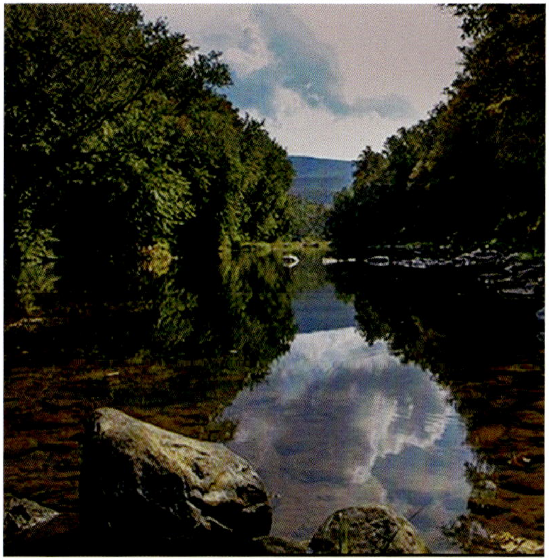

STEPHANIE SABOURIN

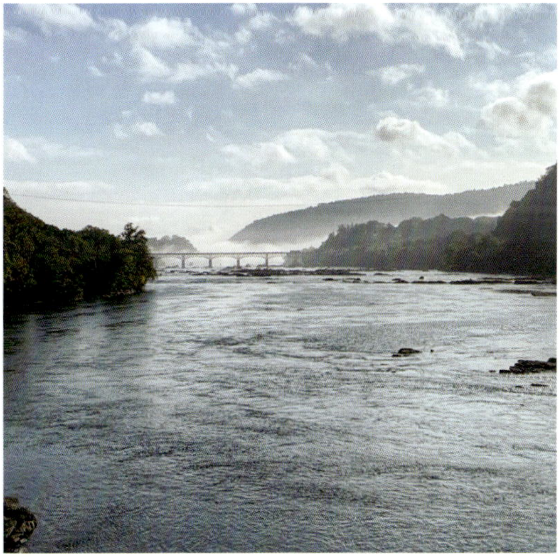

CINDI DUNN

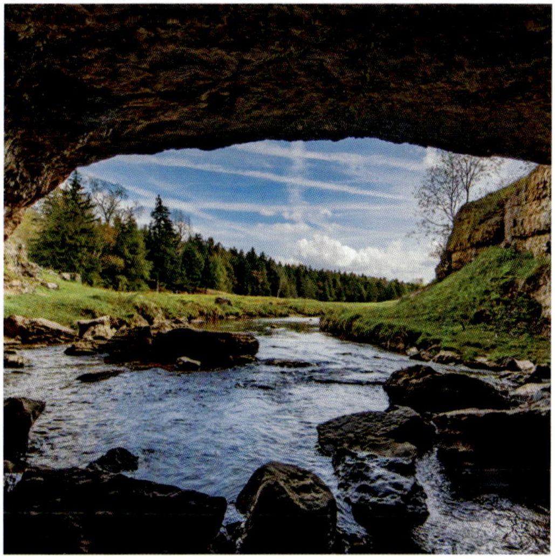

DAVID PROCTOR

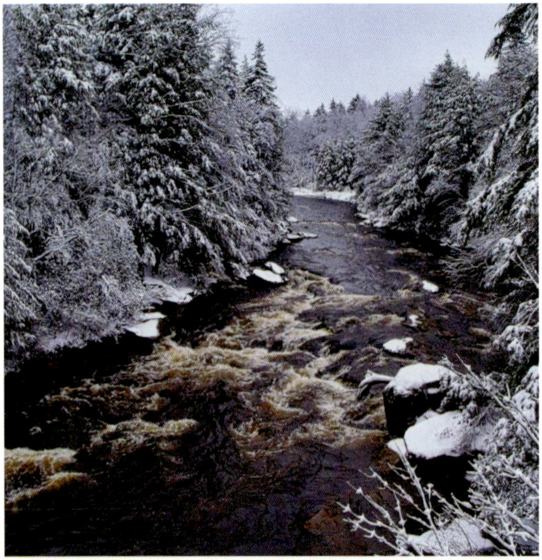

KENDALL BRUMBAUGH

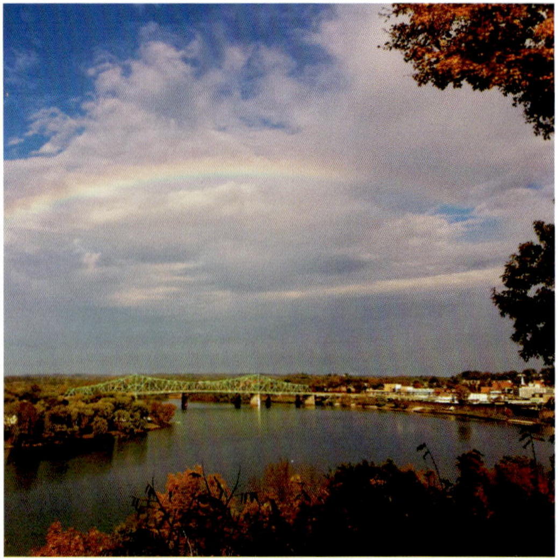

STEPHANIE CARPENTER

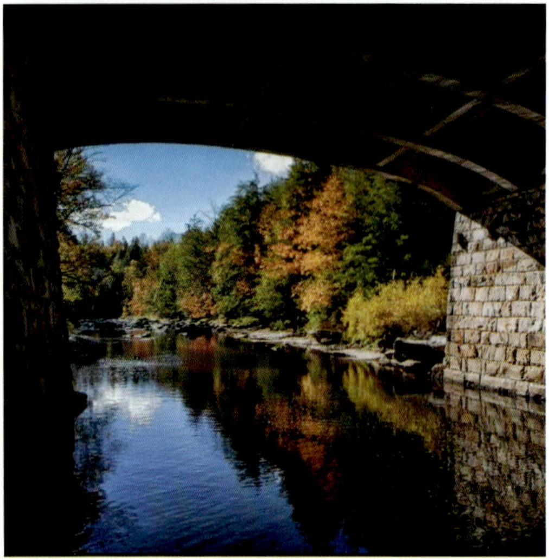

TOM DEAN

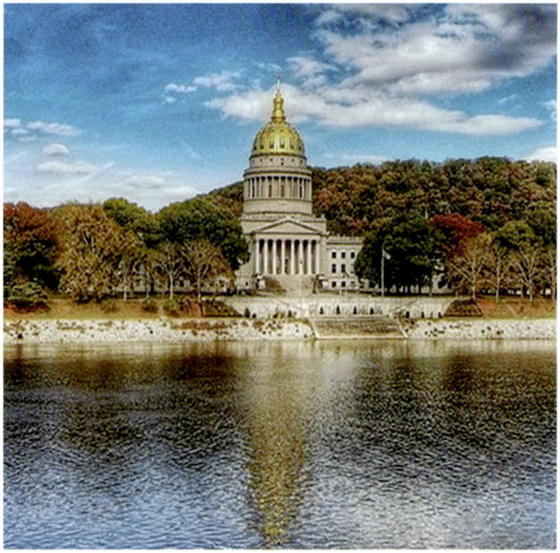

EMILEE GREATHOUSE

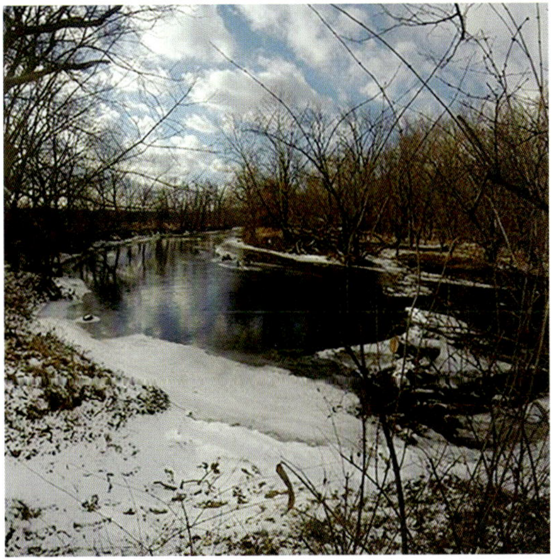

KATIE RICHARD

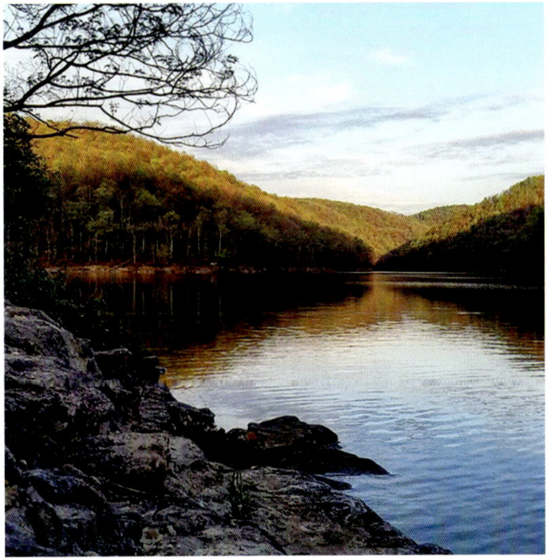

JUSTIN FRAME

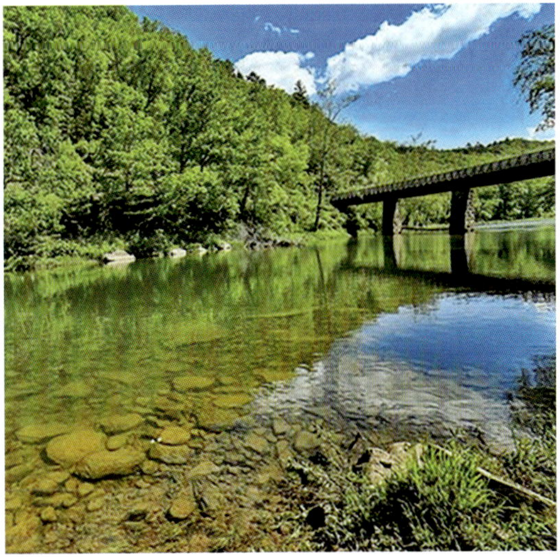

BRENT SCHNUPP

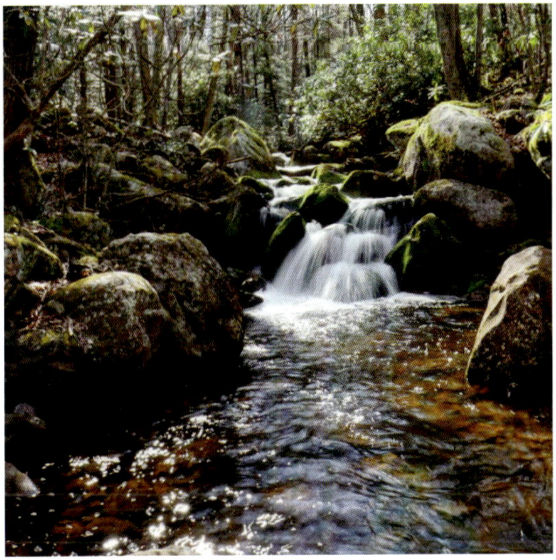

JULIE RATLIFF

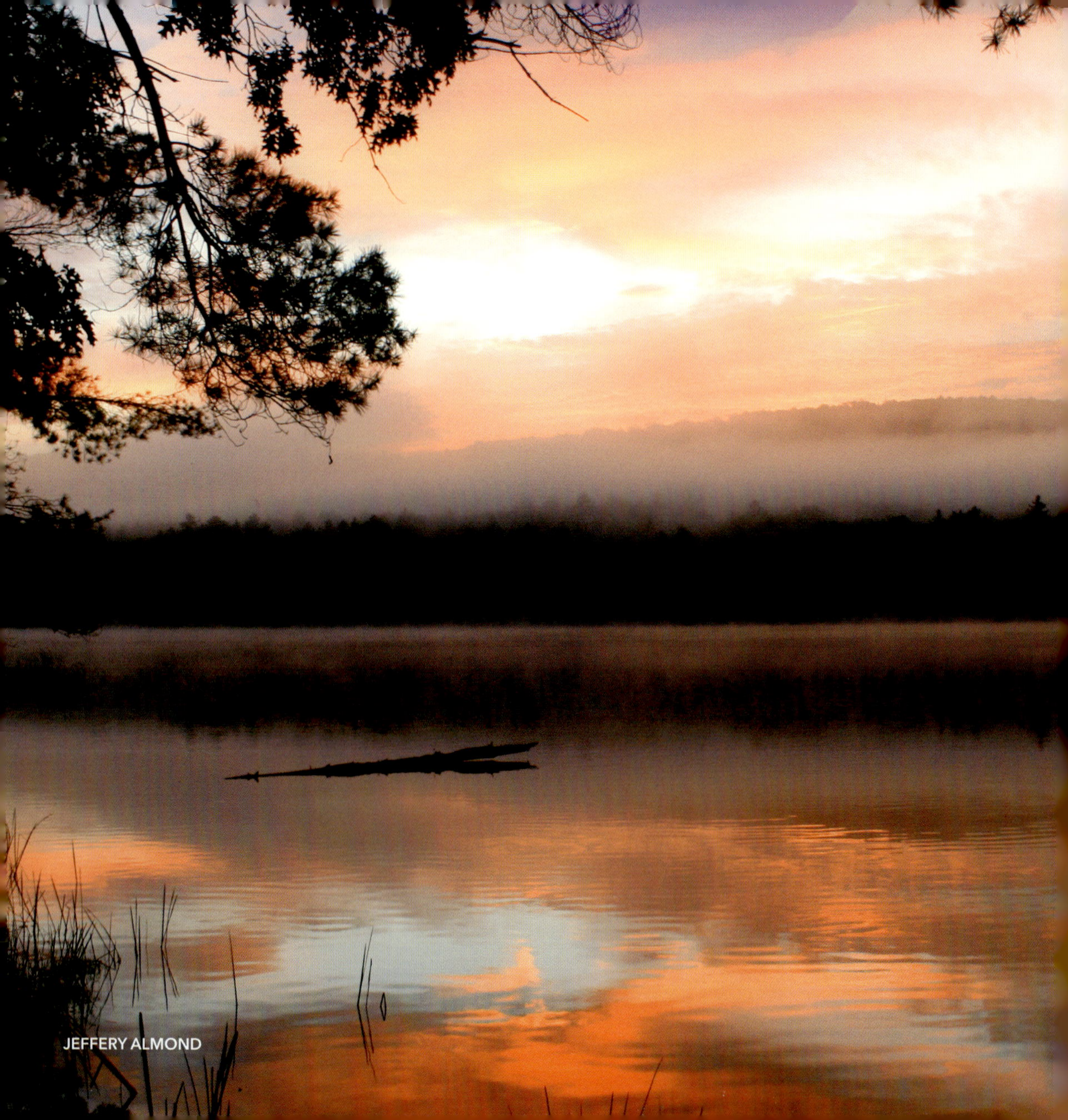
JEFFERY ALMOND

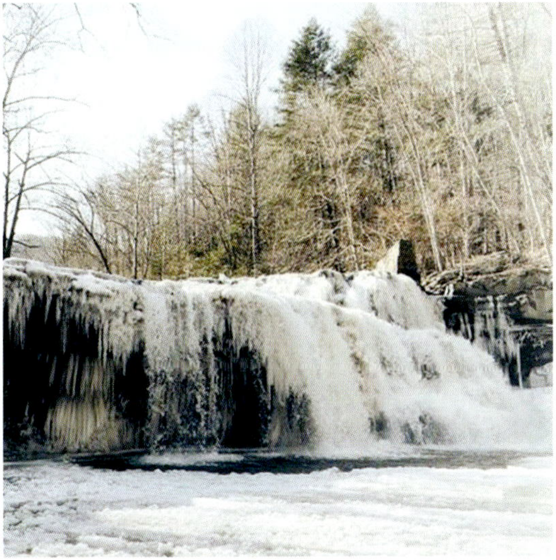
KAYLA DAWN

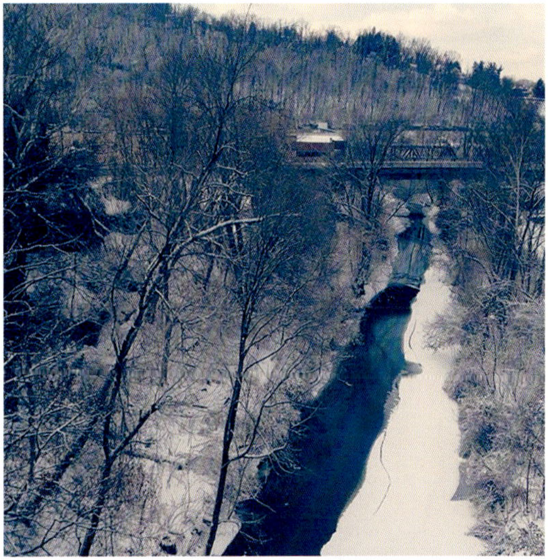
LAURA WILCOX

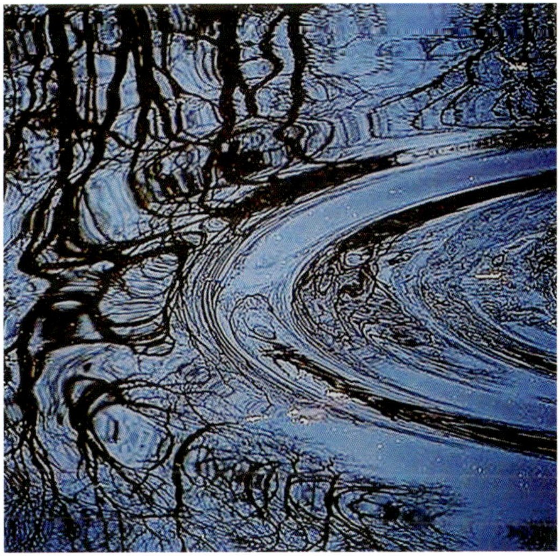
ELAINE CLARK

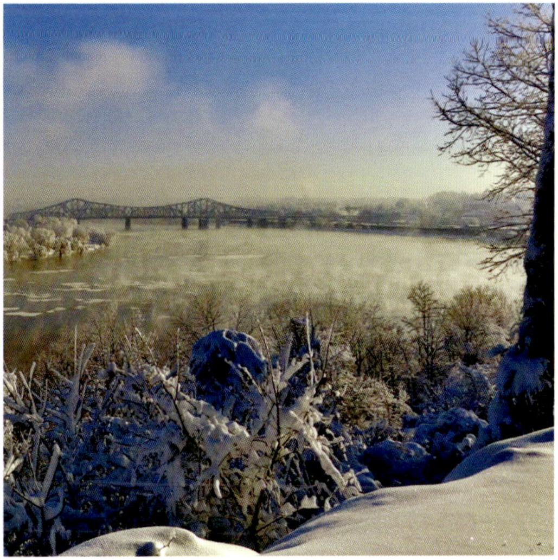
STEPHANIE CARPENTER

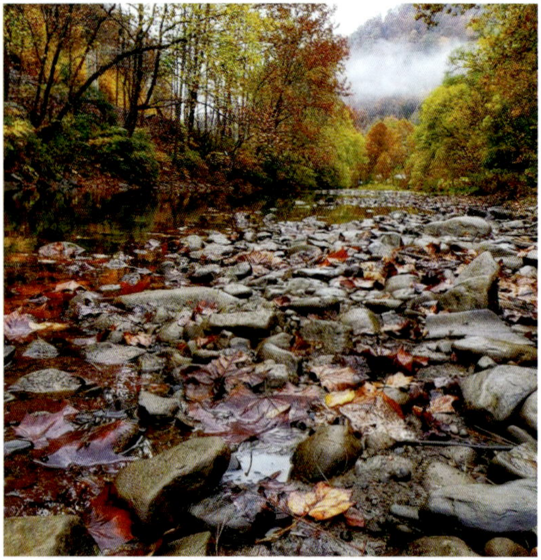

EMILEE GREATHOUSE

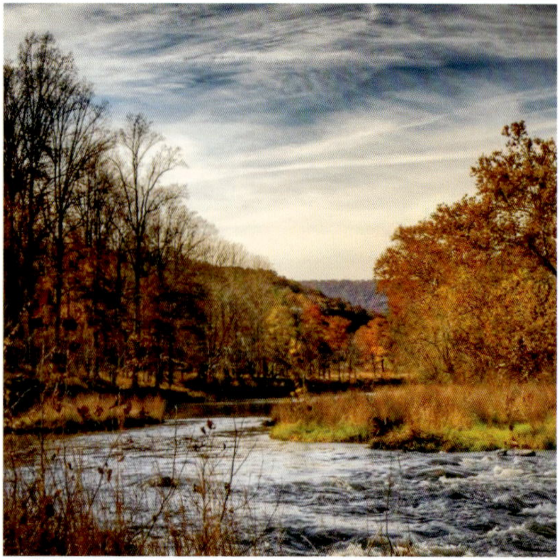

STEPH SABOURIN

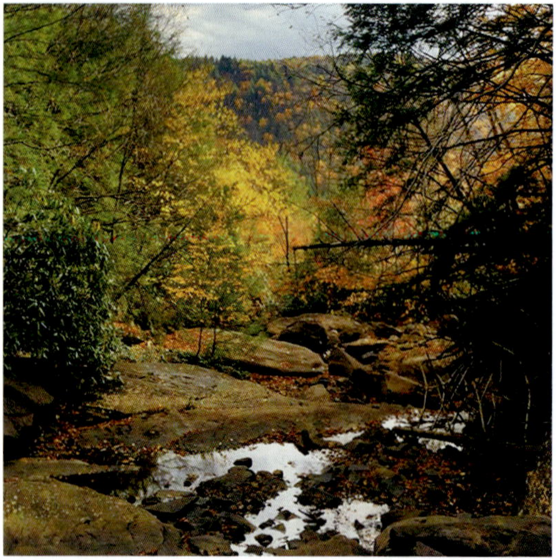

RENAU LUCAS

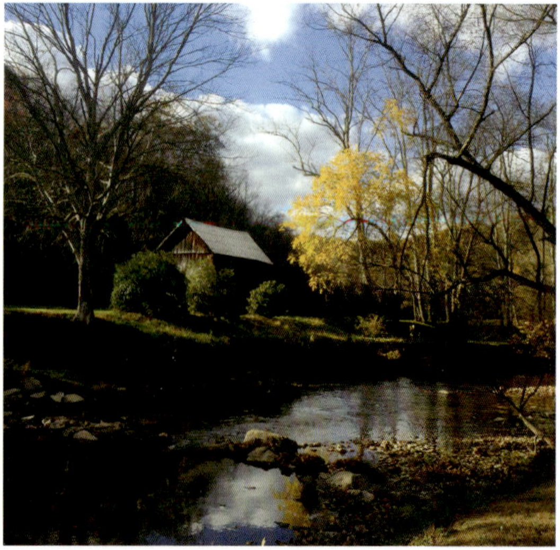

KERRY BLACK

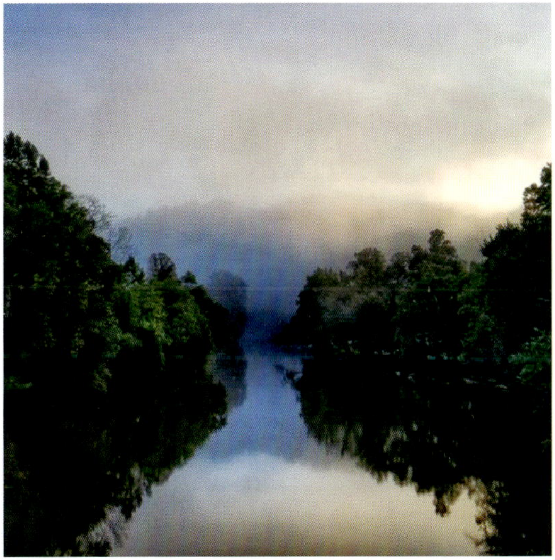

EMILEE GREATHOUSE

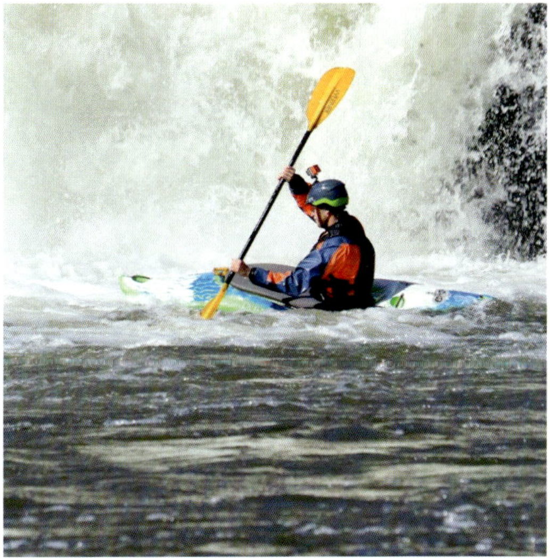

MELISSA EISENHAUER

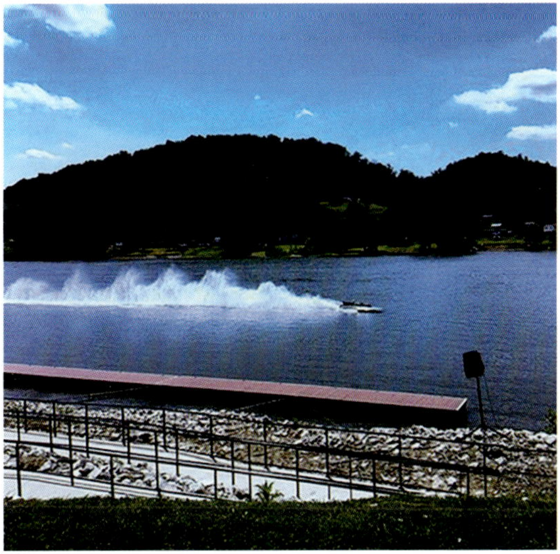

WESLEY PHILP

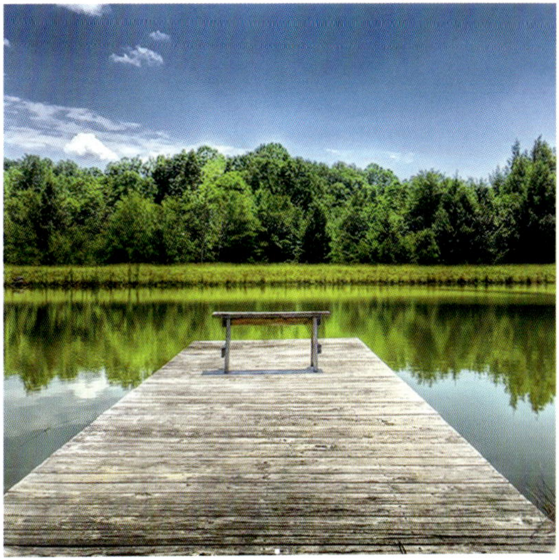

LORI TURNER

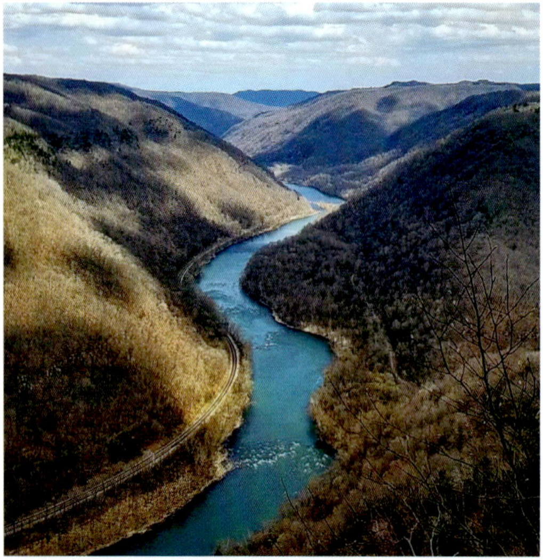

CONNIE BOLEY-LILLY

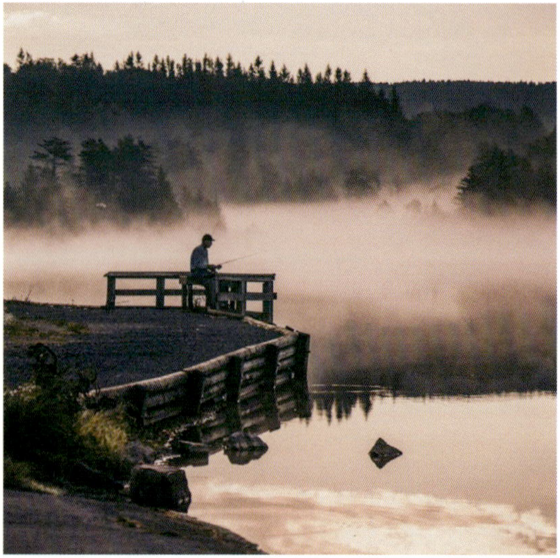

WENDY PARKS

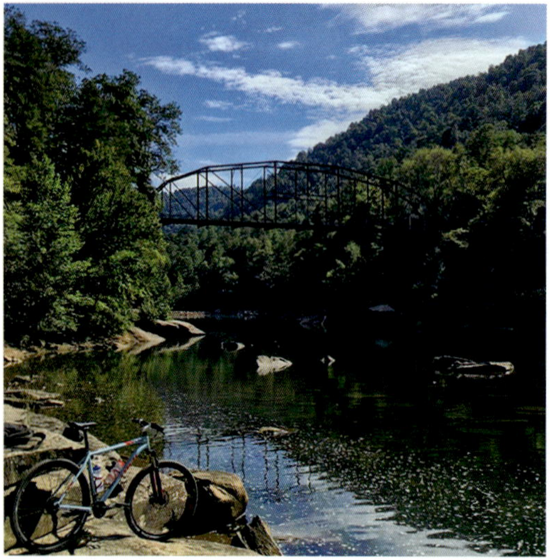

DON DEQUASIE

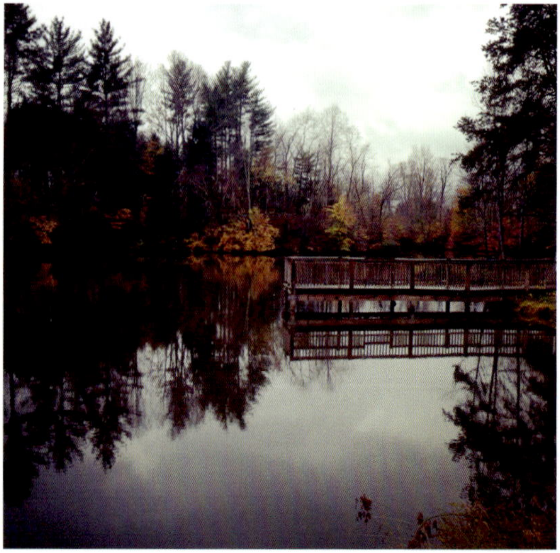

HEATHER ROSE

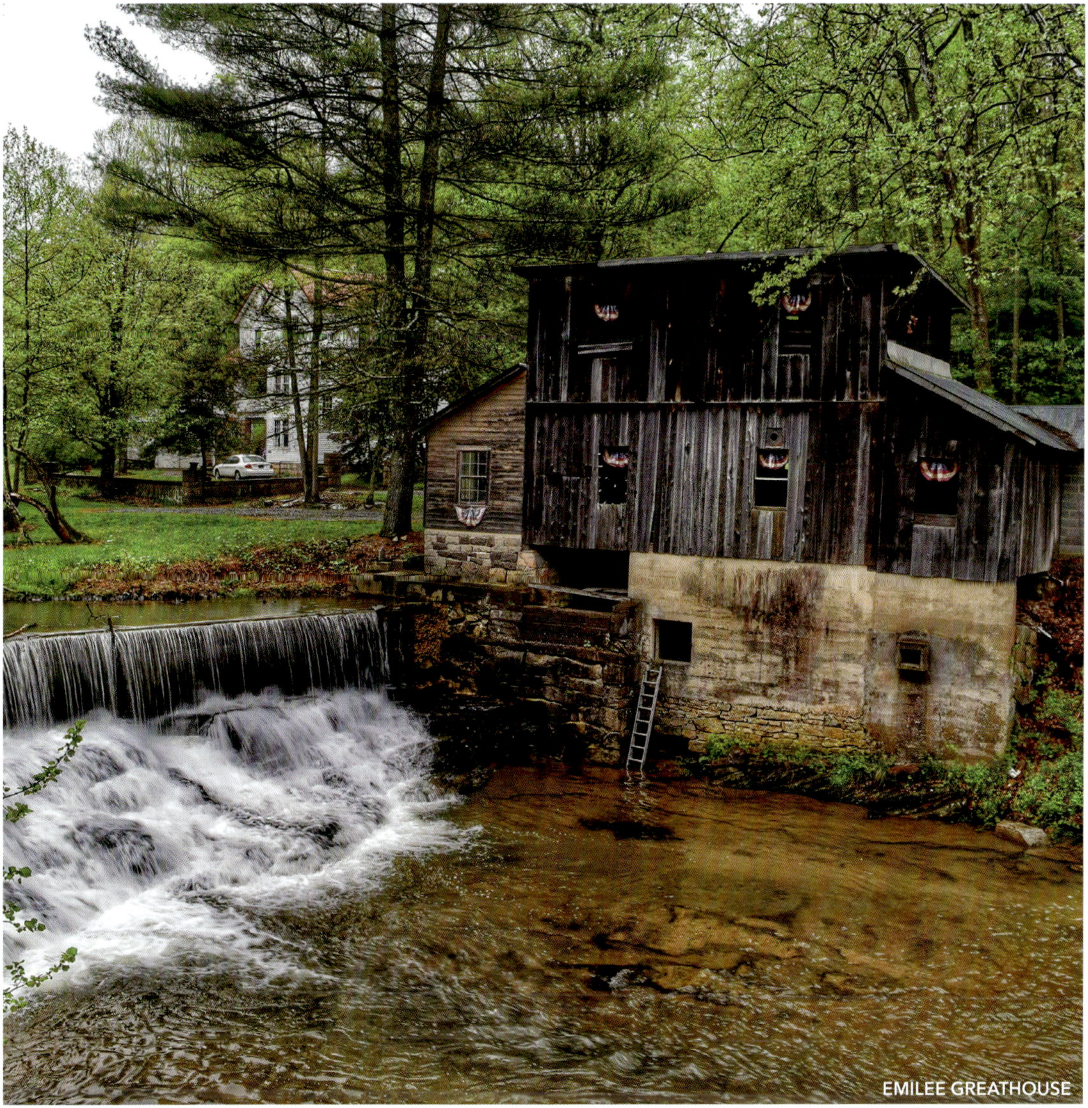
EMILEE GREATHOUSE

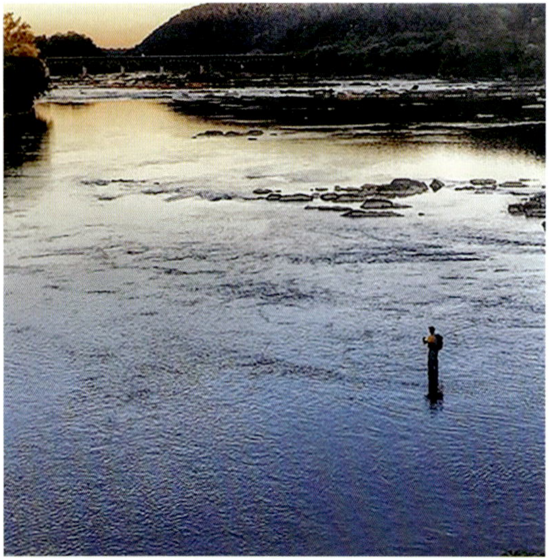

CINDI DUNN

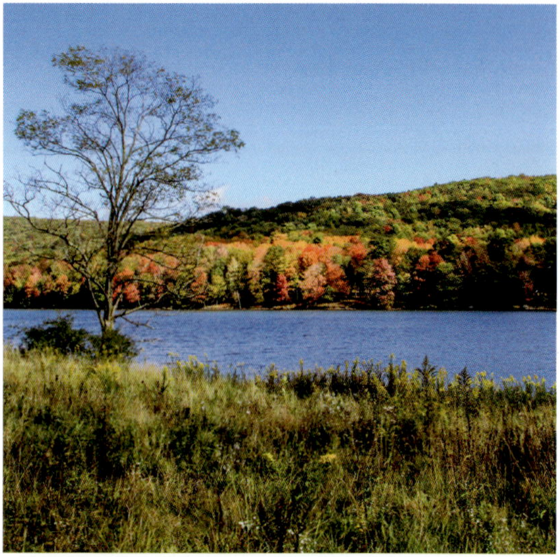

CANDY THOMPSON

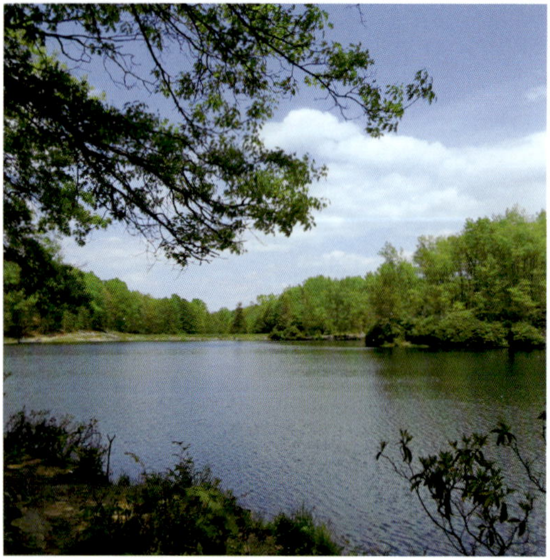

PATTY MOLES

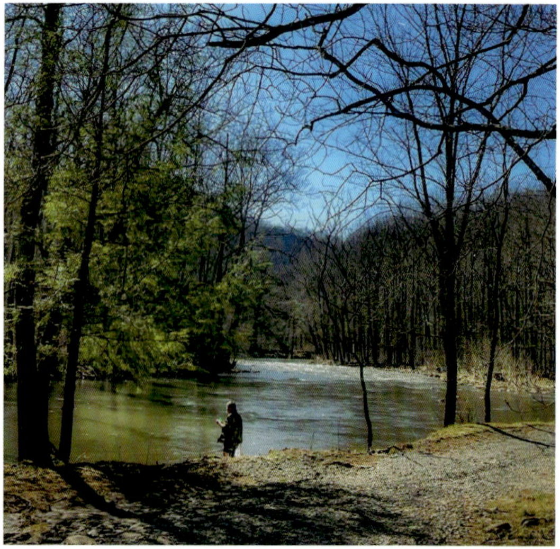

CHARMAGNE AYOTTE

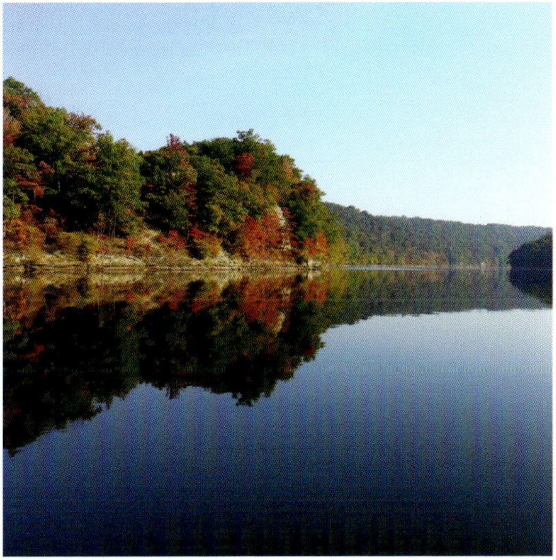

RELLA CVETICAN

KENDALL BRUMBAUGH

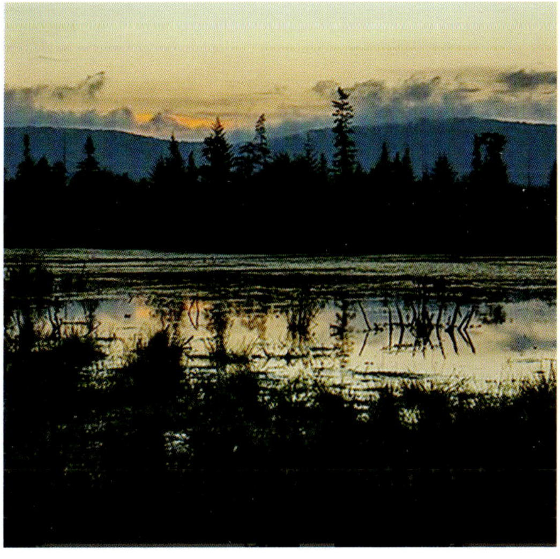

BRIAN BOYCE McCOY

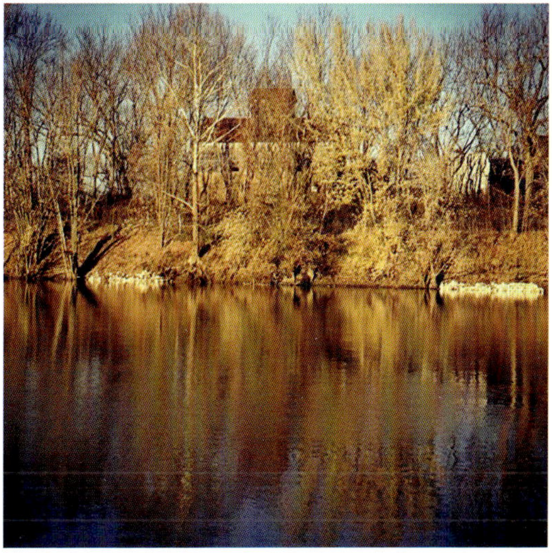

CHRISSY LITTLER

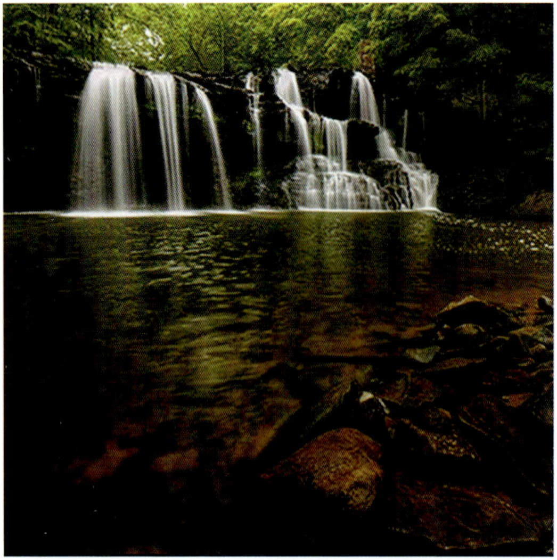

TOM DEAN

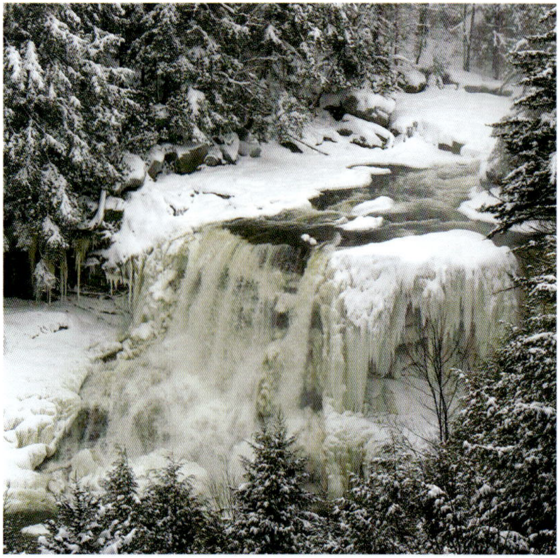

LAURA MOUL

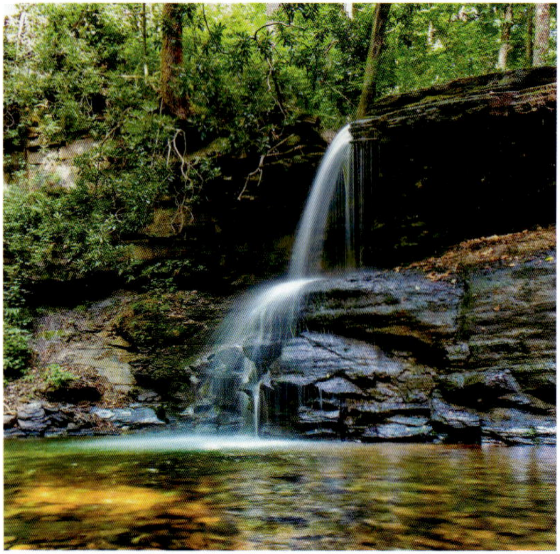

CHARMAGNE AYOTTE

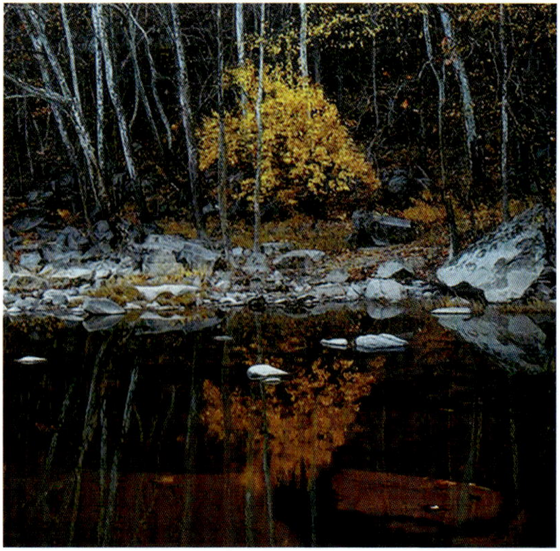

KEVIN JACK

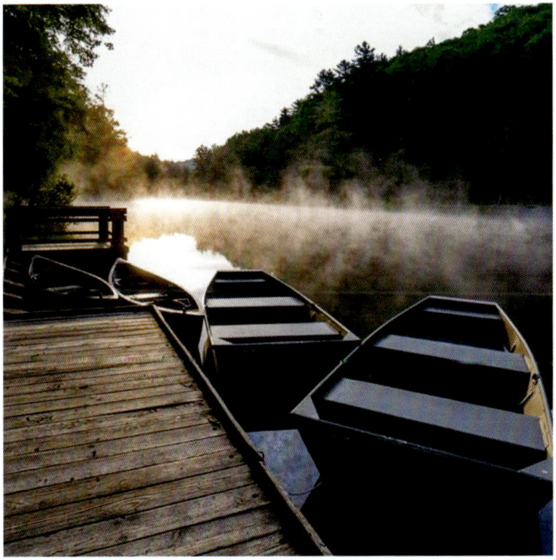

JESSE THORNTON

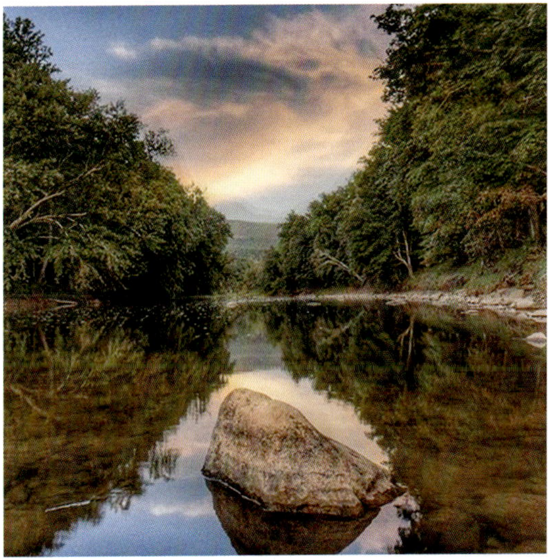

STEPHANIE SABOURIN

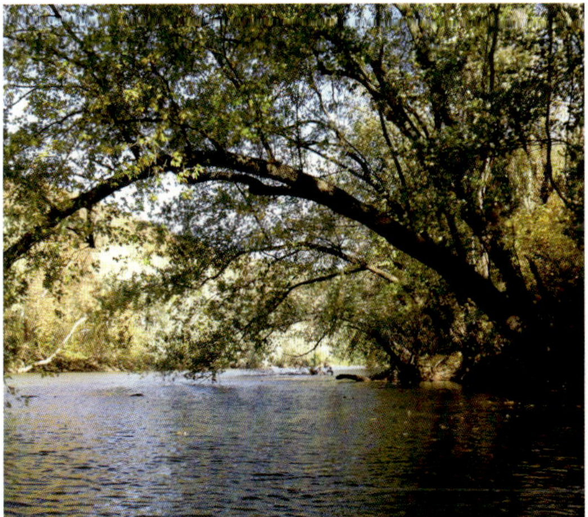

GEORGE R. BOHACH

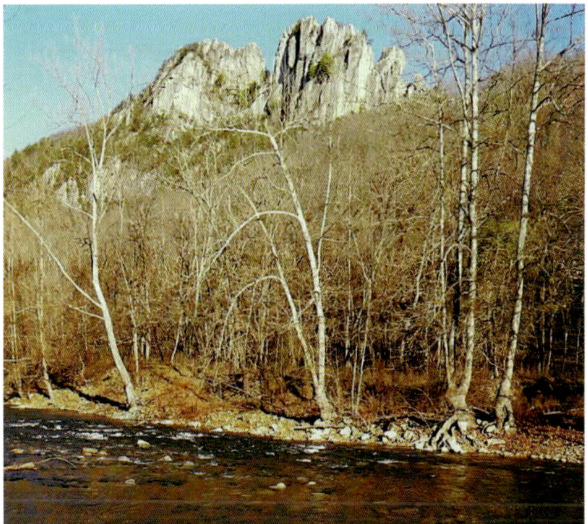

KATIE RICHARD

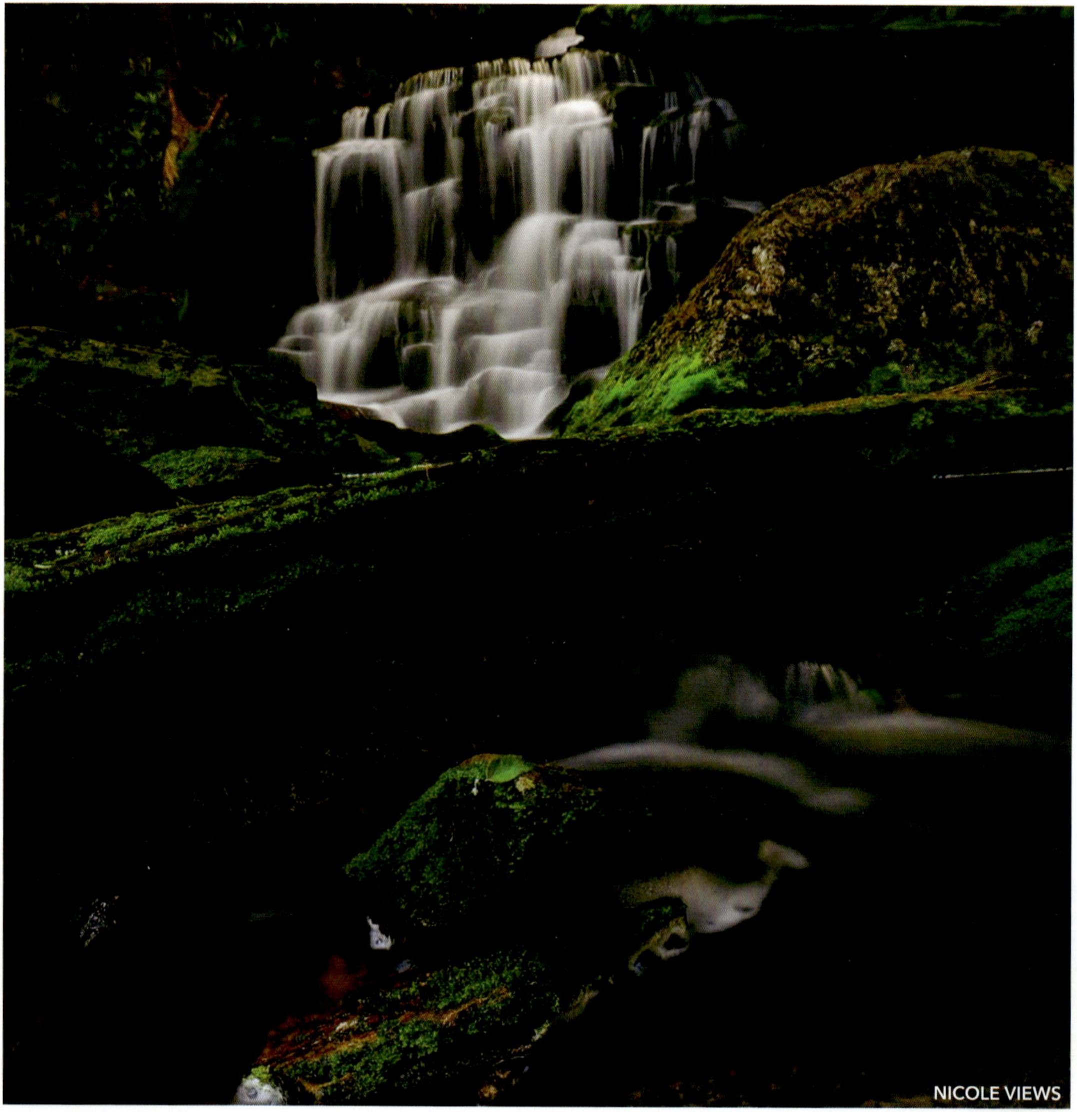
NICOLE VIEWS

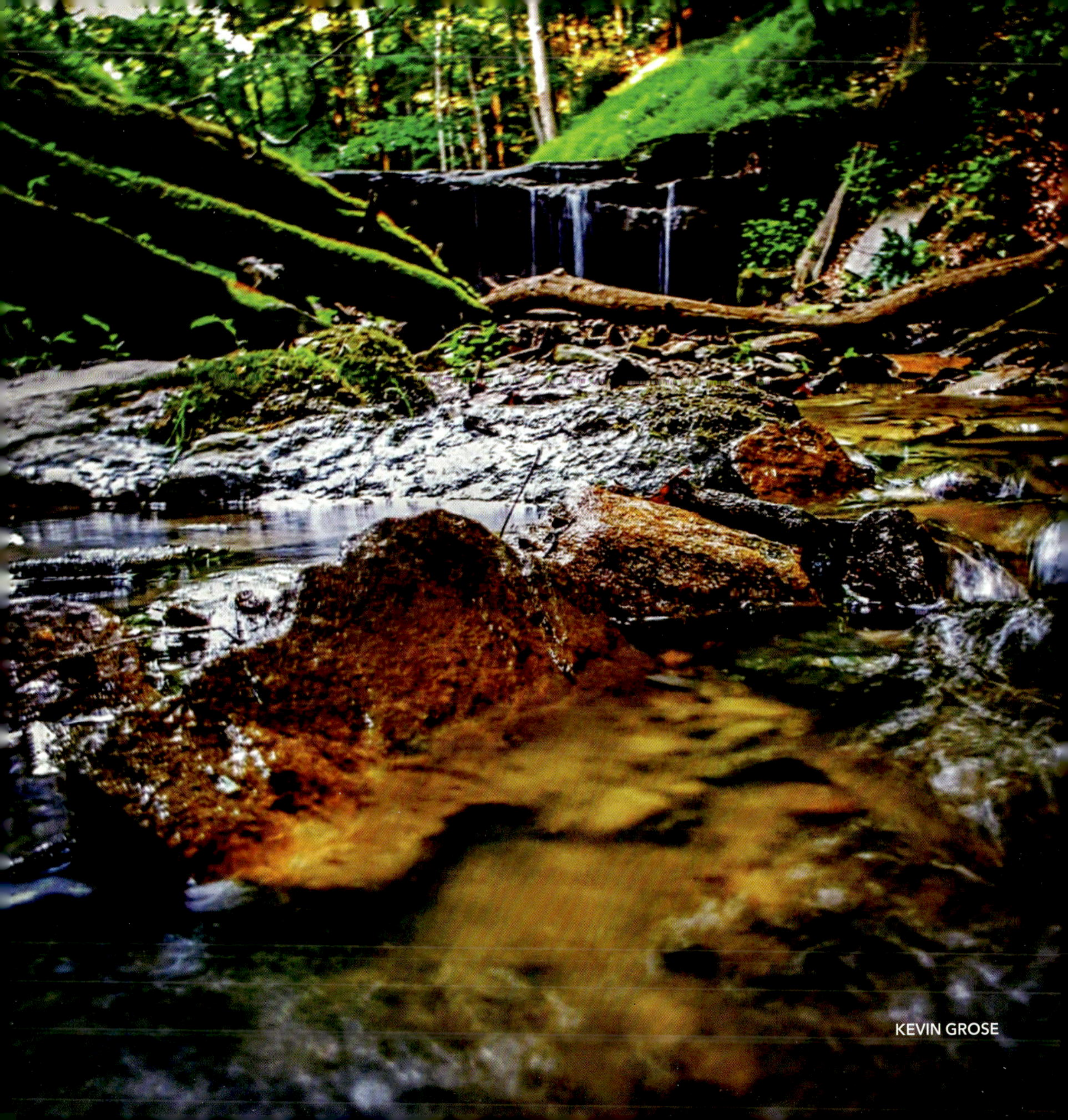
KEVIN GROSE

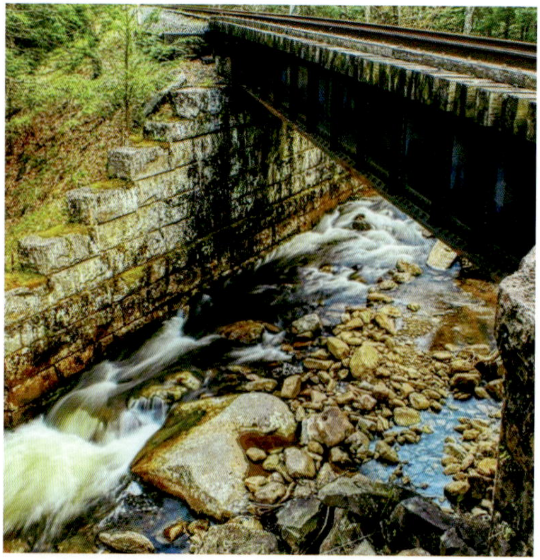

KENDALL BRUMBAUGH

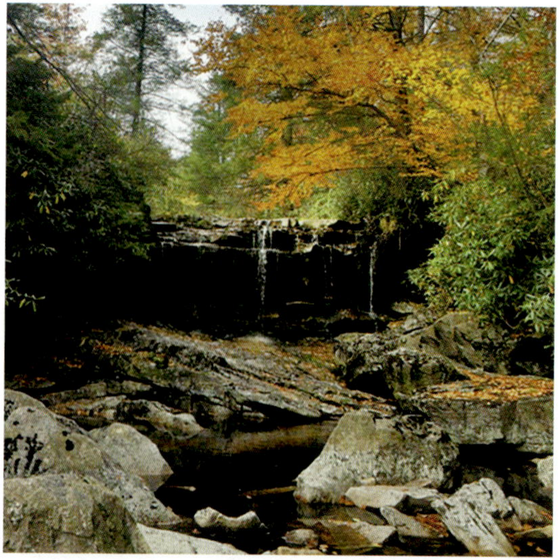

RENAU LUCAS

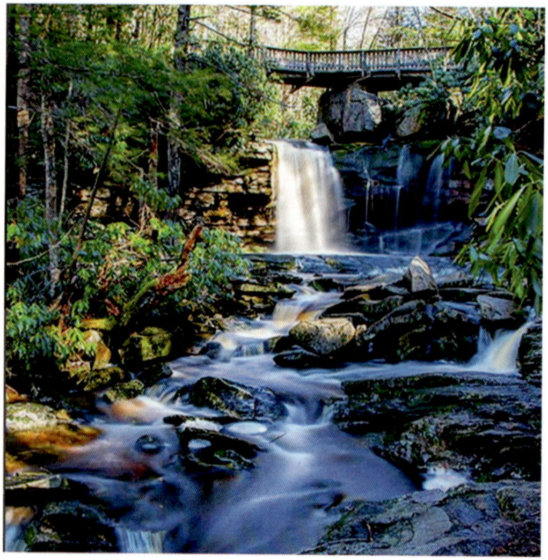

SARAH E. BAILEY

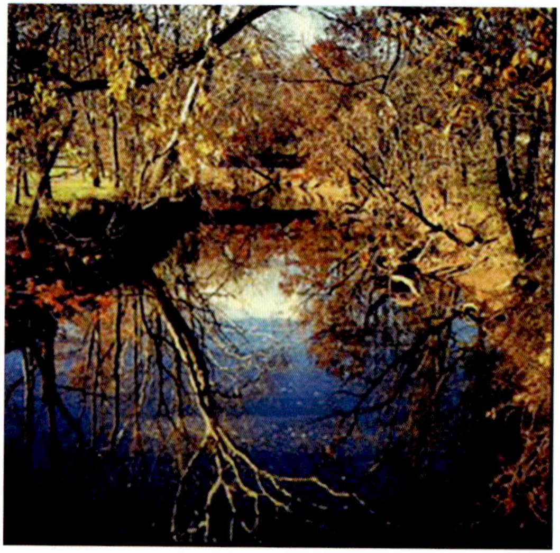

CAROL M. JOHNSON

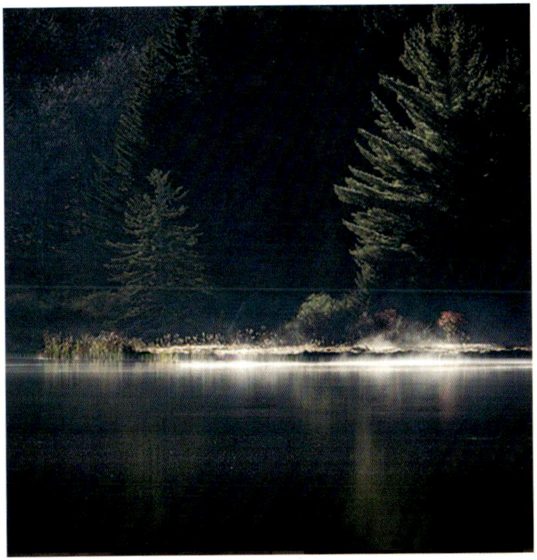

WENDY PARKS

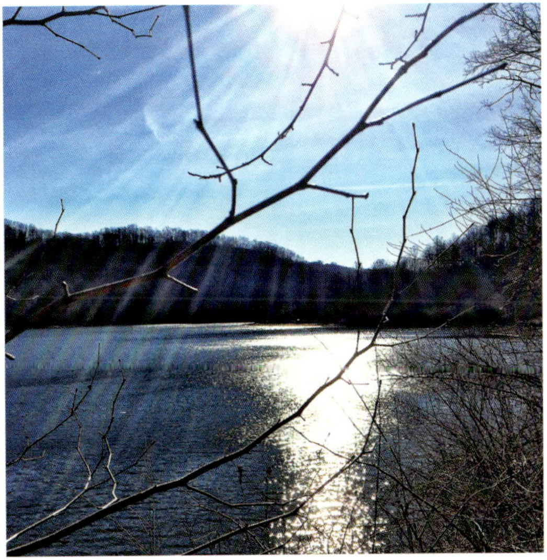

JADON MILLER

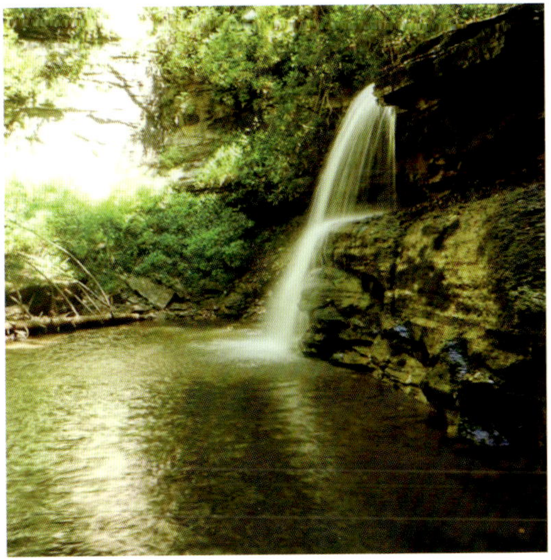

JULIE RATLIFF

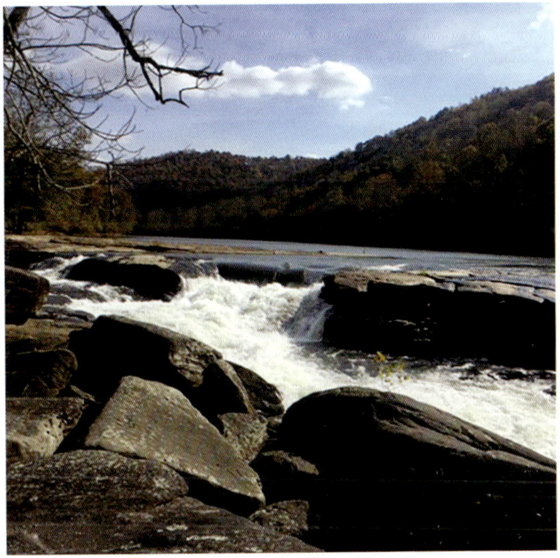

JENNIFER D. RANDOLPH

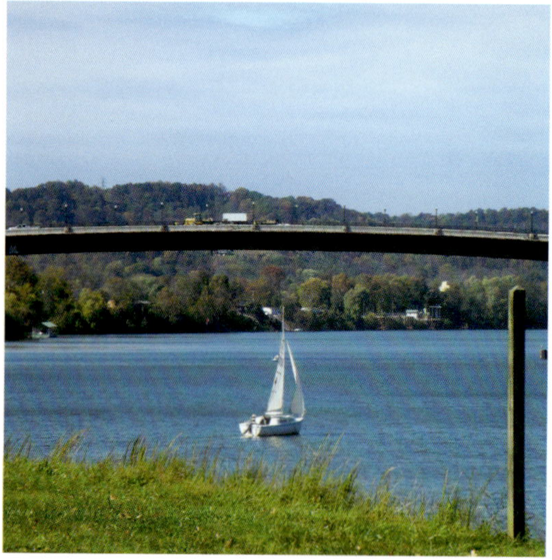

NEIL RICHARDSON

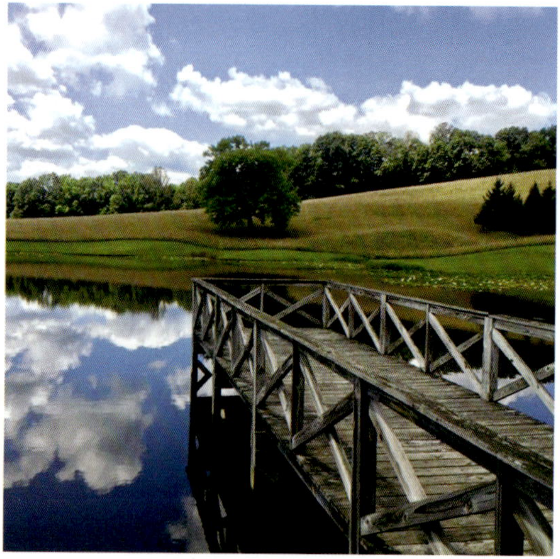

ASHLEY McCOY

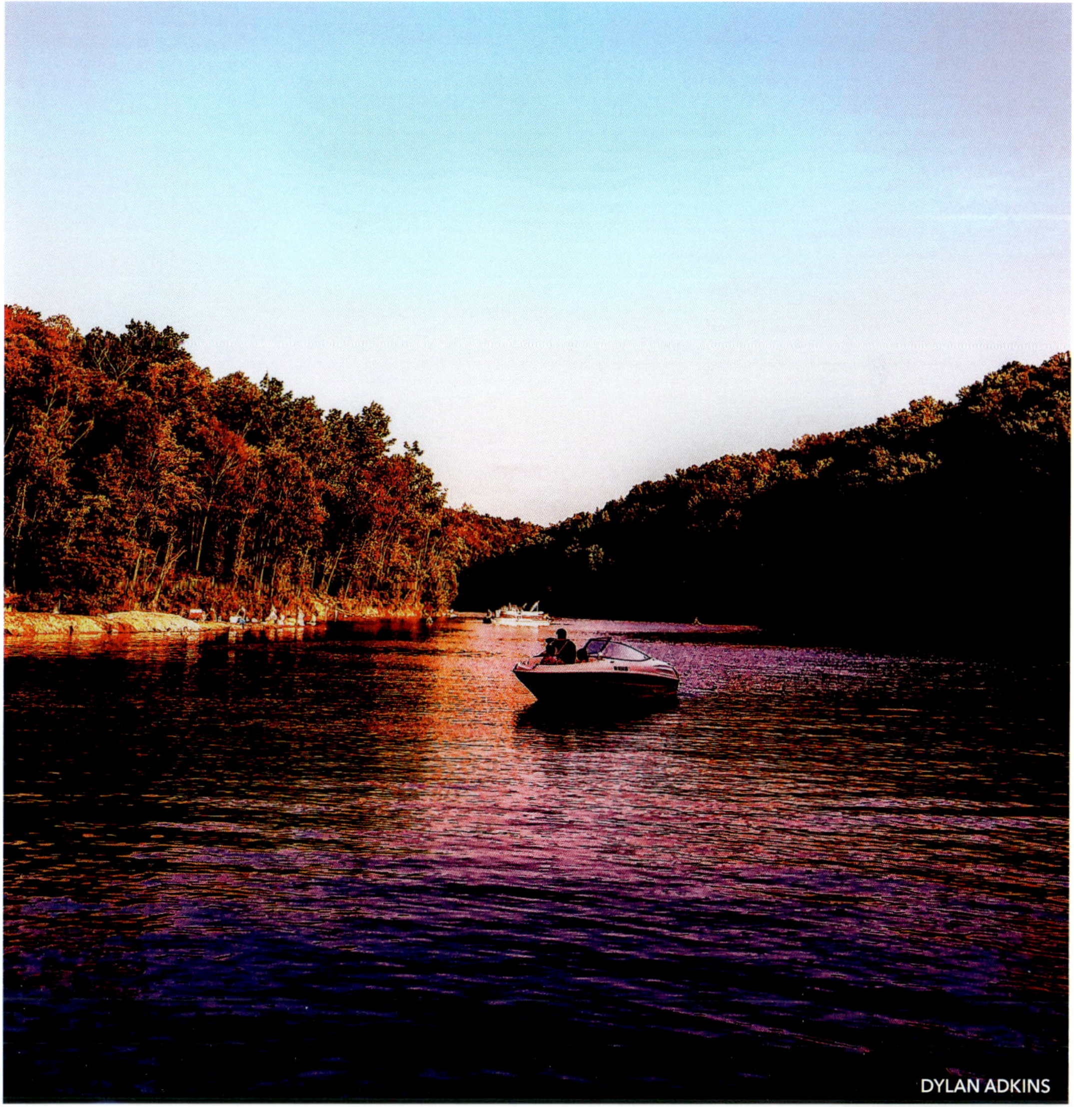
DYLAN ADKINS

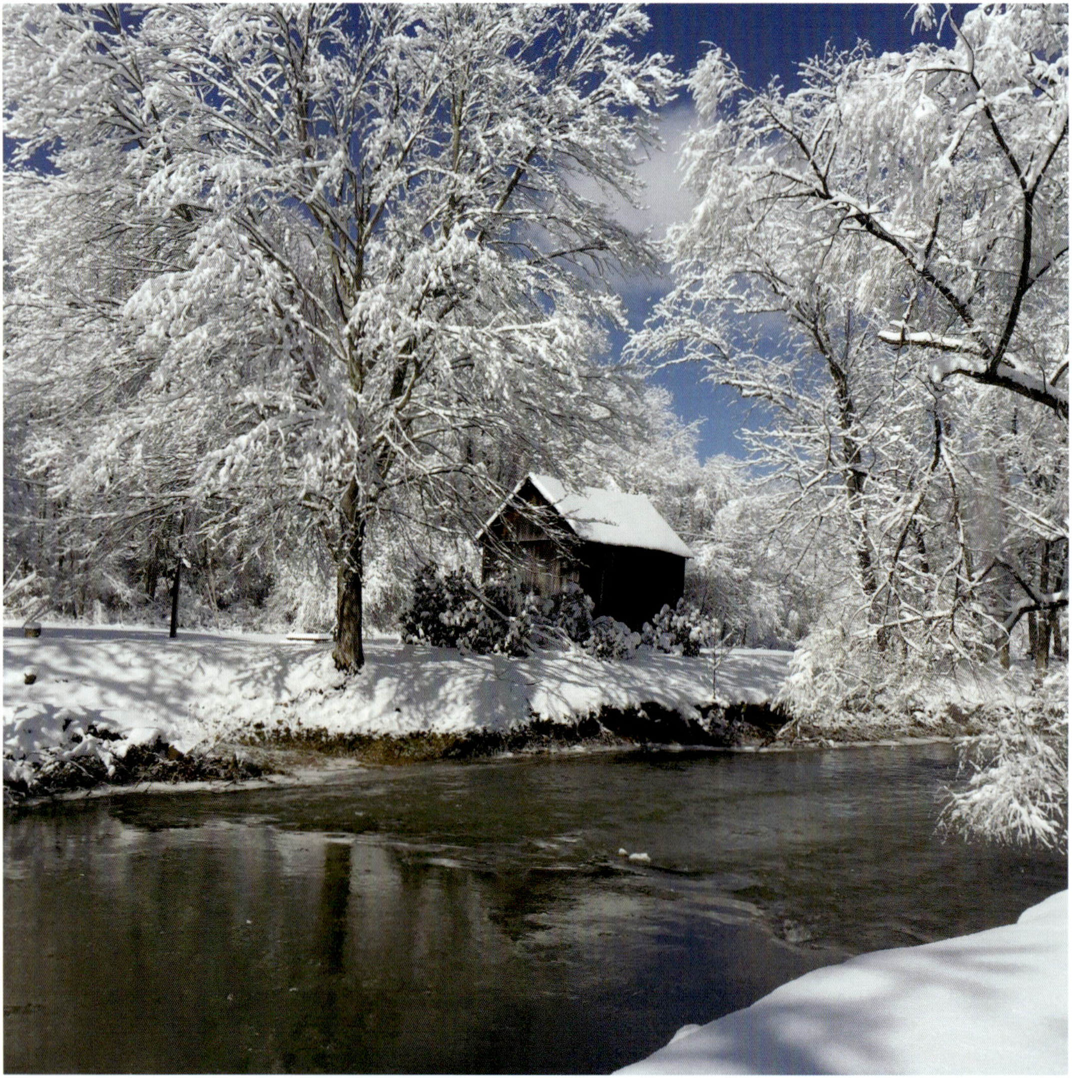

KERRY BLACK

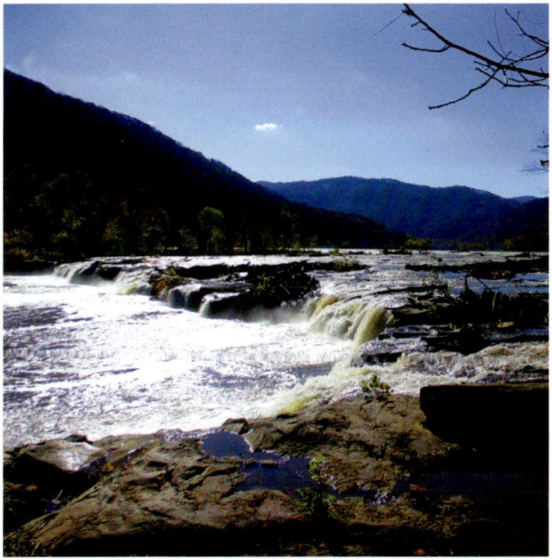

JAMES W. LILLY

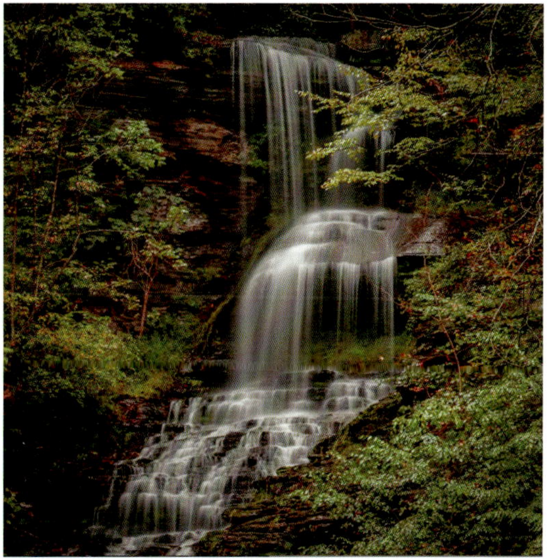

WENDY PARKS

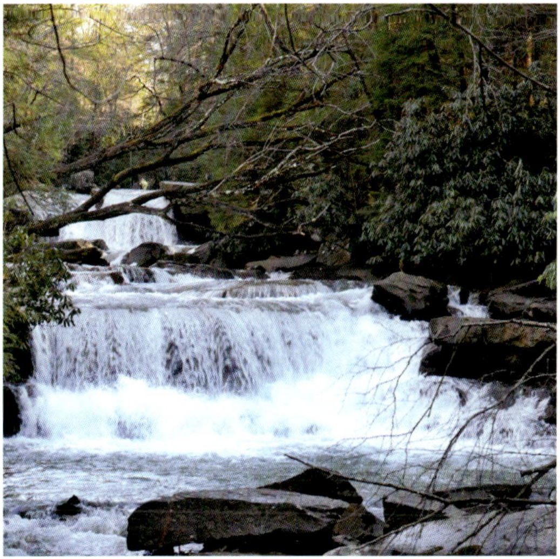

KIMBERLY FOWLER

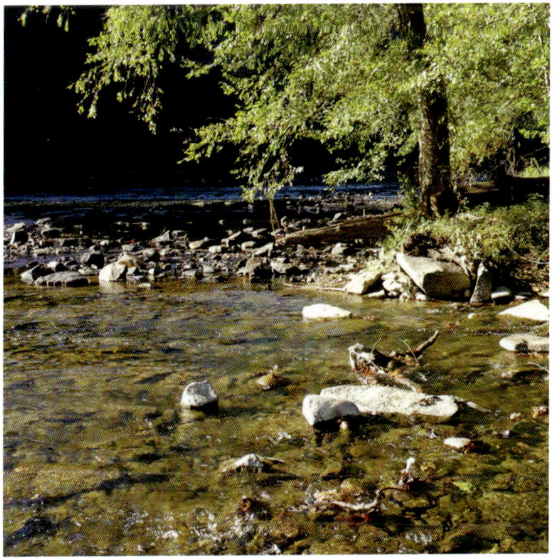

PAULA WALTERS

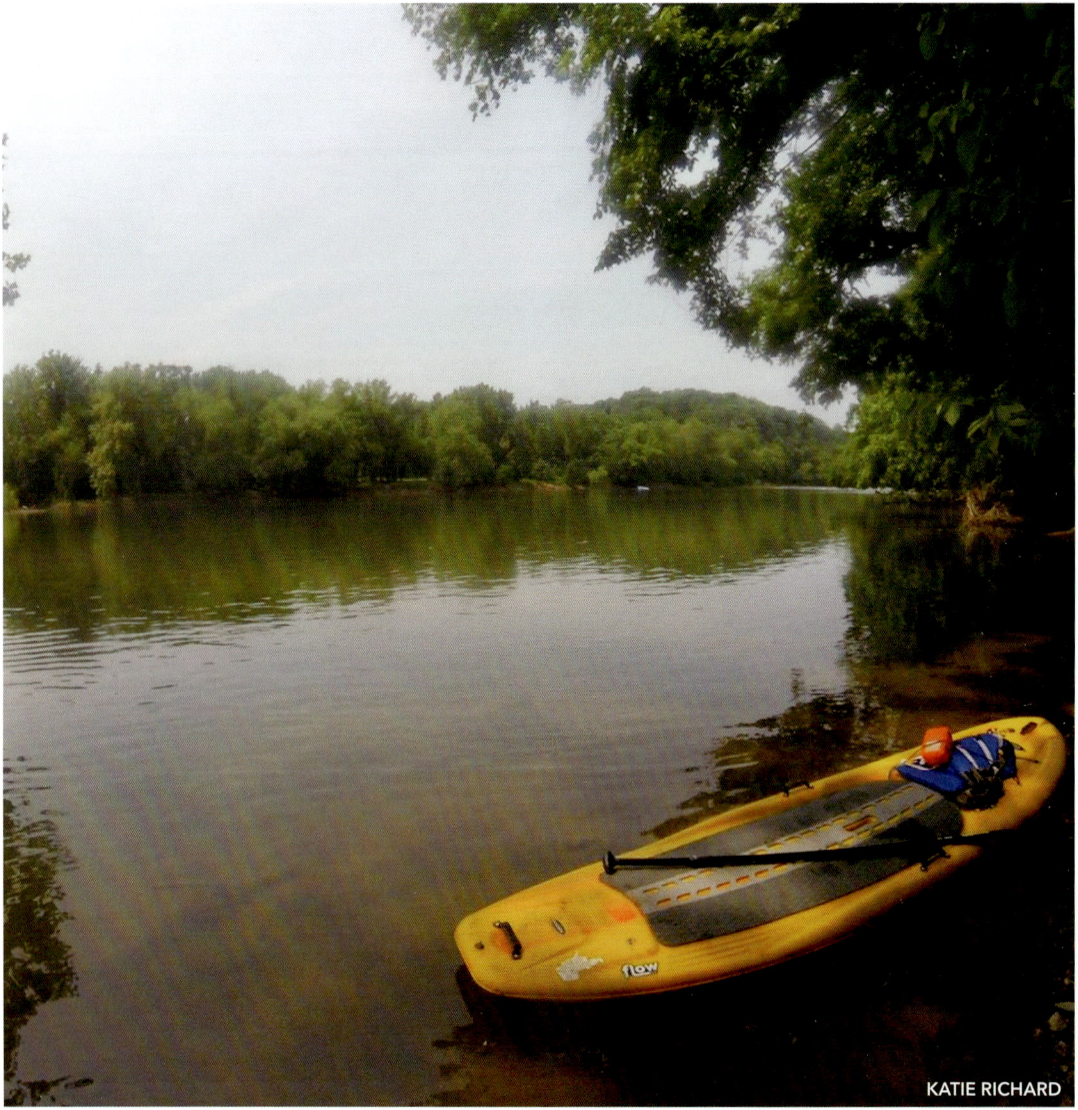

KATIE RICHARD

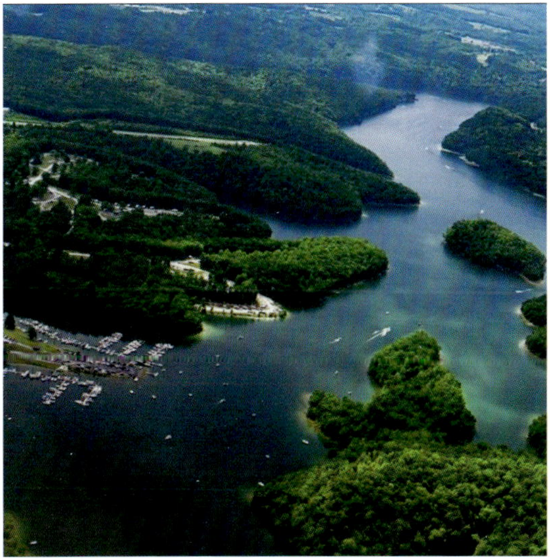

SHEILA JENKINS

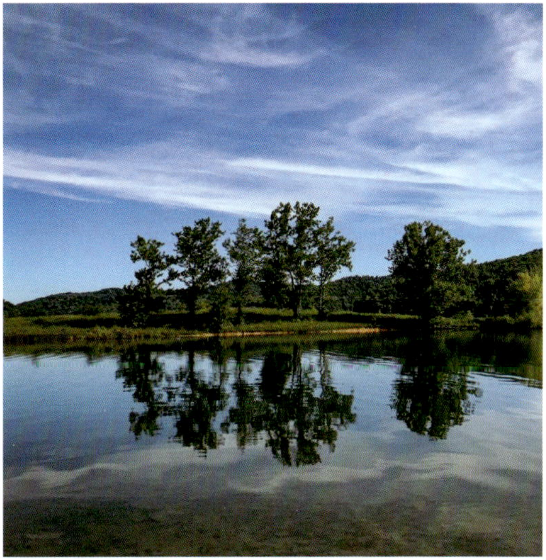

JOE HILDRETH

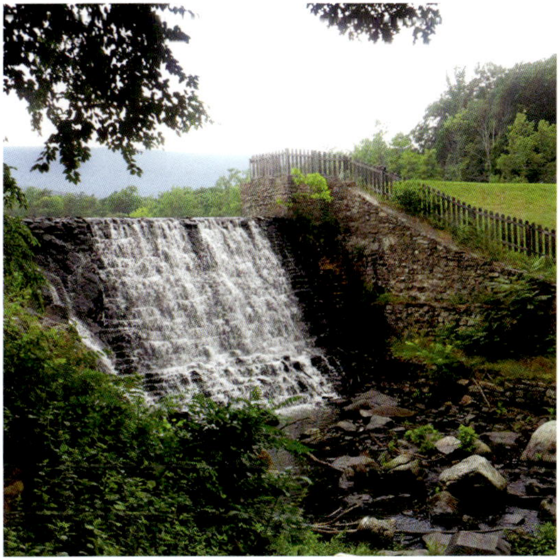

JENNIFER CARPENTER

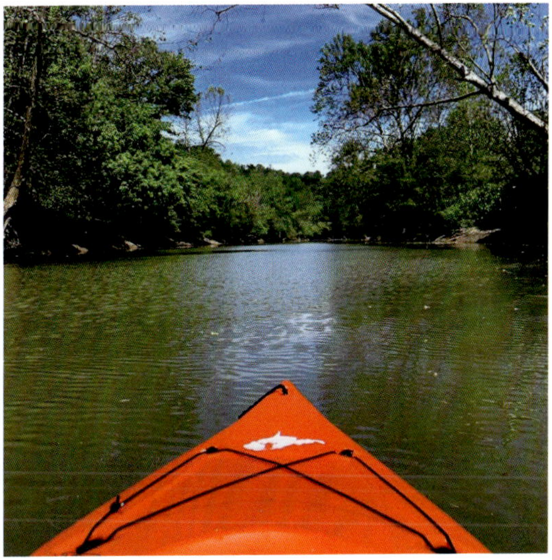

WESLEY PHILP

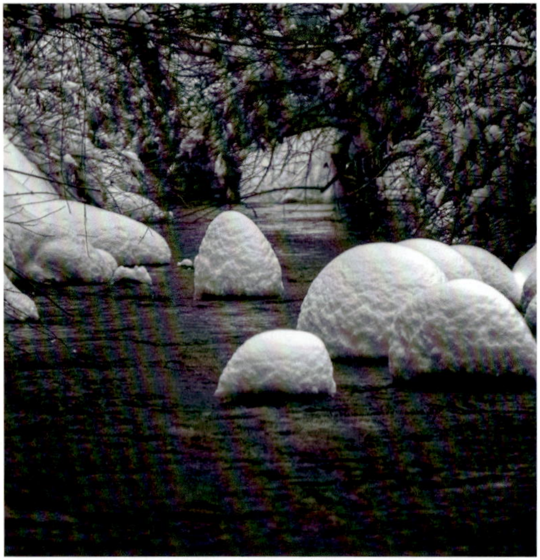

CLAYTON SPANGLER

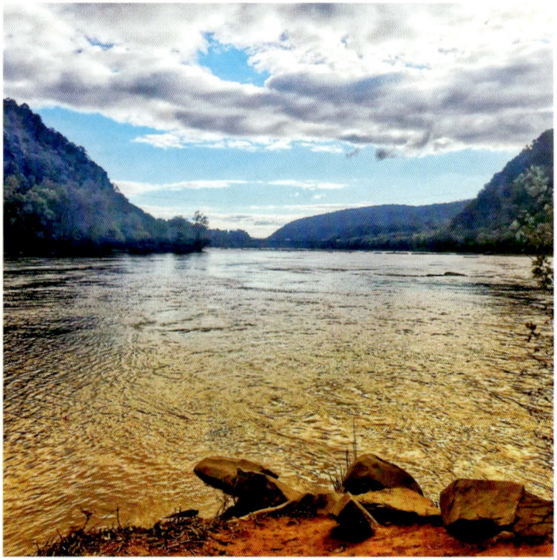

CINDI DUNN

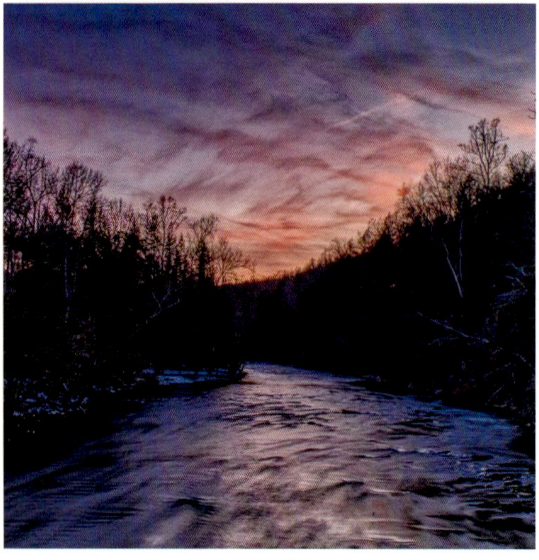

ERIC BRUMBAUGH

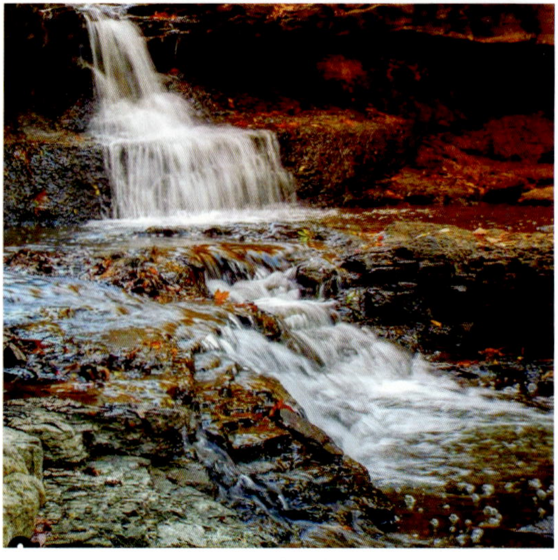

KEVIN GROSE

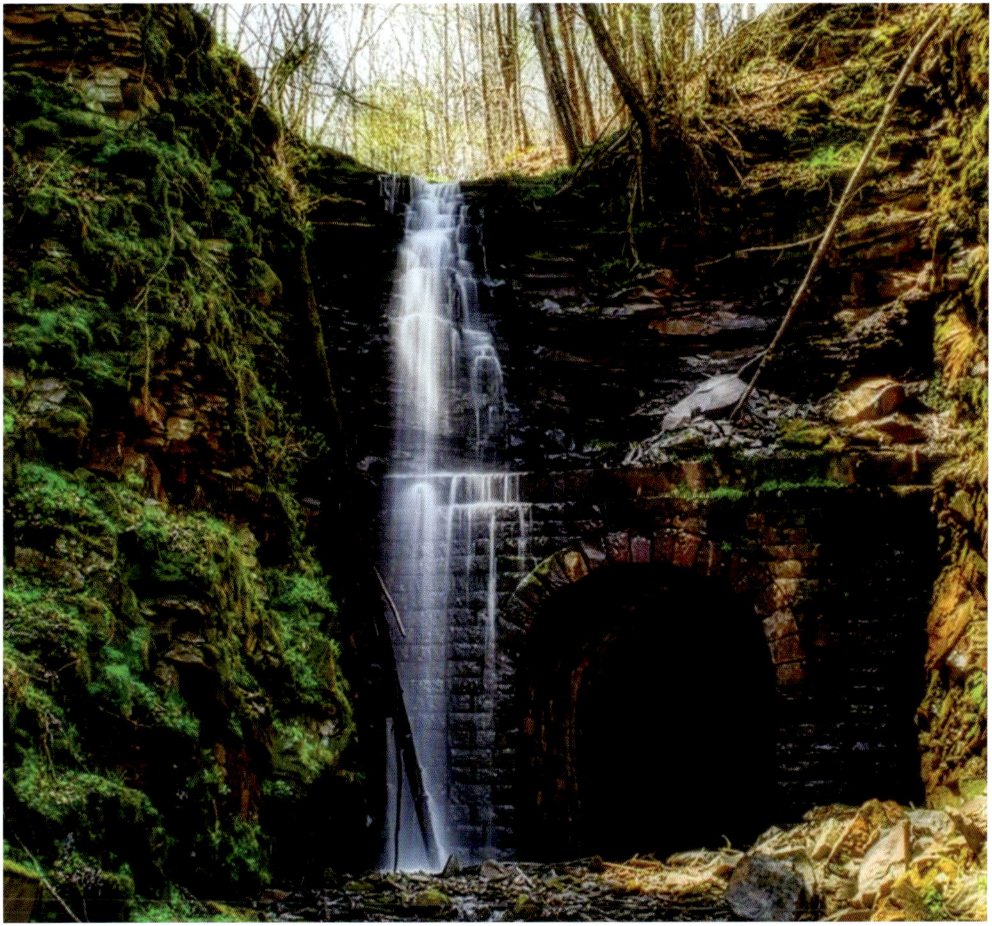

ERIC BRUMBAUGH

places

Photography takes an instant out of time, altering life by holding it still.

- DOROTHEA LANGE

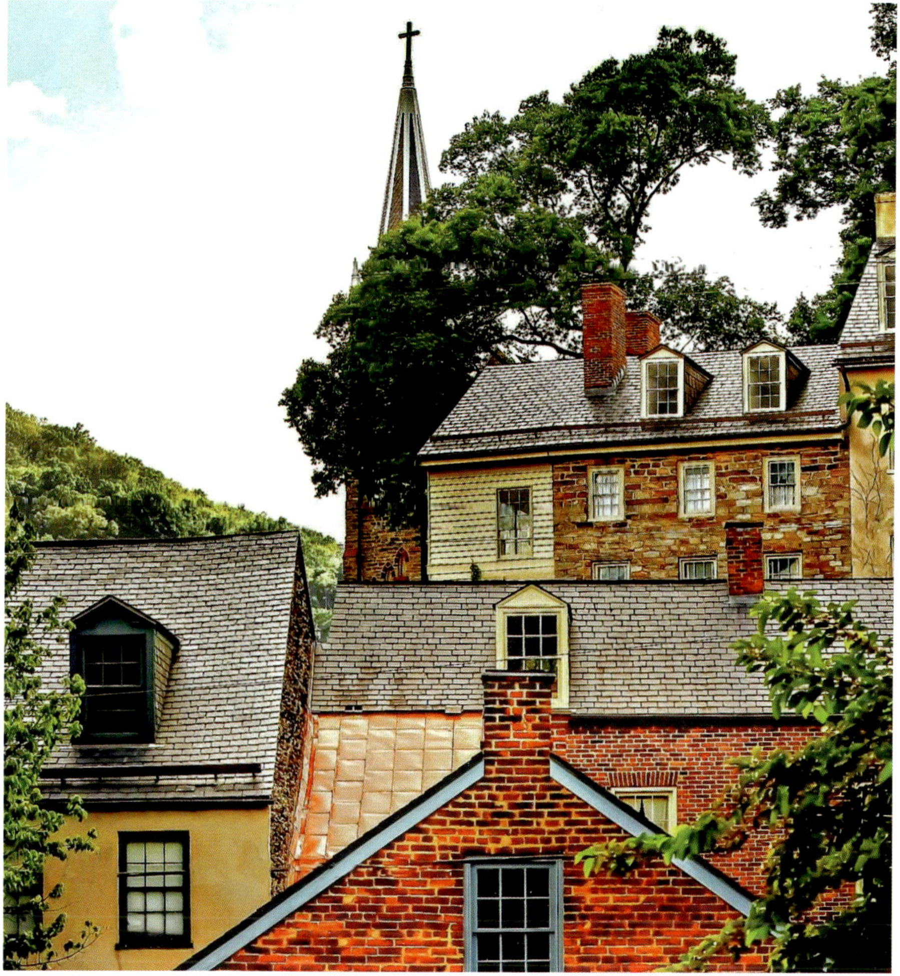

CINDI DUNN

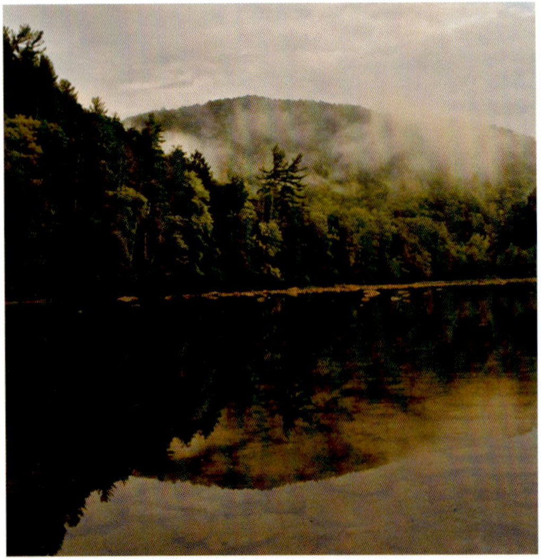

TANNER FARNACK

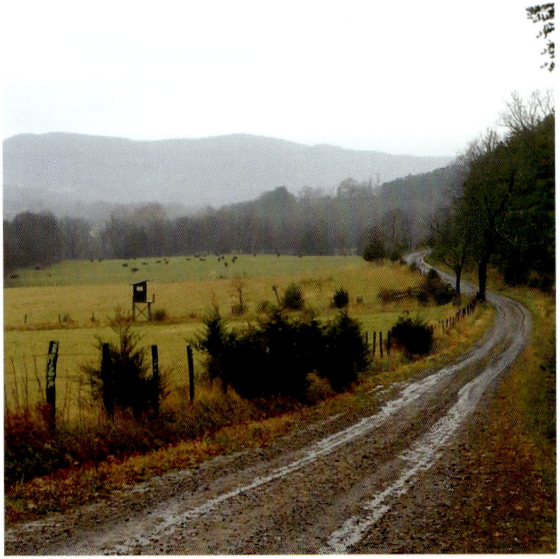

PAT SMITH

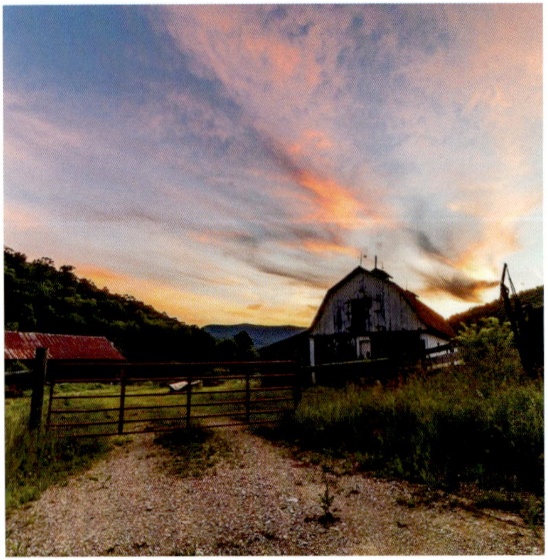

ERIC BRUMBAUGH

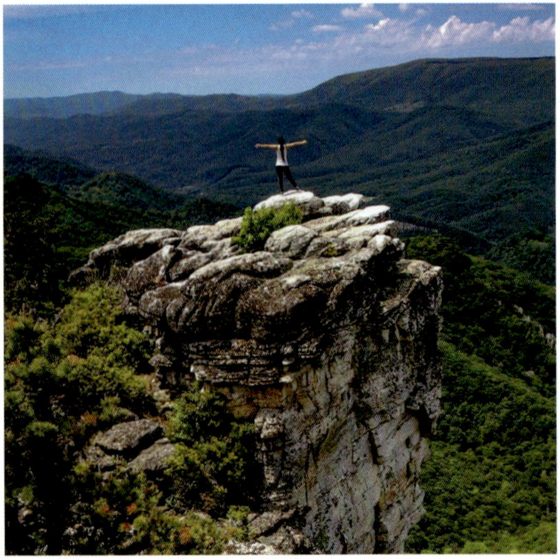

KIMBERLY BYARD

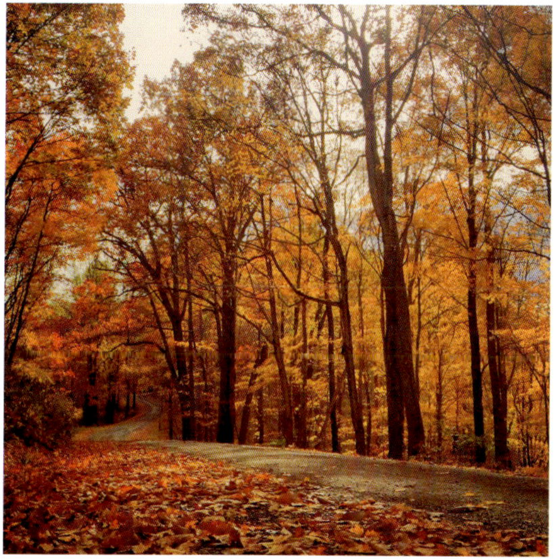

JESSICA STALNAKER

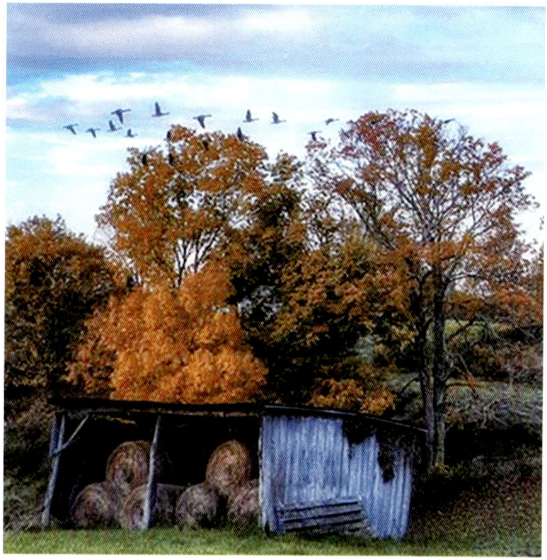

WENDY PARKS

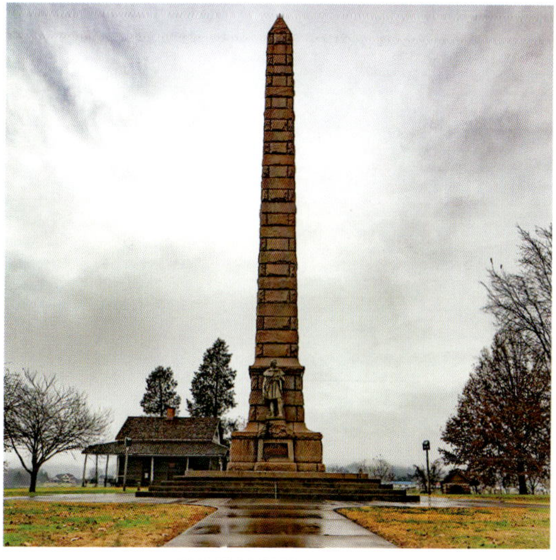

CHARMAGNE AYOTTE

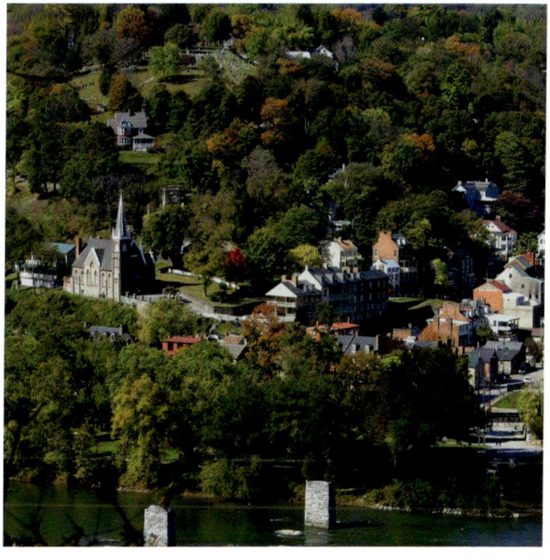

DOUG CRAZE

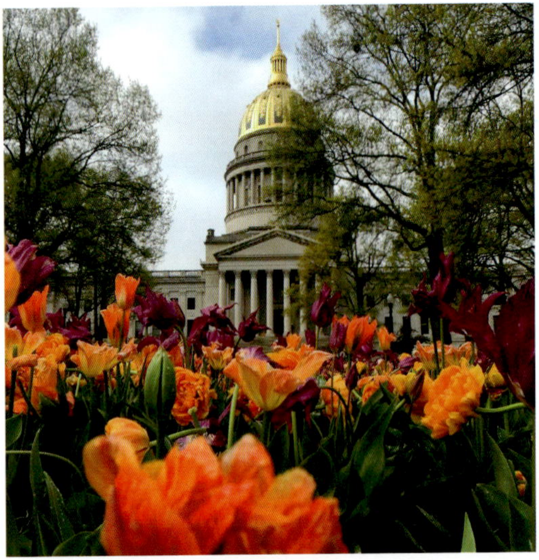

AMY DAMRON

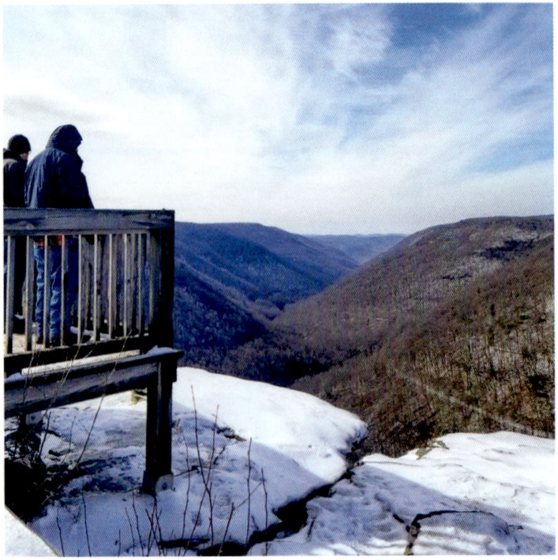

SARAH E. BAILEY

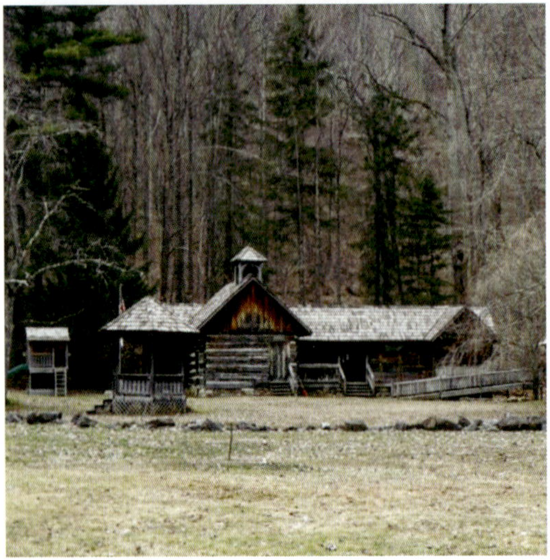

JULIE RATLIFF

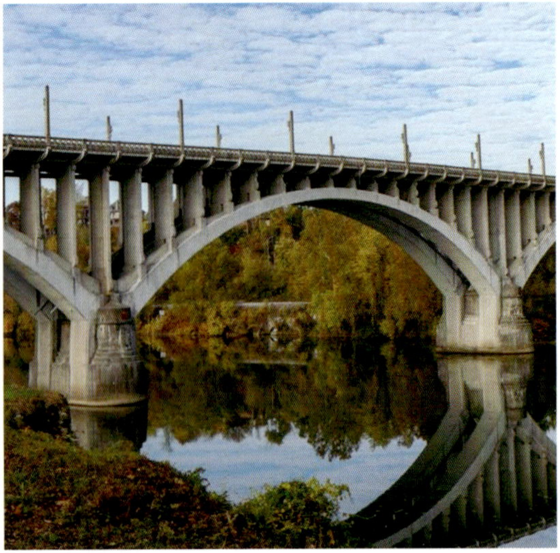

WENDY PARKS

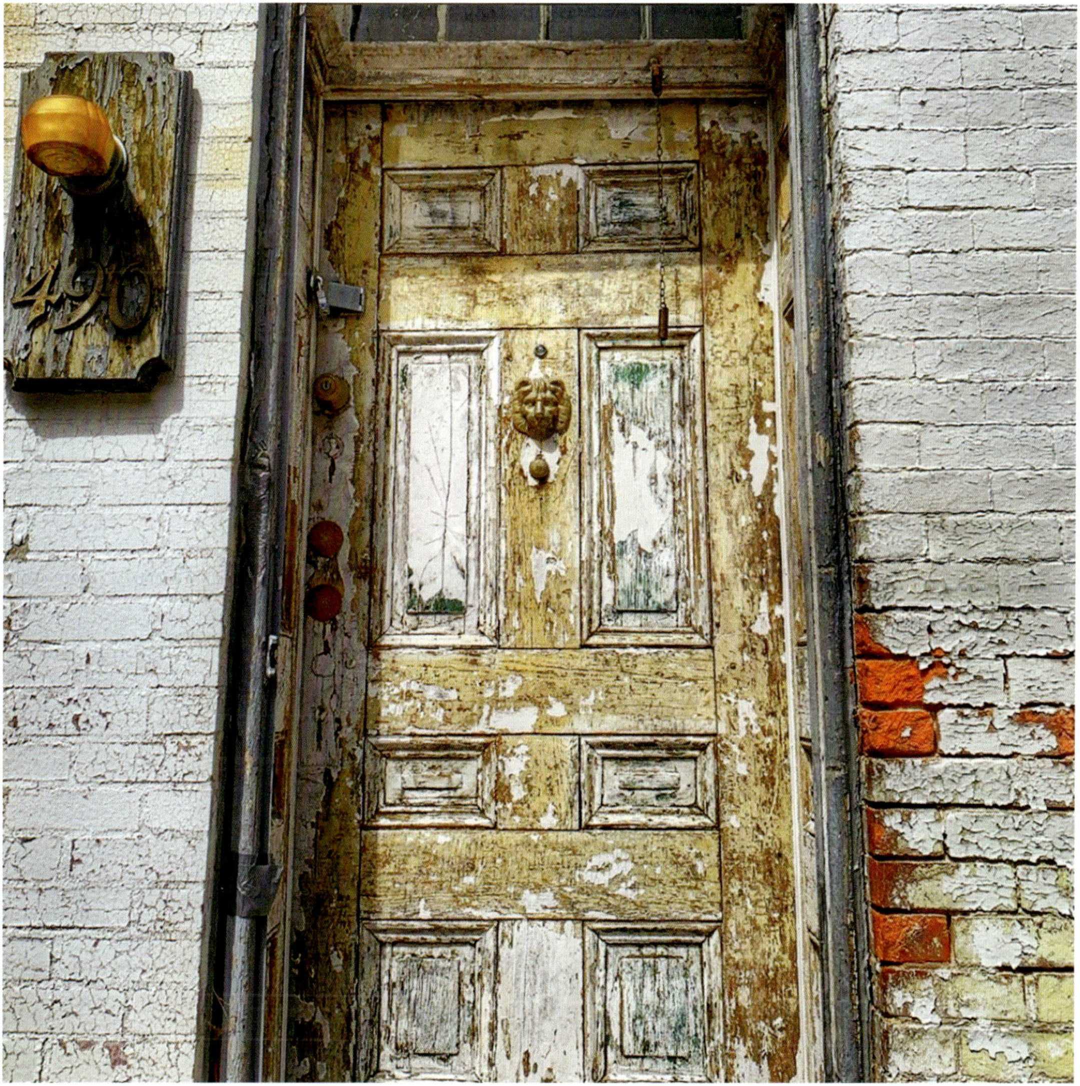

CINDI DUNN

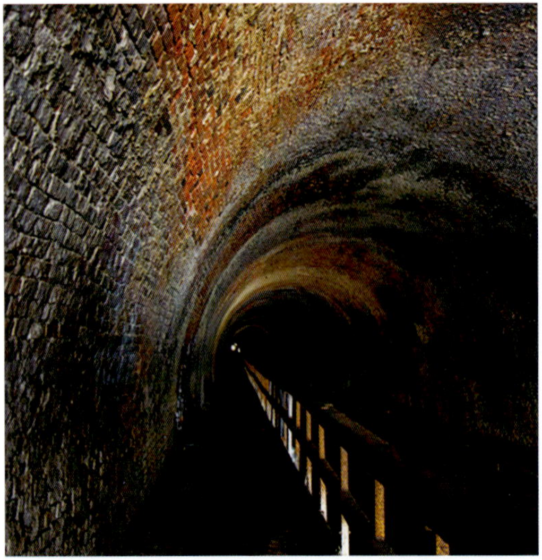
JOHNNIE C. WALTER

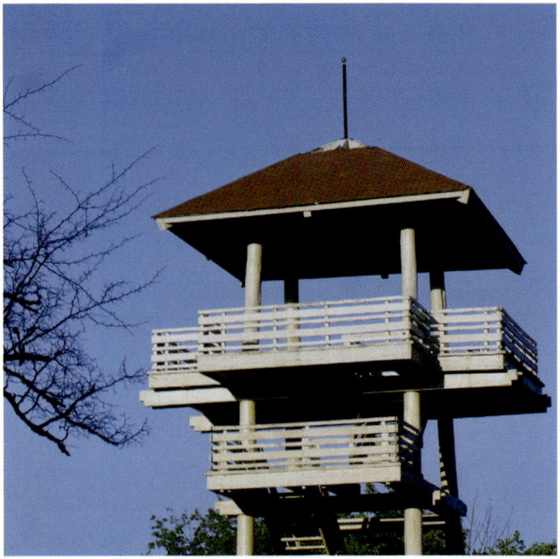
THOMAS C. SEITZ, JR.

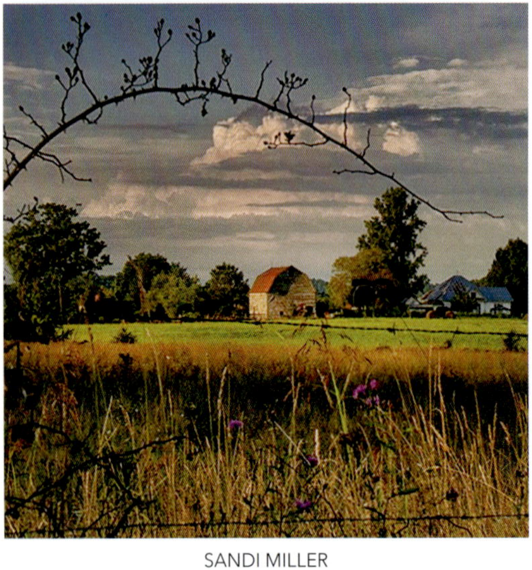
SANDI MILLER

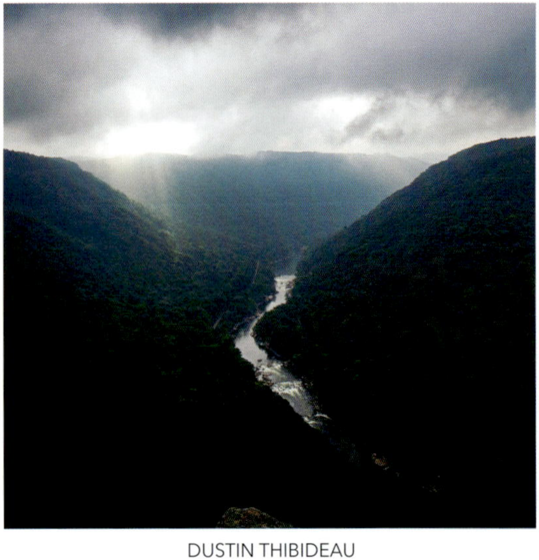
DUSTIN THIBIDEAU

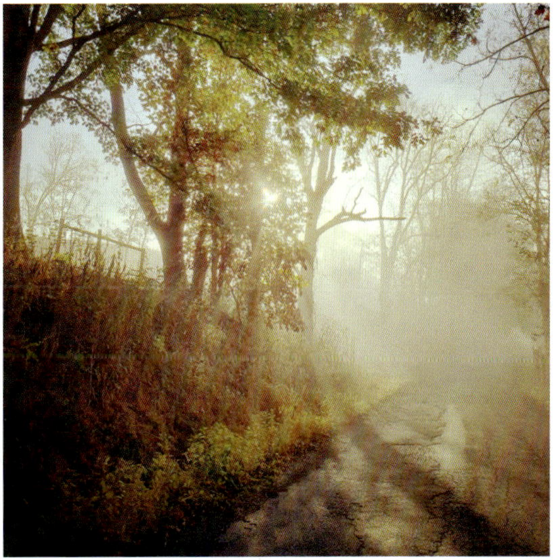

MARLENE COLE

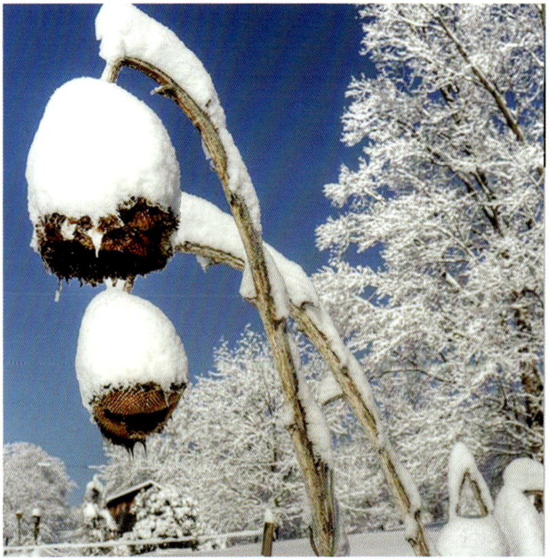

DANNY SNYDER

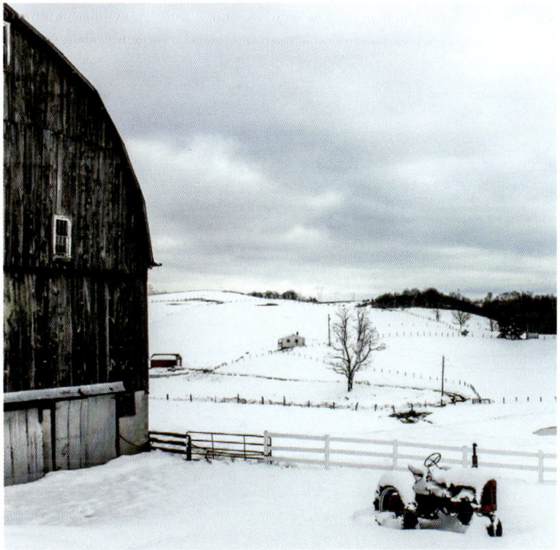

JENNIFER (STONE) TAYLOR

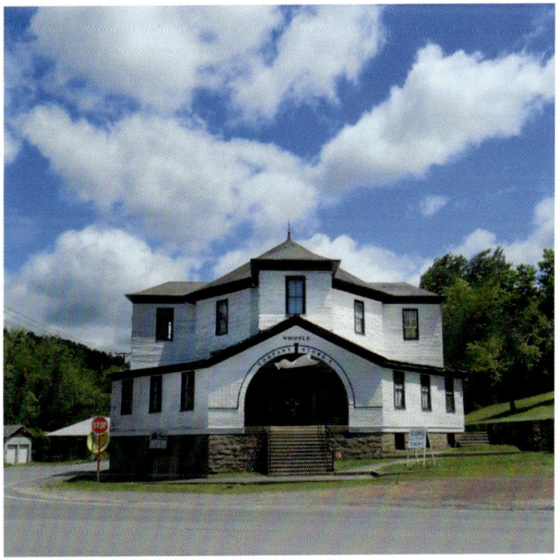

VAL CARNELL

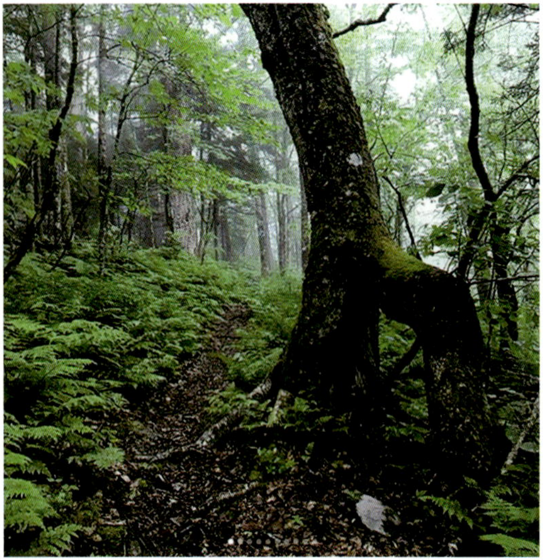

BRENT SCHNUPP

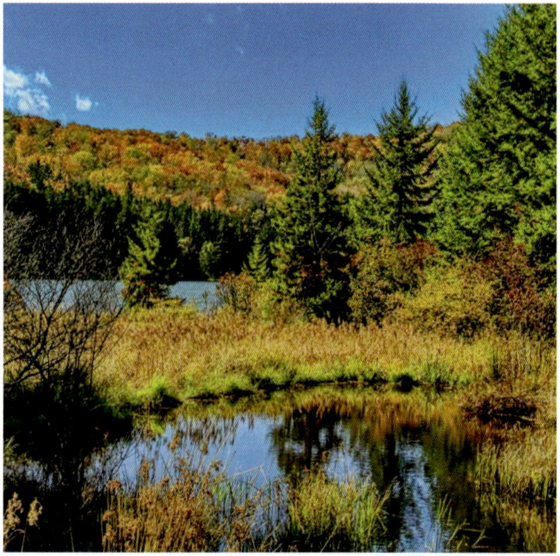

KENDALL BRUMBAUGH

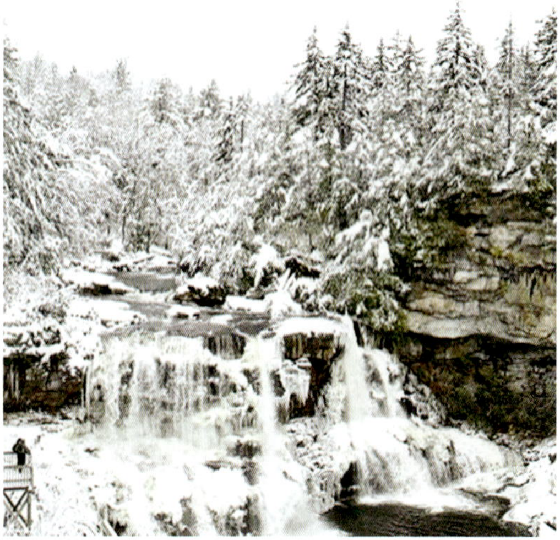

LYDIA FACH

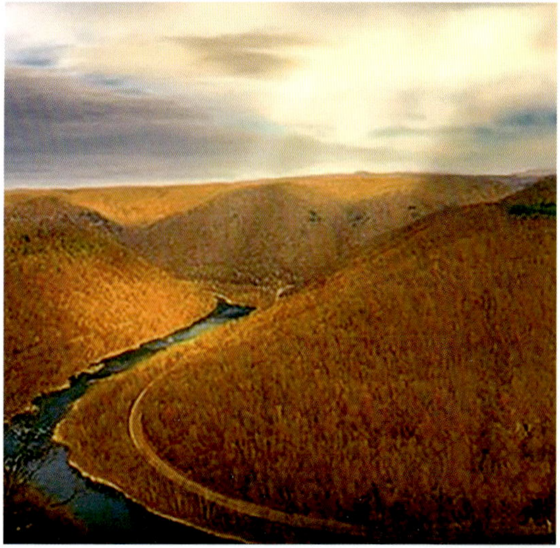

JAMES NICHOLS

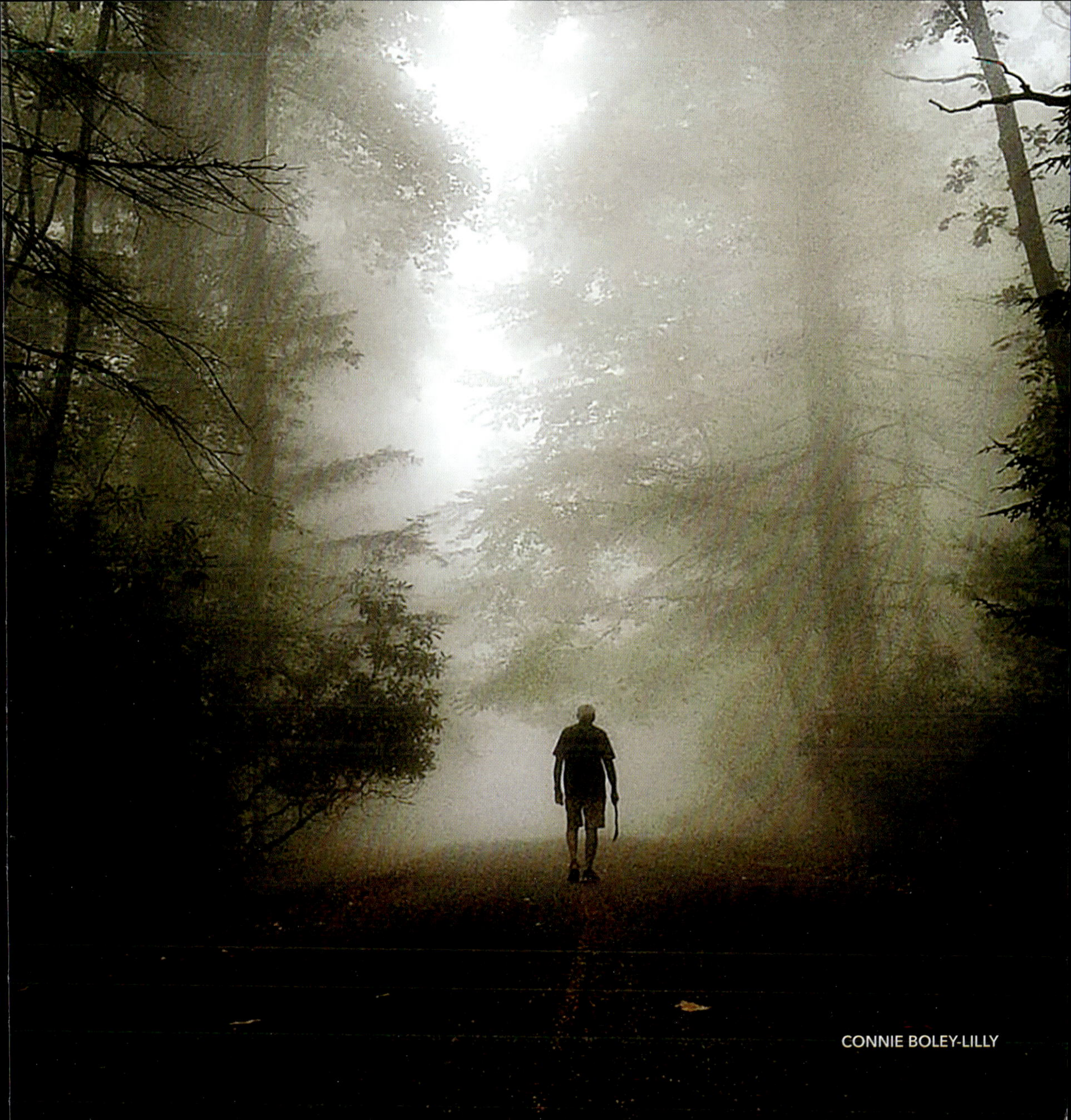

CONNIE BOLEY-LILLY

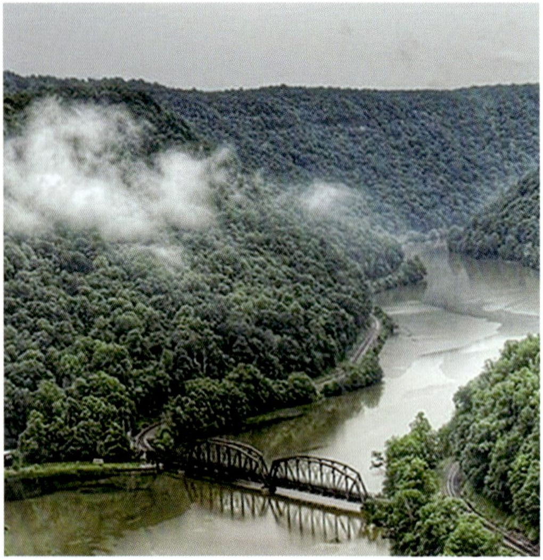

EMILEE GREATHOUSE

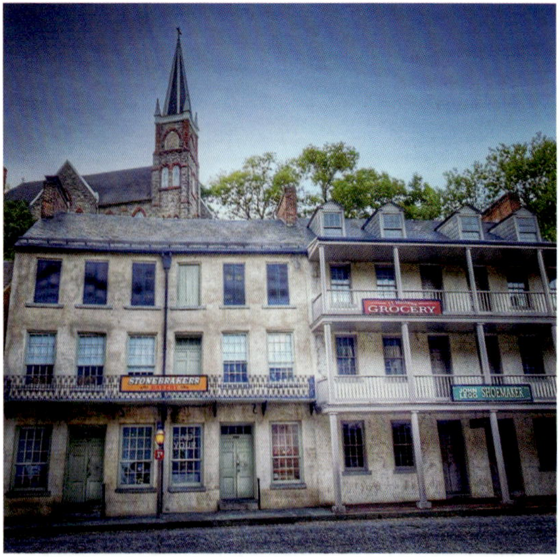

CINDI DUNN

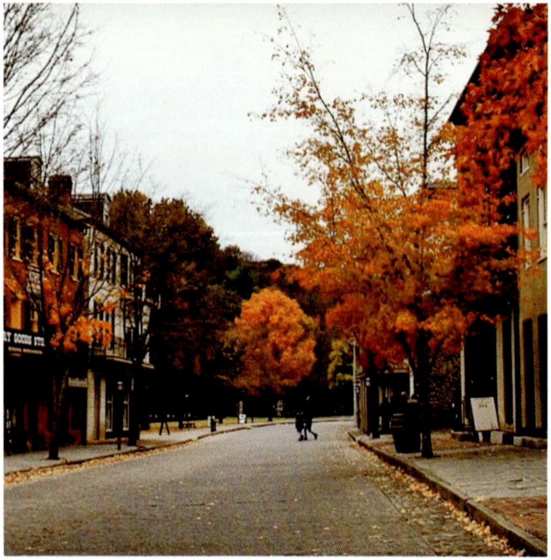

AMBER MESSICK

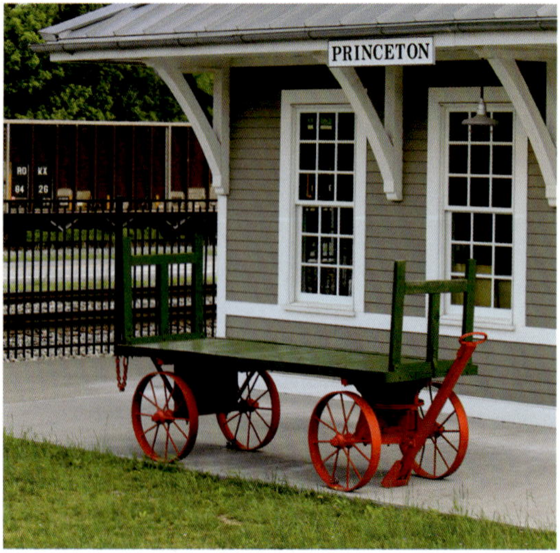

STAN WIKLE

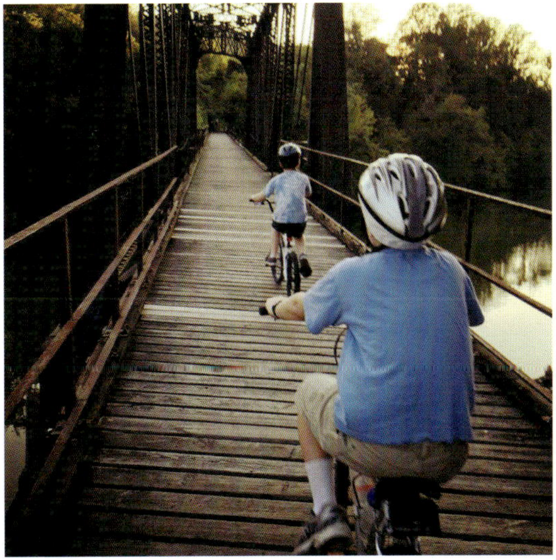

DON DEQUASIE

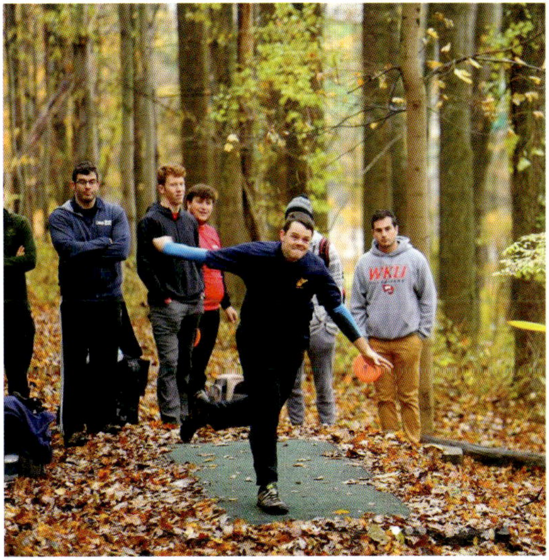

BRIAN BOYCE McCOY

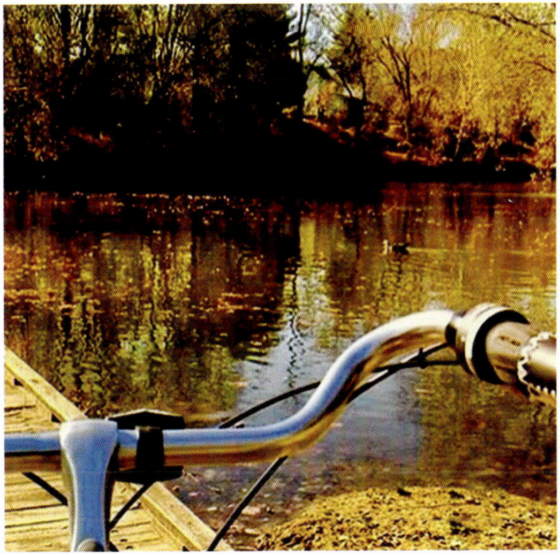

WESLEY PHILP

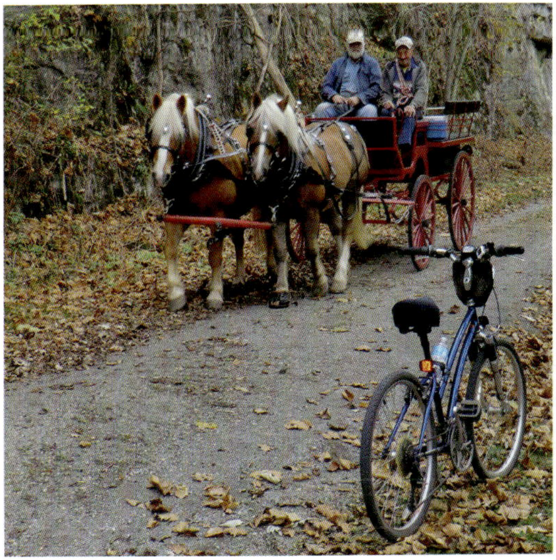

CORALETTA HOUCK

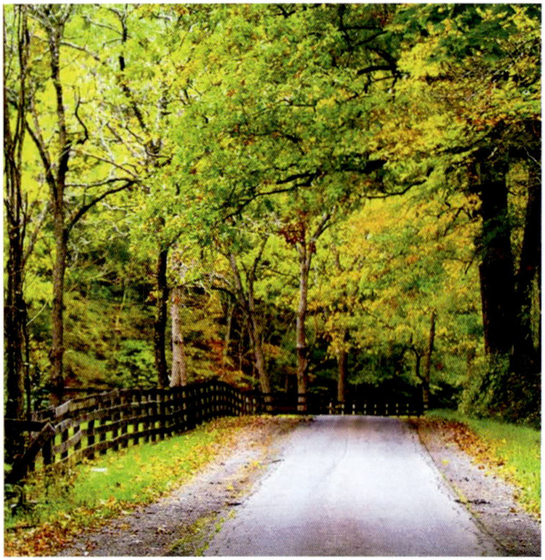

JENNIFER AYERS

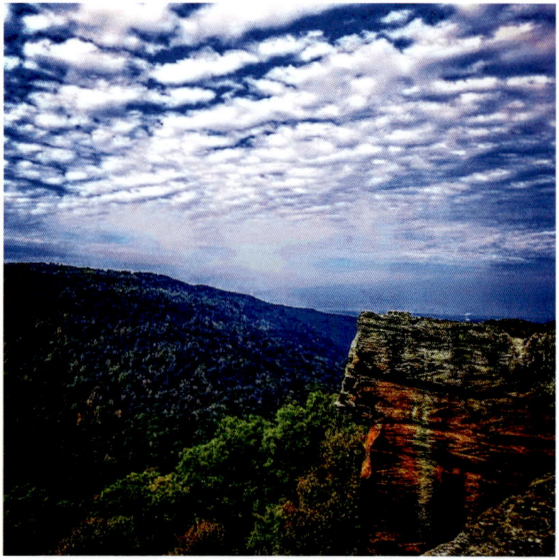

KEVIN GROSE

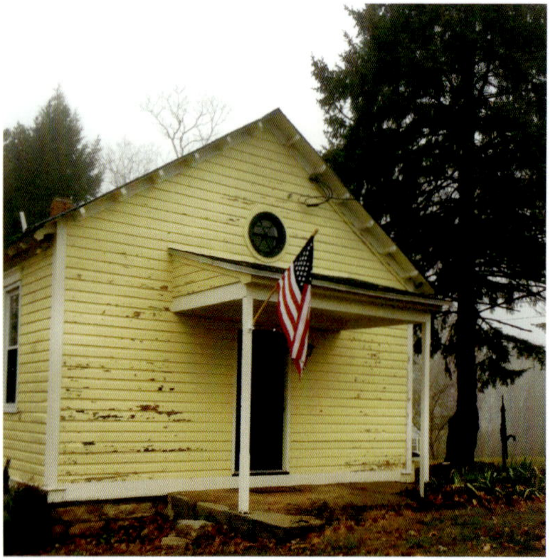

TERESA YOST

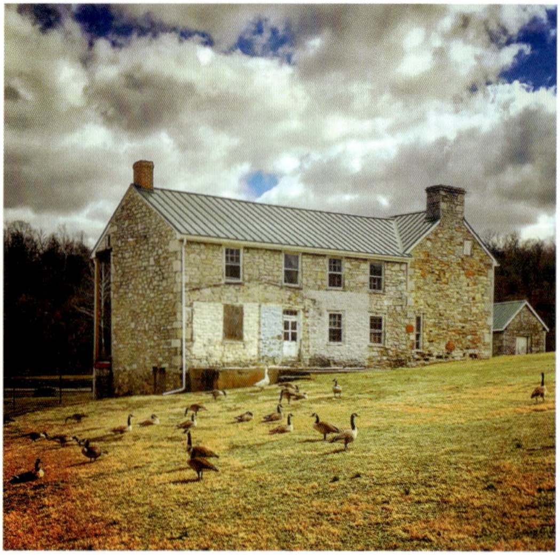

ELAINE CLARK

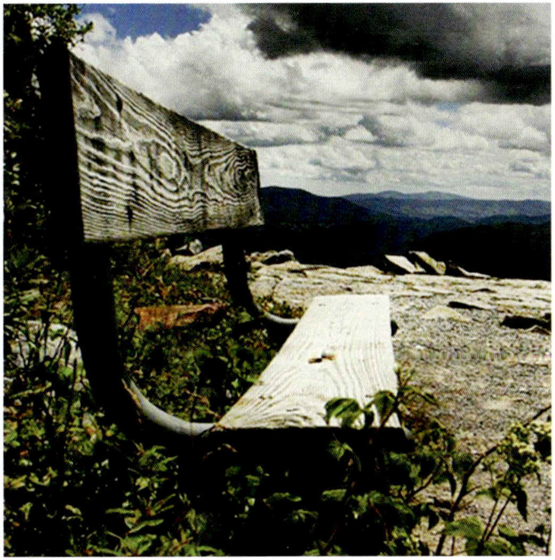

AMBER BALSINGER

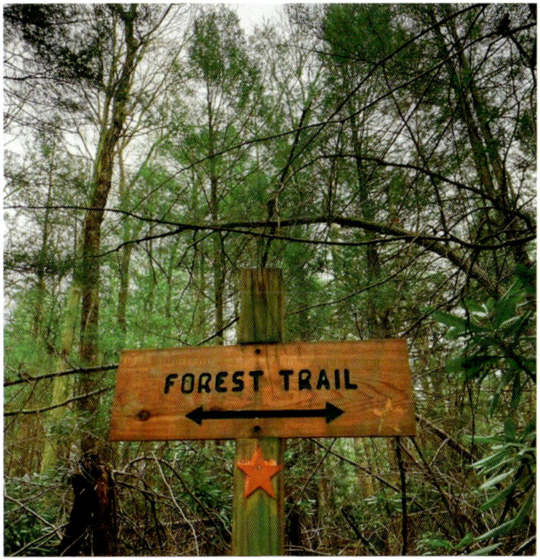

HUNTER BAUER

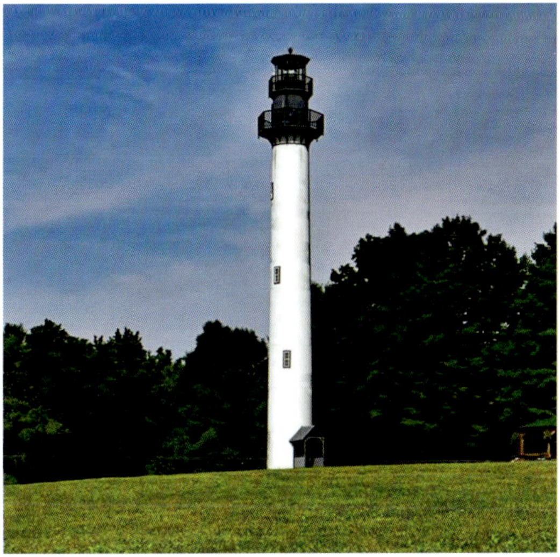

RONDA LEGG

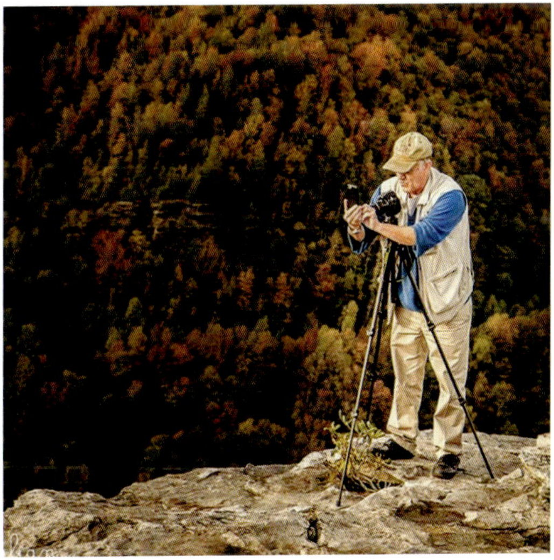

DENISE POWERS FABIAN

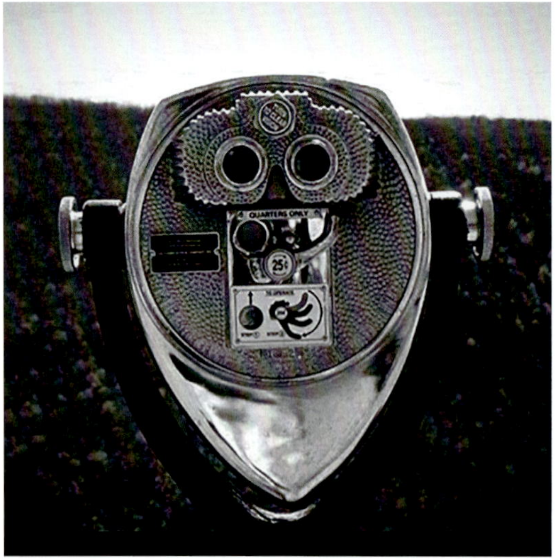

AMBER BALISINGER

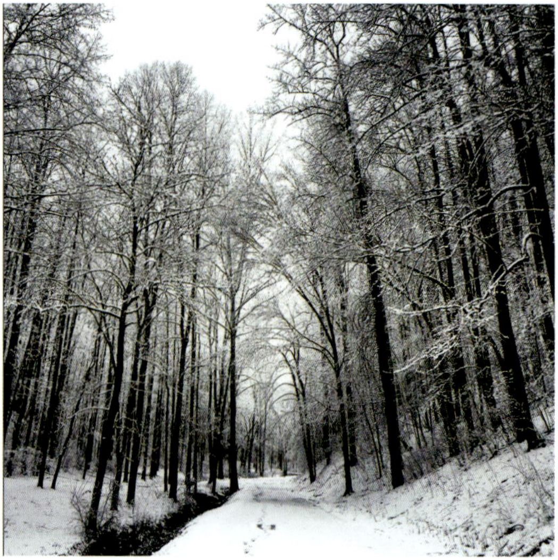

BO KENNEDY

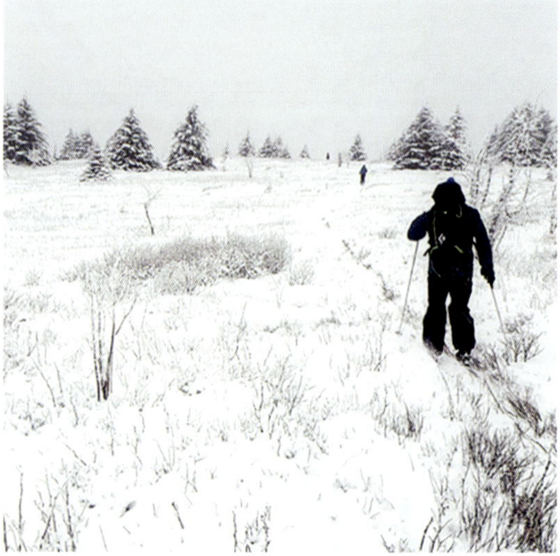

LIZ STOUT

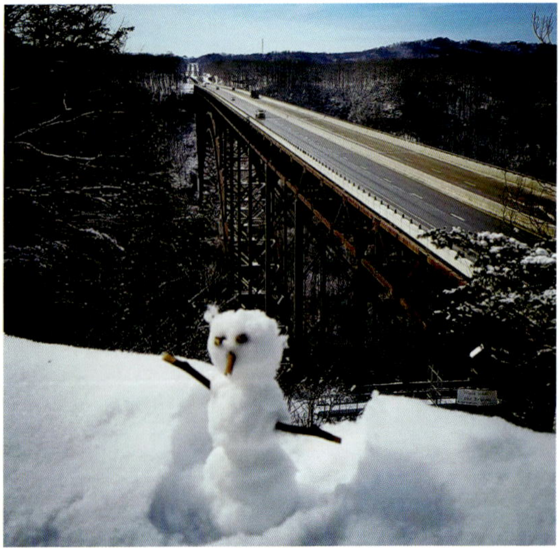

CONNIE BOLEY-LILLY

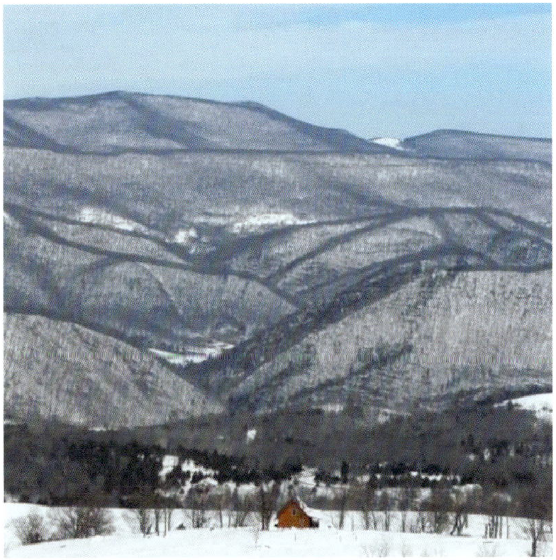

CYNTHIA MULLENS

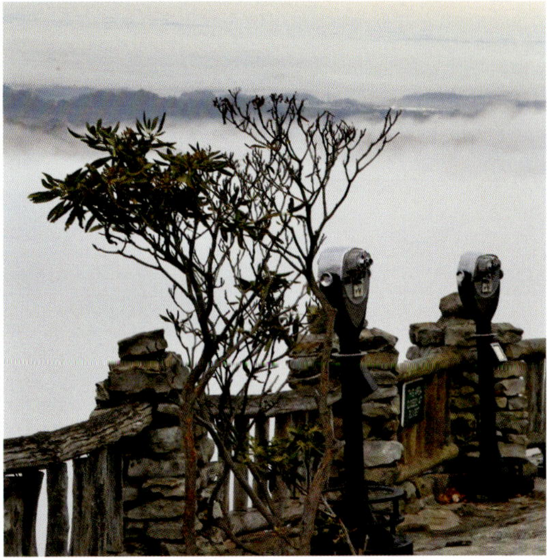

KIMBERLY FOWLER

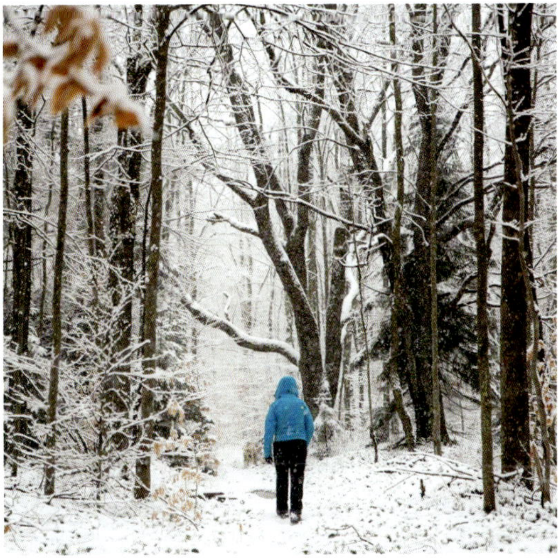

LIZ STOUT

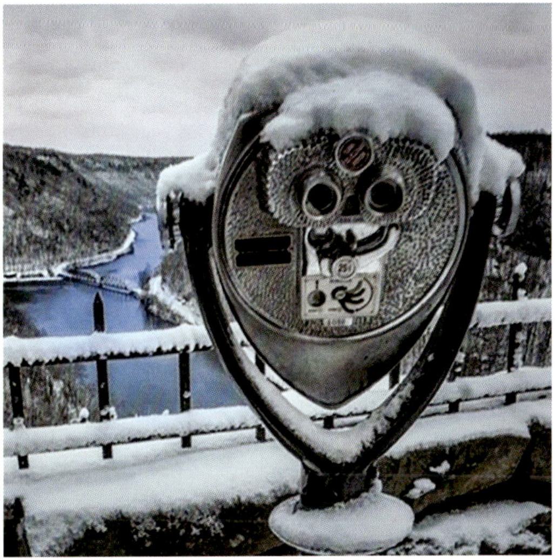

TOM DEAN

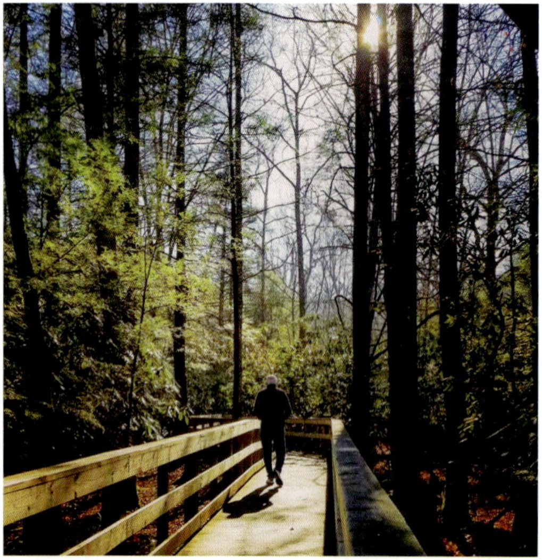

CONNIE BOLEY-LILLY

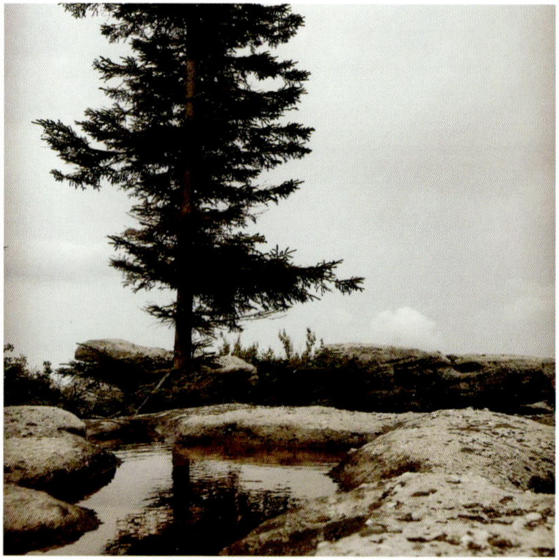

AMBER MESSICK

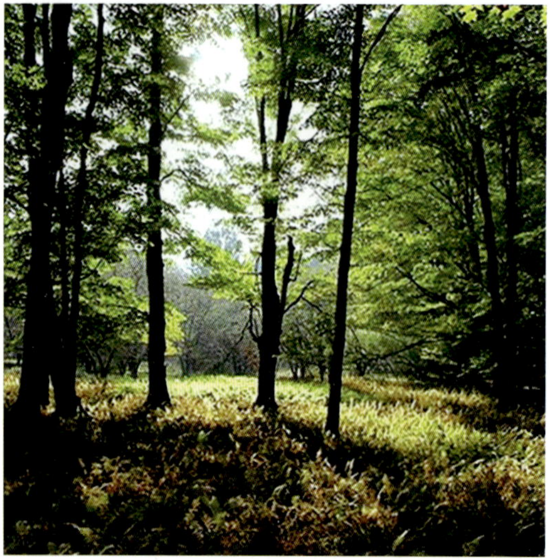

RENAU LUCAS

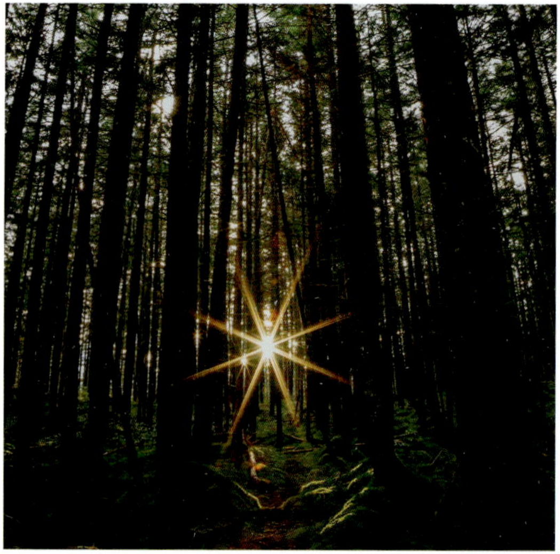

NICOLE VIEWS

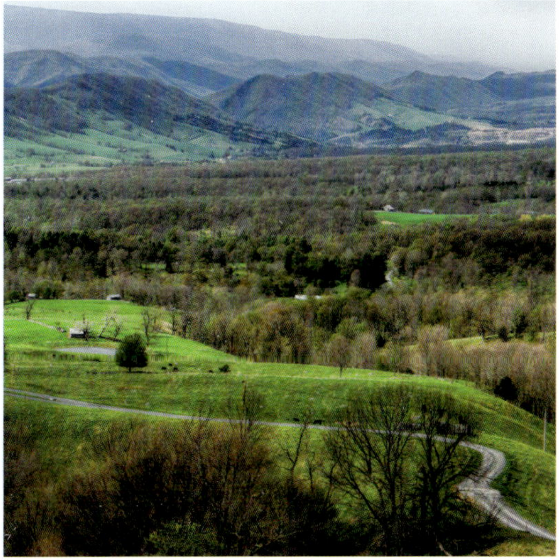
LAURA MOUL

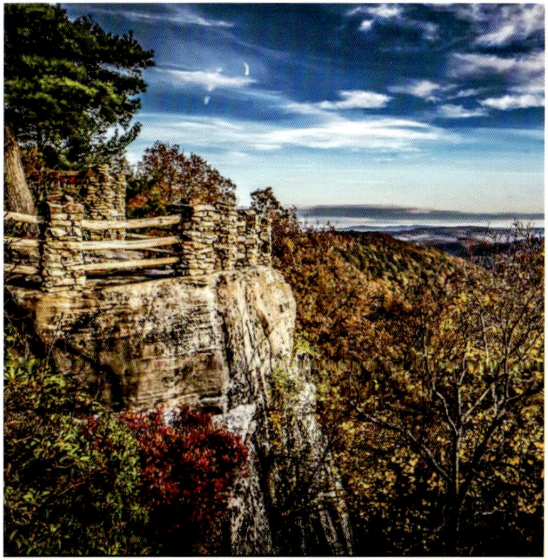
WENDY PARKS

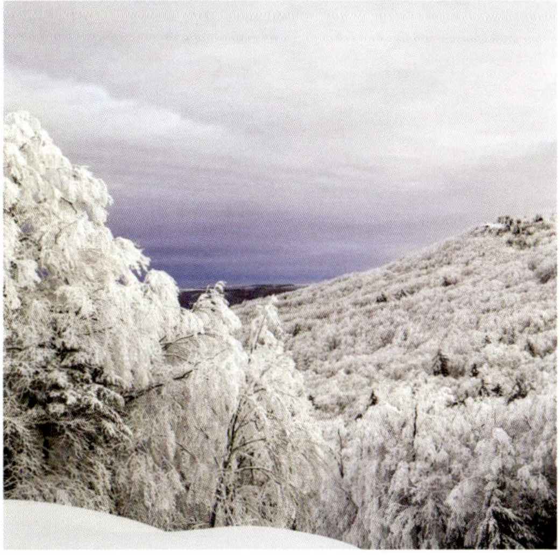
LIZ STOUT

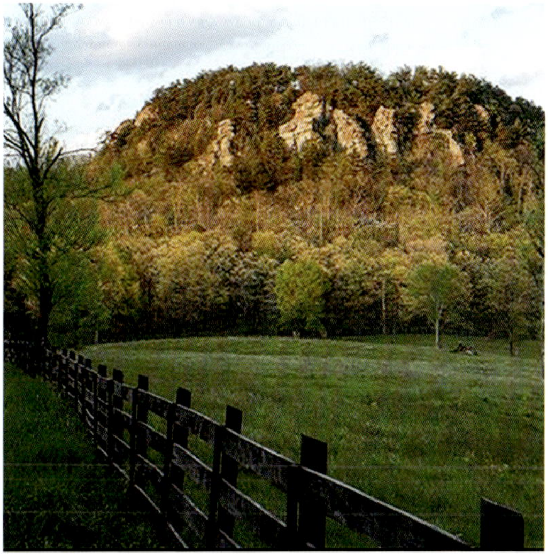
BRIAN BOYCE McCOY

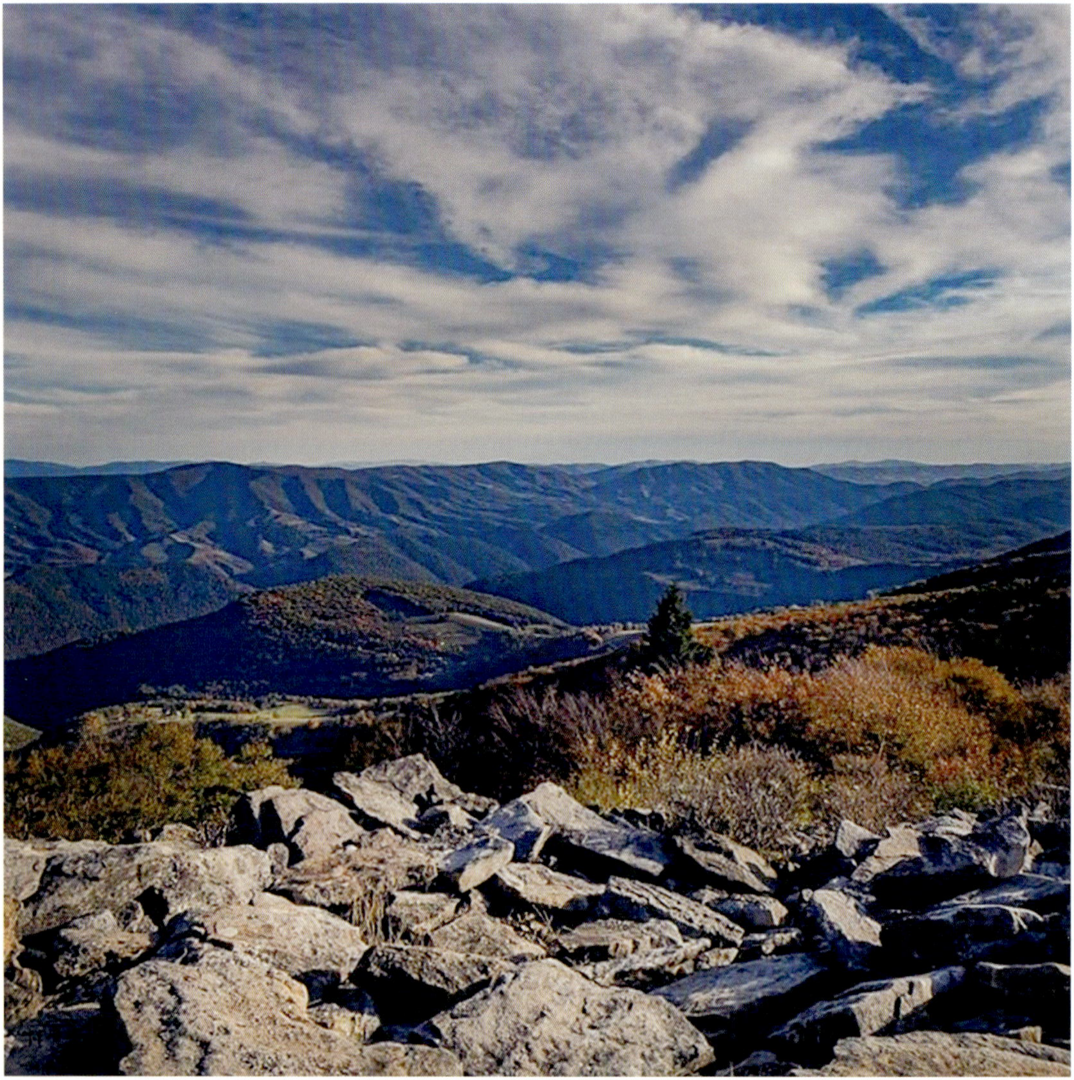

BRENT SCHNUPP

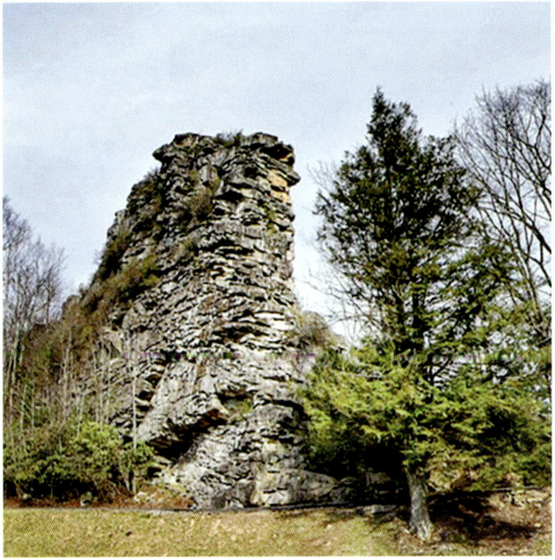

EMILEE GREATHOUSE

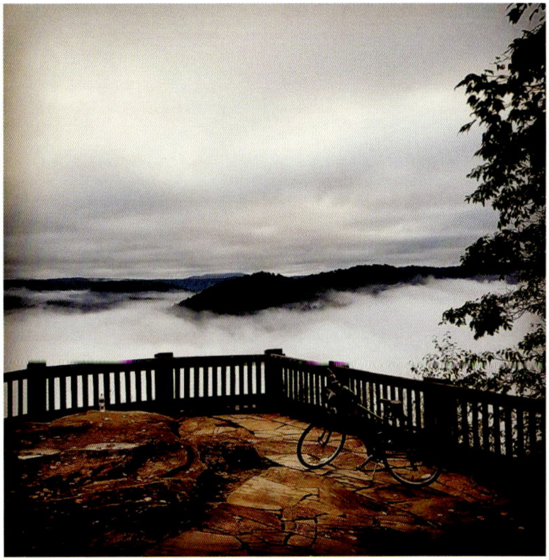

CONNIE BOLEY-LILLY

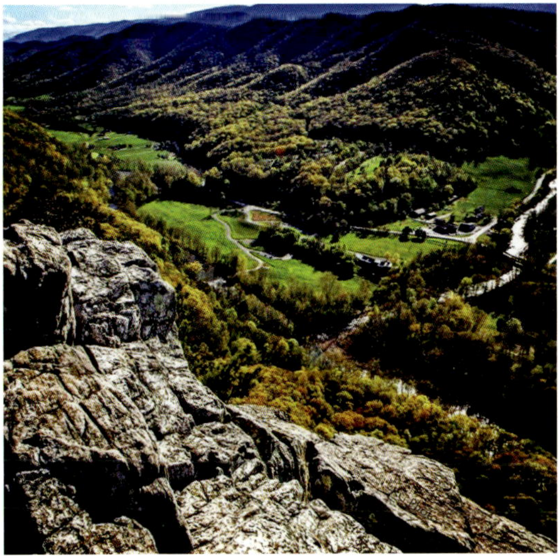

KEVIN GROSE

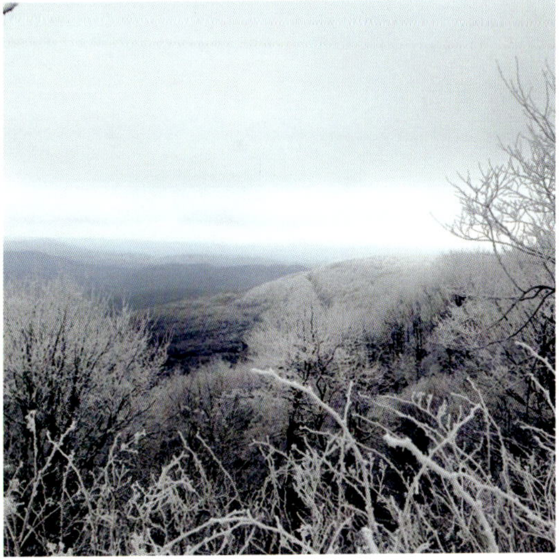

JEANNIE HANNA

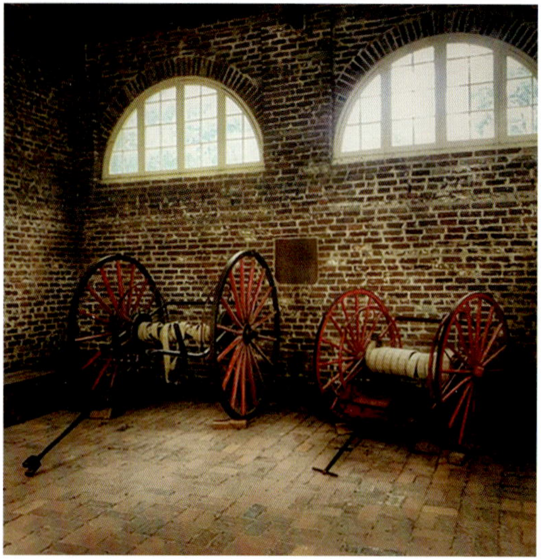

CINDI DUNN

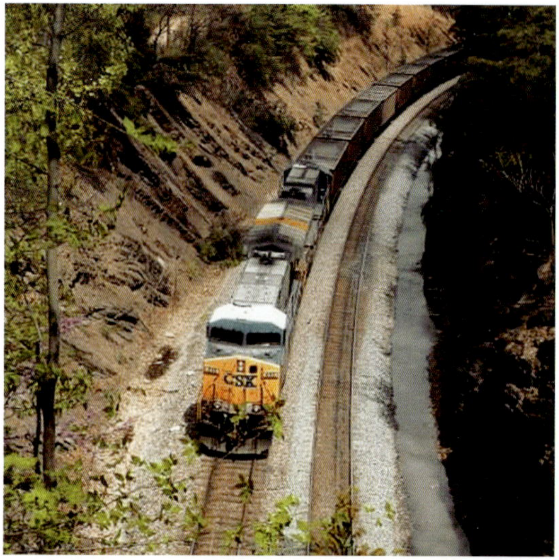

BOBBIE JO DeHAVEN

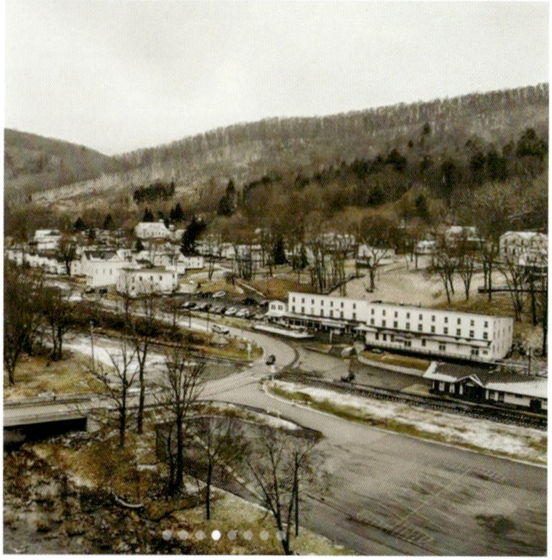

BRENT SCHNUPP

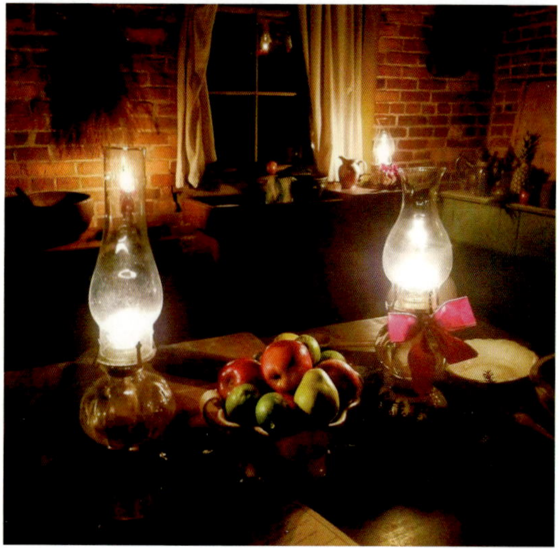

WENDY PARKS

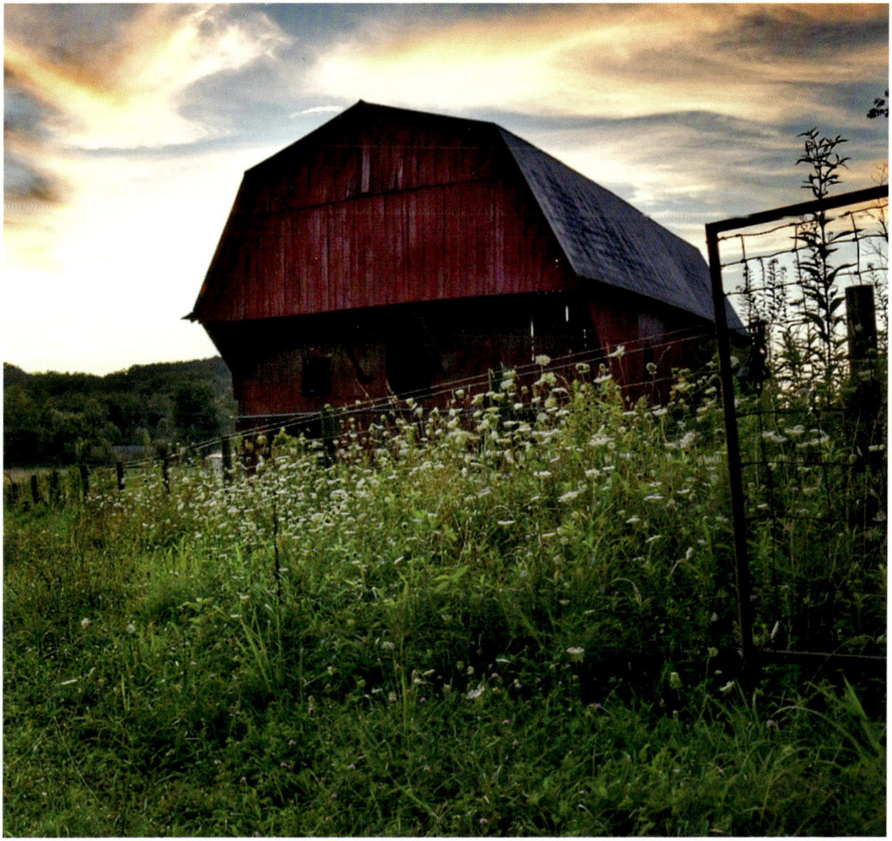

EMILEE GREATHOUSE

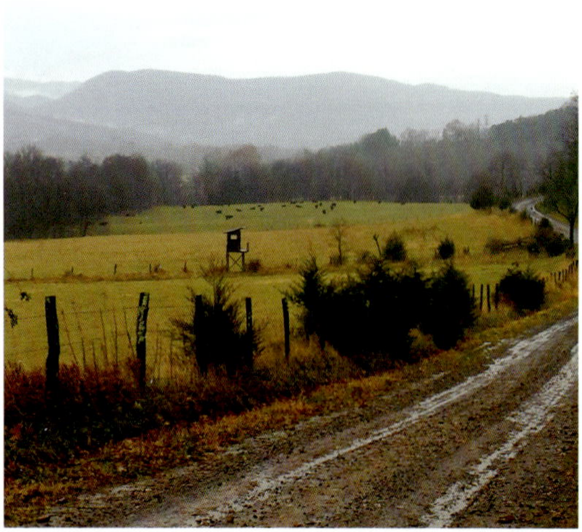

PAT SMITH

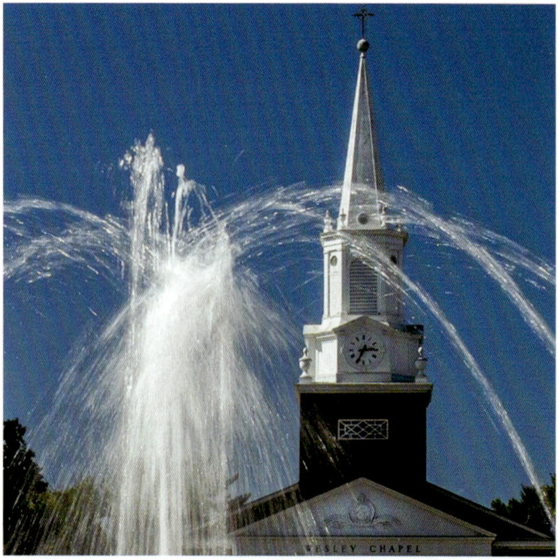

SANDI MILLER

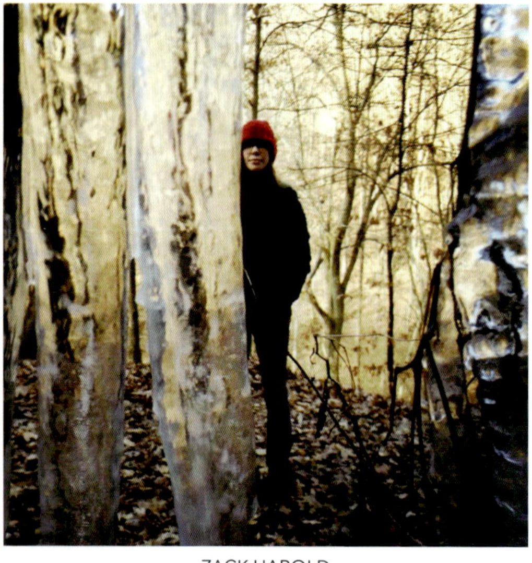

ZACK HAROLD

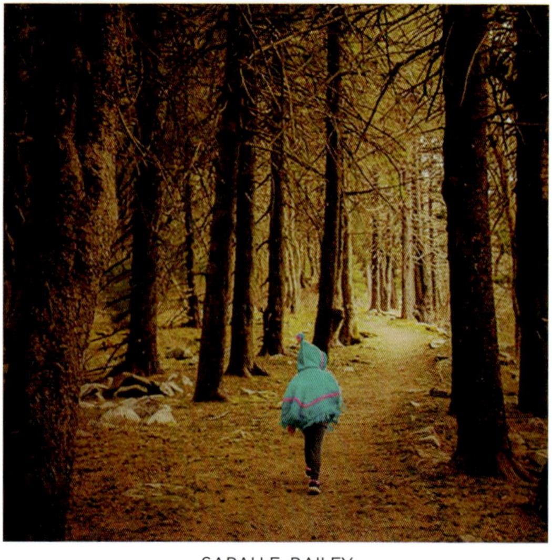

SARAH E. BAILEY

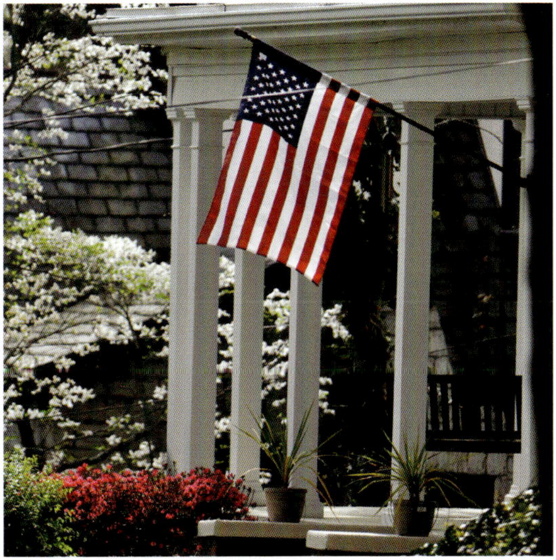

TOM HINDMAN

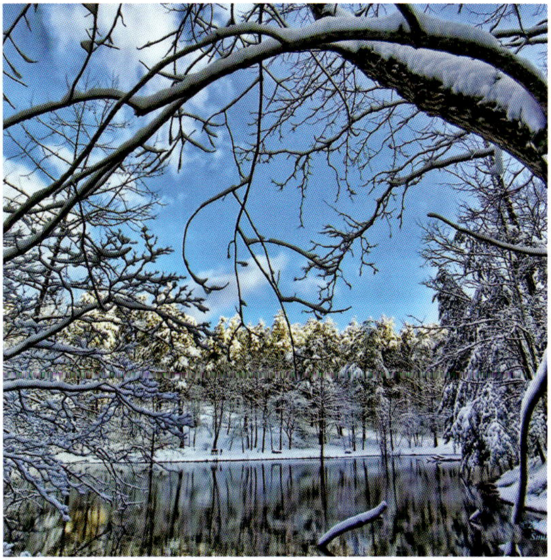

RICHARD MARLOW

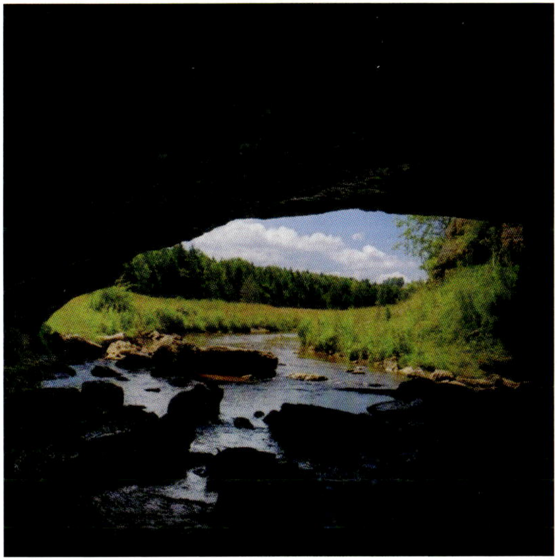

TOM DEAN

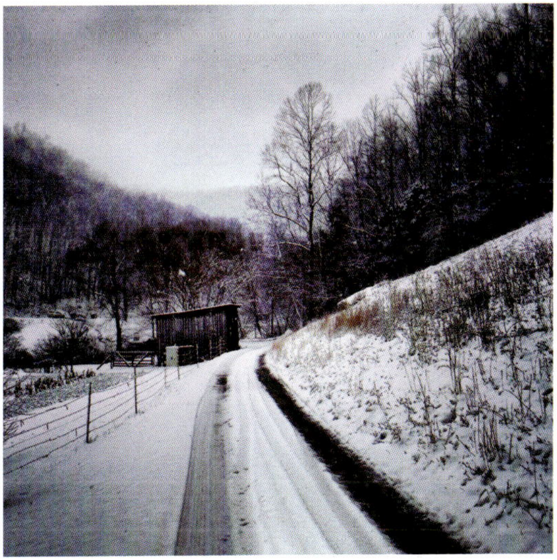

DIANA KEES

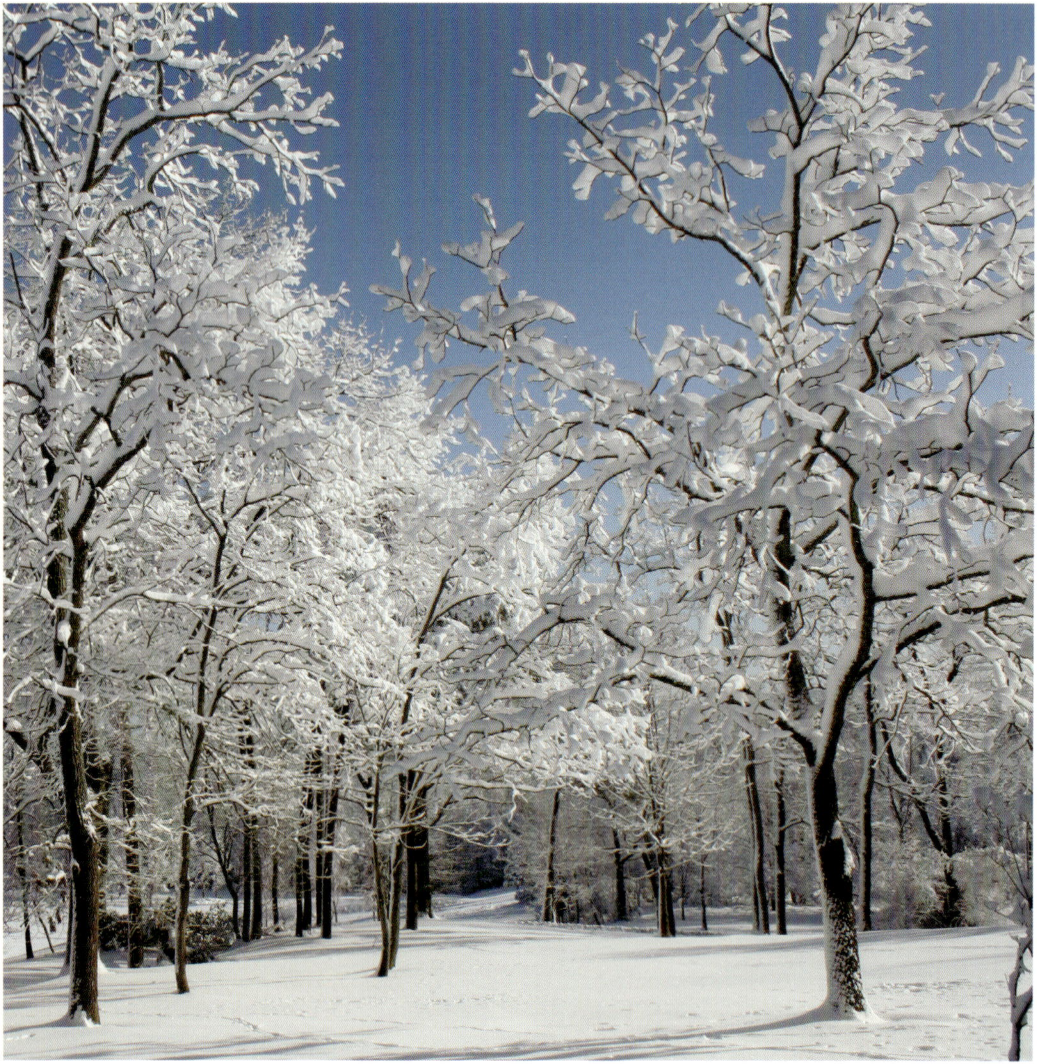

CARLETTA JOHNSTON

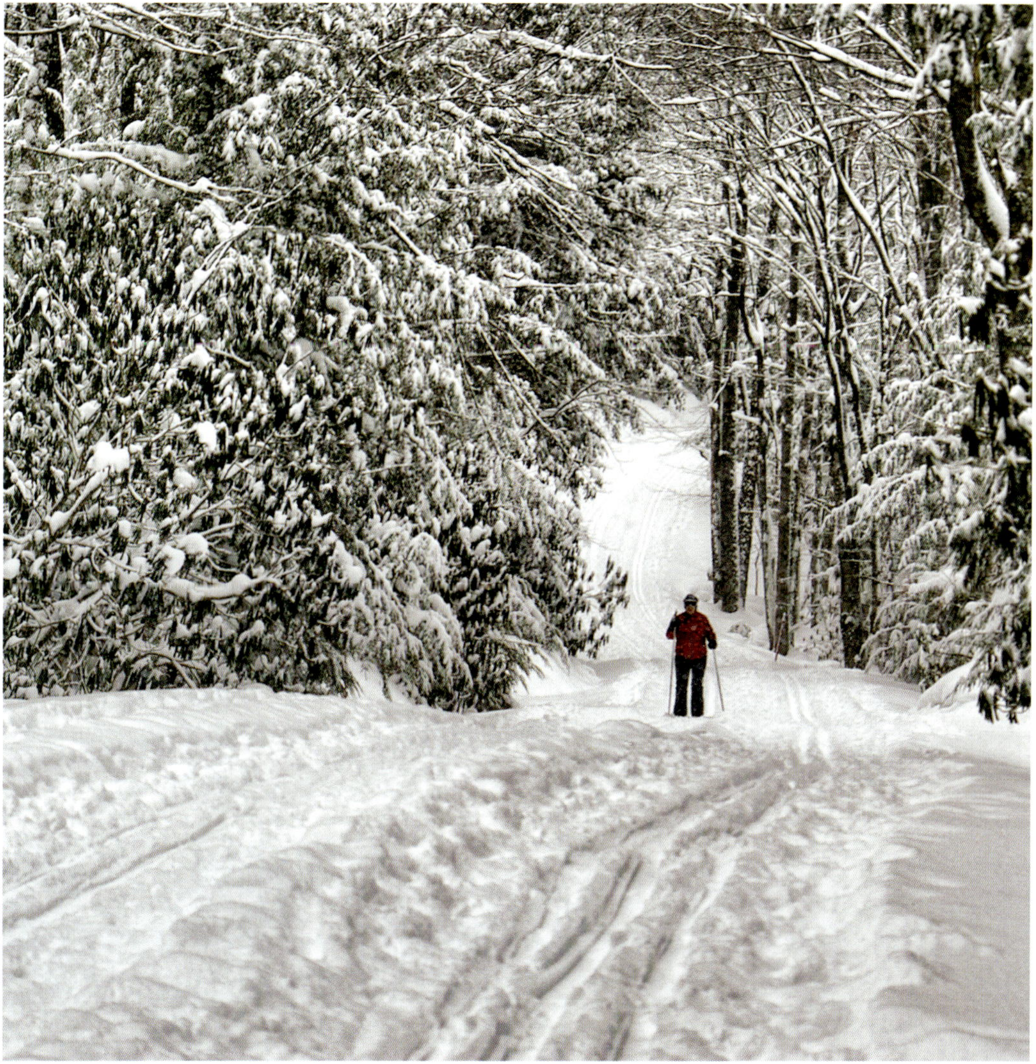

LAURA MOUL

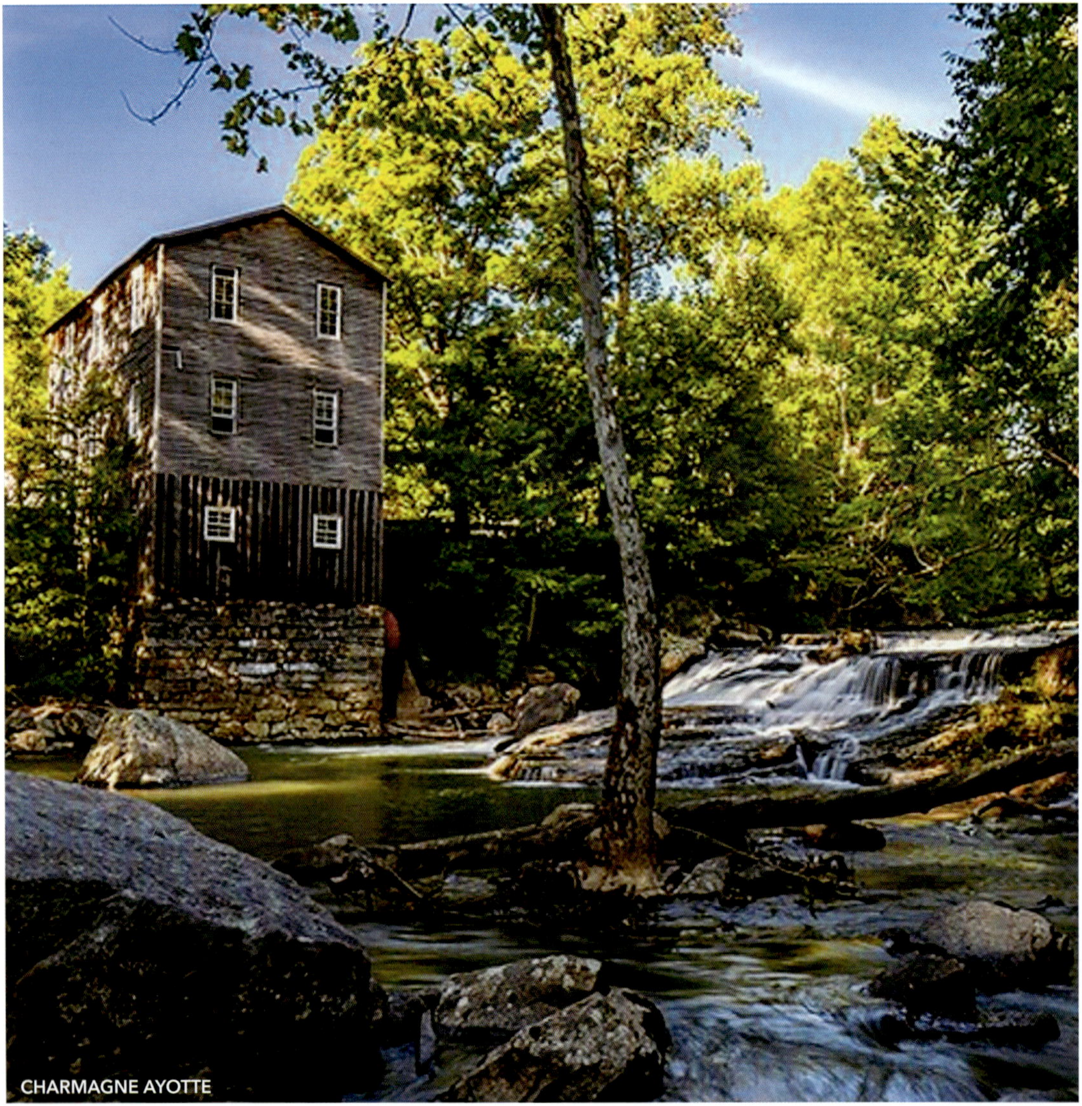
CHARMAGNE AYOTTE

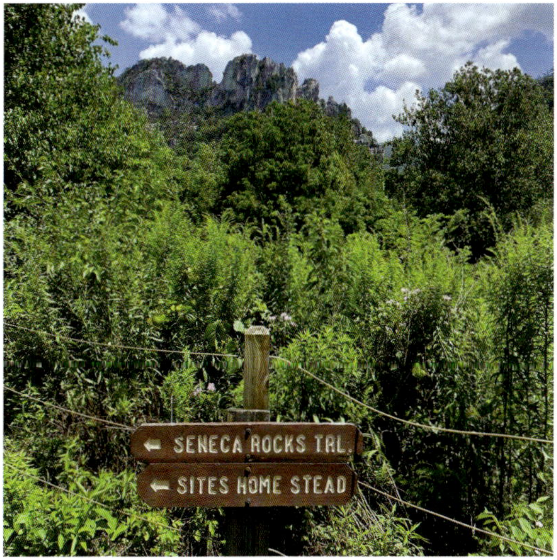

HUNTER BAUER

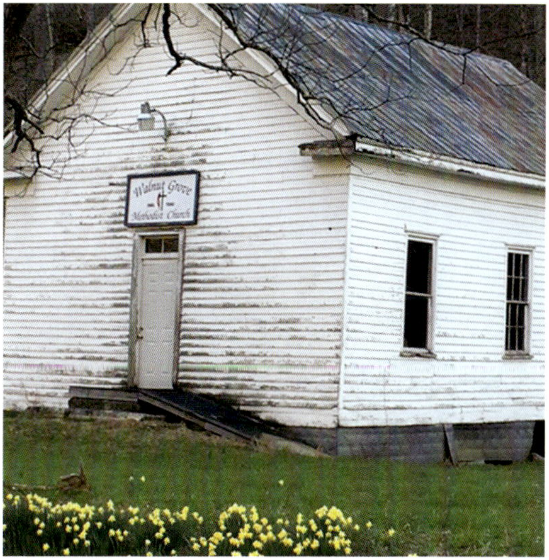

JEANETTE CHAMBERS

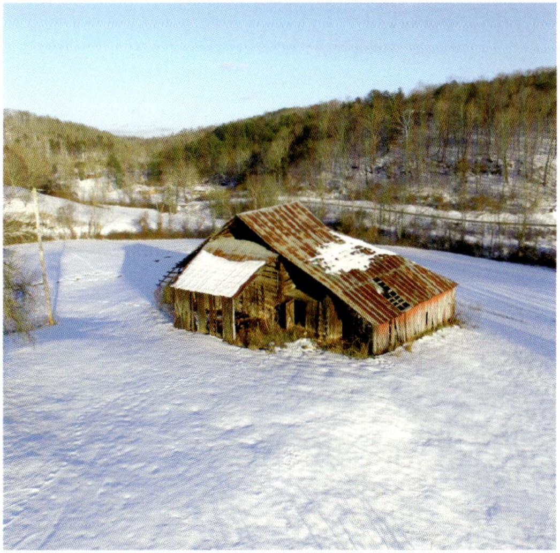

ROBERT LOVEJOY

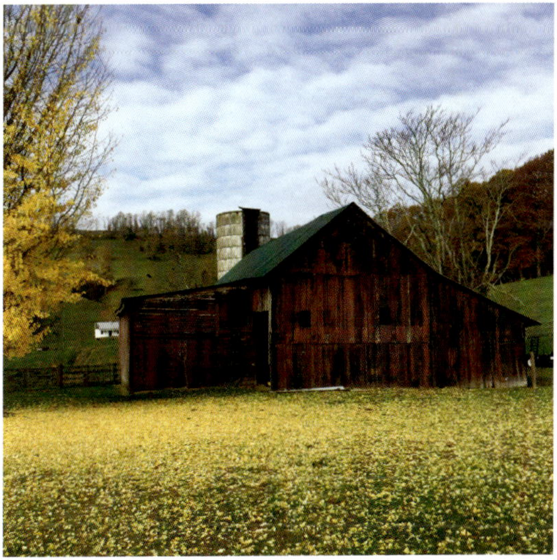

CHRYSTAL SKINNER

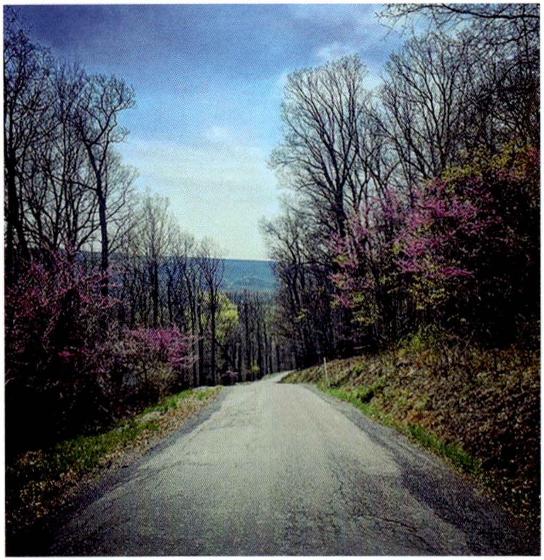

ELAINE CLARK

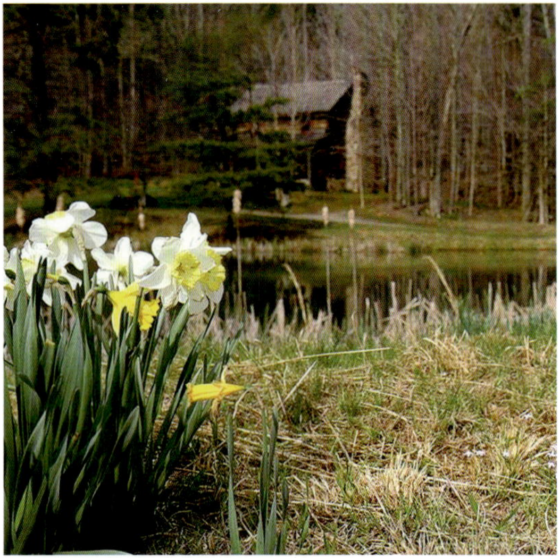

SHARON KAY CARPER

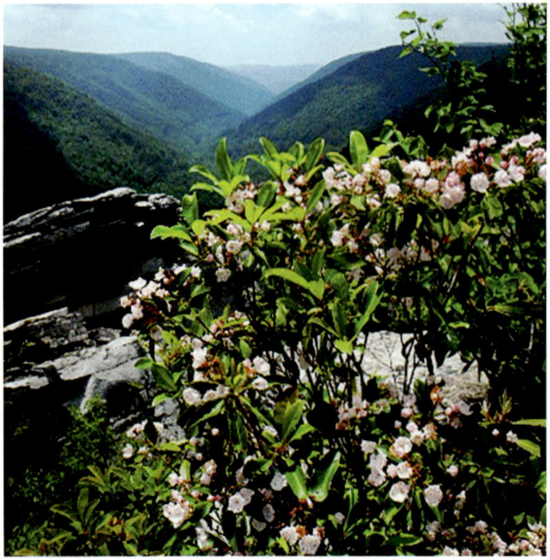

ARNOLD PARRISH

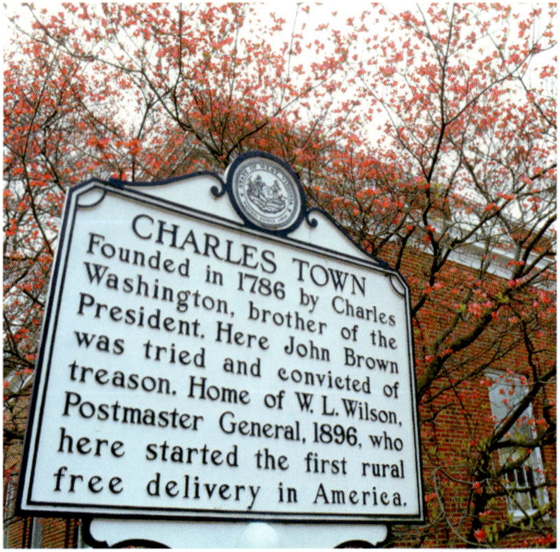

JANICE SCOTT

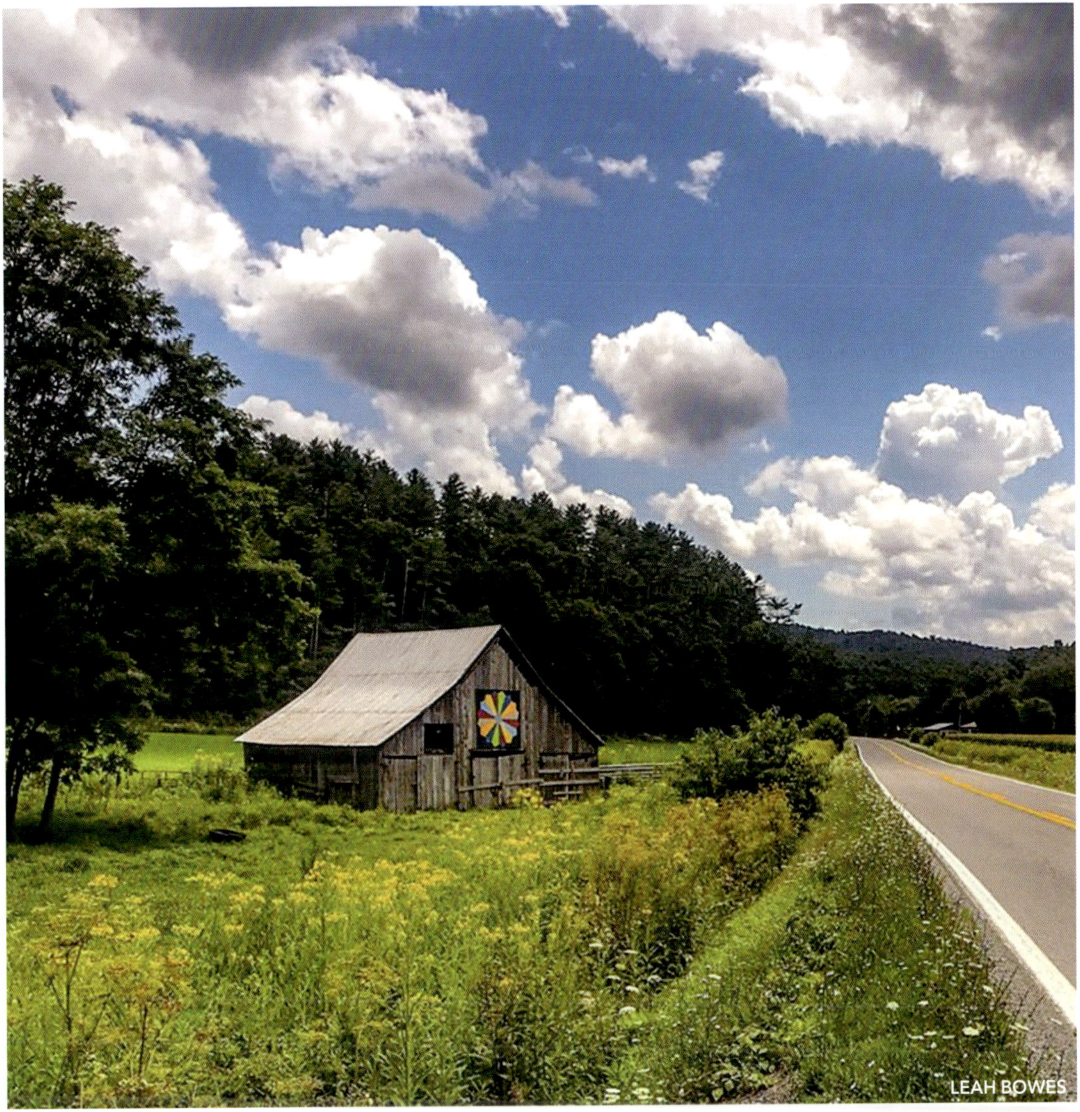
LEAH BOWES

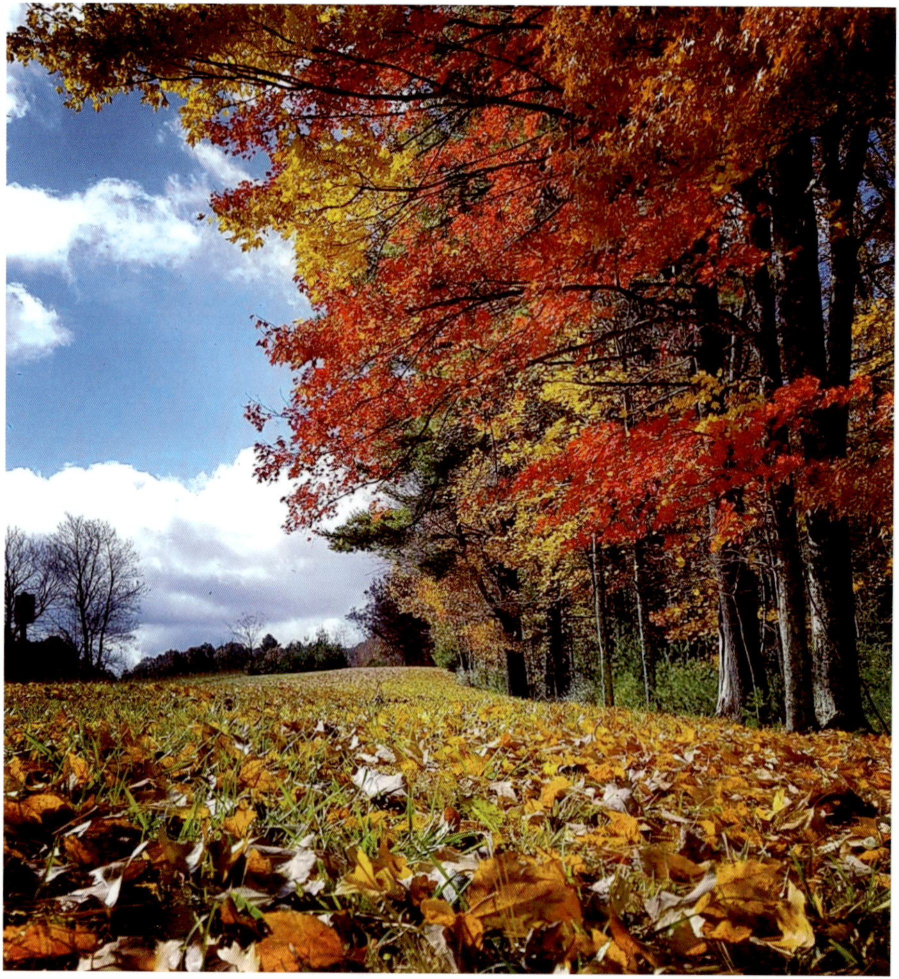

CONNIE BOLEY-LILLY

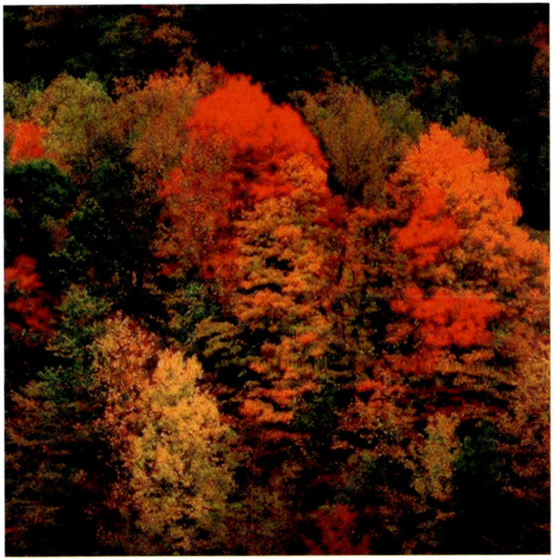

BILLY BOWLING

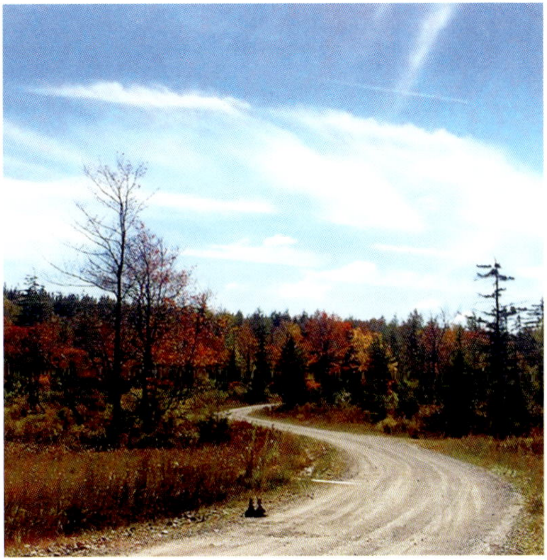

RENAU LUCAS

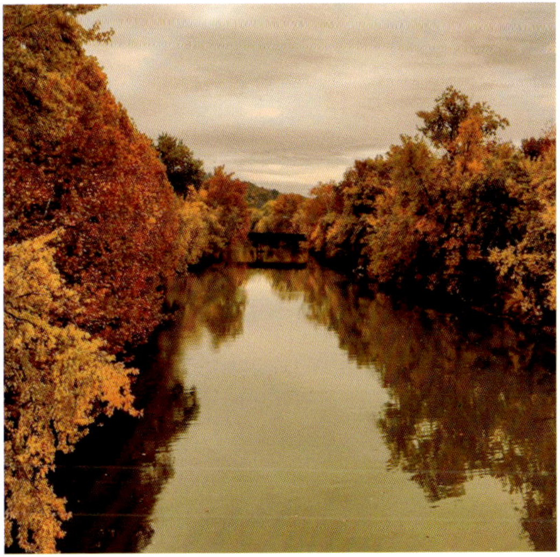

WESLEY PHILP

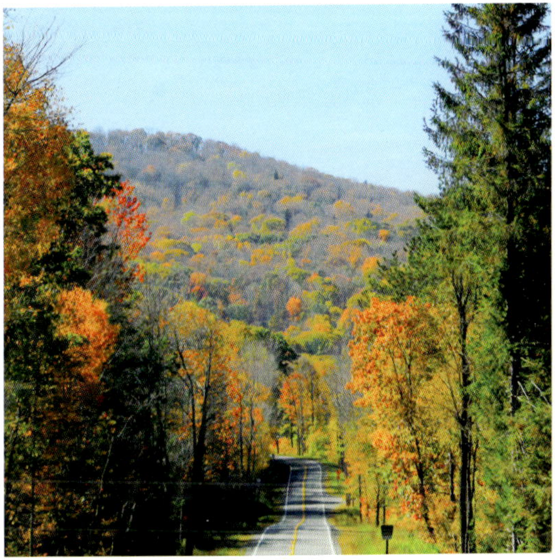

BRIDGETT BARRE

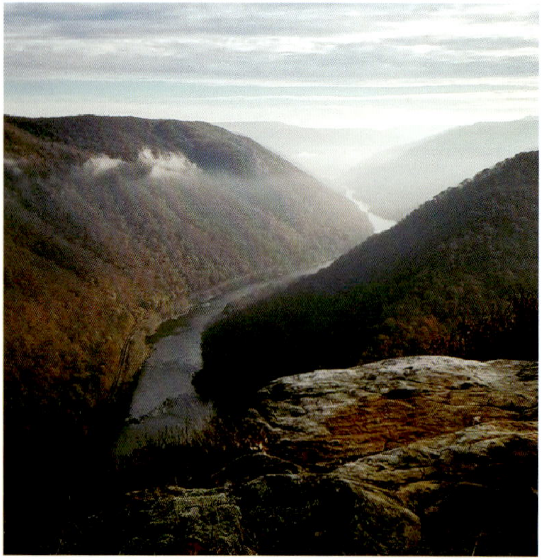
CONNIE BOLEY-LILLY

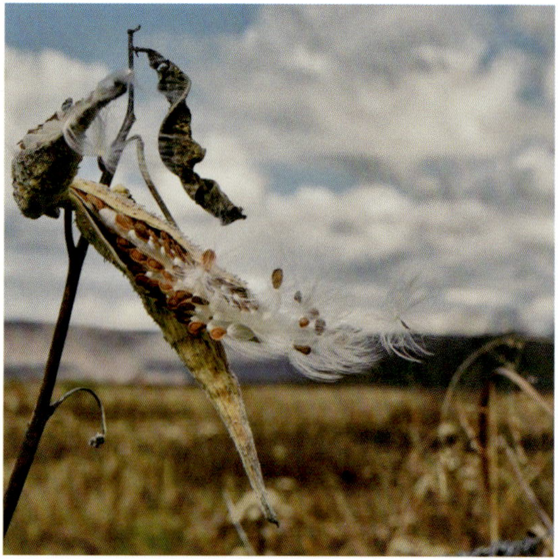
KATIE RICHARD

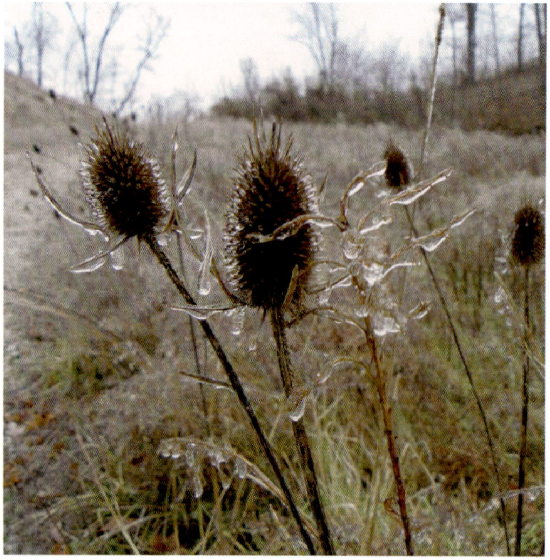
STEPHANIE CARPENTER

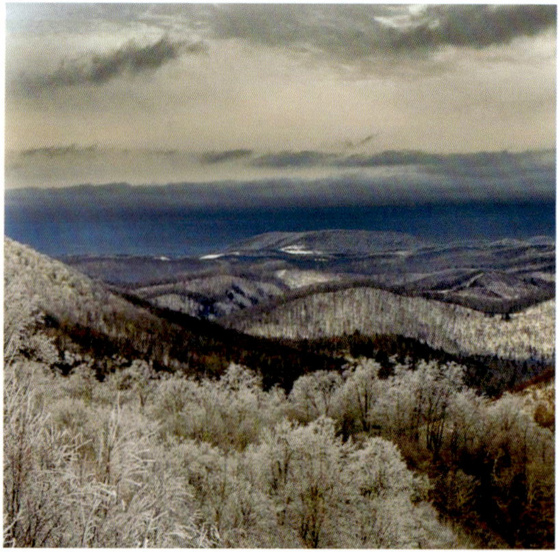
BETH SPENCER

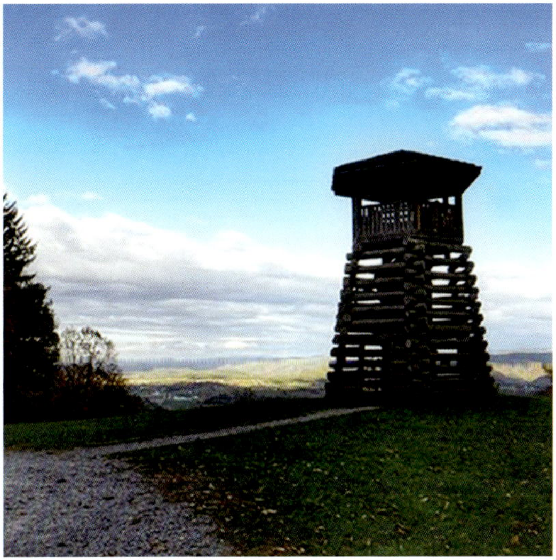

EMILEE GREATHOUSE

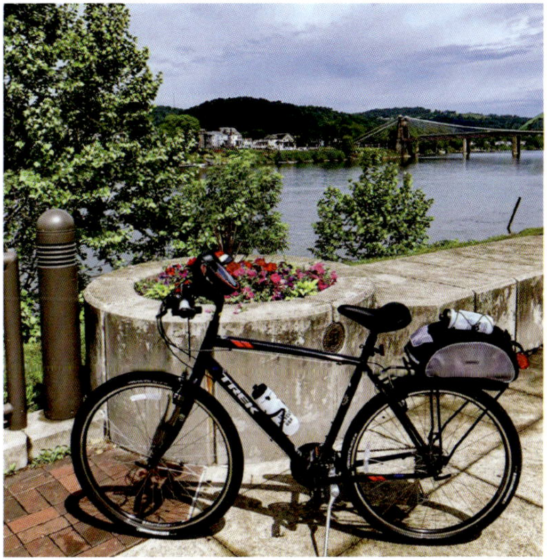

WES PHILP

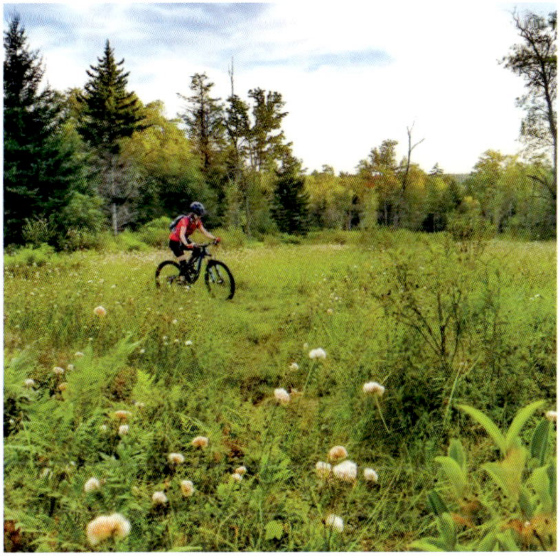

LIZ STOUT

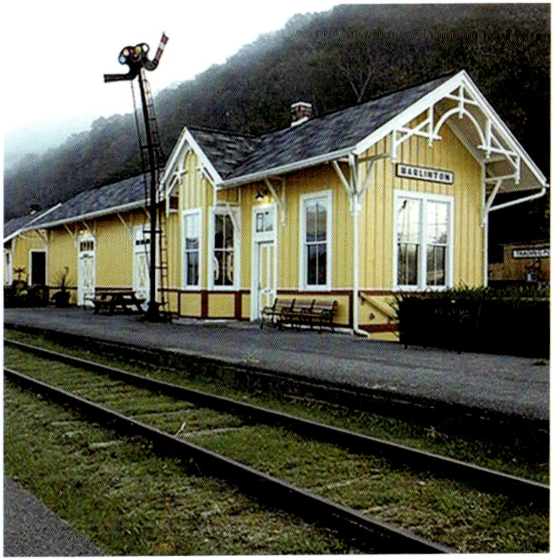

BRENT SCHNUPP

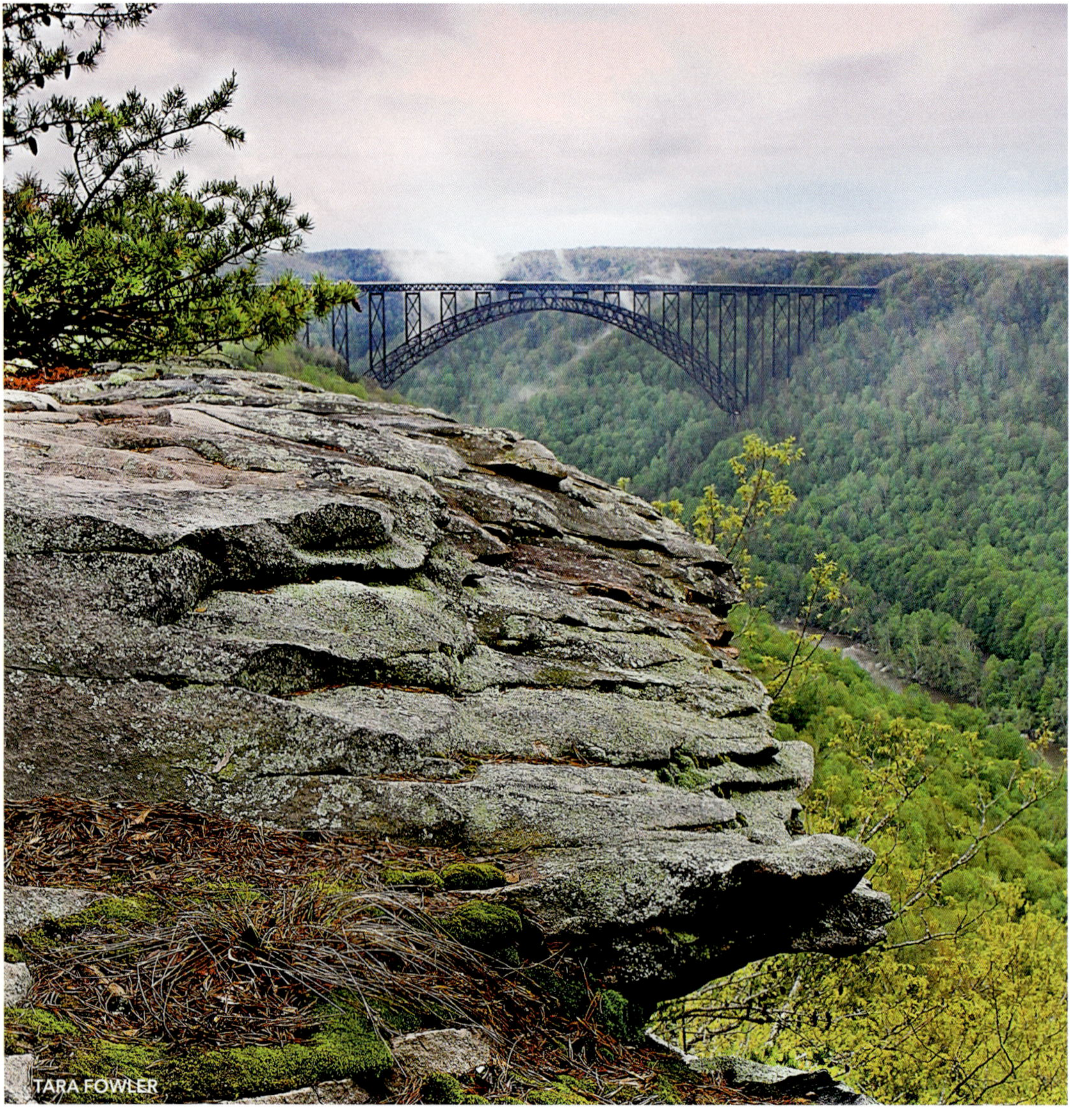
TARA FOWLER

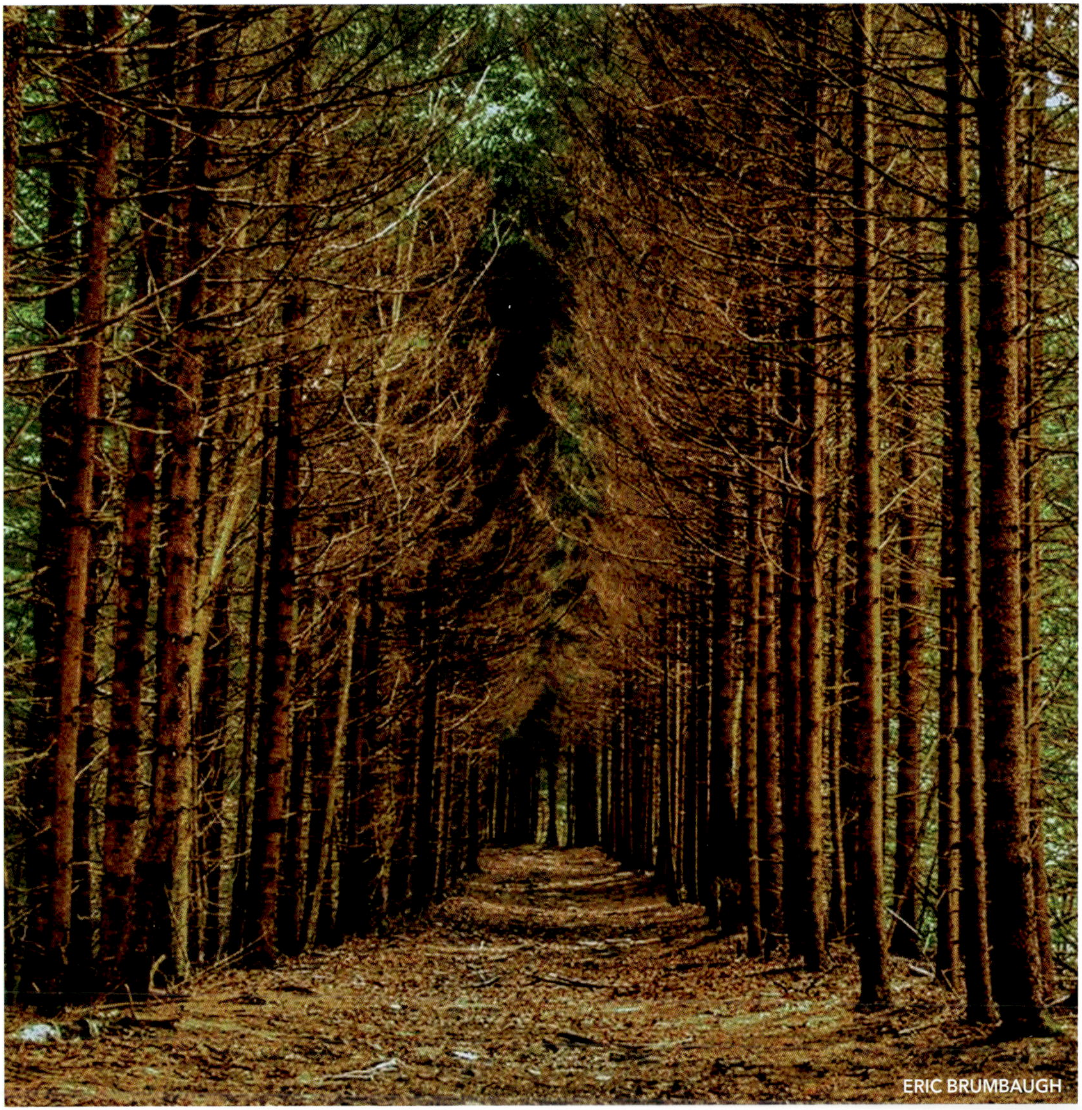
ERIC BRUMBAUGH

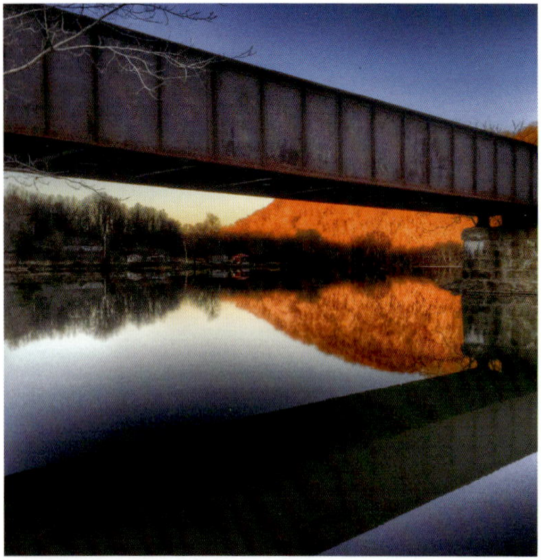

ROBERT PHIPPS

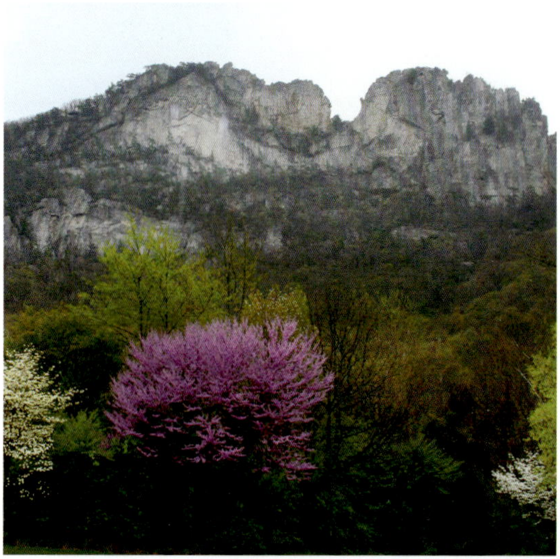

LAURA MOUL

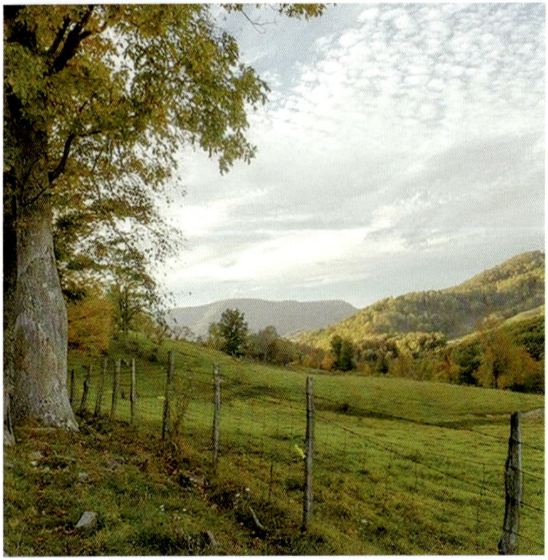

DENISE POWERS FABIAN

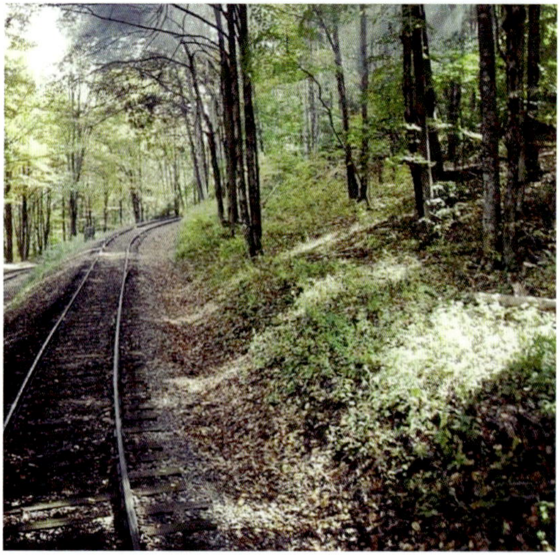

AMBER HEATH

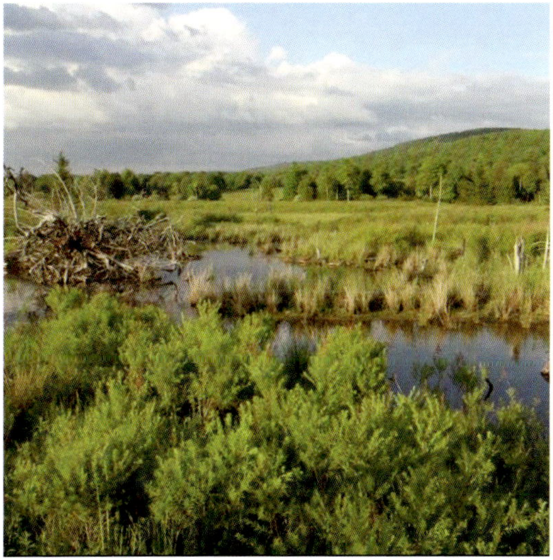

ELIZABETH SEELEY

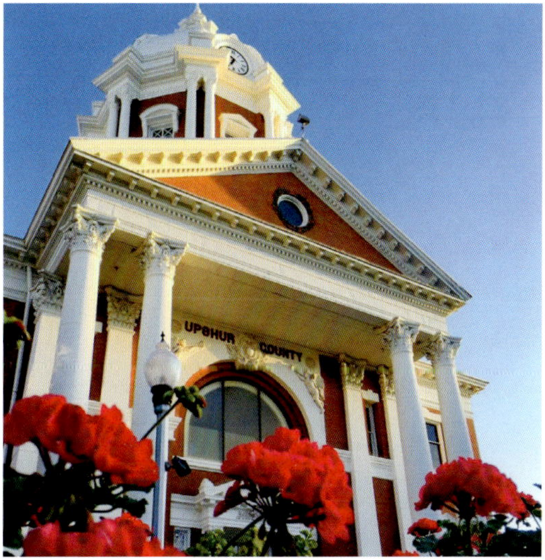

SANDI MILLER

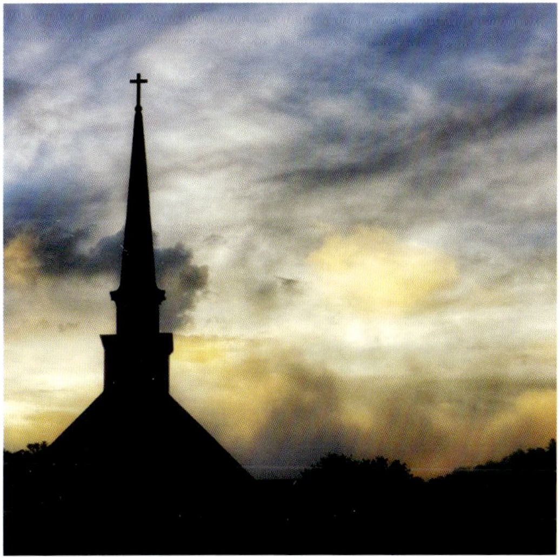

EMILEE GREATHOUSE

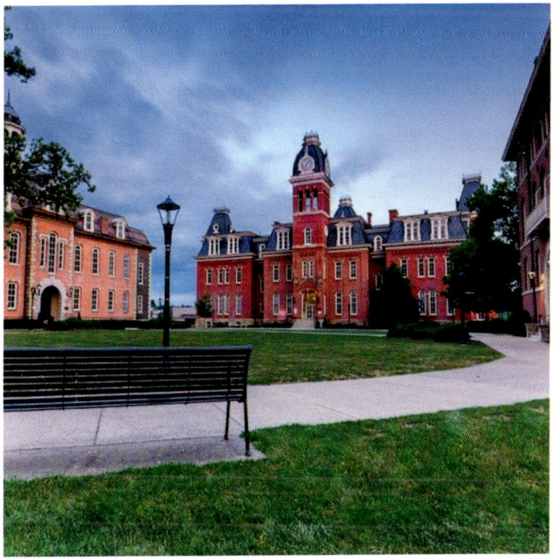

JAMES PRUTILPAC

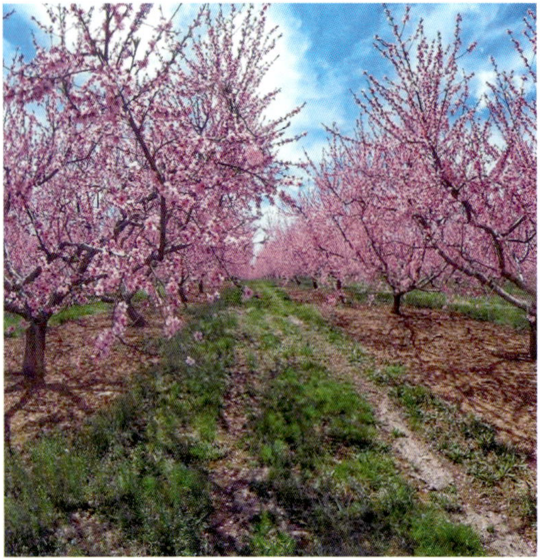

KATIE RICHARD

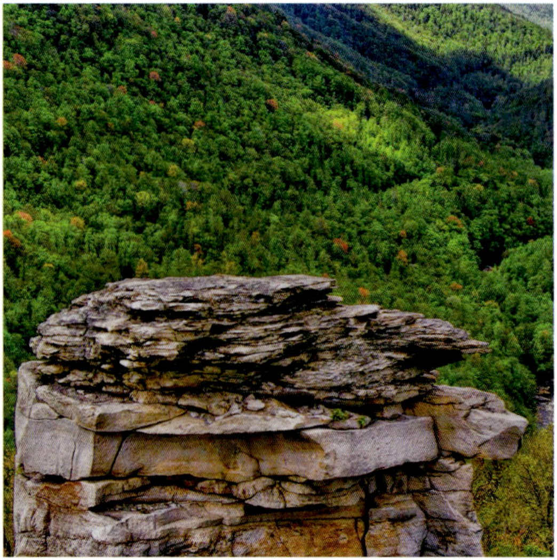

LAURA MOUL

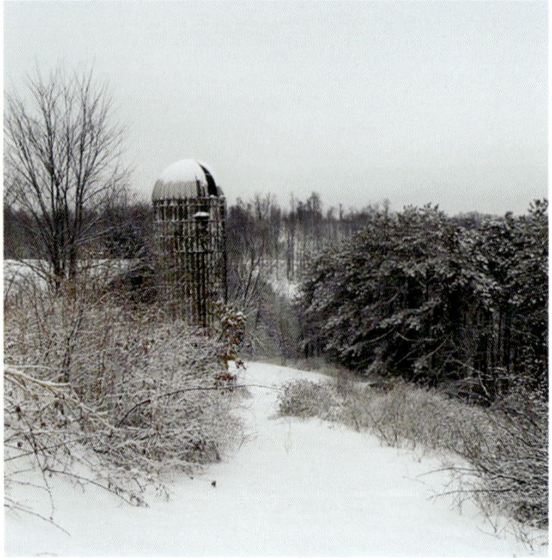

CANDY THOMPSON

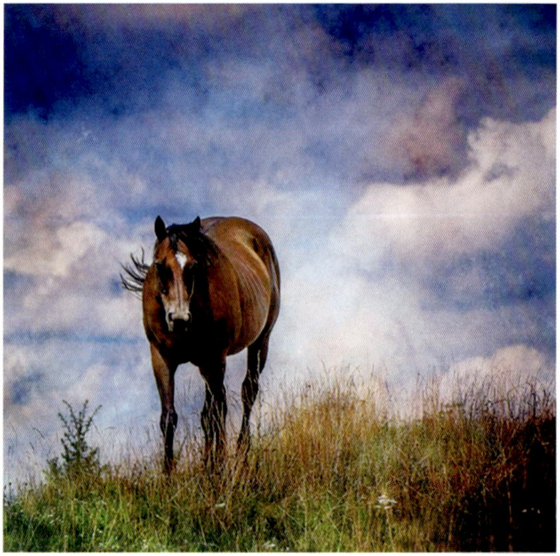

KEVIN JACK

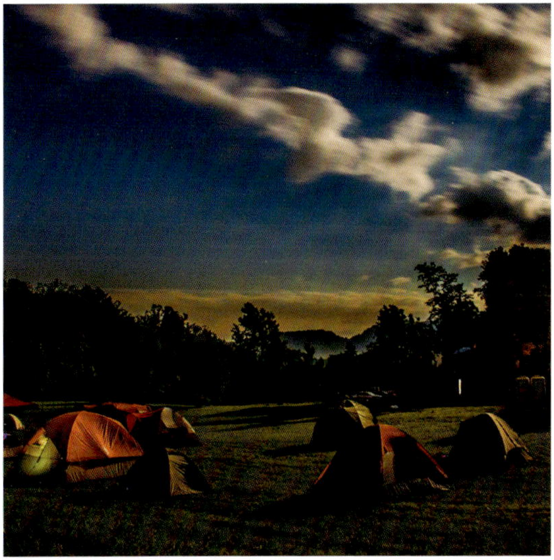

JAYSON HARRIS

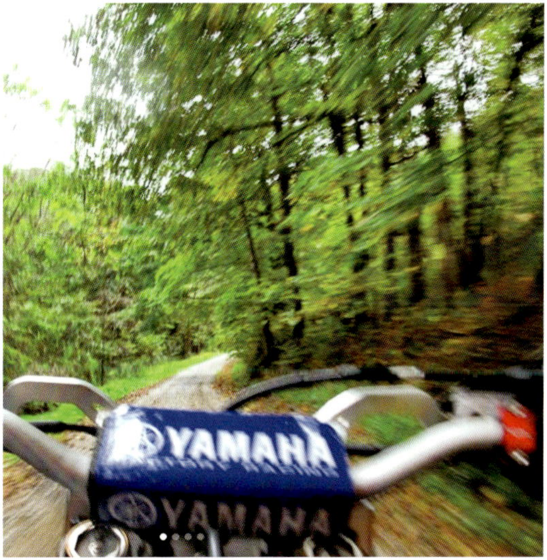

DON DEQUASIE

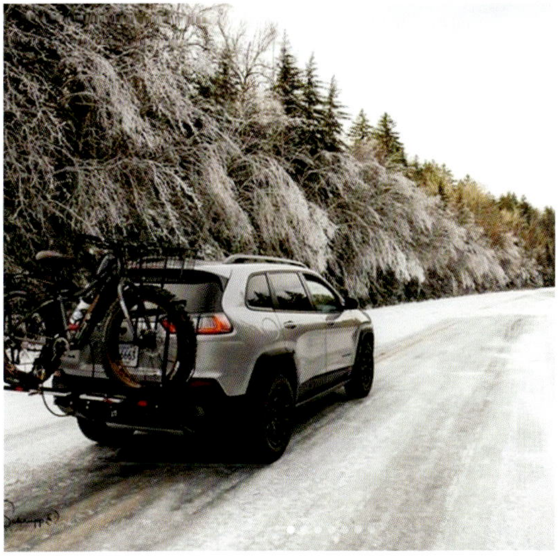

BRENT SCHNUPP

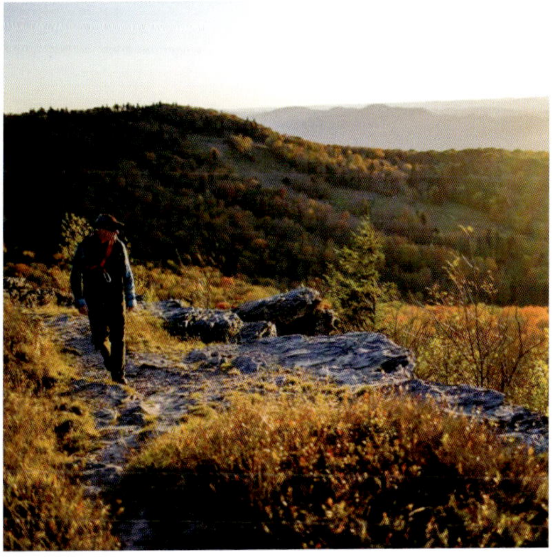

LIZ STOUT

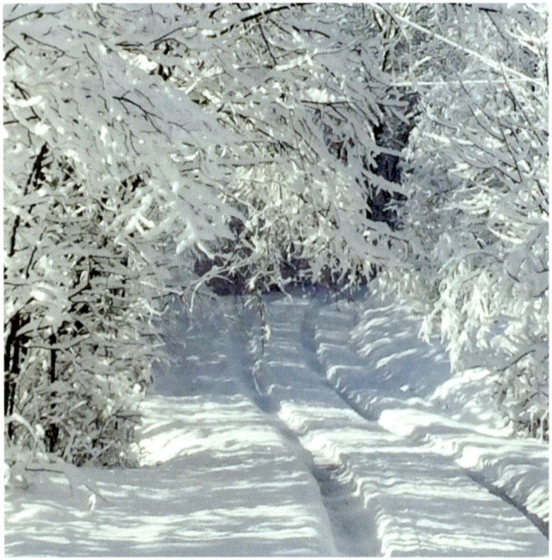

CAROLYN MITCHELL

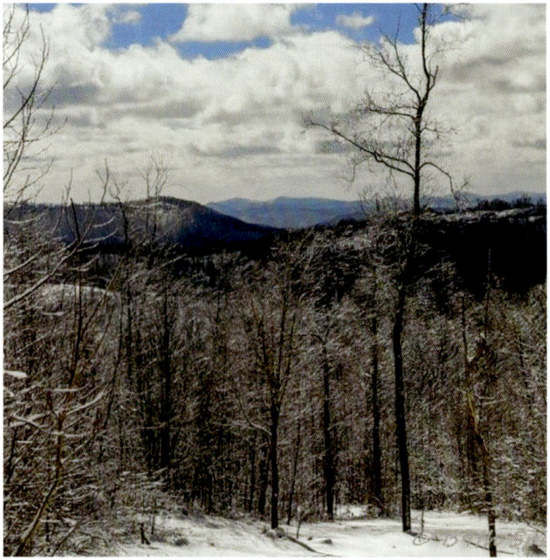

BETH SPENCER

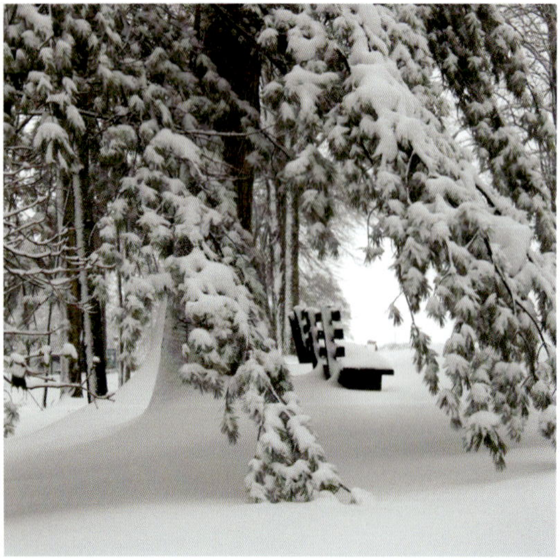

JEFFERY ALMOND

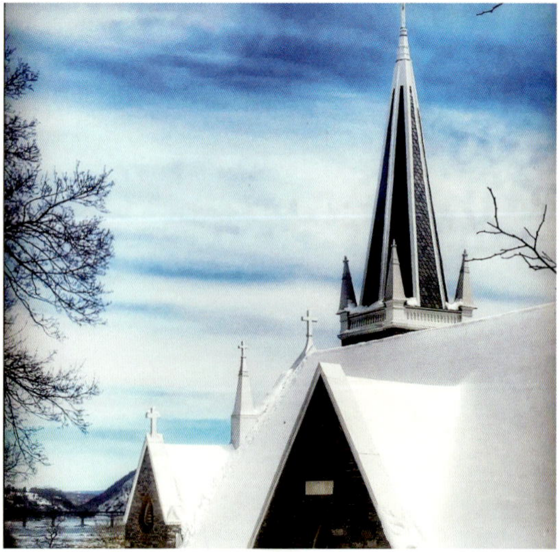

CINDI DUNN

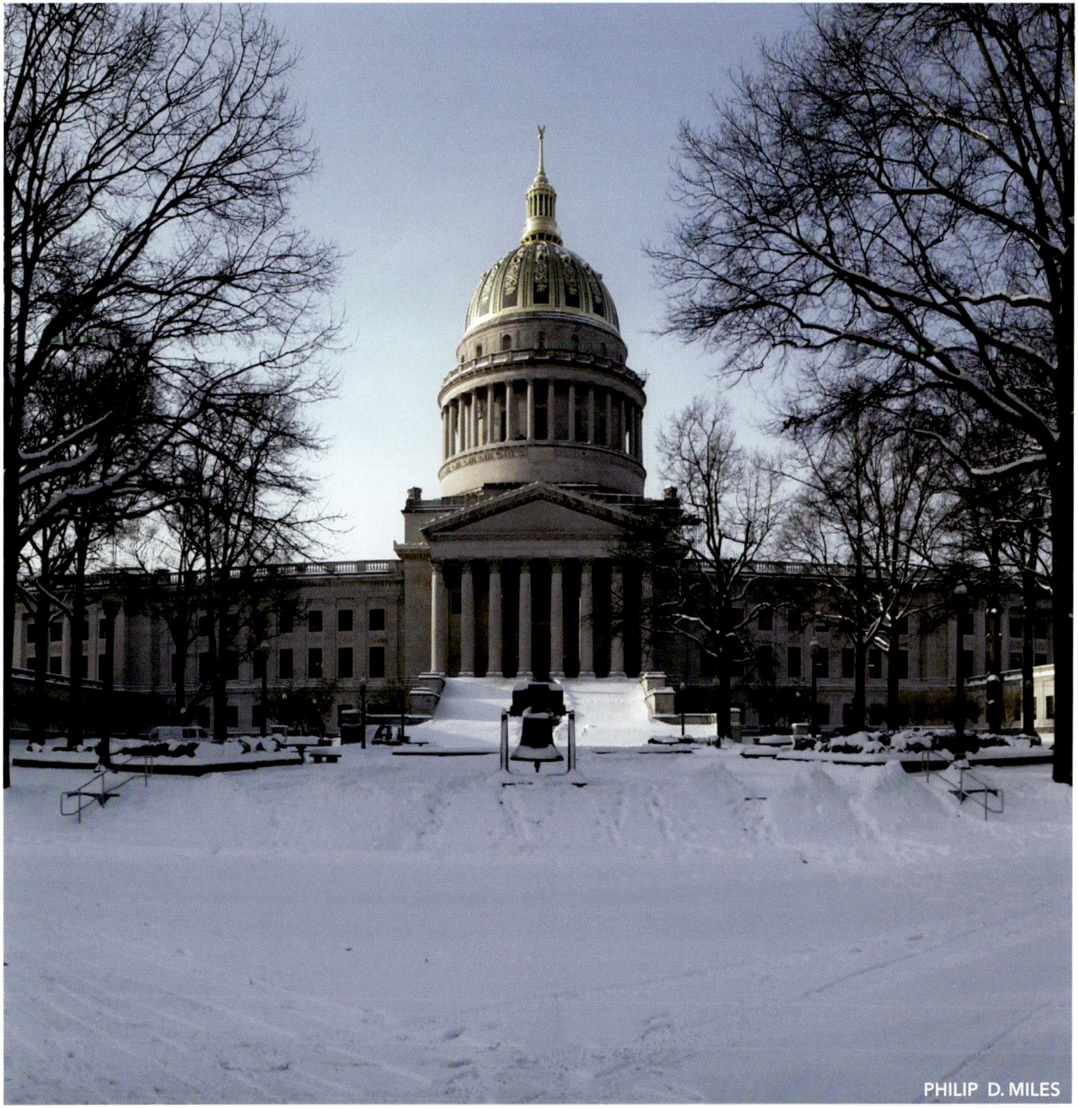
PHILIP D. MILES

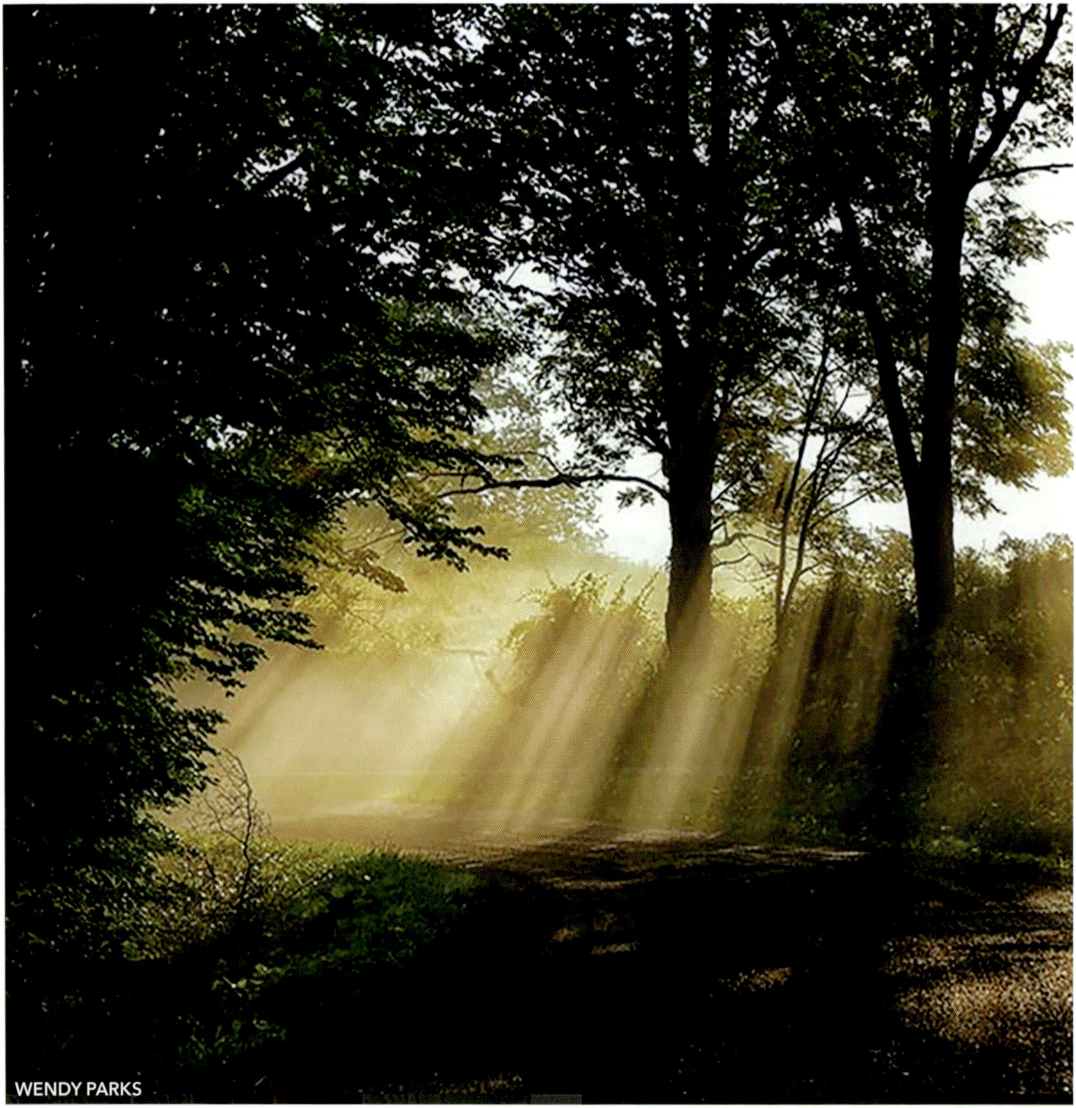
WENDY PARKS

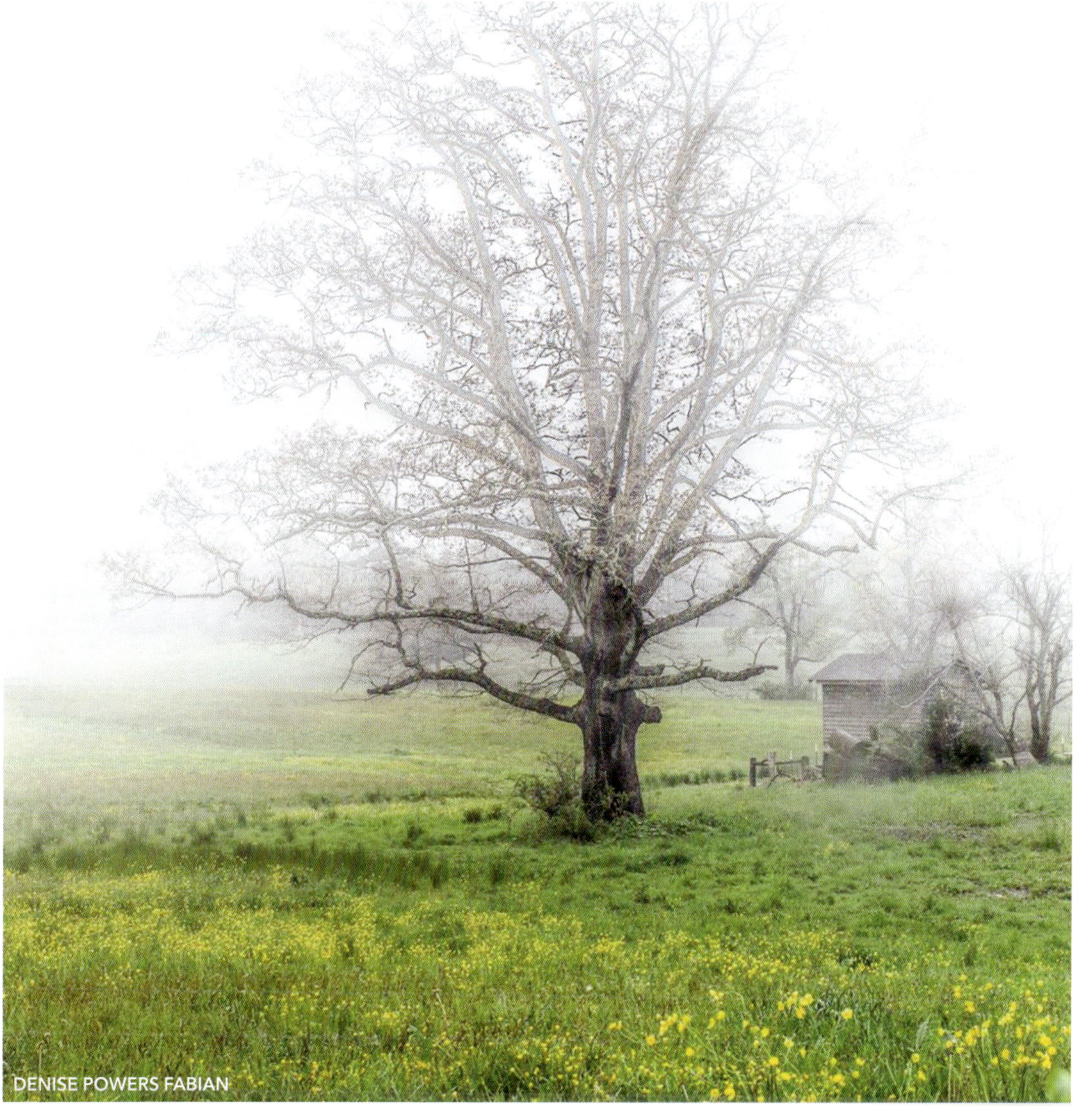
DENISE POWERS FABIAN

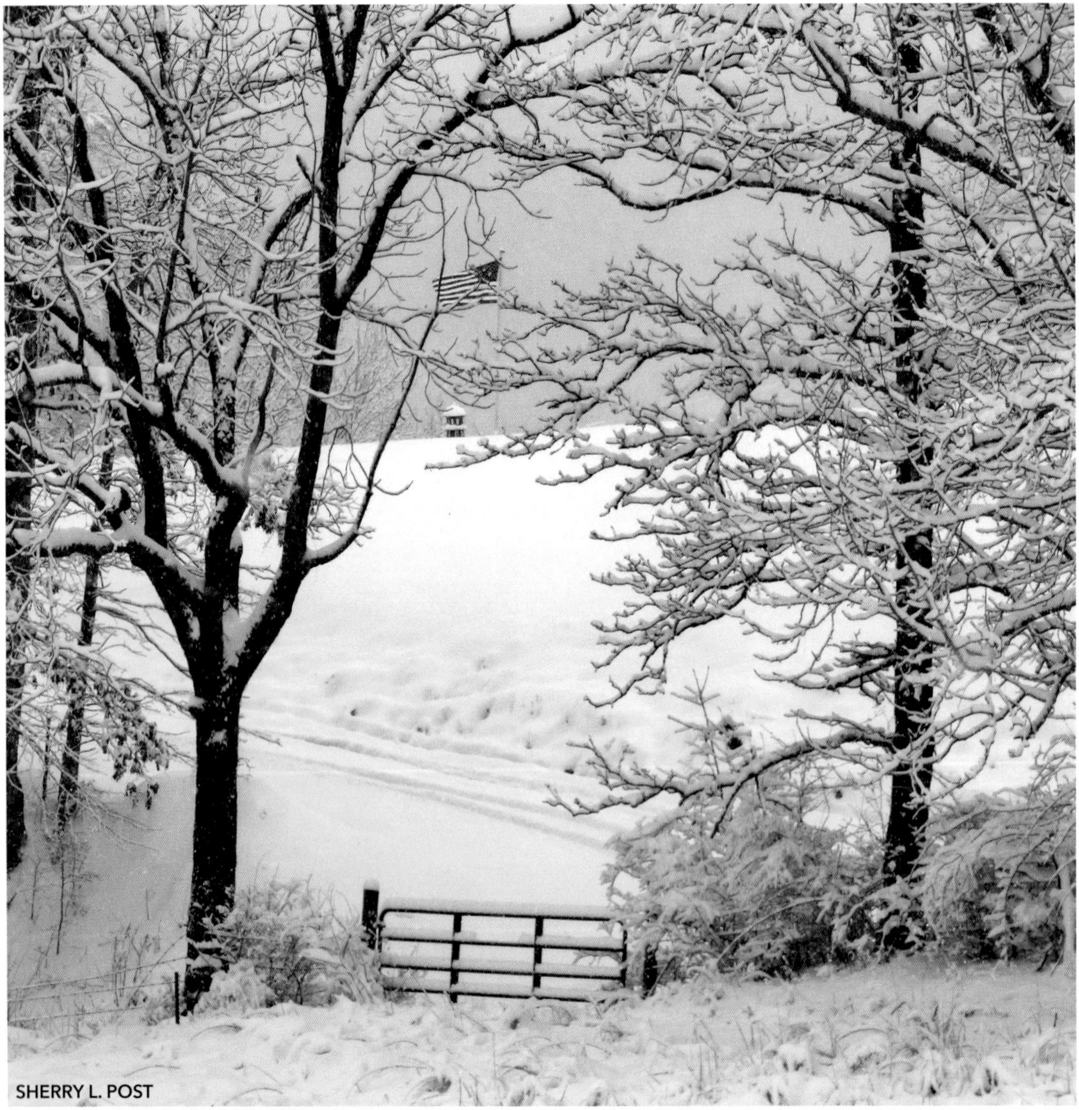

SHERRY L. POST

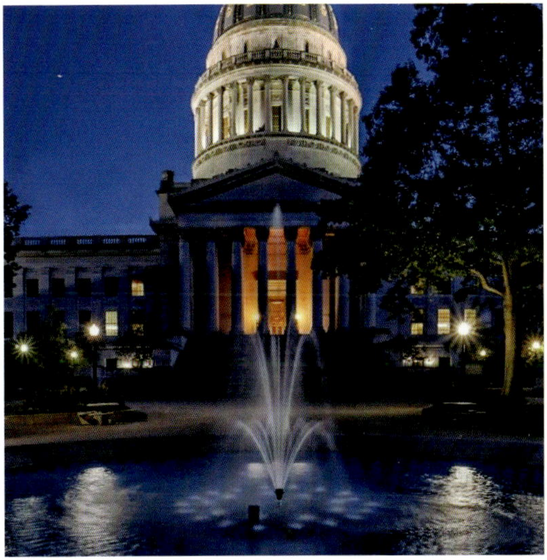

TOM DEAN

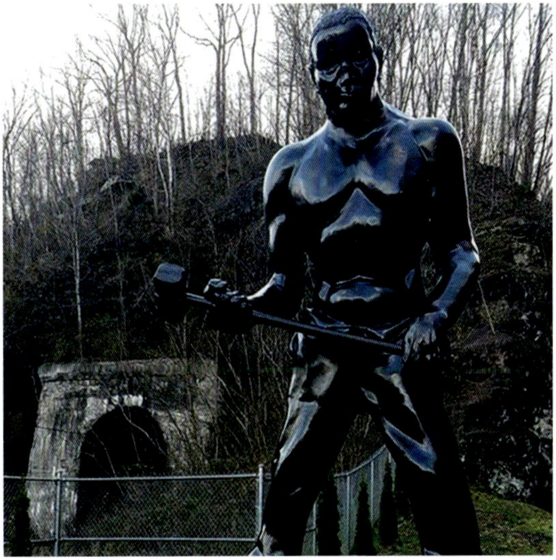

JUSTIN FRAME AND JUDITH BOYCE

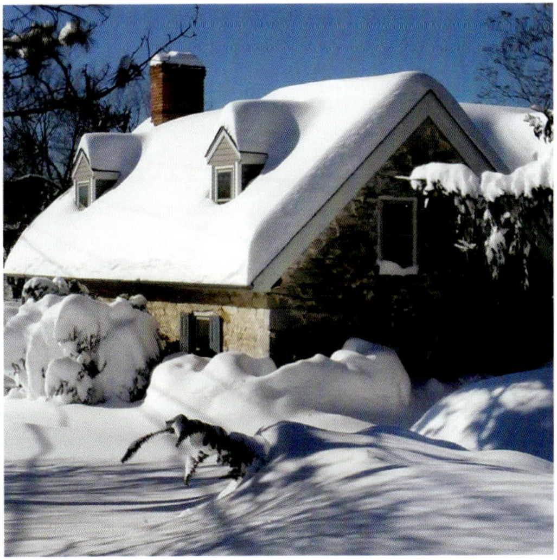

RICHARD CARSON

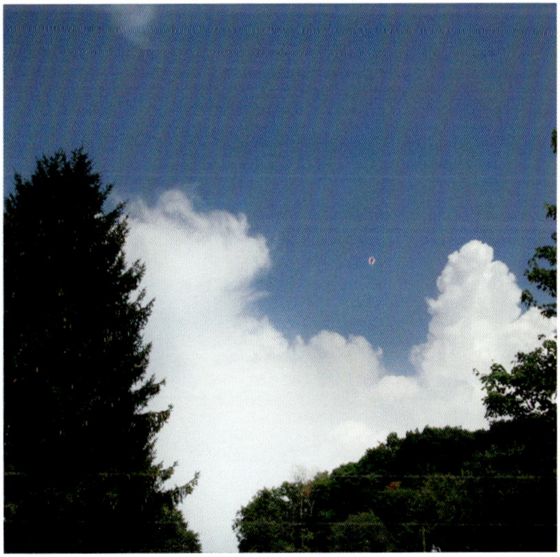

TERRY A. WELLS

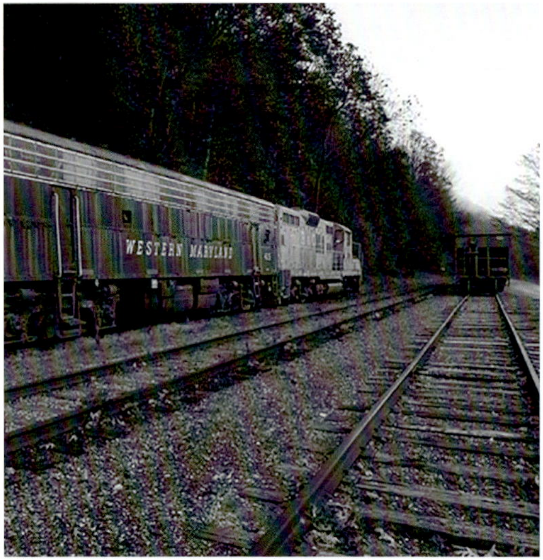

BRENT SCHNUPP

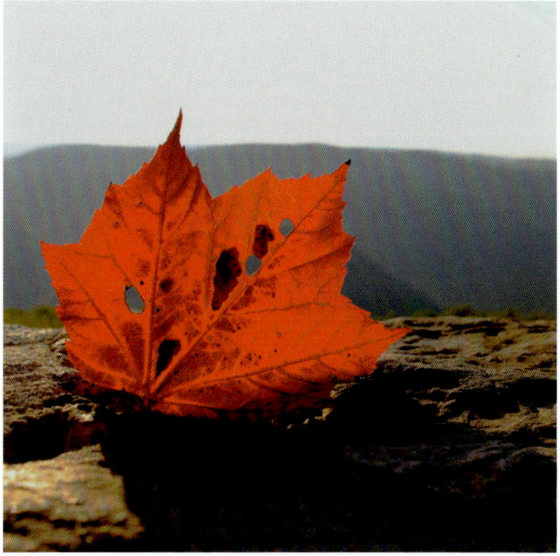
STAN WIKLE

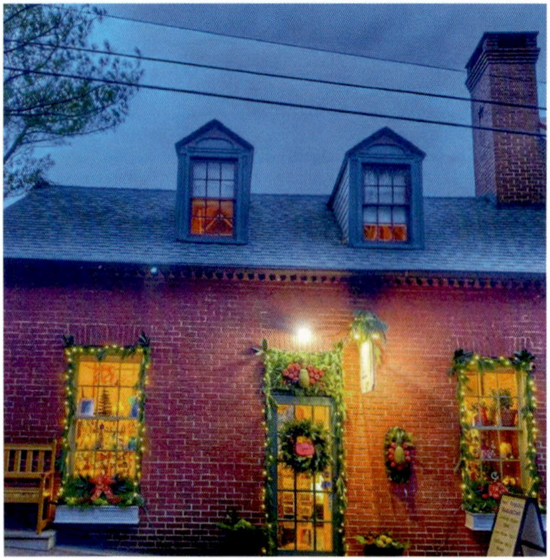
CINDI DUNN

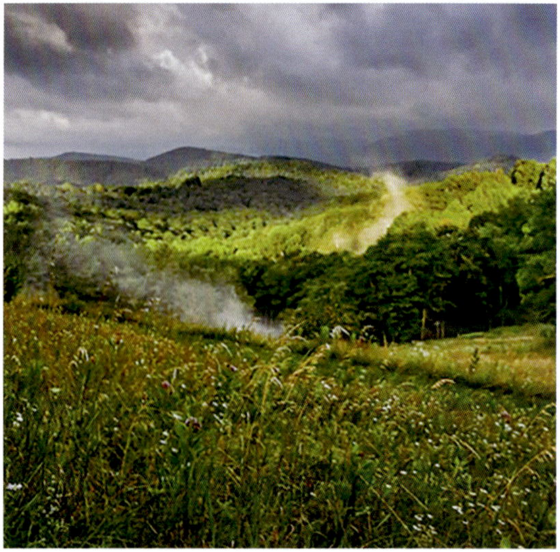
WENDY PARKS

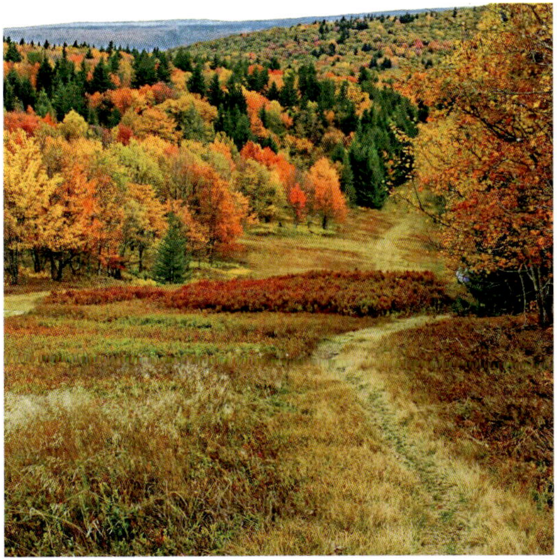

ARNOLD PARRISH

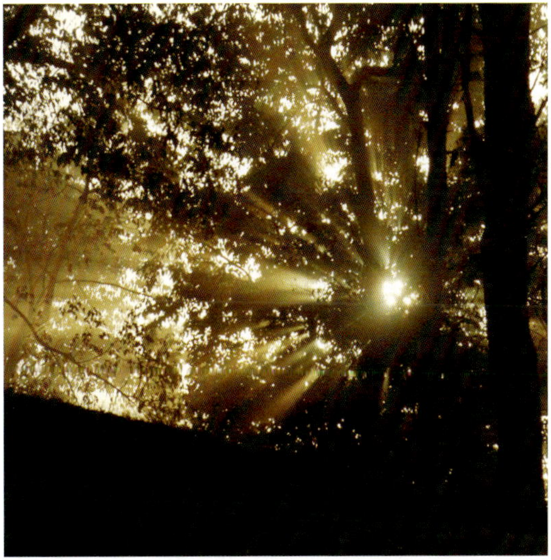

STEPHANIE CARPENTER

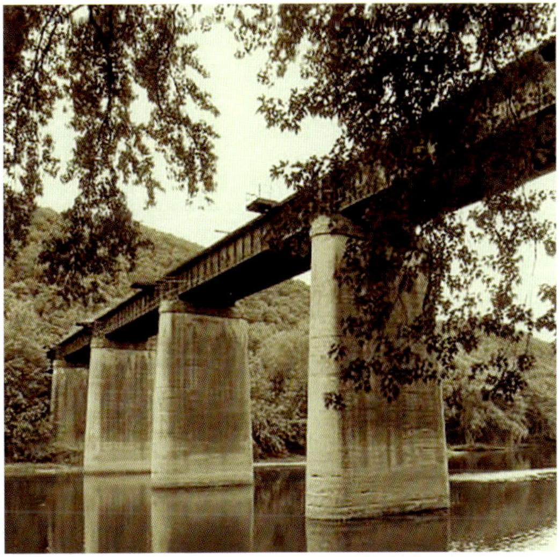

BOBBIE JO DeHAVEN

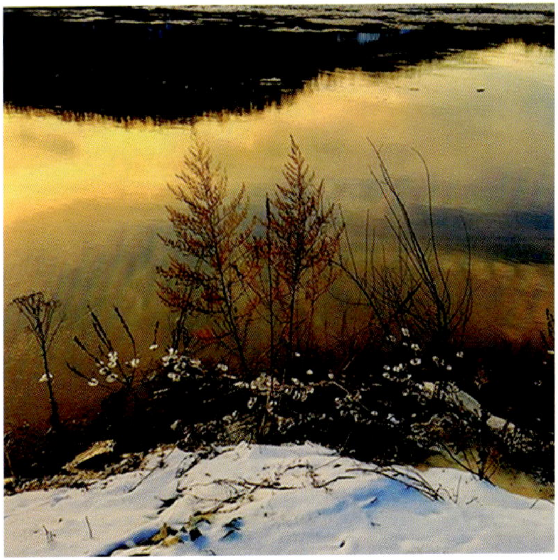

WESLEY PHILP

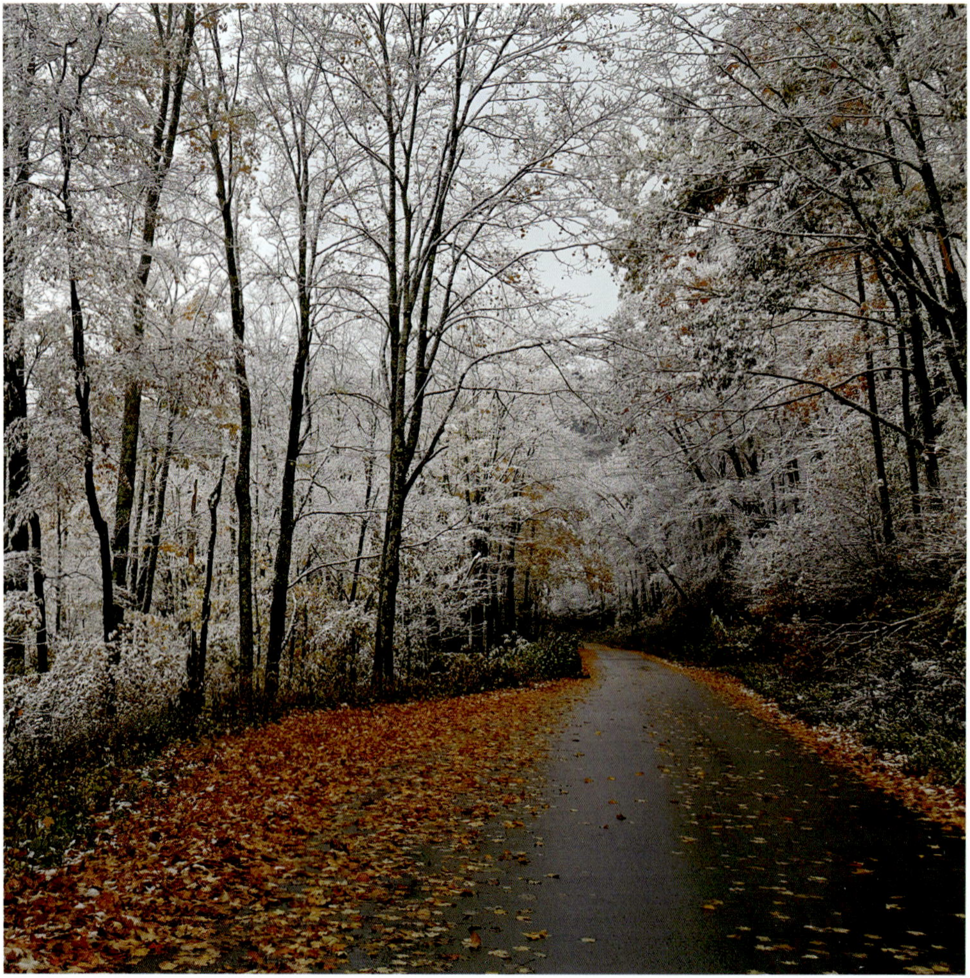

VARSHA BIDARE SHIVARAM

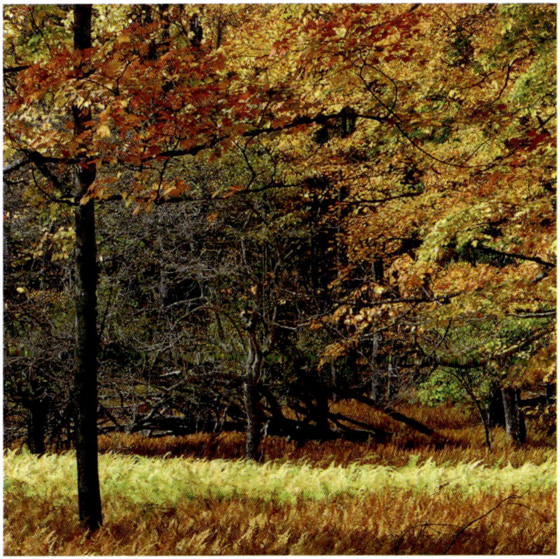

JENNIFER HONEYCUTT

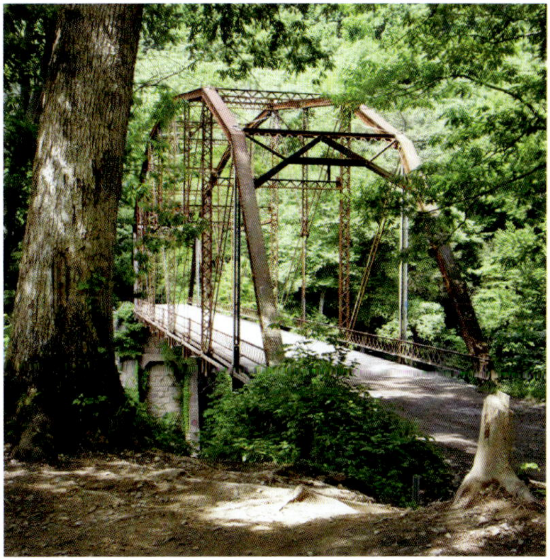

CANDY THOMPSON

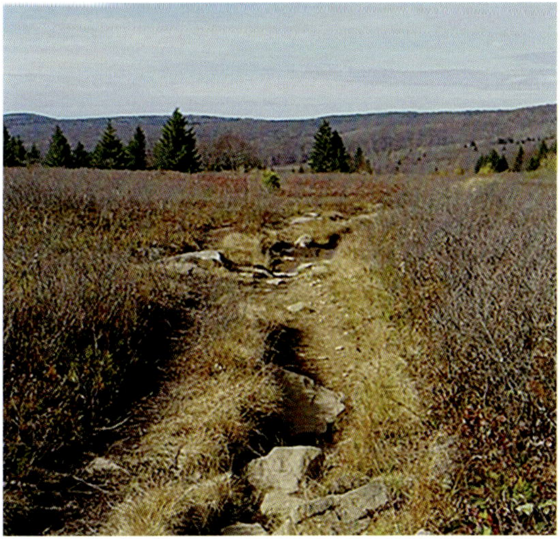

KATIE RICHARD

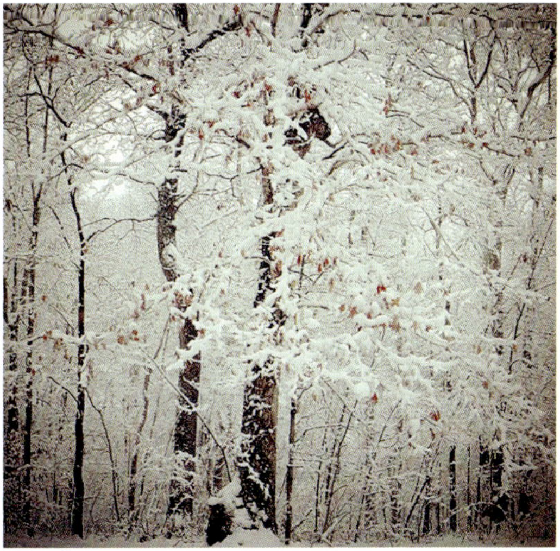

ELAINE CLARK

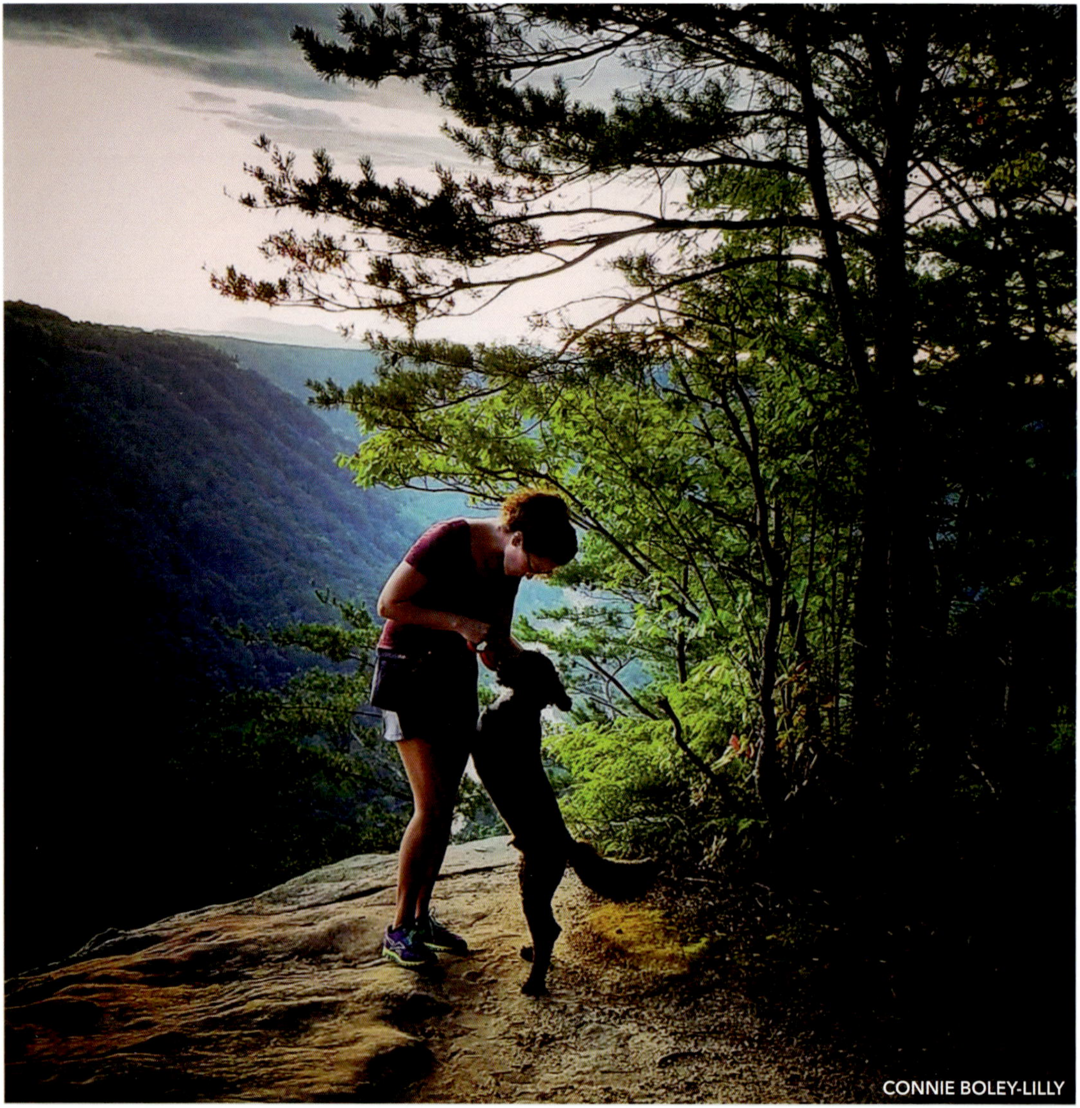
CONNIE BOLEY-LILLY

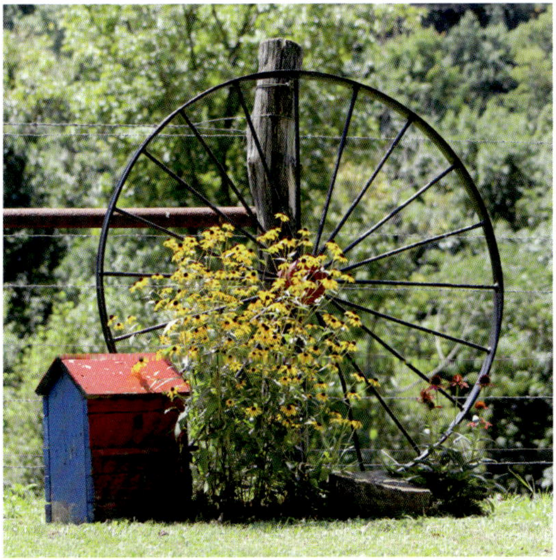
PAM BURNS

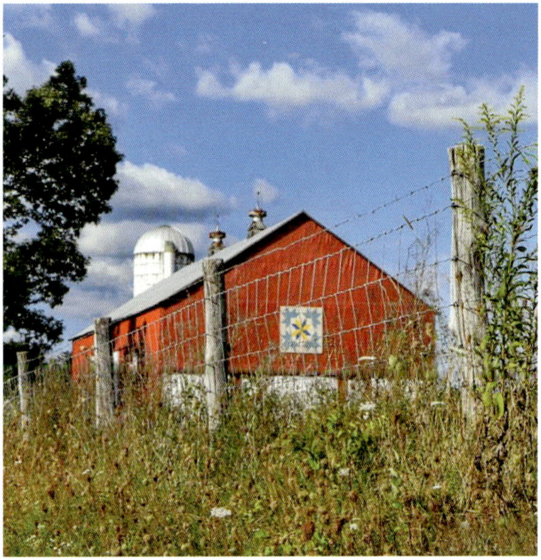
EMILEE GREATHOUSE

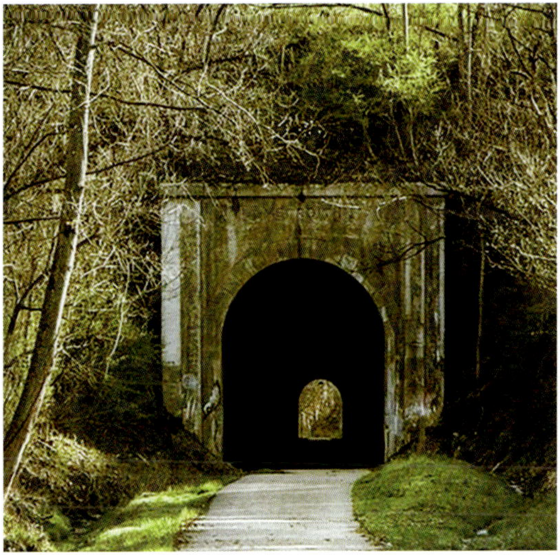
WENDY PARKS

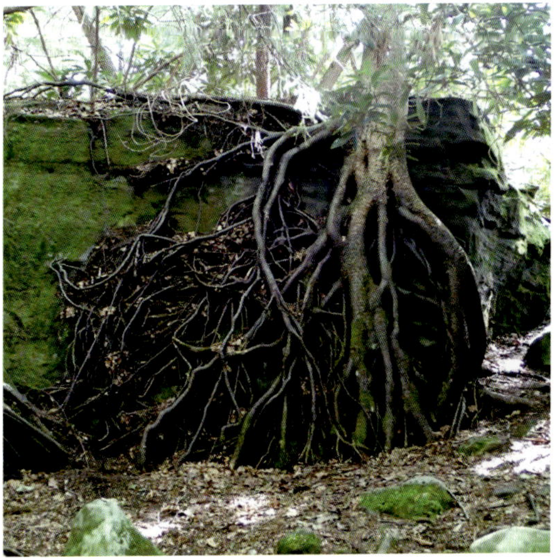
MARK REASOR

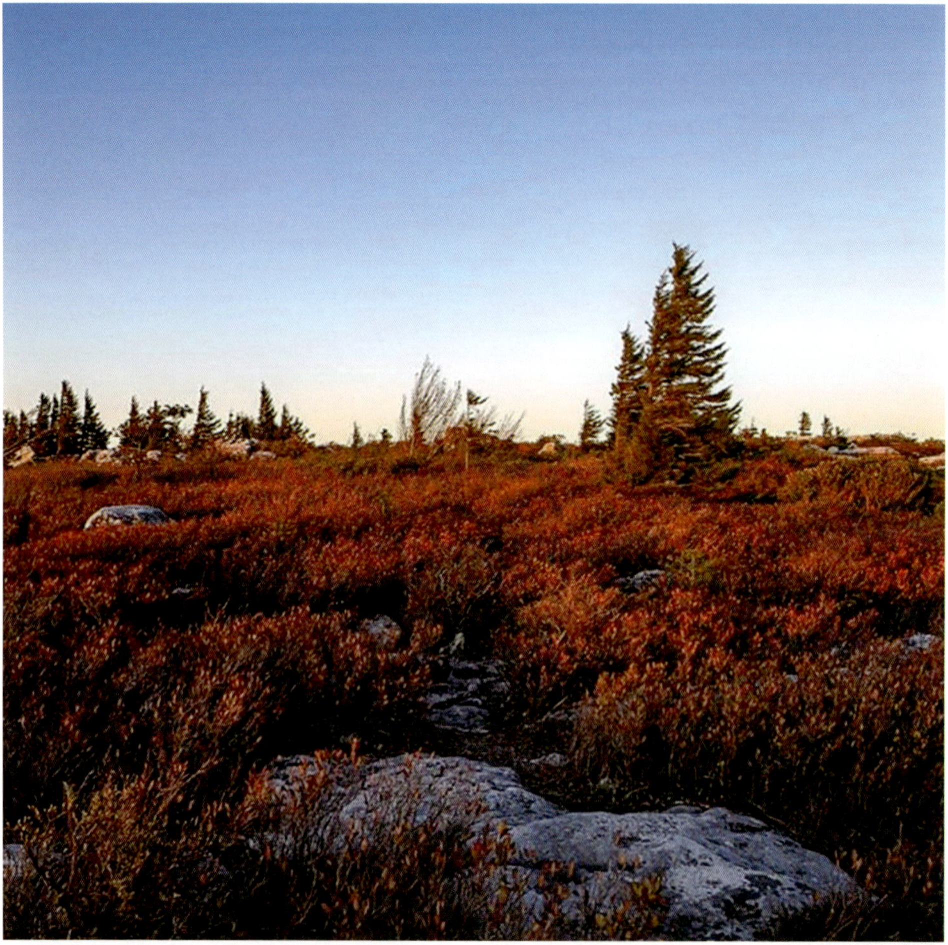

BRENT SCHNUPP

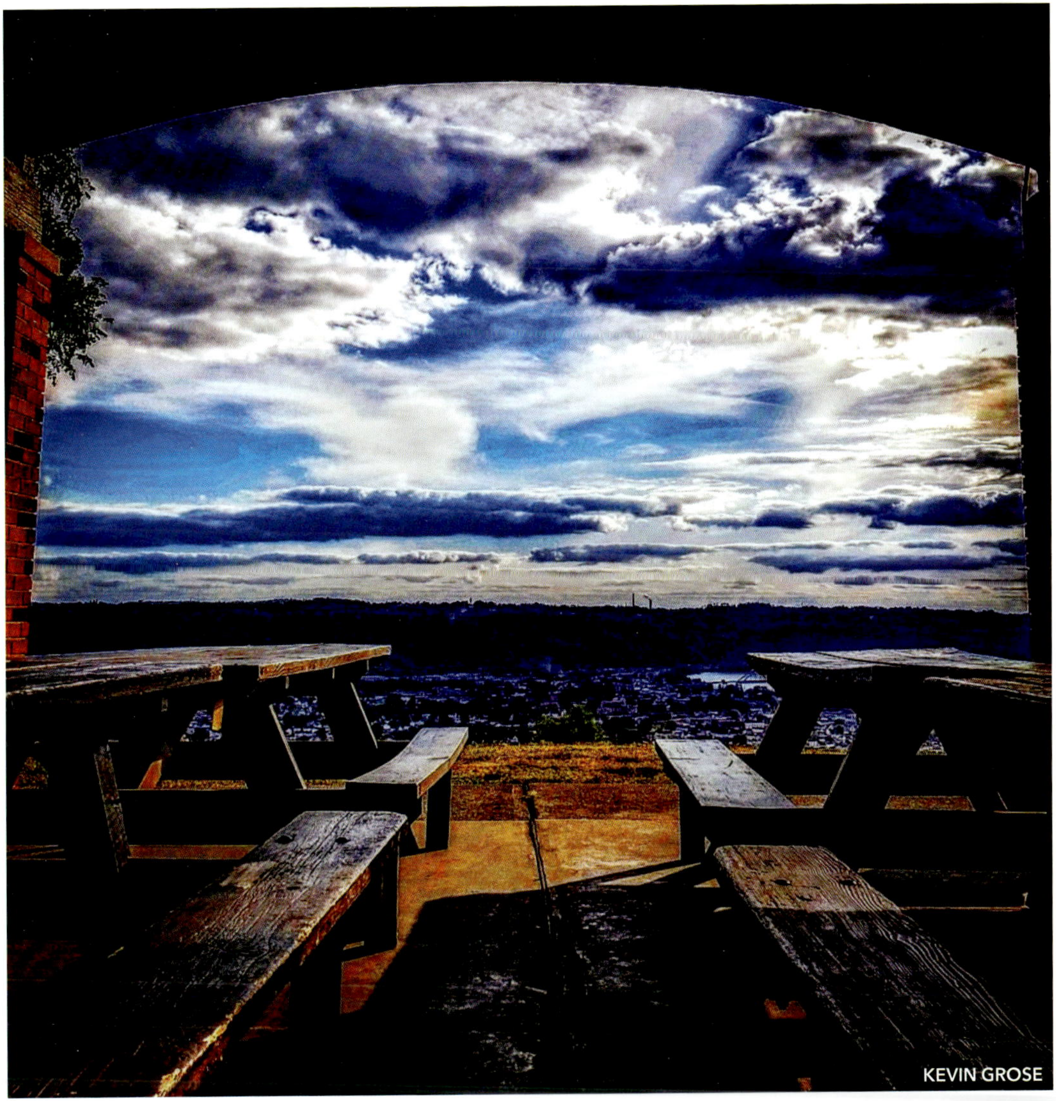
KEVIN GROSE

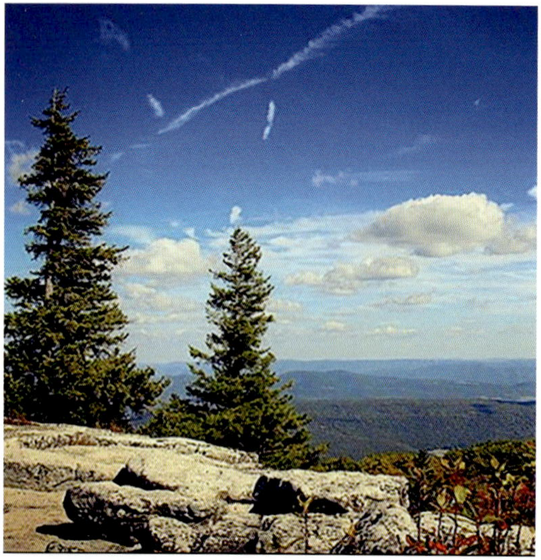

SARAH E. BAILEY

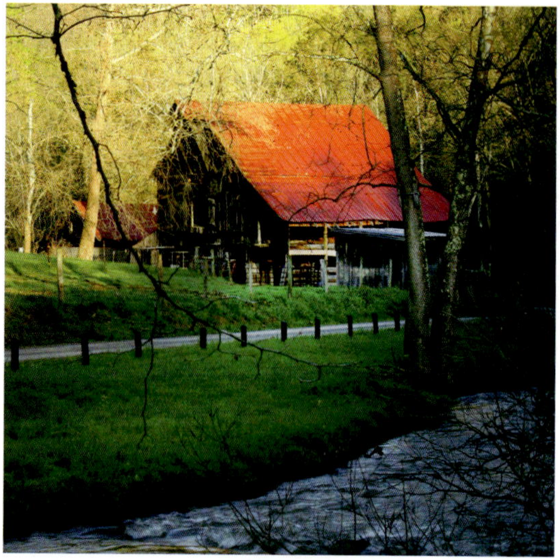

SANDI MILLER

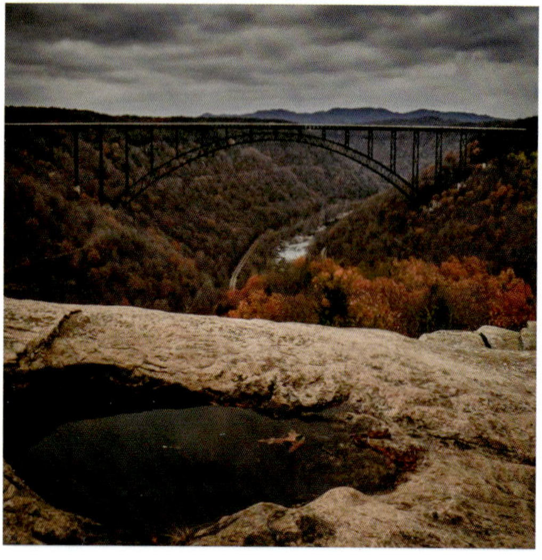

NICOLE VIEWS

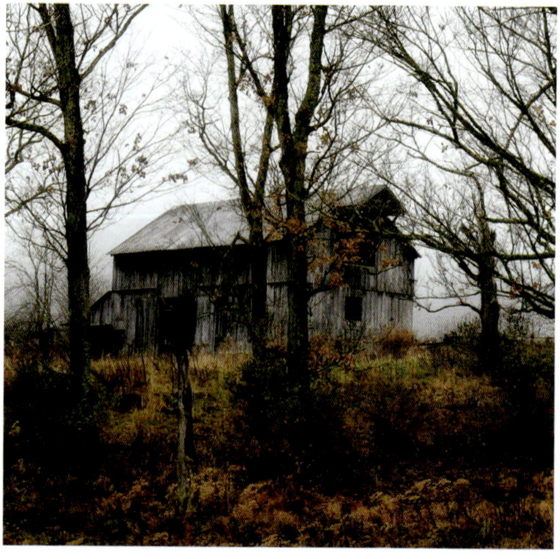

EMILEE GREATHOUSE

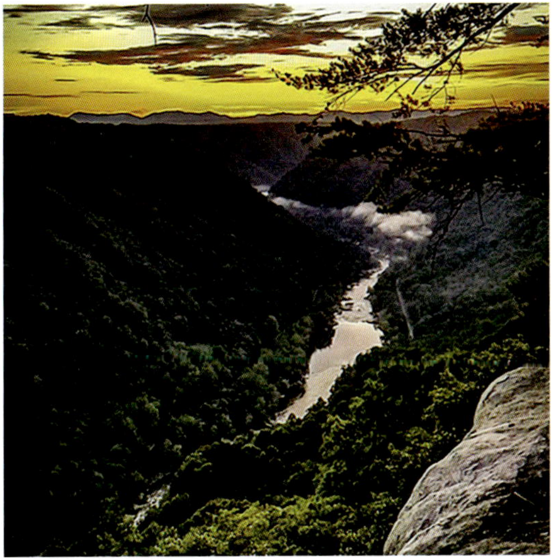

CONNIE BOLEY-LILLY

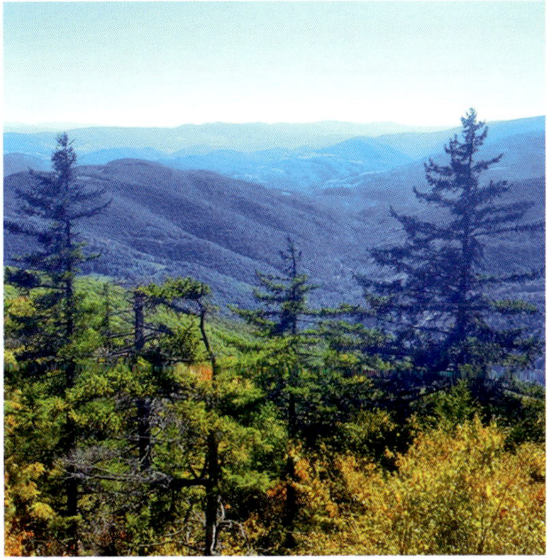

LIZ STOUT

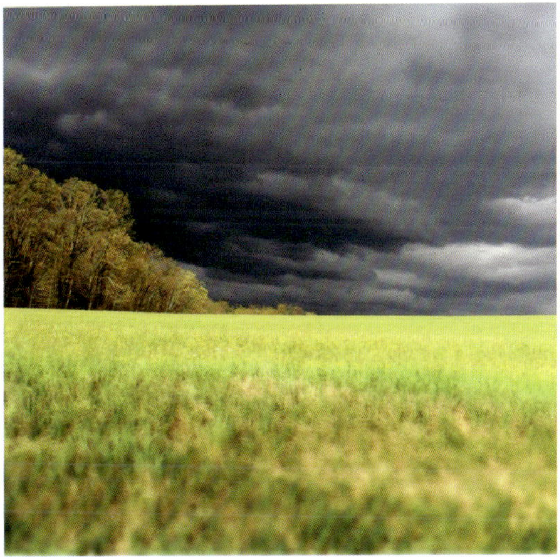

PAULA COLEMAN

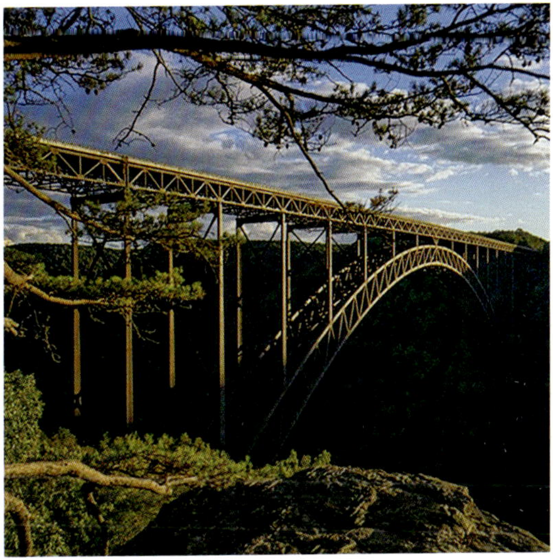

TOM DEAN

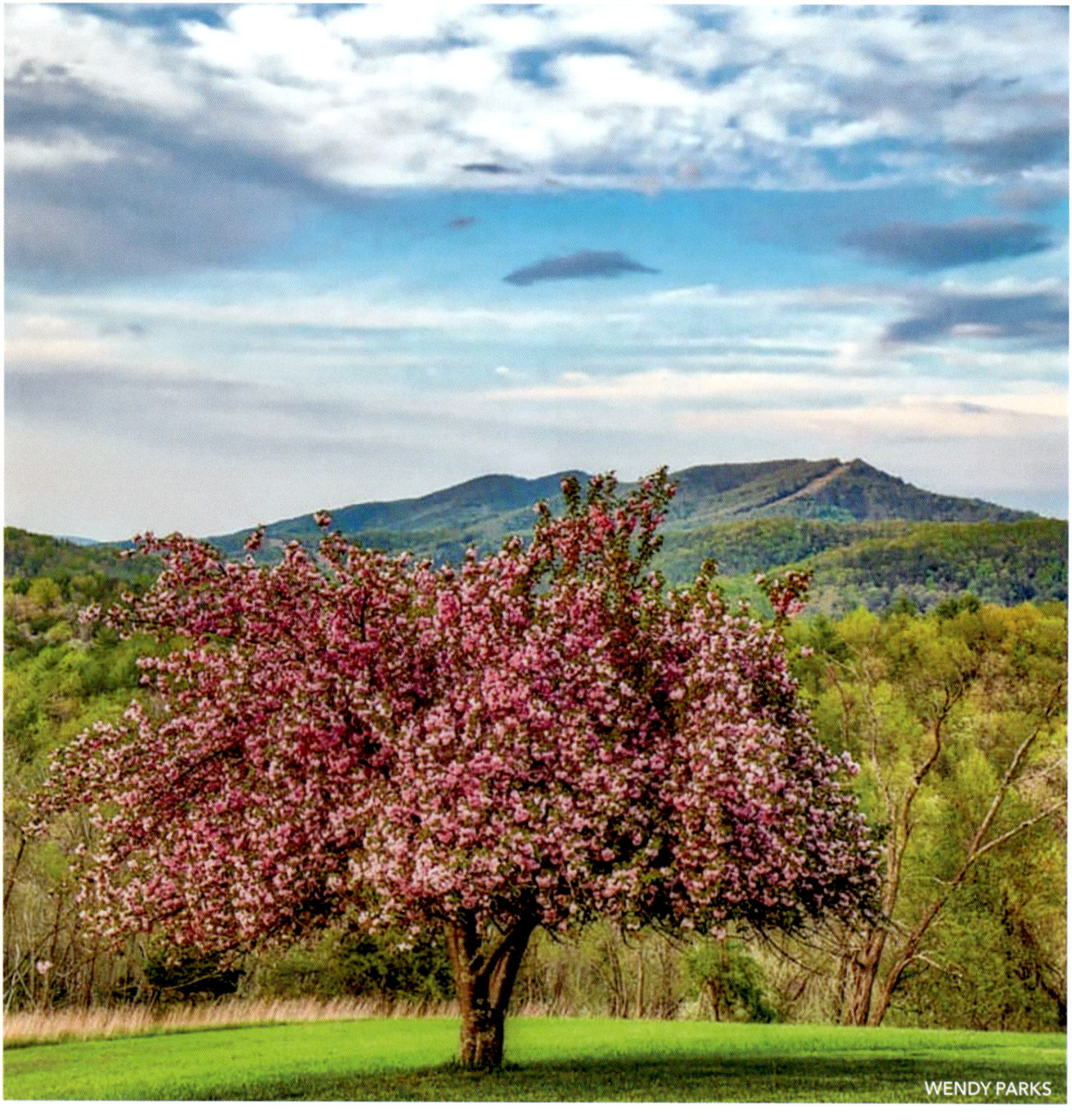
WENDY PARKS

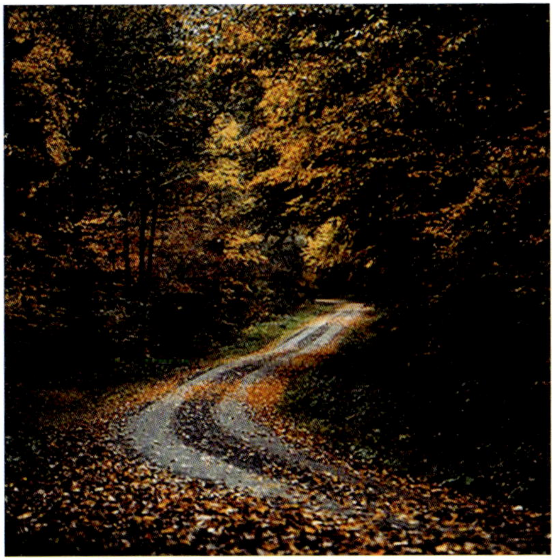

KEVIN JACK

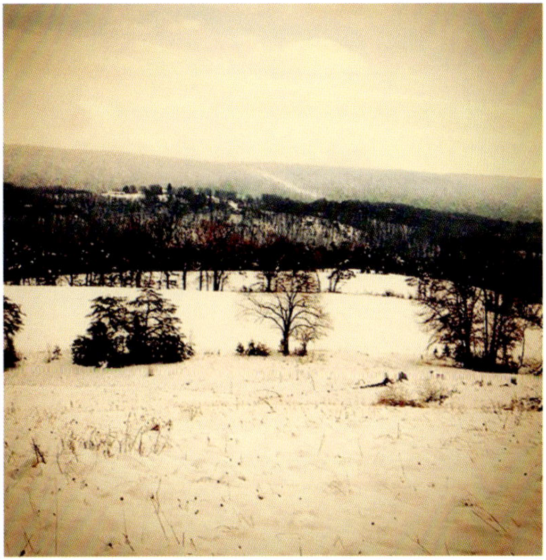

ELAINE CLARK

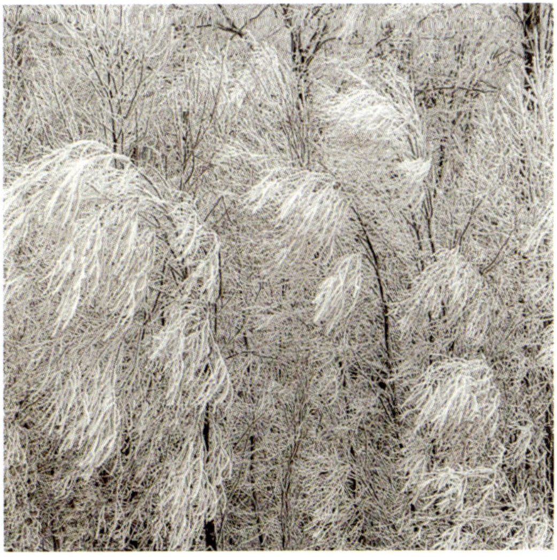

BETH SPENCER

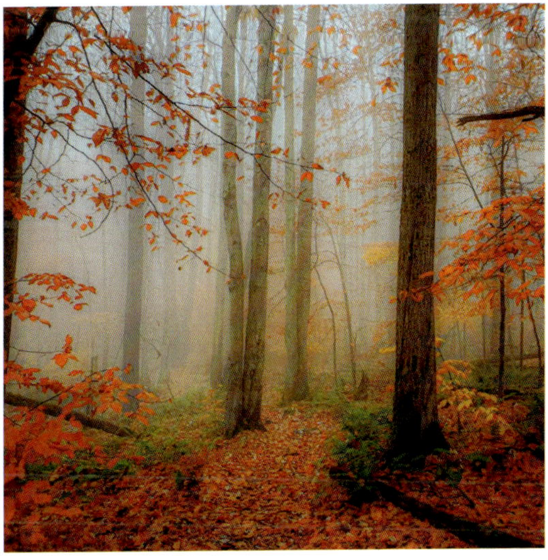

KEVIN GROSE

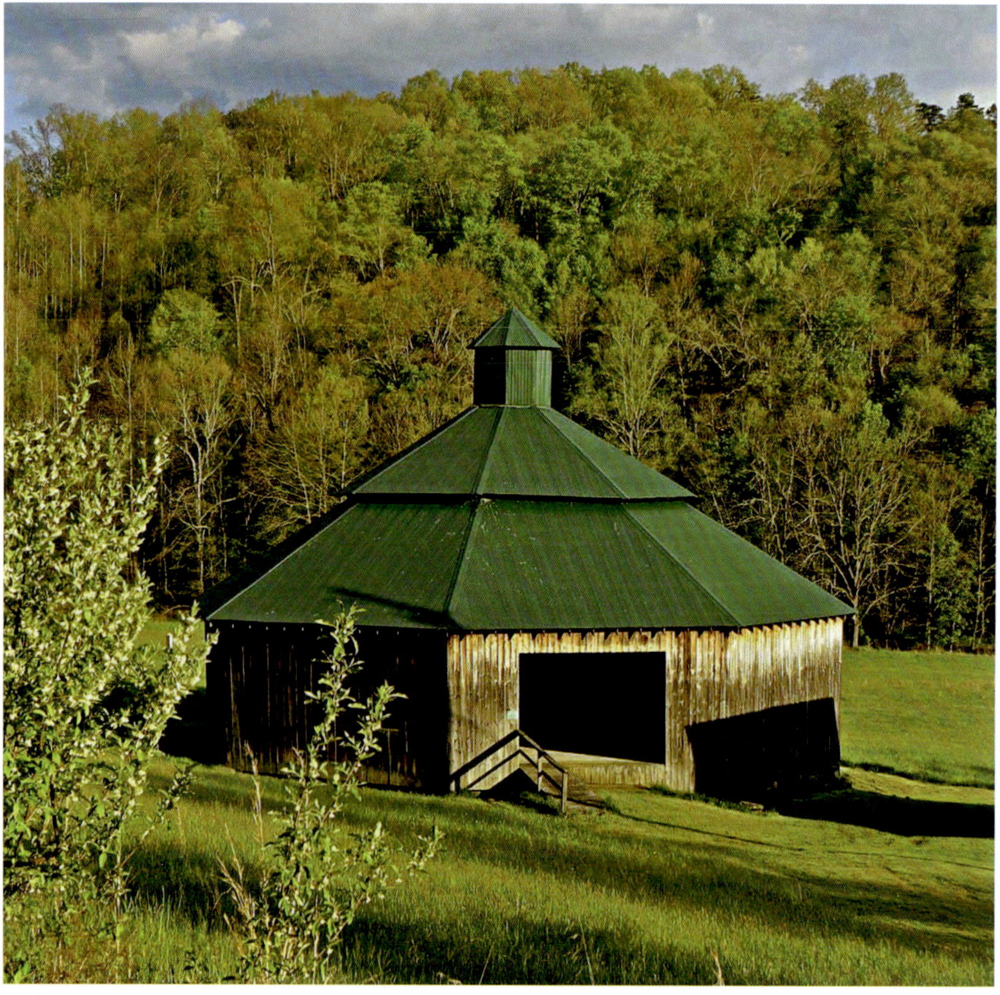

VAL CARNELL

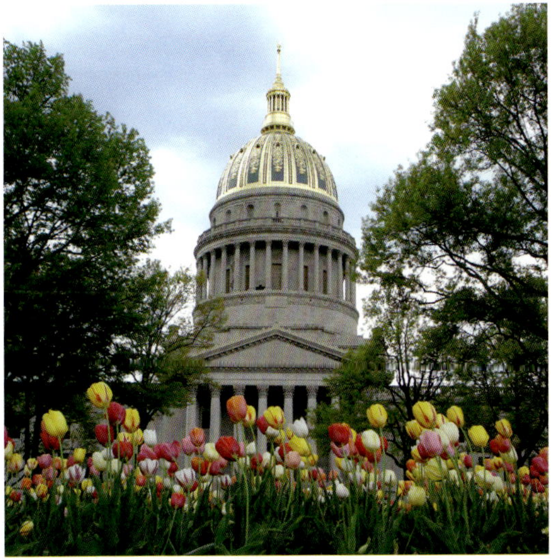

PHILLIP D. MILES

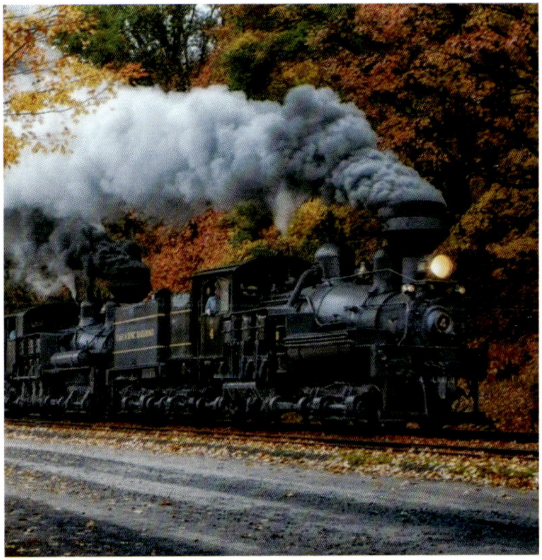

TOM DEAN

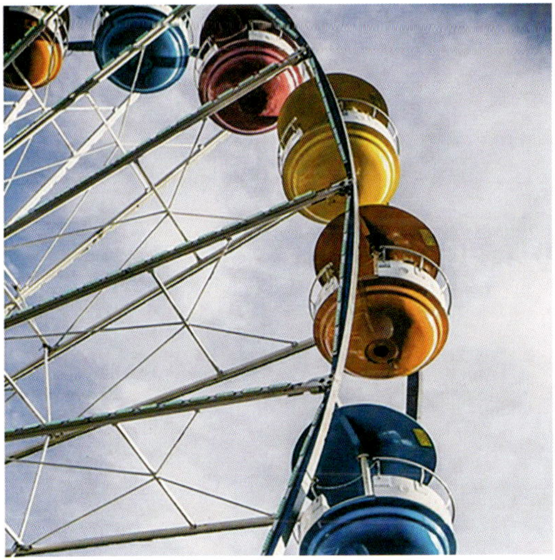

KEVIN JACK

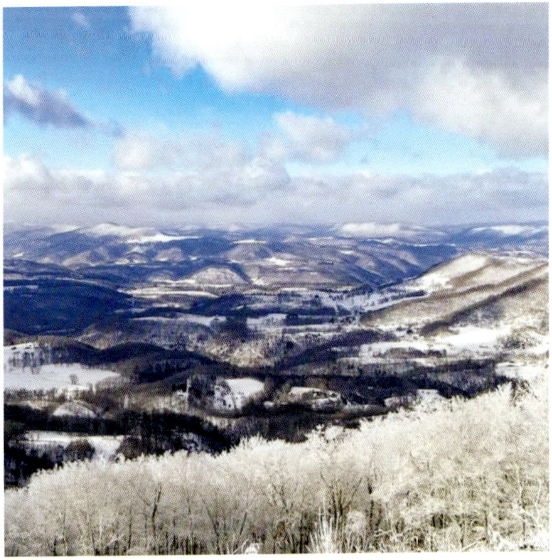

LIZ STOUT

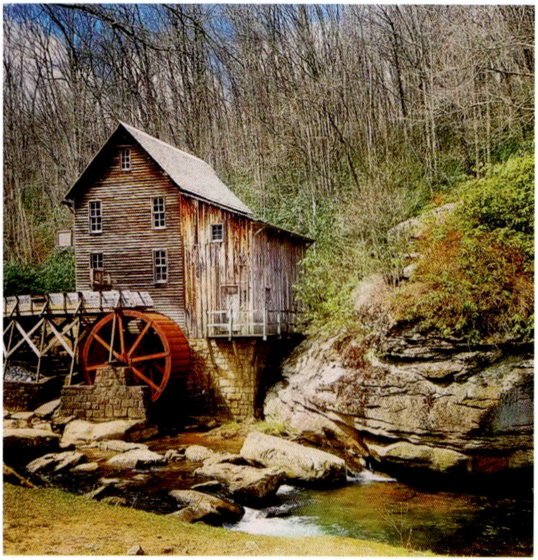

CONNIE BOLEY-LILLY

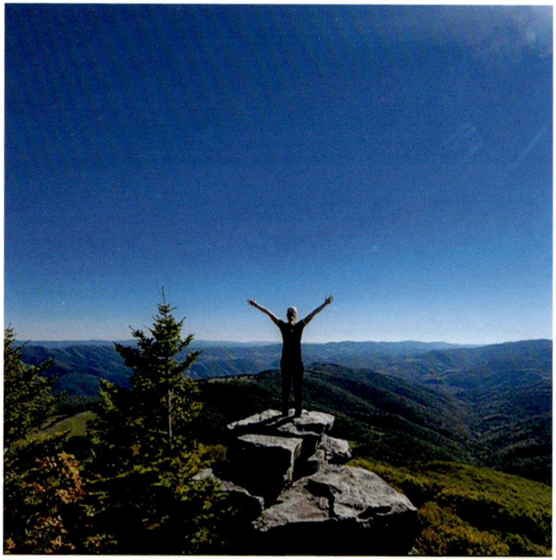

LIZ STOUT

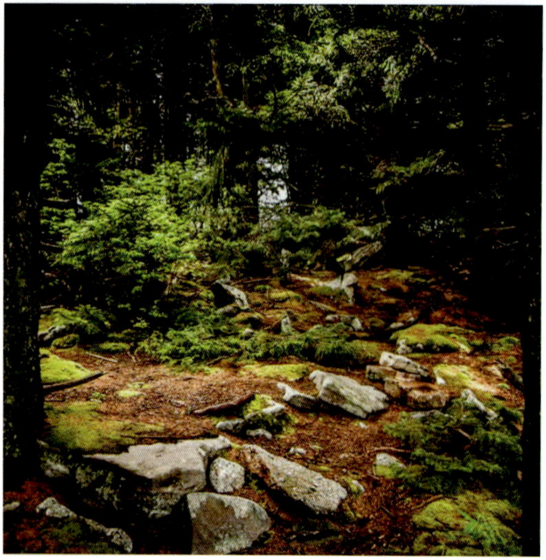

WENDY PARKS

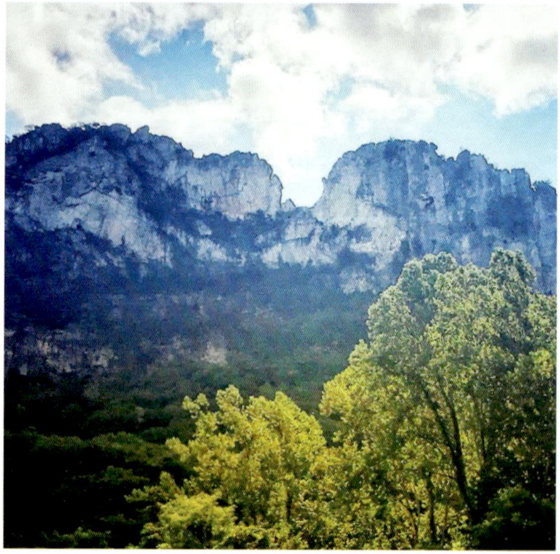

CINDI DUNN

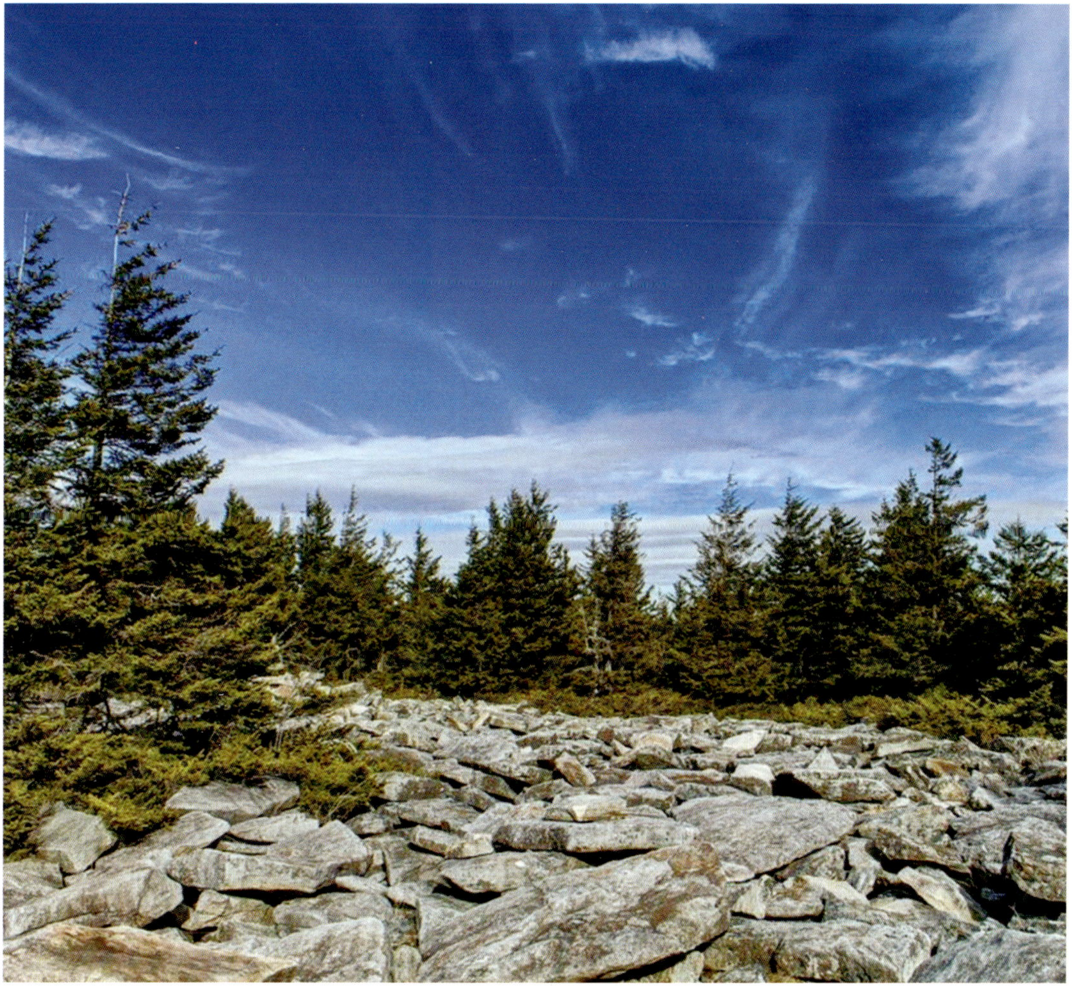

ERIC BRUMBAUGH

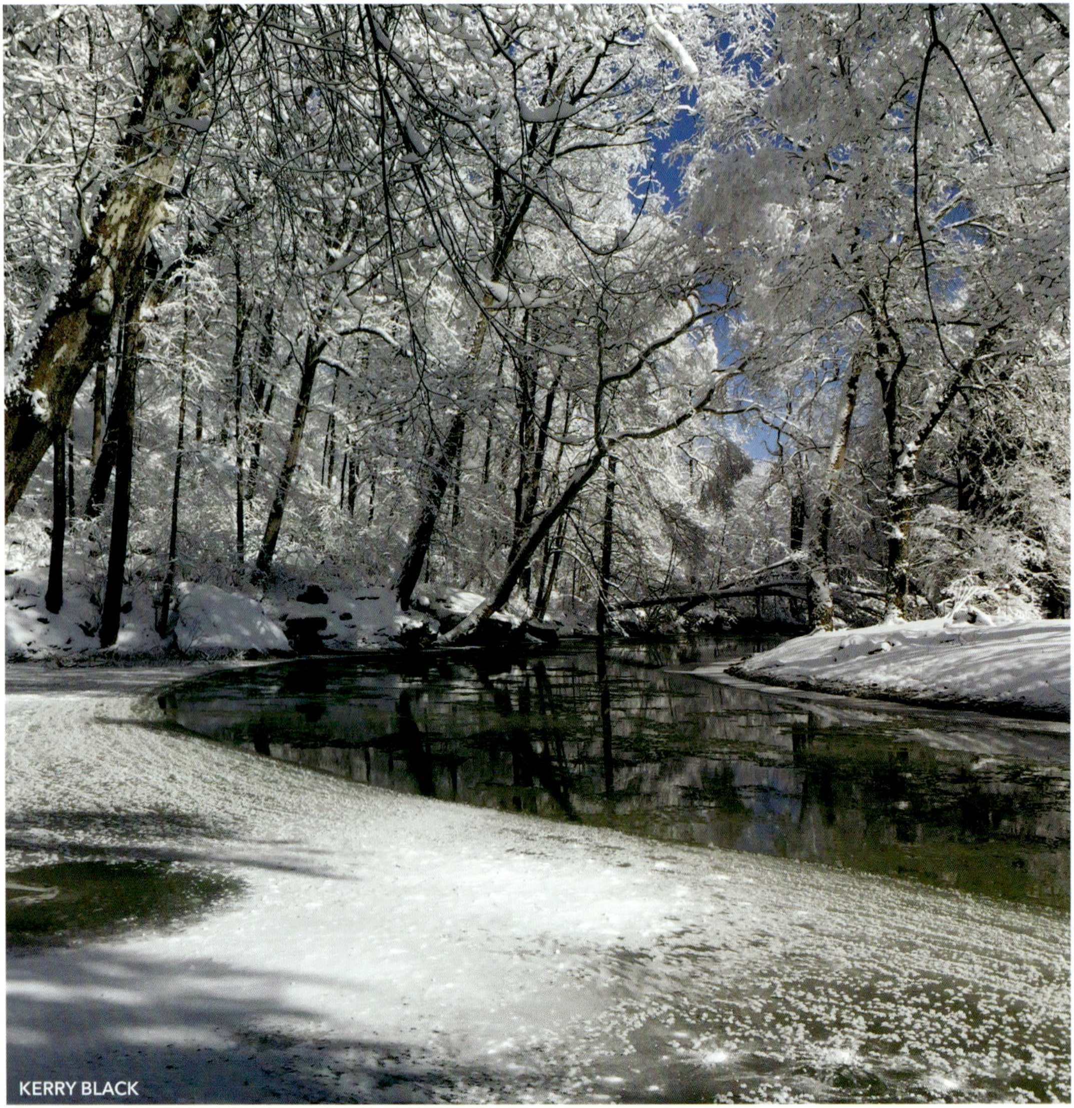

KERRY BLACK

miscellaneous

Today everything exists to end in a photograph.

- SUSAN SONTAG

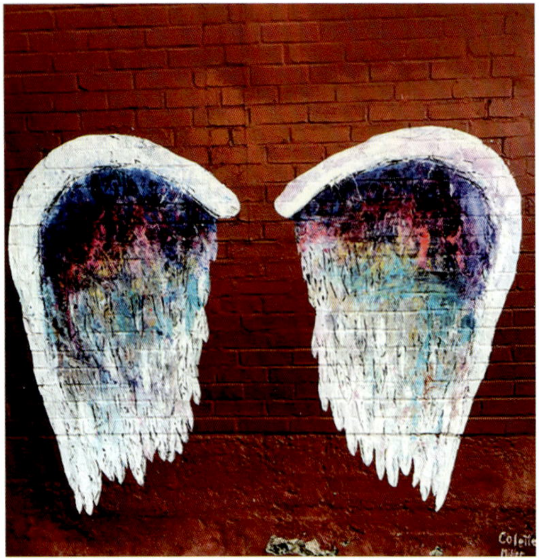

AMBER BALSINGER

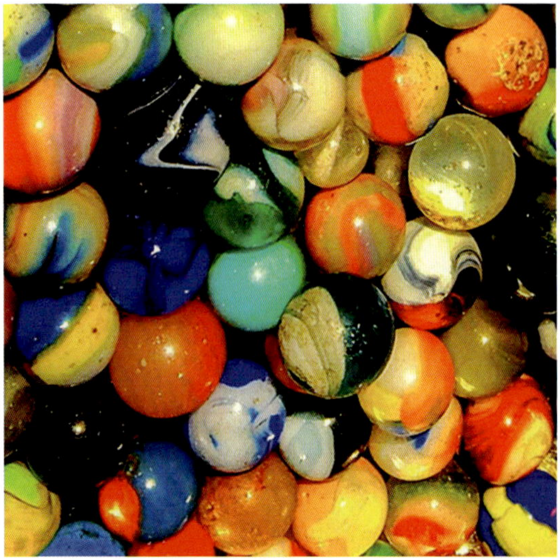

WESLEY PHILP

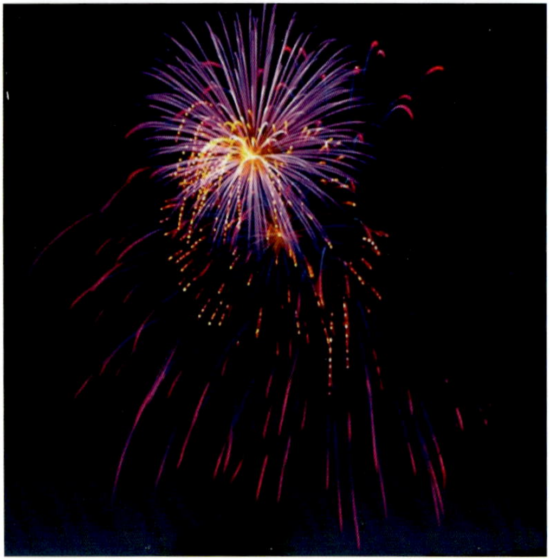

BETH SPENCER

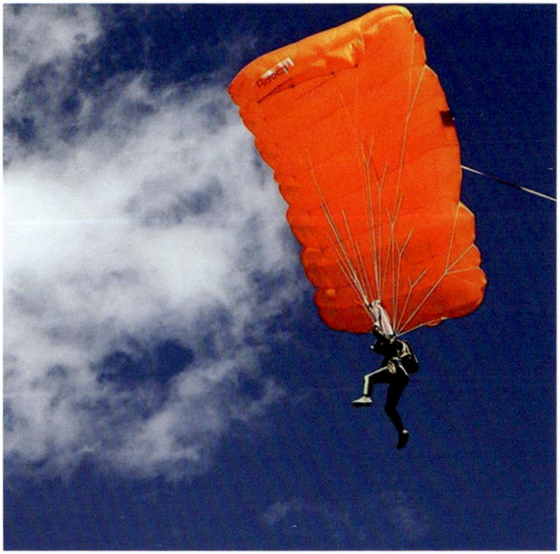

BRIAN BOYCE McCOY

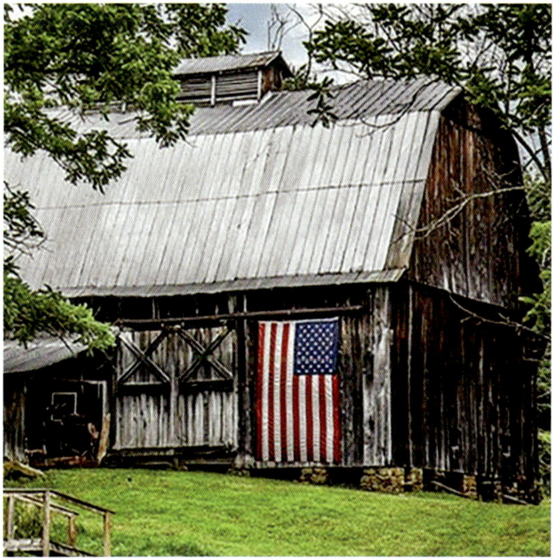

WENDY PARKS

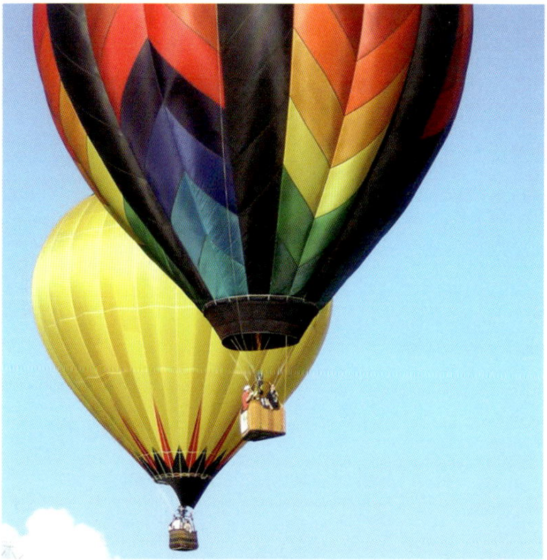

JENNIFER LOHMAN

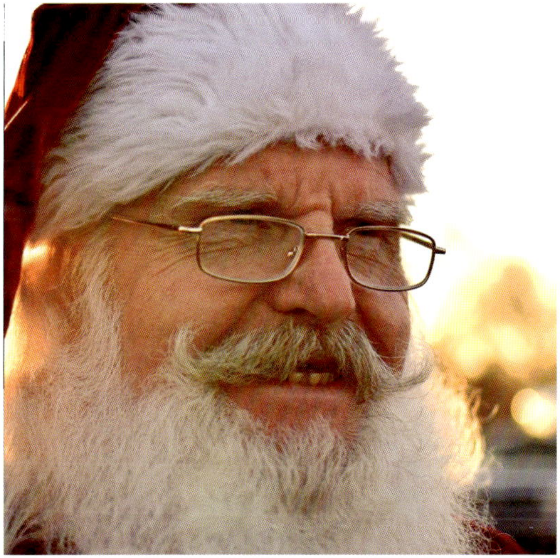

VANESSA HOCHARD

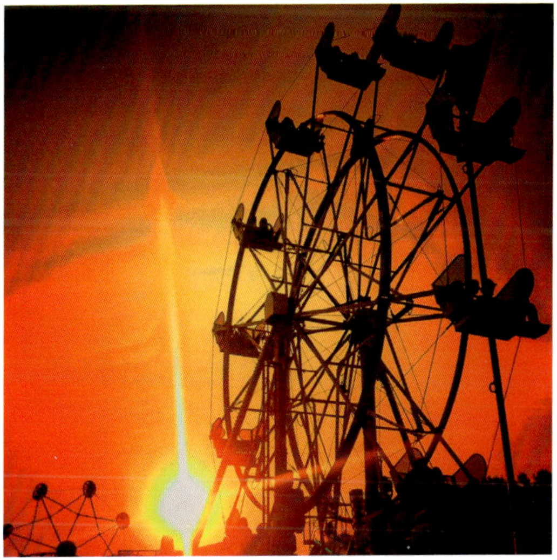

KEVIN GROSE

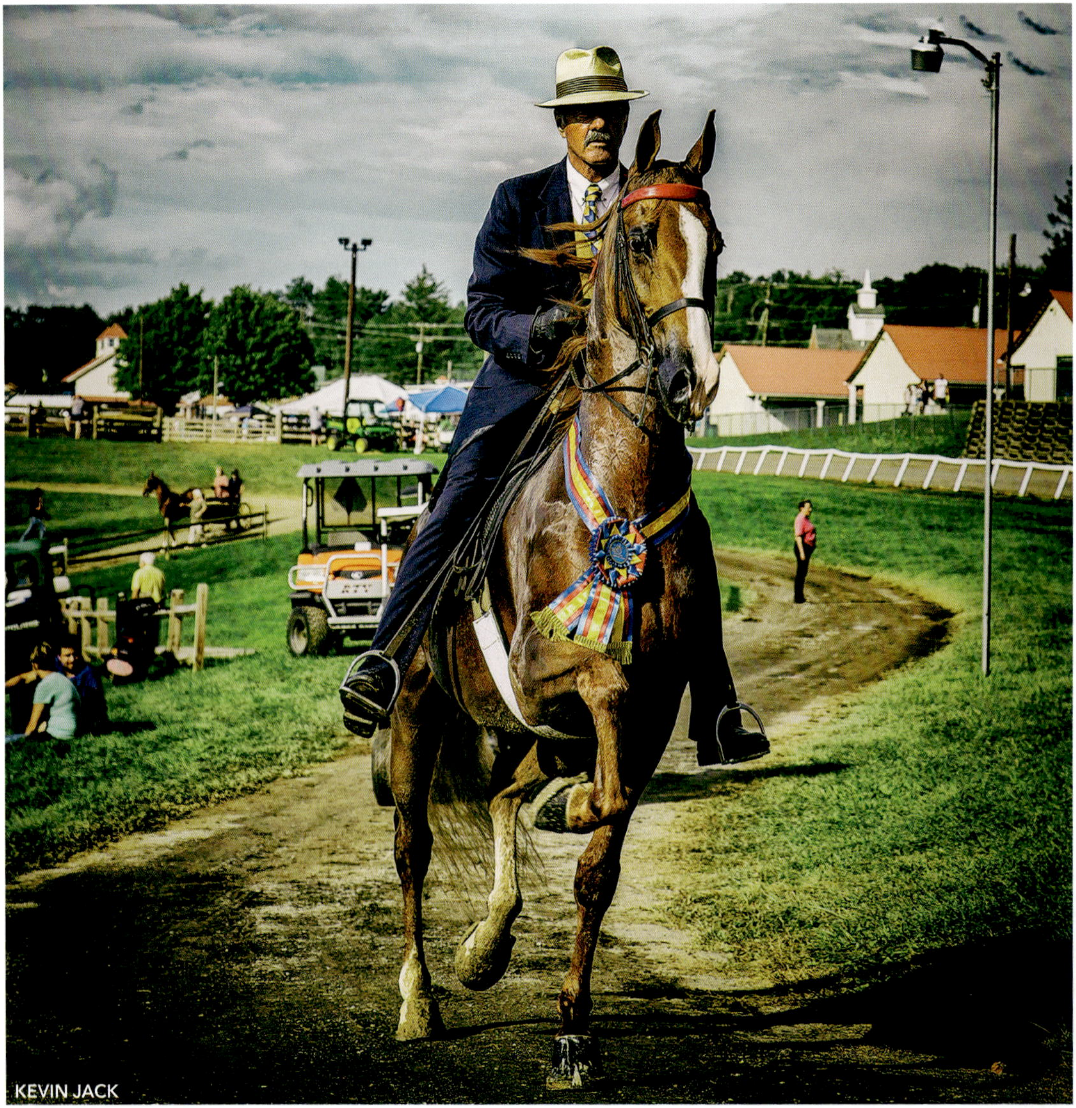
KEVIN JACK

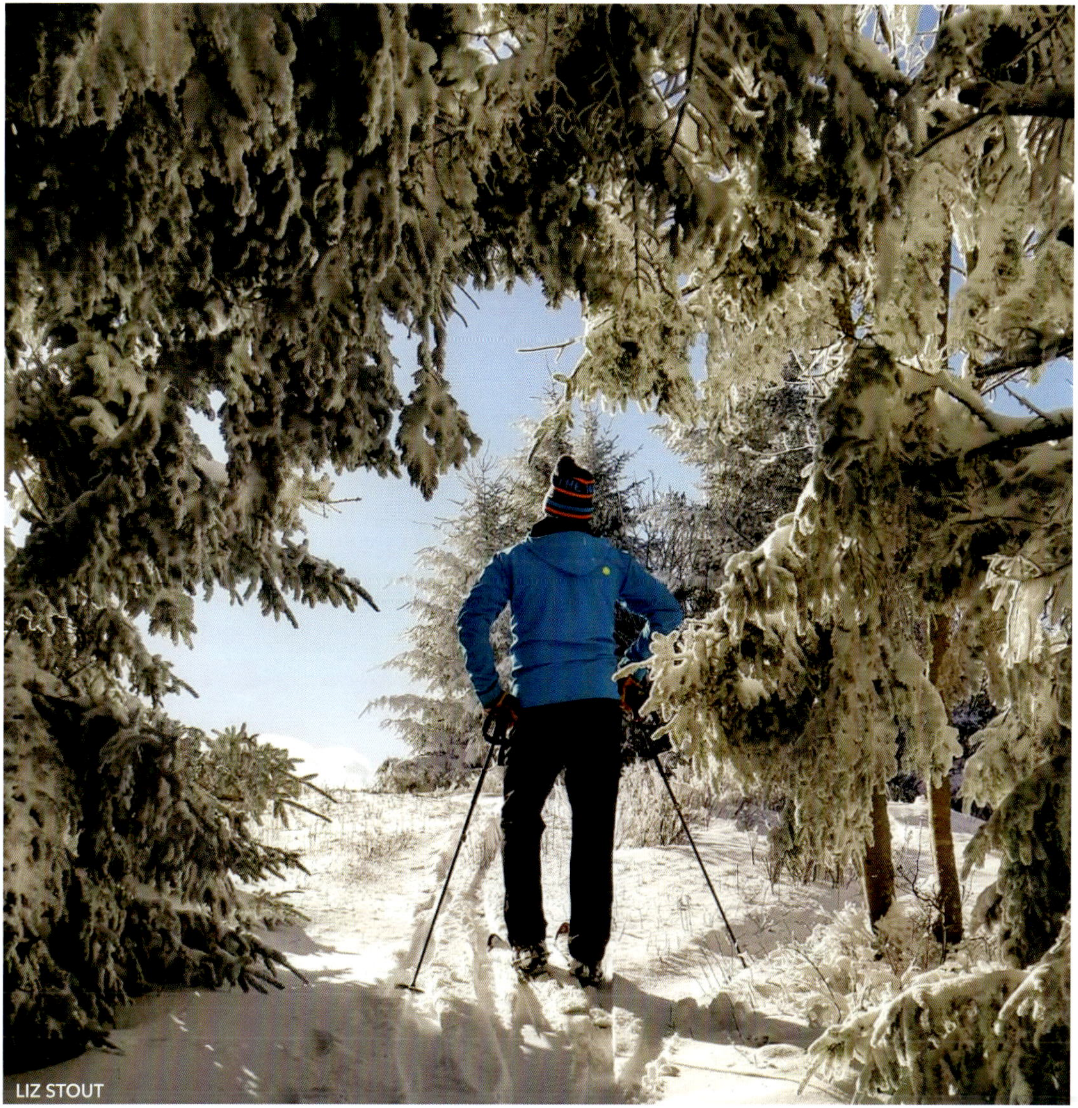
LIZ STOUT

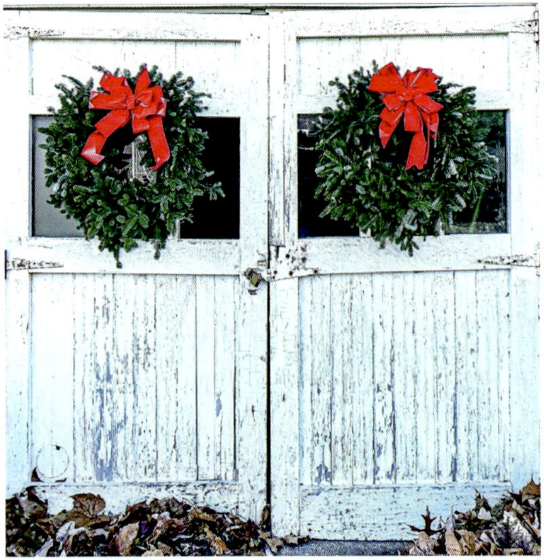

WESLEY PHILP

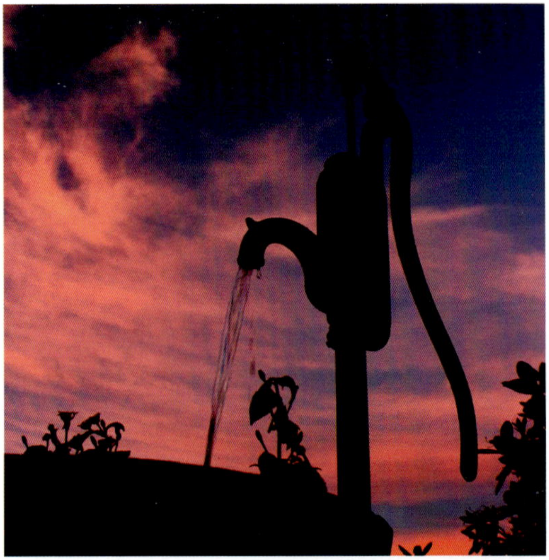

STAN WIKLE

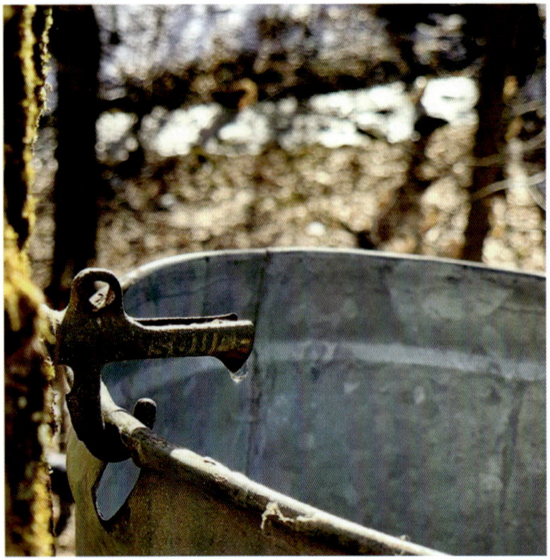

SHEILA JENKINS

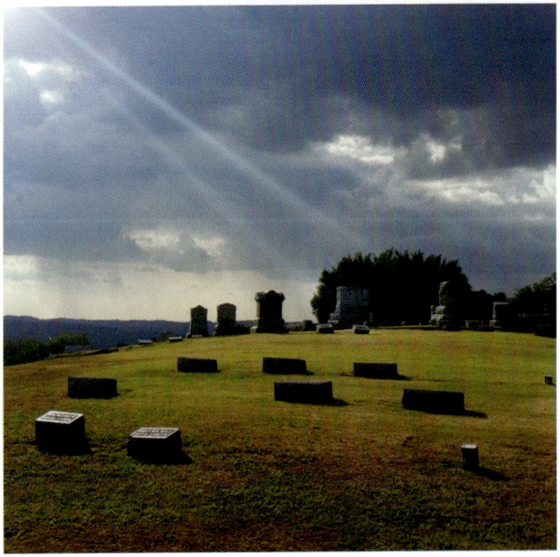

CYNTHIA MULLENS

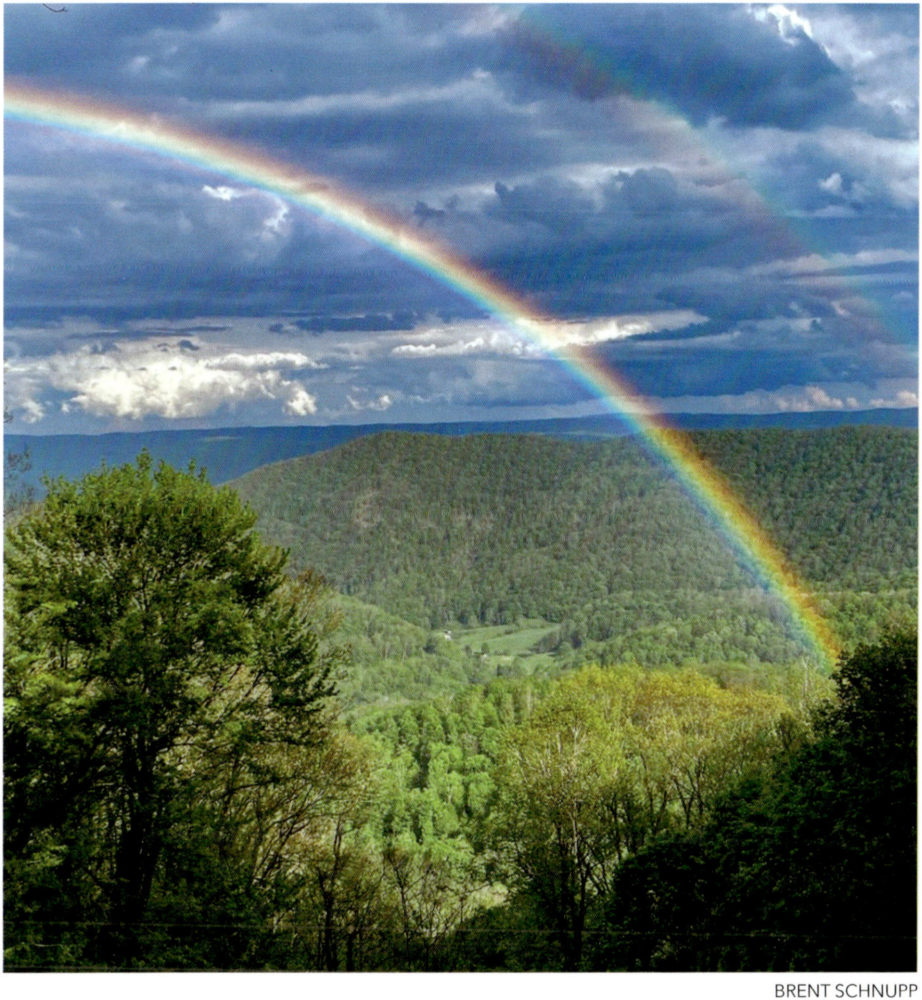

BRENT SCHNUPP

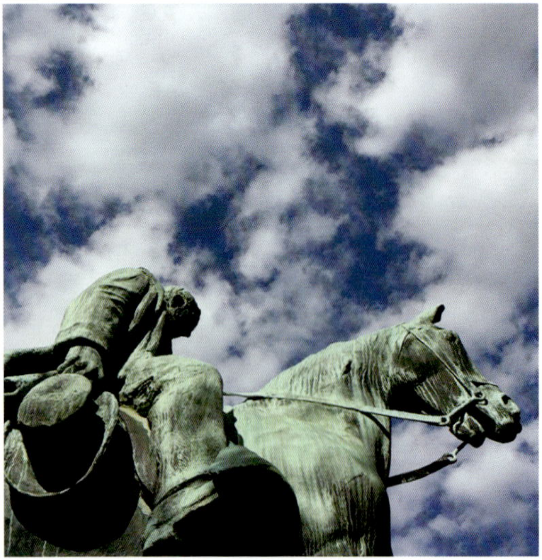

BENJAMIN MISHOE

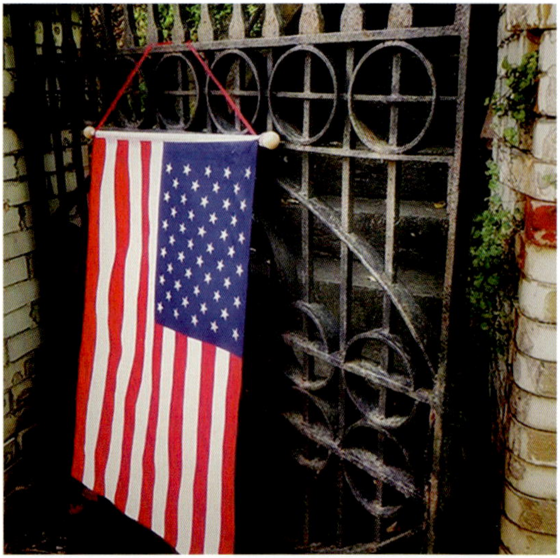

CINDI DUNN

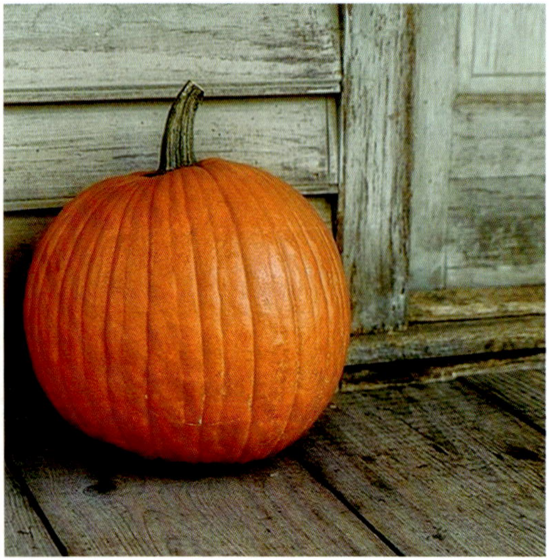

DENISE POWERS FABIAN

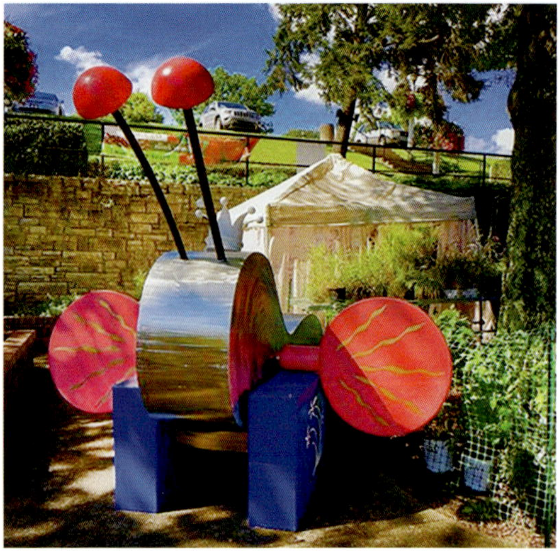

WESLEY PHILP

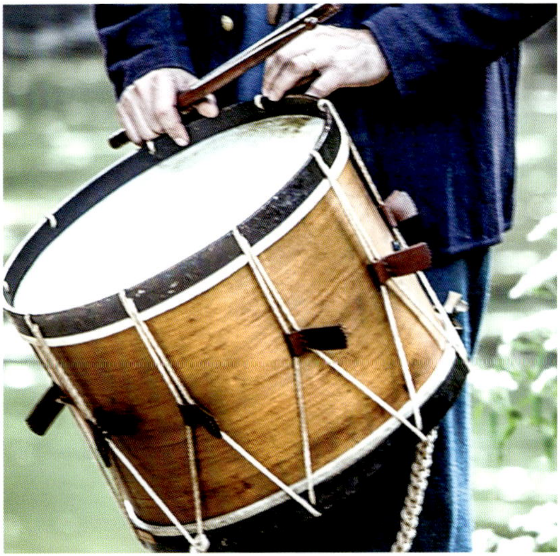

CINDI DUNN

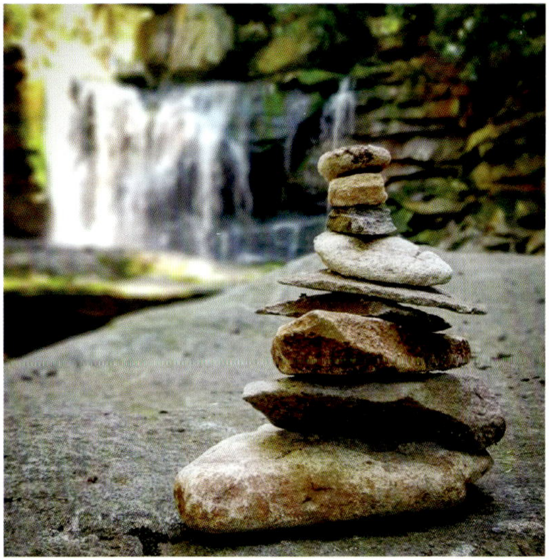

KEVIN GROSE

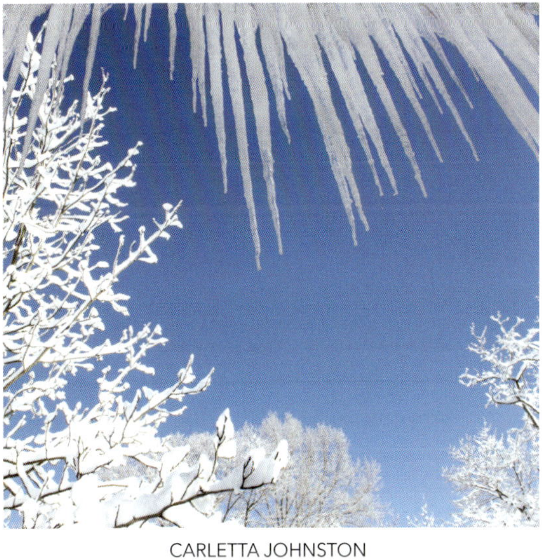

CARLETTA JOHNSTON

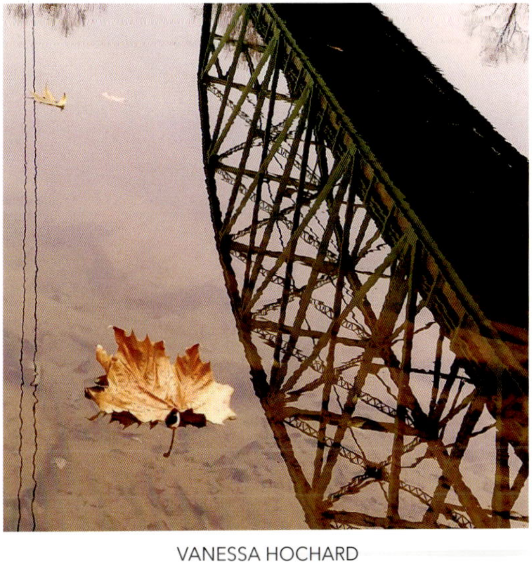

VANESSA HOCHARD

ISBN: 979-8-9858583-0-3

NEW SOUTH MEDIA
1135 Main Street, P.O. Box 279
Granville, WV 26534
newsouthmedia.com